A Companion Guide to
Brasses & Brass Rubbing

Also by Richard J. Busby

BEGINNER'S GUIDE TO BRASS RUBBING

A Companion Guide to Brasses & Brass Rubbing

RICHARD J. BUSBY

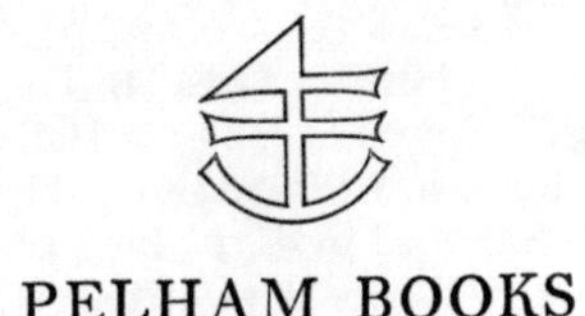

PELHAM BOOKS

First published in Great Britain by Pelham Books Ltd
52 Bedford Square, London, W.C.1
1973

7207 0436 7

Set and printed in Great Britain by
Tonbridge Printers Ltd, Peach Hall Works,
Tonbridge, Kent, in Bell eleven on thirteen point,
on paper supplied by P. F. Bingham, Ltd,
and bound by James Burn at Esher, Surrey

To my Mother and Father

Contents

Illustrations

Acknowledgements

This book could not have been written without the help of a great number of people, particularly during the compilation of the two Appendices at the end. Whilst it is impossible to name all of these many archivists, curators, librarians, officers of archaeological and historical societies and others who replied to my questionnaires and letters, or supplied photocopies of material in their care, a few merit special mention. To all of these, to those I have not named and others, I extend my sincere thanks.

Amongst those to whom I owe thanks are the following. For ease of reference alphabetical order has been adopted for individuals:—

Mr A. E. Barley, Archivist and Librn, S.P.C.K.; Mr James Brown, Verulamium Museum, St Albans; Dr H. K. Cameron, MA, BSc, PhD, FRIC, FSA (President of the Monumental Brass Society); Mr H. Carr, Secretary, Quatuor Coronati Lodge No. 2076, London; Mr R. H. Clark, ALA, Area Librn., Christchurch Branch Lib., Christchurch, Hampshire (for much info. on Herbert Druitt); Miss Florence Connolly, Curator of Fine Arts, Boston Public Lib., Boston, Mass., U.S.A.; Mr Peter Curnow, BSc, FSA; Lt Col W. E. C. Davidson-Houston; Mr A. G. Davies, BA, Curator, Hertford Museum; Mr M. T. Dowdell, ALA, Torbay Public Lib., Devon; Dr P. W. Gathercole, MA, AMA, Curator, University Museum of Archaeology and Ethnology, Cambridge; Mr Henry W. Gray, MVO (for some of the photographs and much other help); Mr S. B. Halmann, ALA, Admin. Librn, R.I.B.A. Library; Mr A. R. Hewitt, FLA, Librn and Curator, United Grand Lodge of England, Freemasons Hall, London; Mr R. C. Howes, FLA, County Reference Librn, Bucks Co. Lib.; Mr Philip Ireson, Sussex Monumental Brass Society; Mr D. L. Jones, Chelmsford and Essex Museum; Mr I. Kaye, Librn, Royal Society; Mr P. T. Klein, Dept. of Archaeology, Birmingham City Museum; Mrs V. B. Lamb, Hon Librn, Sussex Archaeol. Society; Mr M. J. Macpherson, Asst Sec., Sussex Archaeol. Soc.; Mr G. E. Moodey, FSA, Hon Sec., East Herts. Archaeol. Soc.; Dr Malcolm Norris, MA, FSA; Miss L. V. Paulin, OBE, MA, FLA, County Librn, and the Staff of Hertfordshire County Library; Mr J. R. Pike, FLA, Borough Librn, Torbay Public Lib., Devon; Mr E. O. Reed, J. P. FLA, Borough Librn and Curator, Chelmsford and Essex Museum; Mrs

S. J. Reiser, Asst Registrar, Fogg Art Museum, Harvard University, Harvard, Mass., U.S.A.; Mr F. P. Richardson, FLA, Librn, Law Society; Mr and Mrs P. Scott, Licencees, King's Head, Pebmarsh, nr Halsted, Essex; Miss E. M. Spencer, BA, ALA, Librn, British Dental Assn; Mr F. B. Stitt, BA, BLitt, Staffs. C.R.O.; Hon. Guy R. Strutt, BA (for help in my efforts to trace some missing mss belonging to J. A. Sparvel-Bayly (see Appx II below)); Mr P. Sykes, DMA, ALA, Librn, Nottingham Public Lib.; Mr H. O. Wilson, ALA, Librn, Greater London Record Office and Library; Mr M. Winton, BA, Dip Ed, ALA, Local History Librn, Borough of Kings Lynn, Norfolk (for the supply of so much info. about the Beloe family); also to Birmingham P.L.; Dept of Western MSS, Bodleian Library, Oxford (for permission to reproduce the Stukeley drawing in Pl. 8*a* below and other help); Gloucester P.L.; Local History Dept, Greenwich P.L.; Guildhall Library; Liverpool City Lib.; Art and Architecture Divn, New York P.L.; Royal College of Surgeons of England Library; St Albans City Lib.; Society of Antiquaries of London Library; Westminster City Libraries; Hertfordshire C.R.O.; Monumental Brass Society and Worcester County Museum.

My very special thanks must go to the following: Dr R. A. Kennedy, BLitt, NDA, AMA, Curator, County Museum, Haverfordwest, Pembroke, Wales; Dr D. T. W. Price, until recently Asst Editor, Shropshire V.C.H. (now Lecturer in History, St David's University College, Lampeter) – for his unstinting help in connection with this book and other matters; Mr W. Clay Dove of Sutton-in-Ashfield, Notts, for so much help in many ways during all stages of writing this book, and for the supply of photographs; Mrs Sally Morris, Local Sec. for the South-west of the M.B.S. – for her kindness and for 'volunteering' so willingly to make a rubbing of the Waller brass at Torquay (See p. 41 below); Mr M. C. Spedding, Principal, Dr H. H. Hillman, Deputy Principal, and the Staff of Pitt House Schools Ltd, Torquay (for their invaluable help and co-operation in obtaining details and rubbings of the Waller brass in the School Chapel). Apart from the few mentioned above, nearly all the photographic work for this book was undertaken by Mr Peter Marshall of Hatfield Polytechnic, who gave generously and patiently of his own time and without whose help this book could not have been completed. Similarly, my sincere thanks go to Mrs J. A. Allen, and later Miss Hazel S. Carter, for their unfailing help in the difficult task of typing this manuscript; and lastly to my wife Janet and son David who have suffered with remarkable patience the inherant problems of having a 'part-time' author in the family!

List of Main Abbreviations Used

The following are the most commonly used abbreviations adopted in this book. Any others not listed will be found in most standard lists of abbreviations of which a large number are available.

General List

Acad Academy
aced acedemical
ackn acknowledged
add additional
adds additions
adm admitted
advisy advisory
aet aetatis
ALA Associate of the Library Association
ann annual
antiq antiquary
appt appointed
archaeol archaeology
archit architect(–ure)
ARIBA Associate of the Royal Institute of British Architects
asst assisted (–ant)
attg attaining

b born
BA Bachelor of Arts
bibliog bibliography
biog biography
bk book
Bldg(s) building(s)
BM British Museum (London)
Boase Boase's *Modern English Biography* (6 vols)
Bp Bishop
br(s) brass(es)
Bryan Bryan's *Dictionary of Painters & Engravers*

Bull Bulletin

C Curate
c circa
cent century
ch church(es)
Chap Chaplain
child children
cm centimetres
Co Company
Coll College
colld collected
colln collection
Comm Committee
comp compiler(–ed)
contrib contributor(–ion)
Convacn Convacation
corr correcting(–ion(s))
Corr Corresponding
CRO County Record Office

d(au) daughter
D deacon
DD Doctor of Divinity
Dept Department
Depy Deputy
Dict Dictionary
Dir Director
DNB *Dictionary of National Biography*
drwg drawing

E[Ed/ed] East [Editor/edited]
e.d. eldest daughter

edn(s) edition(s)
Educ Educated(–ion)
elec elected
Encycl Encyclopaedia
engr engraved(–ing)(–er)
e.s. eldest son
esp(ec) especially
estab established
Exec Executive
exhib exhibited(–ion)

FBA Fellow of the British Academy
fd founded
Fdr(s) Founder(s)
FGeolS Fellow of the Geological Society
f.i. foot inscription
fig(s) figure(s)
fl floreat
FLA Fellow of the Library Association
FLinnSoc Fellow of the Linnean Society
fol folio
f.p. facing page
fragt fragment
FRAstS Fellow of the Royal Astronomical Society
freq frequent(–ly)
FRHistS Fellow of the Royal Historical Society
frontis frontispiece
FRS Fellow of the Royal Society
FRSA Fellow of the Royal Society of Arts
FSA Fellow of the Society of Antiquaries(London)

geneal genealogist(–ogy)(–ical)
G.S. Grammar School
Gt/gt Great/great

Harl Harleian
her heraldry(–ic)
hist history(–ical)
H/M Headmaster
Hon Honorary/Honourable
hse house

i/c in charge
illus illustrated(–ion)
imp important
incl including(–ed)
info information
ins inches
inscr inscription
Inst(n) Institute(–ion)
intro introduction

jd joined
J(nl) Journal
jnr junior
jnt joint
JP Justice of the Peace

KG Knight of the Garter
Kt Knight

LDS London Dental School
L.E.A. Local Education Authority
L.I. Light Infantry
lib library
Lib Assn Library Association
librn librarian
litho lithograph(ic)
LRCP Licenciate of the Royal College of Physicians

m married
MA Master of Arts
matric matriculated
m.b. monumental brass(es)
MB Bachelor of Medicine
M.B.S. Monumental Brass Society
MD Doctor of Medicine
memb member
m.i. marginal inscription
Mon Monumental
MRCP Member of the Royal College of Physicians
MRCS Member of the Royal College of Surgeons
ms(s) manuscript(s)
M.S. Mill Stephenson
MSP Member Internationale de Philologie, Science et Beaux Artes

N North
Nat National

nat hist natural history
N.S. New Series

ob died
Obit(s) obituary(–ies)
obtd obtained
O/P Out of Print
op.cit. in the work cited
ord ordained
o.s. only son
Oxon Oxford

p page
palimp palimpsest
pbk paperback
Pl(s) Plate(s)
P.O. Post Office
P.O.Lond Dir Post Office London Directory
port portrait
pp pages
pr priest
Pres President
Procs Proceedings
propd proposed
psh parish
pte private
pub(d) publisher(–ed)
publns publications

Q. Quarterly

R Rector
RA Royal Academy of Art
repr reprint(ed)
res resigned
retd retired
Rev Reverend
rev reviewed/revised
Roy Soc of Lit Royal Society of Literature

Rpt(s) Report(s)
rs rubbings

S South
s son
s.a. see also
Salop Shropshire
Sch School
Scot Scotland
Sec Secretary
Ser Series
sev several
sh shield
Snr Senior
Soc(s) Society(–ies)
Soc of Antiq Society of Antiquaries of London
subscr subscriber(–ed)
surv surviving(–ed)

topog topographical
Trans Transactions
trans translated

Univ University

V Vicar
v very
V&A Victoria & Albert Museum (London)
VCH Victoria County History
vol(s) volume(s)
V.P. Vice-President

W West
w wife

y.d. youngest daughter
yrs years
y.s. youngest son

Periodicals

AAN *Architectural Association Notes*
AASRP *Associated Architectural Societies Reports and Papers*
Abbey Mag *Abbey Magazine* [*St Albans Abbey, Herts*]
Am Hist *Amateur Historian* (now renamed *Local Historian* (q.v.))
Ann Reg *Annual Register*
Antiq *Antiquary*

Antiq J *Antiquaries Journal*
Archeol Archaeologia
Archaeol Ael *Archaeologia Aeliana*
Archaeol Camb *Archaeologia Cambrensis*
Archaeol Cant *Archaeologia Cantiana* [Kent Archaeol Soc]
Archaeol J *Archaeological Journal*
Archit *Architect*
Archit Rev *Architectural Review*
Art J *Art Journal*
Art Q *Art Quarterly*
Athen *Athenaeum*

BAA(Jnl) *British Archaeological Association, Journal*
Beds Hist Rec Soc *Bedfordshire Historical Record Society* (*Publications*)
Berks Archaeol J *Berkshire Archaeological Journal*
Birm & Midland Inst *Birmingham & Midland Institute* (Archaeological Section), *Transactions*
Brit Archit *British Architect*
Brit Dental J *British Dental Journal*
Brit Topog *British Topographer*
Build News *Building News*

Camb Antiq Soc *Cambridge Antiquarian Society, Proceedings*
Camb Antiq Soc Misc Comm *ibid, Miscellaneous Communications*
Ch Bells *Church Bells*
Conn *Connoisseur*
Croydon NH & Sc Soc *Croydon* [Surrey] *Natural History & Scientific Society, Transactions*
CUABC *Cambridge University Association of Brass Collectors, Transactions*
CWAAS *Cumberland & Westmorland Antiquarian & Archaeol. Society, Transactions*

Dental Rec *Dental Record*
DNAAS *Architectural & Archaeol. Society of Durham & Northumberland, Transactions*
Dorset NHFC *Dorset Natural History Society & Antiquarian Field Club, Proceedings*

EAST *Essex Archaeological Society, Transactions*
E Anglian Mag *East Anglian Magazine*
EHAS *East Herts Archaeol. Society, Transactions*
Essex Nat *Essex Naturalist*
Essex Rev *Essex Review*

Gent Mag *Gentleman's Magazine*
Geog Mag *Geographical Magazine*
Gloucs J *Gloucester Journal*
Gloucs N&Q *Gloucestershire Notes & Queries*

Hants FC & AS *Hampshire Field Club & Archaeol. Soc., Papers & Proceedings*
HCM(ag) *Home Counties Magazine*

Herts Archaeol *Hertfordshire Archaeology*

Illus Lond News *Illustrated London News*

J Design & Manuf *Journal of Design & Manufacture*
J Roy Anthrop Inst *Journal of the Royal Anthropological Institute*

LAMAS *London & Middlesex Archaeological Society, Trans.*
Lib Assn Rec *Library Association Record*
Local Hist *Local Historian* (formerly *Amateur Historian*)

MBS Port *Portfolio of the Monumental Brass Society*
MBS Trans *Monumental Brass Society, Transactions*

N & Q *Notes & Queries*
Norf Archaeol *Norfolk Archaeology*

OUBRS *Oxford Journal of Monumental Brasses* (Oxford Univ. Brass Rubbing Society)
Oxford Port *Oxford Portfolio of Monumental Brasses*
Oxon Archaeol Soc Rpts *Oxford Archaelogical Society Reports*

Peterboro NHSAS *Peterborough Natural History, Scientific & Archaeol. Society, Reports & Papers*

Rel & Illus Archaeol *Reliquary & Illustrated Archaeologist*
RIBA Jnl *Royal Institute of British Architects, Journal*
Roy Soc Proc *Proceedings of the Royal Society*
RSA Jnl *Royal Society of Arts, Journal*

SAC *Surrey Archaeological Collections*
SAP *Society of Antiquaries of London, Proceedings*
Shrop Archaeol Soc *Shropshire Archaeological Society, Transactions*
Soc Army Hist Res *Society for Army Historical Research, Journal*
Som &Dorset N&Q *Somerset & Dorset Notes & Queries*
Somerset ANHS *Somerset Archaeol. & Natural History Society, Procs.*
SPEST *St Paul's Ecclesiological Society, Transactions*
StAAS *St Albans & Hertfordshire Architectural & Archaeol. Society, Transactions*
Suffolk Inst *Suffolk Institute of Archaeology, Proceedings*
Sussex A.C. *Sussex Archaeological Collections*
Sussex N&Q *Sussex Notes & Queries*

TLS *Times Literary Supplement*
Topog & General *Topographer & Genealogist*

Wilts Archaeol & NH Soc Mag *Wiltshire Archaeological & Natural History Society, Magazine*
Wilts Gaz *Wiltshire Gazette*
Wilts Mag *Wiltshire Magazine*
Worcs Herald *Worcestershire Herald*

Yorks Archaeol (& Topog) J *Yorkshire Archaeological (and Topographical) Journal*

Introduction

Brass rubbing has reached another crisis point in its history. To-day, events and circumstances which first occurred some one hundred and twenty-five years ago are being repeated – but on a larger scale. Popularity (for which the present author cannot escape some responsibility) invariably inflicts casualties, and the same sentiment expressed by the Rev Charles Boutell in his famous book *Monumental Brasses and Slabs* (1847; intro. p. vii), to 'raise the prevelant amusement of brass rubbing into something of a system', might well be re-echoed to-day. Unfortunately, as then, other results have also repeated themselves, and a growing number of churches are being forced to 'close their doors' to students of the 'chalcotriptic' art (see pp. 84–85 below).

The main reasons for the above circumstances are, however, somewhat different to those of the past, since it is not just the large numbers of people making rubbings, but 'abuse' of the privilege by a regrettably growing number of persons who wish no more than to make financial gain by the sale, or reproduction, of the rubbings themselves, both at home and abroad (and especially in North America). This, allied to the ever present danger of serious damage to the brasses themselves, plus the few people who cause annoyance to the Church authorities by bad manners or behaviour, collectively add up to more and more bans on rubbing, both in the United Kingdom, and, more recently, on the continent as well, e.g. Bruges, Belgium.

In my *Beginner's Guide to Brass Rubbing* (1969), I tried to set down some basic standards and methods to help those new to the subject to learn the techniques of making good rubbings for enjoyment. In this sense it has been moderately successful.

The *Companion Guide* is aimed especially at those who have benefited from the above and are encouraged to take a more detailed look at the brasses themselves in their own right. Much can be learned from the intelligent study of brasses, both historically and artistically, and in this context rubbing the brasses can become of secondary importance. The present work sets out to show how this study can, and is, being applied and extended, both for recreational and educational use, both by individuals or by groups in schools, colleges, Local Education Authority classes, etc., at all levels and stages. Much of this book is inevitably historical in outlook, but does not follow the completely traditional lines of enquiry found in most other books on brasses—this has been, and will be, adequately dealt with elsewhere by other writers better qualified to do so, and whose names frequently occur in these pages.

The aim of this book is, as the title suggests, to be a *Companion Guide* to the study and use of brasses and brass rubbings for both general reader and specialist, summarising past research, indicating future lines of enquiry and chronicling past and present trends, ideas and methods. In order to, in part at least, answer Mr. P. MacQueen's recent plea for a 'bibliography of brasses' (*MBS Trans* 10, iv (1966), 249-53), special attention has been paid to the citing of sources of information quoted in the text, appendices and references. This will not only indicate to those not yet familiar with the *Transactions* of the Monumental Brass Society the scope and extent of this publication, but will also, I hope, help all readers to find their way through the vast literature of this subject and to follow up any special interests of their own. For convenience the textual references have been gathered at the end of the book, rather than adding them as footnotes on each page, and contain much additional and valuable information on specialised topics and sources which might be pursued. Special attention is also drawn to Chapter 3 which contains much of value to those interested in the old and modern methods of reproducing brasses, from the pen and ink sketches of the old antiquaries to the modern rubbing and photolithographic methods. Also, two unique features of the book, Appendix I, listing topographically, historical and other collections of brass rubbings in the United Kingdom (never before attempted); and Appendix II, which records the life (in outline) and written or other work, of many persons who have made a significant contribution to the history or study of brasses from the seventeenth century to the present day. To save too many embarrassing omissions, only deceased persons are included.

The *Companion Guide* is more than 'just another book on brass rubbing' (a favourite phrase of reviewers), and whilst not pretending to be the last word on this fascinating subject, offers much that is unique – especially on 'modern' brasses which are only now beginning to be appreciated. It does not incorporate all new research, but this will be completely covered in Dr. Malcolm Norris' forthcoming book which all are urged to read; it may well alter some of the long held theories on the origin of brasses. Research continues all the time and many sources, especially abroad, still remain almost untapped. Those seriously interested in current developments are urged to join other interested parties in the Monumental Brass Society. With the closure of many churches, thefts from others, plus normal wear and tear, brasses remain constantly 'at risk', and it is the duty of all those professing serious interest to take what steps they can to protect these unique memorials, or to inform those who can do so on their behalf. The M.B.S. has several members who specialise in the repair and relaying of brasses, but they are overburdened with work and lack suitable premises in which to operate and perform this skilled and invaluable task. Another group of members is engaged on the revision and up-dating of Mill Stephenson's classic *List of Monumental Brasses* (see p. 38 below).

The *Companion Guide* offers not only much that is new, but also might be called a 'state of the art'. If it gives those interested in the study and preservation of monumental brasses, ancient and modern, a greater appreciation of the memorials they rub and their history, then it will have achieved its object.

If it is also enjoyed as a work of reference and helps to generate something of the pleasure the present writer has gained from eighteen years study of brasses, then it will be doubly successful.

R.J.B.
Welwyn Garden City,
Hertfordshire,
2nd February, 1972.

CHAPTER ONE

Brasses and the Allied Arts: an Introductory Guide

[1] THE BRASSES

(Note: the reference numbers in the text refer to the Chapter notes, page 134 ff)

It is now generally accepted that the first monumental brasses had their origin in northern France, Germany and Flanders, being a natural development from other funeral monuments, especially the incised stone slab and the cast metal tomb. With the notable exception of Rev Herbert Haines (1826-72), his friend and contemporary Albert Way (1805-74) and the Waller brothers, few writers until recent times have looked at brasses outside their own context, or realised how closely their style and manufacture were related to and influenced by allied arts and crafts. Before illustrating this point, however, it is necessary for me to describe something of the general background to the growth of the brass industry in Europe. Readers must bear in mind that this is a personal view, which should be read in conjunction with the works by other writers listed in the bibliography at the end of this chapter.

The Brass Industry 1100–1700

The indifferent use made of the term 'brass' and its equivalents in contemporary documents and books, often makes it very difficult for one to know exactly what a particular writer is referring to. Terms like "aurichalcum" (L), "cuivre blanq" (Fr.), AEs (L). "coperwerk" (Dutch) and "messing" (Ger. 16th century), were all frequently used to refer to any alloy resembling what we now call brass. The late R. H. D'Elboux wrote a valuable and informative article on this subject[1] in which he cited the various terms used in contemporary documents; one of the earliest references to the actual term 'brass' that he discovered, was in the will of Richard Hunt of Shipley, Sussex (dated 25th August, 1546), who requested 'a stone to be layed over my grave and also a brasse to be nayled on the same stone . . . '.[2] Most references to the sheet or hammered brass used for monumental brasses was, however, to latoun or laton (L), laiton (Fr.) or latten (Eng.), and it is the last term which will be used throughout this book in the above context.[3]

The brass, copper and bronze industries were very closely related (sometimes referred to collectively as 'dinanderie', after the town of Dinant in Belgium, an important early centre) so it is not surprising to find that latten contained a high percentage of copper, and was manufactured by a very similar process to the other two metals. Much of our information on the early brass and copper industries has come from treatises by writers like Rugerus Theophilus (c. 1100), Bartolommeus Angilicus (c. 1475 *et seq*), Vannoccio Biringuccio (1540), Georgius Agricola (1556), Ciriacus Schreittmann (1578), Lazurus Ercker (1580) and Christoph Weigel (1698). Most of their treatises are available in an English translation (*c.f.* bibliog. for details) and it is quite clear from these that, even with the advent of the steam hammer and rolling mill, the basic processes of 'batterie' remained almost unaltered right up until the Industrial Revolution in England, by which time engraved brasses had virtually fallen out of use.

The use of latten throughout the period under discussion was certainly never confined to funeral sculpture, which, in mainland Europe particularly, became to a large extent a secondary industry. The art of making engraved latten plates as memorials grew up as part of an important trade in domestic and ecclesiastical metalwork. Towns like Dinant, Aachen, Antwerp, Bruges, Cologne and Nuremberg attracted some of the finest craftsmen in the world, and were universally known for their copper and brass bowls, ewers (aquaminile), candlesticks, chalices, pattens, lecterns, tryptyches, reliquaries and embossed and carved book covers. Many of these items were also made in precious metals, and allied to the above were the sister arts of enamelling, ceramics, stained glass, manuscript illumination, stone and wood carving, the making of miniatures, and later on, of printing blocks and plates. When plate armour became fashionable, the Milanese armourers passed on their skill in decorating the metal to many craftsmen, not least the engravers of brasses, possibly even drawing the patterns or designing some military brasses themselves. It is worth noting that under the guild system, the Armourers and Brass Founders virtually held the monopoly of all work involving the use of latten or brass for many years.

Each of the above industries and sub-industries was, in turn, jealously controlled by a tight-knit guild of craftsmen, journeymen, apprentices and masters (*c.f.* p. 28 ff. below) and the immensely powerful merchants of the Hanseatic League. Apart from the Italian influence mentioned above (which was not solely confined to the engraving of armour) perhaps the greatest single source of inspiration to the artists and craftsmen of the twelfth to fourteenth century in particular, was that of Byzantium. This, coupled with the ever present religious (and financial) control of the Church, had considerable effect on the work, and mind, of the medieval tradesman.

Early Centres of the Industry

The sites of the earliest brass foundries were largely determined by their proximity to natural deposits of calamine (or zinc) ore and copper; the former was a vital hardening ingredient used in the smelting of copper, and the proportion of one to the other also had some effect on the colour of the final product. The largest deposits of calamine lay in the area between the Rivers Meuse (or Maas) and the Rhine, especially around Aachen, Givet and Liége. Copper was mostly extracted from the Harz Mountains (especially near Gozlar), the Erz Gebirge Mountains (on the present German-Czec.

border) and the Swiss Alps. The mines were mainly owned and controlled from the fifteenth century onwards by the Hanseatic Merchants of Nuremberg and Augsburg in the central/southern provinces of modern Germany, and the fact that one of the earliest surviving brasses is found at Regensburg (c. 1189) near these areas may be no more than coincidence, since the oldest figure brass at Verden (1231) is found well to the north of the above locality.

Later, however, as communications improved and new trade routes opened, the industry gradually moved away from the original centres near the mines to other areas. By the fifteenth century the craftsmen had already established themselves in towns beyond Germany and Flanders, not least in France and England. That trade in latten existed between the south and east coast ports of England and the north-German, French and Dutch ports is already well known. So is the fact that England and Scotland were forced to import their latten from the continent until the discovery of natural calamine deposits in Somerset in 1566. Mr. F. A. Greenhill has shown quite clearly that, on the evidence of a fine indent in Dundrennan Abbey, Galloway, Scotland (probably of early fourteenth century date) not only that brasses were being imported into Britain at a very early date, of which this is the earliest known example, but that the 'English style' with figures and accessories cut out and separately inlaid, was practised by continental engravers earlier than had hitherto been supposed.[4] From c. 1566 onwards, it was therefore possible for English workmen to manufacture the metal for brasses themselves, though too late to save this branch of the industry from the rapid deterioration which had already begun.

The changes in location were not all for economic reasons, as geographical and other factors had an equally important effect. The town of Bruges in Belgium, for example, for many years a major centre and the headquarters of the Hanseatic League (boasting at its height fifty-two craft guilds), declined in importance because by about 1480 its river had become unnavigable and trade moved away to Antwerp instead. The latter town is known to have shipped large quantities of latten to France, Spain, Portugal, Scandinavia and the Baltic countries. Dr. Roland de Beeck in a recent article describing Portugese brasses,[5] mentions the flourishing trade in copper and latten between Antwerp and Portugal, and points out the resemblance in style between some Portugese brasses and other contemporary north European examples. As an example, Dr. de Beeck indicates the similarity in execution between the Flemish brass at Evora of Ruy Paeez and his wife (c. 1530) and the Flemish brasses in England of Andrew Evyngar and his wife (1533), All Hallows, Barking, London, and of Thomas Pownder and his wife (1525) formerly at St. Mary Quay, Ipswich, Suffolk (now in the Ipswich Museum). The direct use and export of a design to different countries has rarely been shown with such effect, as surviving examples are rare.[6] The only other examples which immediately spring to mind are the famous series of mid-fourteenth to early fifteenth century Flemish brasses like those at St. Albans Abbey, Hertfordshire (c. 1360) Lübeck (1350); Schwerin (1347, 1375) and Thorn (1361).

It is interesting to note how closely the development of the monumental brass is reflected in the history of important towns like Nuremberg (Nürnberg), which was the leading west European centre for brassware during the fifteenth and sixteenth centuries. The 'brass beaters', or 'batteurs', arrived at Nuremberg in c. 1370 (probably from Flanders) when monumental brass engraving was almost at its finest; the craft reached its peak there between c. 1500 and 1550, after which it declined rapidly in importance, to have practically died out by the 1630s.

Although it is obviously dangerous to draw any positive conclusions from one example only, it is striking how closely the above pattern reflects the general development of monumental brass engraving and production. Because of the southerly location of Nuremberg, it further suggests a gradual movement of the skilled craftsmen from Flanders, France or Northern Germany, between the early thirteenth and the mid-fourteenth centuries, back to the more southerly provinces. This would appear to substantiate further the theory that northern Europe or France was the original home of the art of producing engraved latten memorials. As Dr H. K. Cameron and other authorities have pointed out, Nuremberg and many other German towns favoured the cast metal tomb or inscription plate rather than the flat latten plate which was possibly a 'foreign influence in Germany'.[7]

The name most closely associated with Nuremberg from the mid-fifteenth century onwards was that of Vischer, whose works made cast metal tombs (usually of bronze) and a number of brasses. Some of the latter have been identified at Meissen, Erfurt and Cracow. It is interesting to note that the fine brass of Cardinal Frederic (1510) in Cracow Cathedral contains two figures copied directly from a contemporary woodcut by Albrech Dürer; the brass itself has been ascribed by Malcolm Norris[8] to Hermann Vischer the Younger. Both Vischer and Dürer were resident in Nuremberg as well as being universally known as great artists in their own fields.

The Craftsmen

Early western art was largely, if not exclusively, controlled by the Church, to whose end most of the work was directed. Indeed, a great deal of the earliest work was carried out in the monastic scriptoria and workshops, e.g. engraved decorative metalwork, manuscript illumination, book production, enamelling, etc., but by the twelfth century there were already many lay craftsmen, and by the first half of the fourteenth century the craft guilds were appearing. Over-emphasis of the skill of monastic craftsmen has caused one authority R. E. Swartwout,[9] to point out quite clearly that the bretheren were not all the 'master craftsmen' hitherto supposed. He quotes many instances (well documented) where lay workmen were responsible for constructing monastic buildings, carving or gilding statues, making tombs, etc. It was only when driven by sheer poverty that a few monks attempted the work themselves, often, in the case of building construction, with disastrous results. Swartwout ascribes the blame to those historians and scholars who, over many years, have misinterpreted or translated too literally the word 'fecit' [made]; in many cases it simply meant commissioned or financed.

Several craft guilds themselves relied heavily on the Church for financial support as well as trade, especially the Goldsmiths, but the fact that their members lived and worked outside the ecclesiastical buildings was significant in itself. Also, the religious 'ties' were often a pretext used for raising prices or wages.[10] By strict rules and limited membership the guilds ensured not only a livelihood and good working conditions for their members, but controlled the tools they used, the apprenticeship schemes (normally lasting six to eight years) and, with the aid of impartial 'searchers', the quality and price of the goods produced.[11] Included in the training of every future master craftsman was the equivalent of the modern study tour. This, allied to the traditionally peripatetic nature of the men both during and after training, was one of the main vehicles for the dissemination of ideas, artistic skill and technical knowledge. This mobility has, until recent years, largely been ignored by writers on brasses, though it has long been recognised in other fields. For example, the famous French architect Villard de Honnecourt (fl. c. 1200) is known, from his surviving notebooks in the Bibliothèque Nationale in Paris, to have travelled to Hungary, Switzerland and other countries.[12] The famous engraver and artist Albrech Dürer (*op. cit.*) travelled to several countries during his formative years.

Within the brass industry itself, which was principally engaged in making domestic ware, i.e. cauldrons, ewers, buckets, etc., (the finer ecclesiastical goods like candlesticks, lecterns, font covers, tryptyches, reliquaries, etc., tended to form a quite separate branch) several trades have been identified. Haedeke (*c.f.* Further Reading (p. 48)) mentions brass smelters, rubbers, turners, founders and beaters (or 'batteurs'), sheet metal workers and braziers. Other sources also mention 'lattoners' and 'workers in yellow metal', and we know from surviving examples that enamelling was practised.

Tools of the Trade

The basic tools of the trade (beyond the foundry equipment common to most metal works) were the burin or graver, the hammer and the chisel. In a recent book by I. B. Barsali (*c.f.* Further Reading (p. 47)) the writer mentions how, in another field, goldsmithing, the craftsmen needed to be skilled in handling and using not only engraving and cutting tools, i.e. grainers, planes, chisels, groovers, scrapers, etc., but had to have a good knowledge of casting, gilding, soldering, sculpting, modelling and enamelling. This could equally well be applied to the master lattoner. Barsali also reiterates how much Byzantine art influenced the early craftsmen (Charles Boutell and Herbert Haines were also quick to recognise this fact), who copied not only the techniques, but the designs, especially of ecclesiastical subjects.

No example has yet come to light showing an engraver at work on an ancient monumental brass. The now famous drawings of some early fourteenth century workmen engaged in engraving an incised stone slab[13] give an excellent picture of what an early brass workshop must have looked like. It is interesting to compare the drawings with the photograph at the end of W. E. Gawthorp's excellent and almost forgotten little book, *The Brasses of Our Homeland Churches* (1923), facing page 107, showing 'A present-day Engraver' at work; the cold chisel and the hammer are still being used, while on the bench in front are various drawing instruments, liners, scrapers, etc. Mr Gawthorp made a special study of engraving methods, as well as being closely associated with a firm who made monumental brasses. Some years previously the Waller brothers made some interesting comparisons between English and Flemish methods of brass engraving (*Series of Monumental Brasses* . . . Introduction p. 11), as each used a differently shaped tool for engraving. They state that, "Simple as it seems to be, this difference of practise has materially affected the character of the designs". Examples are then given.

Who were the Engravers?

Lattoners, like many other metalworkers, rarely signed their work, unlike masons, printers, armourers, sculptors, etc., many of whom used marks similar to those adopted by merchants to stamp their goods. A German metalworker *Hans Apengeter* is a rare example of an early craftsman who marked his work; he reached his peak between 1332-44, but it is not known if he ever made or designed brasses.[14] It seems curious that, when so many other craftsmen or workshops in other fields marked or signed their products, that so few brasses until the seventeenth century were signed. This has meant that students of brasses have relied on iconographic or stylistic similarities to group the products of a particular workshop or individual, or can turn to documentary evidence where it has survived. Cases of the latter so far discovered are almost as uncommon as early signed brasses themselves. Wills, contracts or the chance reference to an individual workman as a 'marbler' or 'latoner' in some contemporary document, are our principal sources of information, though in the latter case it is rarely possible to go beyond general supposition. I have already noted two of the most famous examples in my *Beginner's Guide* (pp. 20-1), and others can be found in the books by Malcolm Norris, J. C. Page-Phillips and in the Monumental Brass Society's *Transactions* (*c.f.* Further Reading (p. 46)). As will be seen below, it is evident that many engravers of brasses worked in other metals and materials, including gold, copper, stone and even wood.

In his fine work *English Medieval Architects: a biographical dictionary down to* 1550 (Batsford. 1954. Out of print) John Harvey lists a large number of craftsmen from other trades, e.g. masons, carpenters who are known to have worked in latten or other metals, and who may well have made or designed brasses. Amongst these Mr. Harvey mentions *Henry Harpur*, carver, of Burton, Staffordshire (fl. 1510), who was contracted to make a tomb with 'an image of Henry Foljambe of copper and gilt'; *William Hyndeley* (ob. 1505), master mason at York Minster who left in his will his tools for 'graving in plaite'; *Stephen Lote* (fl. 1381-1418), mason, described in one document as a 'latoner'; *John Orchard* (fl. 1376-95), a 'latoner' of London; *John Wastell* (fl. (?) 1515), mason, who was requested by Thomas Howard, second Duke of Norfolk, to make 'pictours of us and of Agnes our wife . . . ' for their tomb at Thetford (possibly a brass), costing 'cxxxiij *li.* vj *s.* viij. *d.*.; and *Henry Yevele* (ob. 1400), master mason, who refers in his will to his 'marble and laton goods and my tools therin' (*et de latoun ac instrumenta mea ibidem*). At Sudborough, Northamptonshire, one of the children of William and Joan West (1415) is named on an inscription as 'William West, marbler' (ob. 1430) and may well have been responsible for making or designing the whole brass.[15]

On the continent, few signed brasses have survived, and most of these are late examples. The earliest know attributable brasses are those made by the Vischer works at Nuremberg (their mark of a fish appears on some examples); those at Bamburg (1464) and Erfurt (1505) are good examples of their work. Another early German engraver is known from a brass formerly in the Kupferstich Kabinett, Berlin, (1477) which was signed '*Wolfgang, aurifaber*' (see Dr. Cameron's List, p. 46). In France, a little known brass inscription (c. 20 ins. × 10 ins.) was noted by Rev. Herbert Macklin attached to the cenotaph of William VII, Duke of Aquitaine (with sculptured effigy above) in the church of Montierneuf, Poitiers; the inscription was signed 'BONNIOT SCVLP.', suggesting a workman in metal and stone.[16]

Also in France, a Crucifixion scene on the brass of Jean de Thellier and his wife (1604) at Moyvillers, is signed by *Jacques de Nainville*, the brass having been made at Beauvais. A late inscription at Rouen (1711) was engraved by *P. Renault*, a local workman. In Holland, the brass of Canon R. Thienan (1617) at Sittart, is signed '*Fredericus Malders Maeseikeñ sclpt*, 1617'; Malders was a young goldsmith.[17] Like the palimpsest example at Great Berkhamsted, Hertfordshire (obv. 1558, rev. c. 1500), the plate is finely engraved. Names of other continental engravers have been found in wills and similar documents and are mentioned by Malcolm Norris to whom readers are referred for further details.[18]

The most interesting example Mr. Norris quotes is a contract which required the engraver, *Tawchen*, to copy his design from an earlier brass in another church (p. 65).[19] Another writer mentions a document of 1451, referring to *Alard Genoix*, marbler of Tournai, Belgium, as 'ouvrier de lames et de sepultures de laiton', another clear example of one workman engaged in both metal and stone engraving.[20] Mr F. A. Greenhill notes that this dual practice was particularly noticeable amongst draughtsmen of the fourteenth century, especially those designing brasses and incised stone slabs.[21]

Returning to England itself, most of the remaining examples are of seventeenth and early eighteenth century date. Yorkshire, Lancashire and Somerset offer some of the best examples. Most of those in the north of England are from the workshops of *Thomas Ainsworth* (or Aynesworth) in Lancashire and *Joshua and Thomas Mann* of York, and are mainly inscriptions only, sometimes with an achievement of Arms. Examples from the former workshop can be seen at Altham (1677); Lancaster, St. Mary's (1684); Whalley (1693) and Prestwich (1704). Also at Prestwich is an earlier inscription in memory of Anne Allen (1634) with an achievement of Arms which is palimpsest and has on the reverse another achievement signed '*Thos. Aynesworth sculp.*'; this may have been a workshop waster, and suggests that the workshop had been in existence for at least seventy years.

The Manns' workshop(s) was also quite old and the signed examples more scattered. Several brasses signed '*J. Mann, Ebor. sculp.*' can be seen at Colne, Lancashire (1660); Bedale, Yorkshire (1681) and St. Michael-le-Belfry (1680, 1683), St. Sampson (1680) and St. Michael Spurriergate (1681), York. At Bessingby, Yorkshire, is an inscription of 1668 signed '*Thomas Mann fecit*', and signatures of *Richard Crosse* and *Philip Briggs* of York, can be seen at Bedale (1694) and Barton-near-Croft (1680), Yorkshire. Other examples by T. Mann, mostly signed '*Tho: Mann Eboraci sculp.*' occur at

Lowthorpe (1665); Normanton (1668); Helmsley (1671); Ingleby Arncliffe (1674) and Rudstone (1677), all in Yorkshire. Macklin[22] says that a Thomas Mann of York, architect, in his will dated November 27th, 1680 (proved March, 1681) gave to his brother Joshua Mann "all such tooles of mine as he now worketh with . . .". This would seem an unusual combination of professions, although as I have shown earlier, the link between the two arts is not really so distant as one might at first suppose. Macklin and Esdaile also mention other engravers including *Nicholas Stone; Gerard Johnson; Richard Haydock; Gabriel Hornbie* (Yorkshire); *Francis Griggs* (Essex, Shropshire and Yorkshire); *Robert Thorpe*, carver of Sheffield, Yorkshire (Darley, Derbyshire); *George Baldwin* (Munslow, Shropshire);[23] *Richard Mosok* (Ormskirk, Lancashire). The places named in parentheses are the places or areas where signed examples of their work has been found; all are of seventeenth century date.

In the south of England one of the few signed figure brasses of later date is that of Sir Edward Filmer and his wife (1629) at East Sutton, Kent. This is signed by the King's Master Mason, *Edward Marshall.* (ob. 1675).[24] A lesser known name occurs on the curious brass of Dorothy Williams (1694) at Pimperne, Dorset, which is signed '*Edmund Colepeper fecit*'[25]. Two late examples in Somerset are mentioned by the late A. B. Connor at Yeovil (1662) and Crewkerne (1741), which are signed by *George Genge* and '*R. Bannister sculp*', respectively.[26] A third example of better quality at South Brewham, Somerset (1694) is signed '*Gulie. Cockey de Wincalton sculpsit*'.[27] At Marsworth, Buckinghamshire, the brass and tomb of Edward West (1618) bears the famous name of *Epiphanus Evesham*, being signed 'Euesham fecit'.[28]

One last example from this period which cannot go unmentioned is the fine series of portrait busts at Llanrest, Denbighshire in Wales (four of which are excellently reproduced in Trivick[29]). Two of these are signed by the engravers *Silvanus Crue*, a goldsmith, and *William Vaughan.* Although this far from exhausts the list of examples enough has been said to give students a good idea of the scope in this field, and it is an interesting exercise for follow up each of those named in more detail.[30] Modern brasses of the nineteenth and twentieth centuries are only now receiving due attention, and many of the inscription plates bear the maker's name, but few of them were engraved brasses in the above context. Firms like Gawthorp; Heaton, Butler and Bayne and Messrs. Waller (of which more will be said later in this chapter) were the exception rather than the rule.

Contracts for Brasses

Regrettably few original contacts for the making of a brass have survived (as distinct from mentions in wills and other documents) and so those that have are already well known. Those like the 'Sandys Contract' of 1536[31] between *Sir William Sandys* and the Dutch tombmaker Arnout Hermanszoen are already well documented. Also well known is the ledger of the Scottish trader *Andrew Halyburton*, who, between 1493 and 1503 imported brasses and incised slabs from the Low Countries into Scotland, notably the brass (now lost) of Archbishop William Schives of St. Andrews (ob. 1497).[32] Scotland has also produced records showing costs associated with the brasses of Dr. Duncan Liddel (1613), St. Nicholas' Church, Aberdeen[33] and the palimpsest brass of James Stewart, Earl of Murray (1569), St. Giles', Edinburgh.[34] The former was engraved by the Flemish artist *Gaspard Bruydegoms* of the Antwerp mint, while the latter was the work of *James Gray*, goldsmith, who was paid *xx li* 'for ingraving of ane platt of bras' (?) supplied by *David Rowane* at a cost of *vii li*. The design of the obverse of the Stewart brass is very similar to the ornate printed title pages of contemporary books.

Probably the most famous of all contracts is that between the sculptor *Gerard Johnson* of Southwark (1541-1612) and the fastidious John Gage of Firle, Sussex.[35] Not only have Johnson's original sketch and notes survived, but so has the finished product incorporating Gage's alterations. Gage made a particular fuss over the style of bonnets worn by his wives, and even went to the length of sending a specimen to London in a box for Johnson to copy! In Johnson's notes of the contract is specified '. . . a Stone to be of marble enlayed, the pictures and stouchtions* with the epitaphs to be of Brasse . . . the marble appteyning to thes thre platts are to be made of Mr. Gage his own.'. Gage commissioned three tombs in all, of which his own bears the inscription '*Johes Gage qui hic jacet fecit hec monumenta* 1585'. The use of 'fecit' in this context bears out Swartwout's comment on the danger of too literal translation of this word (see p. 29 above). Johnson's workshop must have had a considerable output, as styles and designs similar to the above have since been identified in a number of other churches.

Space does not permit the inclusion of further examples, but readers interested in this aspect are strongly recommended to refer to the notable work of Mrs K. A. Esdaile in this field, to whom the present writer is much indebted. Unfortunately, her work is now long since out of print (see bibliog. for full details). Many other references can be found (all too often) in the footnotes of Haines' *Manual*, and, to a lesser extent, in Waller (1864), Macklin (1907) and Norris (*op. cit.*). Contemporary wills have also provided a large number of references to brasses, many since lost (or never executed), but few provide the engraver's name. There are many others where it is not certain that a brass is actually what is required. As an example, the will of Thomas Parker (ob. 1501), Rector of Dean, Bedfordshire, requests that a marble stone be placed over his body 'with an effigy, at the discretion of mine executors . . . '.[36] In this case the brass, showing Parker in almuce, with inscription under and a representation of the B.V.M. and Child (now lost) still survives on an altar tomb in Dean church showing that his will was carried out properly. In other cases, the deceased's wishes are specifically altered.

In Finchley parish church in north London, is an inscription of 1509 giving an extract from the will of Thomas Sanny, while at Bobbing, Kent, the brass of Sir Arnald Savage (ob.

* i.e. escucheon (shield)

1410) was laid down at the request of his son, also Sir Arnald (ob. 1420), in the latter's will.[37] Ordering of brasses posthumously by friends or relatives was not uncommon (as distinct from those individuals who ordered brasses for themselves during their own lifetime), and two good examples come from monastic houses. The first example has been well documented and states that Abbot Thomas de la Mare of St. Albans when ordering his own magnificient Flemish brass (*vide illus.* in my *Beginner's Guide*, Plate 4) also ordered one of similar size for his predecessor Abbot Michael Mentmore, Abbot from 1335-49, of which the slab only now remains.[38] The second example dating from the same period, c. 1360-80, comes from the records of Meaux Abbey, Yorkshire, where Abbot William of Scarborough (1372-96) ordered brasses for *three* of his predecessors, Hugh de Leven, fifteenth abbot; Robert de Beverly, sixteenth abbot; and William, abbot of Dringhowe, seventeenth abbot; (*ordinavitaque lapides tres marmoreos laminis aereis cum imaginibus abbatum sculptos . . .*).[39] This was but one of many extravagencies in which Abbot William indulged, for when he resigned in 1396 his expensive 'tastes in art and splendour' left the House in debt for 360 *li.*

Finally, an extract from the will of Archbishop Samuel Harsnett, whose fine brass lies in Chigwell Church, Essex (1631). His will, made February 13th, 1630-31, is quite specific in its requests for, ' . . . a Marble stone layde uppon my grave wth a Plate of Brasse moulten into the stone an Ynche thicke haveinge the effigies of a Bysshoppe stamped uppon it wth his Myter and Crosiers Staffe but the Brass to be revited and fastened cleare throughe the Stone as sacreligious handes maye not rend off the one w^th^oute breakinge the other . . . '.[40]

The good Archbishop had obviously witnessed the havoc wrought in many ecclesiastical buildings following the Dissolution, to which end Queen Elizabeth I passed two Acts to try and halt the destruction. The comments of the antiquary John Weever (*q.v.*) in his famous book *Ancient Funerall Monuments* (1631) are often quoted in this context. Unfortunately, another ten years after the Archbishop's death his fears were proved to be founded, and probably resulted in one of the greatest single loss of brasses than at any other time in European history. Fortunately the Archbishop's brass has survived[41].

Modern Brasses

Only very recently have Georgian, Victorian and later brasses received the attention due to them by students of this subject. September 26th 1970 marked the first meeting of the full committee set up by the Monumental Brass Society to organise and carry out the revision and extension of Mill Stephenson's invaluable *List of Monumental Brasses* . . . The aim is not only to up-date the existing *List*, but to record, for the first time, all modern figure brasses up to the present day and inscriptions up to 1850; in addition, all remaining indents of brasses of all dates are to be recorded in detail, and although the publication of this latter work may prove too expensive, the information will be made available to serious students. The present writer is on the above committee as well as being a Regional Controller for Hertfordshire. The task is a mammoth one and cannot be undertaken lightly as churches of all denominations are to be visited, and accuracy is essential.

The rectangular brass plate, both plain and decorative, remained the most common design from the late seventeenth century onwards. By the mid-nineteenth century new manufacturing processes resulted in the almost universal use of coloured pigments and enamels (especially red and black) both in the letters and in border decoration, blazons of Arms, etc. Also, the large plain or decorative-headed cross enjoyed a renewed popularity, especially in larger churches, usually placed within a marginal inscription.* Many nineteenth century and later brasses are the work of local funeral masons, and are usually found either screwed directly to the wall or tomb, or placed in a stone framework.

* This may well have been the result of A. W. Pugin's recommendations in his famous *Apology for the Revival of Christian Architecture in England* (1843), pp. 33–7

During the first half of the eighteenth century the ledger stone, marble monument or sarcophagus, and the mural tablet of white or veined marble gradually out-moded the latten plate. A visit to Bath Abbey, Somerset, whose walls are almost covered with examples of the former type, will bear good testimony to this change. Conversely, a visit to Winchester Cathedral will reveal modern brass plates in equal profusion. Figure brasses, however, are less common, and such as there are have largely escaped the comments of writers on brasses or the interest of students—partly, perhaps, because they cannot generally be rubbed, more probably because of their comparative 'newness'.

Designs

In the eighteenth century many brasses consisted solely of a well engraved Achievement of Arms, complete with embellishments, similar in design to contemporary stone monuments and book-plates. Sometimes the inscription is on the same plate, sometimes cut in stone below, e.g. Richard Poley, knt. (ob. 1765) and his wife Elizabeth (ob. 1792), Rochester Cathedral, Kent.[42] It is also worth notice, that both figure and other brasses were finding their way beyond Britain and Western Europe, first, perhaps, to the United States with the early settlers in New England. The indent of one such brass has only recently been recorded (with a photograph) by Dr H. K. Cameron at Jamestown Memorial Church, Jamestown, Virginia.[43] Dating from c. 1630, it shows the indent of a man in armour, foot inscription, scroll, one shield and a marginal inscription. The figure may represent Sir George Yeardly (c. 1580-1627), Governor of Virginia, and apart from its obvious importance, is the only old latten memorial known in North America to date. The remainder are mainly nineteenth century and later, several being very fine, notably that of Thomas Messenger (1820-81) in St. Anne's Protestant Episcopal Church, Brooklyn, New York,[44] and a less ornate example to Louisa Boldern (1826), St Paul's Church, Halifax, Nova Scotia.[45].

The Gothic Revival

The debt of antiquarians to Richard Gough is now well known, for apart from his published works and manuscript notes and drawings in the Bodleian Library, Oxford, he is generally credited as being largely responsible for the first serious study and appreciation of monumental brasses. The interest he generated manifested itself in Victorian times not only in literary form, but in the first experiments in brass rubbing (as distinct from impressions and dabbings) in the 1840s, and not many years later in a new vogue in figure brasses. The printed works of Charles Boutell, Cambridge Camden Society, John Carter and Rev. Herbert Haines were the first fruits of the revival in our own context. In general terms the so called 'Gothic revival' was inspired by the works of men like John Ruskin (1819-1900) and A. W. Pugin (1812-52) whose books were widely read and admired. Pugin himself designed a number of Victorian 'Gothic' brasses for the firm of John Hardman & Co. of Birmingham and other specialist firms; many were typically ornate in design and abounding in foliation, crocketed and panelled buttresses and canopies, and black letter inscriptions. Two good examples of Pugin's work are the brasses at Clipsham, Lincolnshire (Rev. Matthew Stow, Rector, and his six sisters, 1843-47)[46] and Horbling, Lincolnshire (Rev. Thomas Brown, ob 1849, aged 81).[47]

Victorian manufacturers of brasses

Apart from Messrs. Hardman above, there are a few names in this context that have remained familiar to all serious students of brasses. Amongst these are Messrs Waller; Heaton, Butler & Bayne; and T. J. Gawthorp. The Waller brothers, Lionel A. B. and John G. are probably best remembered for their fine series of engravings of monumental brasses (*q.v.*), but were also responsible for the design and execution of many modern brasses as well as the repair of numerous old ones. Perhaps their most famous work at the time was the brass they designed and made for the Great Exhibition in Hyde Park in 1851, valued, according to the

Gentleman's Magazine[48] at 'not less than 1000 *l*.'. An illustration of the brass can be seen in the *Art Journal's Illustrated Catalogue 'The Industry of all Nations'*, p. 304 (1851; repr. David & Charles, £3.25, 1970; and Dover: Constable, £2.25, paperback, 1970). Examination of the brass soon shows parts of it to bear close resemblance, especially in the design of the canopy, to that of Sir Hugh Hastings, 1347, Elsing, Norfolk. After the Exhibition the brass was used as a memorial to J. G. Waller's mother, sister and a friend in the chapel of St. Raphel Convalescent Home, Torquay, Devon.[49] Another brass to his mother is in Hove Church, Sussex. Among Messrs Wallers' other activities, they were frequently asked to restore, repair, or reproduce old brasses, at which they became great experts. Notes on some of their work appeared in the early volumes of the Monumental Brass Society's *Transactions*. A good example of a partial restoration is the brass of Sir William and Lady Bagot (1407), which they repaired and re-enamelled at the direction and cost of a later Lord Bagot. They went to great pains to achieve accuracy in detail, using either old rubbings or impressions, or, at second best, original prints or drawings, as in the above example.[50]

Whether it was the Wallers or the next important firm to be mentioned, Messrs T. J. Gawthorp of 16, Long Acre, London, who were responsible for the fine modern brass of Edmund Tudor (ob. 1456) in St. David's Cathedral is not certain. For a restoration it is an excellent example of the best Victorian work in the medieval style, and only recently (1970) has the rubbing of it been firmly restricted. Placed on an altar tomb it is said to be a copy of the original brass brought there at the Dissolution in 1536 from the church of the Grey Friars at Carmarthen. I have been unable to substantiate this fact from documentary evidence to date, or to establish a date for the brass being made. It was presumably placed there during Sir Gilbert Scott's restoration of the Cathedral between 1862 and 1878.

Messrs Gawthorp was founded by Thomas John Gawthorp of Addiscombe, Croydon, Surrey, who was to become art metal worker to H.M. Queen Victoria. From his works in

Long Acre, London, he produced a vast number of brasses, mainly consisting of inscriptions only, or inscriptions and crosses. He usually signed his work nominally or with the firm's trade mark. In the Victoria and Albert Museum's Art Library is a *Catalogue of memorial brasses engraved by Gawthorp* . . . , of c. 1865, shewing a series of sepia photographs of examples of their work. A later catalogue of 1881 could not be traced at the British Museum Library when I requested it. T. J. Gawthorp's son, Walter Edmund Gawthorp (1859-1936), also entered the firm where he remained until his retirement in 1935. Walter not only made a special study of ancient brasses, especially their method of engraving and enamelling, but wrote many papers and a book on this subject. With his father, he was also largely responsible for carrying out repairs to a large number of old brasses in the early part of this century notes on some of which are in Vols. 5 and 6[51] of the *M.B.S. Transactions;* amongst these was the repair and relaying of all the brasses at Tattershall, Lincolnshire. One interesting side-light on this work was W. E. G.'s note on the 'silvery appearance' of the metal observed when drilling holes in the majority of old brasses. In the case of most of those at Tattershall, he carried out an analysis of the metals from various brasses, which showed a much higher proportion of tin in the later examples, which he concluded accounted for the 'silvery' appearance.

Two other firms require more than a cursory mention in this field, namely, Messrs Heaton, Butler and Bayne of London and New York; and, Messers Hart, Son, Peard & Co. Ltd. of London and Birmingham. Both firms were flourishing at the beginning of this century, and both also made stone tablets; in the former case stained glass, mosaics and other church decoration were also undertaken. Like Gawthorp's, Heatons also held Royal Warrants, and advertised their metal for brasses as '*genuine "latten" . . . Brass—the fine old metal engraved in Flemish, and afterwards in English, workshops of nearly seven centuries ago — . . . remains to-day the only suitable material for memorial brasses.*'. It would be interesting to analyse one of their 'latten' plates to test the validity of this statement. One of their catalogues of c. 1910 is in the V. and A. Museum Library, and contains examples of their work, ranging in price from $90 for a small inscription on an oak board, to $1,270 for figure brasses like that of Bishop William Reeves of Armargh, N. Ireland (1815-92). The most famous brass in our context made by Heaton's is that of Rev. Herbert Haines (1826-72), author of the invaluable *Manual of Monumental Brasses*, in Gloucester Cathedral. This is described by me in my new introduction to the reprint of Haines' *Manual* (Adams & Dart. 1970).

The catalogue of modern brasses is endless as examples abound. Hart, Son, Peard & Co. Ltd., appear to have specialised in mural brasses and tablets, and I have not found any example of a figure brass by them. Again, a twenty-page illustrated catalogue of specimens is in the V. and A. Museum Library, of c. 1900. I can think of no more valuable exercise in the above context than a detailed study of the firms manufacturing brasses in the nineteenth and present centuries, including details of any patents registered; search for any surviving company records, papers, drawings, etc., of work carried out or commissioned, and so on. Both Hart's and Hardman's still survive (see Appx. II below).

The names of individual designers of modern brasses, other than those already mentioned, are rarely recorded and also require much further study. In the *Journal of the British Archaeological Association*, Vol. I (1846), p. 44, is a note of a Mr Thomas King of Chichester, who was then making an ecclesiastical brass of a priest, 'copied from a monument at Dieppe of 1447'. It is a pity no more details were included, as it makes tracing the brass almost impossible, assuming it was finished.[52] The brass of Rev. Herbert Haines (op. cit.) was designed by a friend, Capel N. Tripp, while that of another great writer on brasses, William Frederick Creeny (1825-97) in St Michael-at-Thorn, Norwich, Norfolk, was the work of a local artist Mr W. R. Weyer of Norwich.[53] Both are fitting tributes to their respective subjects.

Other nineteenth century or later names to which I have found reference include a 'Mr Matthews', referred to by Sir Henry Dryden in his classic paper on fixing brasses (see p. 46 below for details). Also, an advertisement in the early issues of the *C.U.A.B.C. Transactions* (1890 ff.) refers to *Culleton's Heraldic Office*, 25, Cranbourn Street, St Martin's Lane, London, W.C., who made 'Monumental Brasses designed and engraved in Mediaeval and other Styles, and supplied ready for fixing . . . ' Firms who just made brasses were very rare and most, therefore, supplied other types of memorial in stone, glass or wood, as well as a range of ecclesiastical metal-work. The small local firm of monumental masons, as at the present day, would normally only be able to supply stone slabs and plaques or simple brass wall plates. I have in my possession an undated catalogue of an organisation called '*Sculptured Memorials and Headstones*, 12, Lower Regent Street, London, in which is reproduced a rubbing of one of their brasses designed by Julian P. Allan and in memory of Henry Barry Hyde (ob. 1932), Prebendary of Exeter and Archdeacon of Madras. The rest of the catalogue is filled with examples of stone memorials. Other firms whose names appear frequently in the above context and are often seen on brasses include Singers of Frome; T. Thomason & Co., Birmingham; Barkentin & Krall, London; Cox & Buckley, London; G. Maile & Sons, London (now of Canterbury)[54].

Lastly, mention must be made of Rev. A. Wyon (Vicar of Newlyn, Cornwall in 1952) who designed the fine modern brasses of Bishops Walter Howard Frere (ob. 1938) and Timothy Rees (ob. 1939) in Truro and Llandaff Cathedrals respectively, and of Mr Francis J. C. Cooper who designed a large and skilfully executed brass of Bishop M. N. Trollope, S.T.P. (ob. 6th Nov. 1930), to be placed in the Cathedral of Korea where the deceased held the See. A short but interesting account of the execution and design of the brass (made of 'Latin metal' and requiring three castings before a perfect result was obtained) is in *Metal Industry*, Aug. 25th, 1933, p. 167 (Lamb, H.A.J. 'Modern Brasses'), together with an illustration. The Bishop, we are told, was himself a keen brass rubber as a boy, making the memorial of 'particular aptness'.

I think I have said enough now for the student to realise that every brass, old or new, is of potential interest. How this interest can be exploited and extended is shown in a later chapter. I hope I have indicated sufficient lines of thought to inspire at least some readers to follow up this important work with their own researches—there is still much to be done. A great deal of information can be learned from formal and informal discussion with other interested colleagues both inside and outside the Monumental Brass Society. The Society's week-end conferences, for example, are an excellent forum. Conversely, a great deal more information is secreted in the pages of forgotten books, journals, and manuscripts. If this chapter has suggested what can be done, and still remains to be done, then ith as achieved its purpose. It will be doubly successful if it makes many more people realise that there is much more to be gained from brasses than simply making rubbings of them.

Having dealt in some detail with the manufacture of brasses I will now look at the allied arts to which brasses owe so much and of which they formed so important a part. For those readers who wish to follow up these notes with further research or reading, I am adding below a select bibliography of sources, supplementing or enlarging on those already given as footnotes. Regrettably, many of these works are out of print (prices are not given in these cases), or are readily available only through libraries.

FURTHER READING

Brasses

BOULTER-COOKE, M. A. 'Monumental brasses'. *Churchman,* Dec 1919, 679–84

CAMERON, H. K. *List of Monumental Brasses on the Continent of Europe* (Monumental Brass Soc. 1970)

DRYDEN, Sir Henry E. L. 'On the Ancient method of fixing Sepulchral Brasses' *AASRP* XX (ii) Dec. 1889, 89–93. Illus.

EVANS, H. F. O. 'Fixing of brasses' *MBS* X, ii (Dec. 1964), 58–62. Illus.

FORSTER, W. C. 'Monumental Brasses and the Evangelistic symbols'. *London Naturalist* 1935, pp. 55–60. Illus.

Discusses correct and incorrect order of symbols in relation to inscription (with comparative tables); notes on origin of symbols.

GREENHILL, F. A. *Incised Slabs of Leicestershire and Rutland* (Leics. Archaeol. and Hist. Soc. 1958)

A classic study, admirably illustrated and a basic work of reference; valuable historical introduction showing clearly the corellation between the engraved metal plate and incised stone slab. Good bibliography. The same author has also contributed many valuable papers and notes to the *MBS Trans* both before and since the date of this book, notably on Scottish incised slabs and lost brasses.

JENKINS, C. K. 'Beauty in Brass'. *Apollo* XLIV (Aug. 1946), 32–4; XLVI (Nov. 1947), 118–20; XLVIII (Nov. 1948), 113–5. Illus.

MARTYN, Margaret. 'English Monumental Brasses' *Country Life*, CIII (16 Jan. 1948), 130–31. Illus.

Incl. notes on engravers of brs. and allied objects. (See also letter ff. above article *ibid* 20 Feb. 1948, p. 388 correcting point of detail)

NORRIS, M. 'Mediaeval trade in monumental brasses' *Geog. Mag.* XXVIII, 2 (Mar. 1956), 519–25

Ibid 'Schools of brasses in Germany' *BAA* 3 Ser., 19 (1958), 34–53

Ibid Brass Rubbing (Studio Vista. £2.10.1965)

WEIMAR, Wilhelm *Monumental Schriften . . . c. 1100–1812* (Hamburg. 1899) 16p.+68 plates incl. sev. of brasses (e.g. Verden, 1231).

Reference has also been made to the following

ANSON, P. F. *Fashions in church furnishings 1840–1940* (Studio Vista. £3.15 2nd edn., 1965. Illus. bibliog.

AUBERT, Marcel *High Gothic Art* (Methuen [Art of the World Series]. 1964) Illus. Good bibliog.

DELABORDE, Henri *Étude sur les Beaux artes en France et en Italie*. 2 vols. 1864

Eastlake, C. L. *History of the Gothic revival in England* (1872 repr. Leics. U.P. £5.50. 1970)

Encyclopaedia of World Art (McGraw Hill. 15 vols. 1959–69)

Many valuable articles, most with comprehensive bibliog. espec. useful for articles on medieval art in individual countries like Germany,

Belgium and France, and for subjects like Metalwork, Gothic Art (vol. VI, pp. 627–35), engraving. No separate heading for brasses.

FRANKL, Paul *Gothic architecture* (Penguin [Pelican Hist. of Art] 1962)

GAUNT, William *Flemish cities: their history and art* (Elek. £4.20. 1969) Illus.; bibliog.; Includes sections on Bruges, Ghent, Antwerp and Brussels; gives names of many artists, metalworkers, etc. practicing in these towns during 14th and 15th cents.

HARVEY, John *Gothic World 1100–1600* (Batsford. 1950 (o/p); repr. in pbk. by Harper (N.Y.), Colophon Books Series. $2.75. 1969)

HENDERSON, George *Gothic* (Penguin. 1967)

KIDSON, Peter *Medieval world* (Hamlyn. £1.50. 1967)

MAYER, Ralph *Dictionary of Art Terms and Techniques* (A. & C. Black. £3.50. 1969)

OSBORNE, H. *(ed.) Oxford Companion to Art* (Oxford University Press. £6.00 1970. Incl. comprehensive bibliog. of sources)

PEVSNER, N. *Studies in Art, Architecture and Design.* 2 vols. (Thames & Hudson. £9.00 set 1968)

THOMPSON, Paul *William Butterfield* (Routledge. £10.00. 1971)

VAN PUYVELDE, Leo *Flemish painting from the Van Eycks to Metys;* trans. by Alan Kendall (Weidenfeld & Nicolson. £9.25. 1971)

WEBB, Geoffrey *Architecture in Britain; the Middle Ages* (Penguin [Pelican History of Art Series) £4.20 (pbk.) 1956)

For information on manufacture of 'latten' and other metals

AGRICOLA, George *Georgius Agricola de re metallica: trans. from the First Latin Edition of 1556, with biographical introduction . . . By H. C. Hoover and L. H. Hoover* (1912 repr. 1950. Dover: Constable. £5.95)

BARSALI, Isa B. *Medieval goldsmith's work* (Hamlyn [Cameo Books] £0.75. 1969)

BIRINGUCCIO, Vannoccio *The Pirotechnia of Vannoccio Biringuccio; trans. from the Italian with an Introduction and Notes by Cyril S. Smith and M. T. Gnudi* (M.I.T. Press. £1.65 (pbk.) 1942 repr. 1966)

CAMERON, H. K. 'Metals used in Monumental Brasses' *MBS* 8, iv (Dec. 1946), 109–30

ERCKER, Lazarus. *Treatise on ores and assaying, trans. from the German Edition of 1580 by A. G. Sisco and Cyril S. Smith.* (Univ. of Chicago P. 1951)

HAEDEKE, Hanns-Ulrich *Metalwork* trans. by V. Manes. (Weidenfeld & Nicolson (Social Hist. of the Decorative Arts Series) £4.20. 1970) See esp. Pt. II on bronze and brass industries; Ch. 4 The Renaissance, and Notes on pp. 200 and 201. Valuable work of reference, well documented and illustrated.

HAMILTON, Henry. *English Brass and Copper industries to 1800.* (Longmans. 1926. 2nd edn. with new intro. by J. R. Harris. F. Cass. 1967)

HONOUR, Hugh. *Goldsmiths and silversmiths* (Weidenfeld & Nicolson £5.75. 1971)

Esp. pp. 30–7 describing and illus. work of Nicholas of Verdun (fl. 1181–1205). 'one of the greatest and most adventurous artists of his period' (p. 30). His enamelled copper panel on altar of Kepsterneuberg and his 'Moses return from Egypt' exhibit designs later adapted or copied on brasses and other monuments.

SCHREITTMANN, Ciriacus. *Probierbüchlin, Frembde und Künst Van Wage und Gewicht, auch von allerhandt Proben auff Ertz, Golt, Silber . . .* (Frankfurt. 1578)

SOYRES, B. de. 'History and Particulars of the Brass Battery Process' *Trans. Newcomen Soc.*, XXVIII (1951–2 and 1952–3), 131–35 (Paper

PLATE 1

(*a*) Bishop Yso Wilpe (1231), St Andreaskirche, Verden, nr Hanover, Germany. The earliest surviving figure brass; the design may well have been copied from a contemporary drawing or another tomb. The original brass is now very dark, badly cracked across the centre and secured to a concave-shaped wall with large-headed nails. Size: 101.5 cm (40 ins) high by 78.75 cm (31 ins) at top; 73.6 cm (29 ins) wide at base. Rubbing by Sally Morris. Photo (taken from slide) by Peter Marshall.

(*b*) Bishop Otto von Braunschweig (1279), Hildesheim, Germany. Although nearly 50 years later than the Wilpe brass, shows little progression in design or execution; appointed Bishop in 1260 when only aged 14, Otto died at the early age of 33 years. Photo Peter Marshall (after Creeny).

(*c*) A 16th century metal foundry. Copper formed a high percentage of the content of the 'latten' used for monumental brasses, and scenes such as the above are typical of what a 'brass' foundry would have looked like. 'AEs or Brass', says Sir John Pettus in his *Essays on Words Metallick* (1683), 'is not a proper Metal' but a compound of copper and 'lapis Calaminaris', whilst Latten is but 'Brass Tin'd over'.

(*d*) Detail from the Braunche brass (1364), St Margaret's Church, King's Lynn, Norfolk. Showing head of dexter wife with the usual blank, staring eyes and 'fiddle-bow lips' (as J. C. Page Phillips calls them) common to Flemish brasses of this period and school, with quaint little figure of a 'mourner' in the side shaft in a 'mini-tunic'. Rubbing by the author. Photo Peter Marshall.

(a)

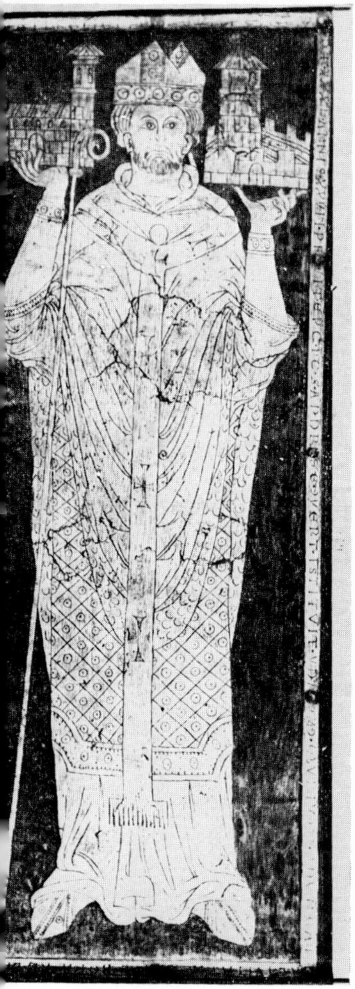

(b)

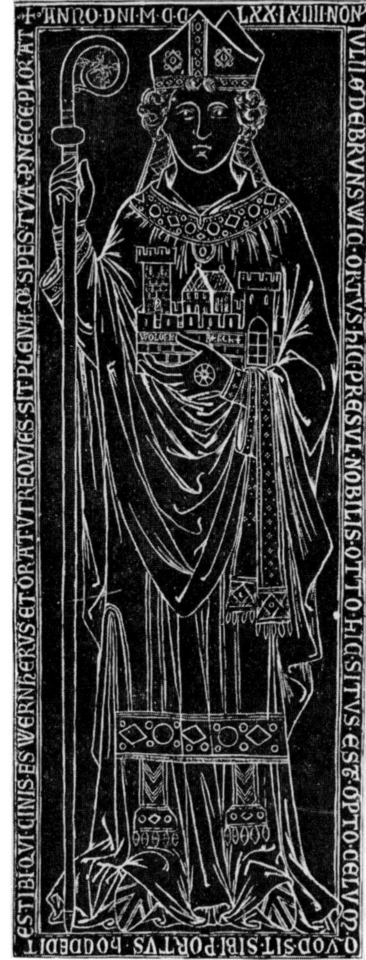

(c)

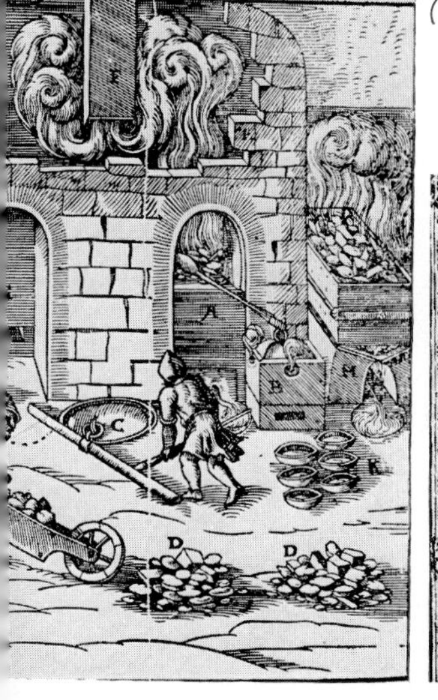

(d)

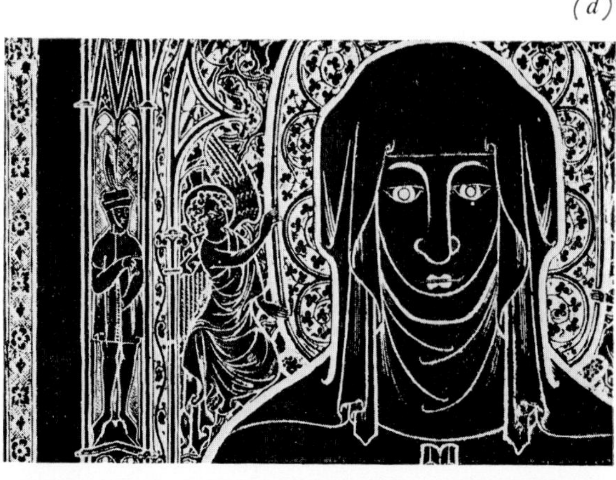

Plate 2

(*a*) William de Kestevene (c. 1360), N. Mymms, Herts. (*b*) Sir Simon de Wensley (c. 1365), Wensley, Yorks (N.R.). Both figures are shown together to indicate their obviously common source; both are thought to be 'Flemish' school and differ mainly only in size. Both are now mural. Size: (*a*) 121 by 50 cm ($47\frac{1}{2}$ by $19\frac{1}{2}$ ins) overall; (*b*) 163.8 cm ($64\frac{1}{2}$ ins); (*c*) Matthew de Assecheton, Rector, Shillington, Beds (1404). A well drawn figure showing the economy of line typical of English brasses of this period; note the unusual feature of a dog at his feet. Formerly in chancel (see BM Cole MSS 5836), now relaid in north chapel. The M.I. is omitted from the illus. Figure 132.7 cm ($52\frac{1}{2}$ ins). Rubbing by the author. Photo Peter Marshall.

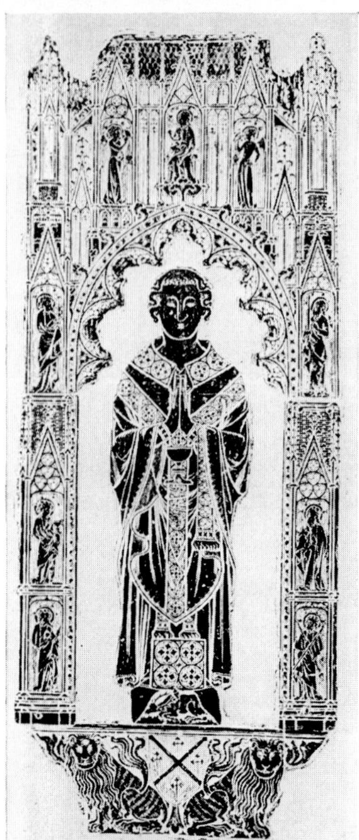

(*a*)

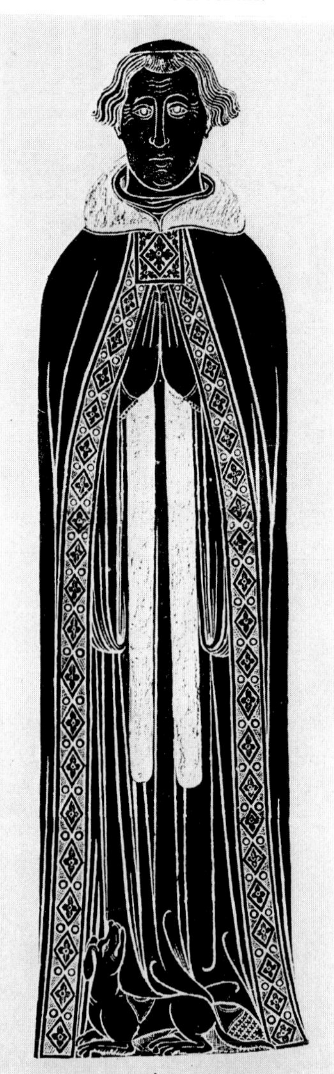

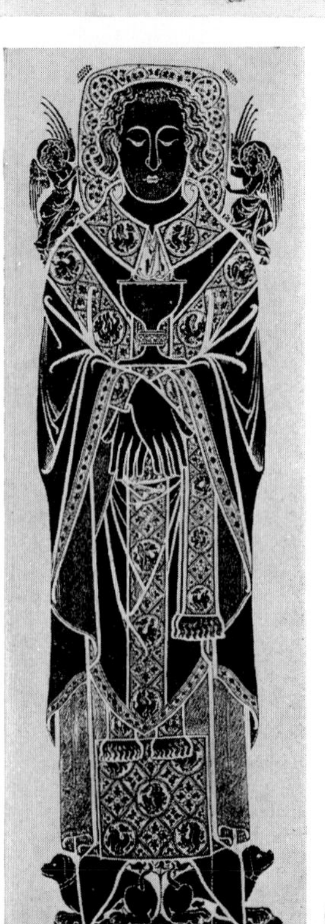

(*b*)

(*c*)

read at Science Museum 17/9/1952)

Historical matter based on H. Hamilton's *English Brass and Copper Industries to 1800,* but with addit. material, mainly on brass industry from about 1700–1800; includes illus, of 'Battery Works' (Plate XIV) of 1764.

TAVENOR-PERRY, J. *Dinanderie: a history and description of medieval art work in copper, brass and bronze.* (G. Allen & Sons. 1910)

Esp. useful are early chapters on Dinant (pp. 17 *ff.*) and for names of brass sculptors mentioned in text.

CHAPTER TWO

Brasses and the Allied Arts: an Introductory Guide

[2] THE ALLIED ARTS

I make no apology for the lengthy discourse above setting out the background to the rest of this section, as it is very important to understand something of the climate in which the art of brass engraving and manufacture developed. The section below aims at indicating some of the sources from other media which were available to, or influenced, the designers of monumental brasses, how these ideas were adapted and transmitted, and how brasses fitted into the general history of their contemporary arts and crafts. The survey will, of neccessity, be brief, and is intended to suggest further lines of enquiry which those interested in this subject can follow. Some is not original, but collectively it has never before appeared under one cover in this form.[1]

Boutell, the Waller brothers, Haines and Way were quick to realise the importance of examining brasses in a broader context, though largely confined their comments to media like the incised stone slab, enamels and printing plates. Generally speaking, the same areas have remained as the only allied arts to be looked at by succeeding writers until very recent times, leaving whole areas virtually unexplored and their influence neglected. The same has also been true of writers on these allied arts themselves, who have omitted to fit brasses into the general context of the history of their subject, or used them for comparative purposes.

The main exceptions to the above were the writers on the history of the printing block and plate. As a result, insufficient emphasis has been placed on the strong artistic influences and traditions which affected designers and engravers of brasses, or indeed, the designs themselves. Although this is partly due to lack of surviving documentary evidence, I hope I will be able to suggest in the notes below how much work is still necessary in order to complete this field of study. To do this, brasses must be looked at in a much broader context than those traditionally adopted by many writers during the first half of the present century.

In all funeral sculpture there remained the very strong influence of the Church. Although a more enlightened attitude to Christian teaching and scientific discovery developed during the period under discussion, the finality of physical death and the belief in the life hereafter still dominated the minds of most men and women. This is borne out by the consistency in the wording of inscriptions; the figures with hands clasped in prayer or kneeling at prayer desks; the frequent use of the traditional symbols or representations of the saints, the Holy Trinity, the Blessed Virgin Mary; the invocatory scrolls, figures of Death, hour glasses and the strange fashion for shroud and cadaver brasses. Many Elizabethan and Jacobean rhyming inscriptions especially, are pre-occupied with wordly benefactions and attributes and the benefits to be accrued from these in the life to come (see some examples in Chapter 4 below).[2] How these traditions were adapted to brasses and other media and how they in their turn affected each other can now be discussed in context; the order below is of no significance.

Stained and Painted Glass

Regrettably, not a great deal of old stained and painted glass in complete condition survives in Britain (cathedrals like York[3] and churches like Fairford (Gloucestershire) are exceptional), though many of the continental ecclesiastical buildings, notably in France, still contain some fine examples. From that which has survived it is not difficult to find designs which bear a close resemblance to those used on brasses of the same period, and there is little doubt that ideas were freely copied or exchanged. It is often forgotten that stained or painted glass was one of the earliest means of visual expression used by the churches for teaching the Bible to the ordinary people; wall paintings, tryptyches, altar frontlas, painted or mural panels and carving were other methods. These in their turn bear close resemblance to the designs in the illuminated manuscripts, drawings, paintings, miniatures and early woodcuts of the period.

In the magnificient work *English Stained Glass* (*c.f.* Further Reading (page 74)) by John Baker, the author notes the "striking similarity" in design and technique between the art of the glazier and the enameller in cloisonné (*q.v.*), but makes no mention of similar work on brasses and incised slabs. Another writer not mentioned by Mr. Baker is the nineteenth century French authority Henri Delaborde, who supports the above statement, but even claims that the process of painting enamels and glass are so similar that the glazier could 'become an enameller by the simple process of substituting a plate of metal for a piece of glass . . . '.[4]

Mr. Baker does, however, suggest some of the sources used by the master glaziers for their designs (pp. 27 *ff.*), including, the Bible; Lives of the Saints; and Dutch and German woodcuts, especially the two famous series in the *Speculum Humanae Salvationis* and the *Biblia Pauperum*. The same is equally true of engravers of brasses, masons, woodworkers and other artists and craftsmen.

One writer on the painted glass in the conventual buildings at Westminster Abbey[5] says that brown enamel used to preserve some thirteenth century glass was so much raised above the decayed surface of the old glass 'that excellent rubbings of the heads of the figures can be taken in the same way as one makes rubbings of brasses'. This is the only reference to 'glass rubbing' I have seen to date! The main similarity between early brasses and painted glass, however, is in the economy of line and the traditional method of depicting folds in costume; the Saints; canopy work and other accessories. Manuscript and early printed work shows the same tendencies.

Architects and Masons

The splendour of the Gothic cathedrals and churches is self-evident, and the wealth of beautiful carving which has survived makes it evident that any work of funeral sculpture or art was strongly influenced by the contemporary architectural detail.[6] In the early Flemish brasses particularly the so called Gothic canopy, with its 'panoply of saints' and weepers in niches around and above the main figure(s) exhibit the strong influence of contemporary stone masonry. Indeed, it has been said by one writer that this wealth of detail was engraved on Flemish brasses 'in an effort to hide the fact that invention and originality were not theirs . . . .'[7] Certainly many of the simpler English canopies of the early fifteenth century especially, are far more pleasing with their slender side shafts, pinnacles and crockets; even those with heavier canopies like that of Dean John Blodwell (1462), Balsham, Cambridgeshire are preferable and more striking than many of the confusing continental designs. Engravers of English brasses were, after all, merely copying the stone counterpart on a flat surface. The fine super-canopy on the famous brass of Prior Thomas Nelond, Cowfold, Sussex, (1433) still presents what is probably the most successful example of this transference from three to one dimension.

I have already mentioned in the previous chapter how some masons also designed or made brasses. John Harvey states[8] that the master mason was also qualified to act as an architect, provided he was capable and of sufficient education. Family connections were also important. These facts, allied to the peripatetic nature of most craftsmen at this time would certainly mean that the inter-action of these groups and individuals caused not only joint practice but free exchange of designs and skills. The seventeenth century architect and engraver Thomas Mann of York (*op cit*) is a good late example; similarly Nicholas Stone and Gerard Johnson were carvers and engravers in several media.[9]

I have also remarked on the way in which early architects copied or adapted designs from artists in other fields, quoting Villard de Honnecourt and Matthew Paris as examples. Manuscripts were used by all craftsmen of the time, and a good example in the above context is quoted by C. J. P. Cave, who shows how a stone mason at Boxgrove Priory, Sussex, copied designs from a French Book of Hours of c 1500. Conversely, several examples have been discovered of work by English masons and carvers of alabaster in places like Nantes and Bordeaux in France,[10] and Portugal.[11] In the case of English brasses found abroad, by far the most famous example is that of Bishop Hallam (1416) in Constance Cathedral, Germany; Dr H. K. Cameron lists one other example in the Musée Lapidaire, Bordeaux, France, to an English merchant John Scott and his wife Christiane (1392).[12] Both these examples, however, were probably imported from England, rather than being engraved on the spot by English workmen.

The wealth of architectural detail found on brasses is mentioned by many writers, but only one, J. S. M. Ward, appears to have made a study in any depth. Not only in his little book on brasses[13] but in two articles in '*The Builder*',[14] Ward mentions especially features like canopies, brackets and crosses.[15] Engravers of brasses were not the only workmen to copy the mason, as the woodworkers mentioned in the next section copied the mason's method of carving until they had fully understood the limits and versatilities of their own medium.

Another link between stone-work and brasses that is only now receiving attention again is the petrology of the material itself. Mr S. E. Rigold in an interesting paper 'Petrology as an aid to Classification of Brasses',[16] shows not only which stones were most commonly used, including stone like Tournai marble, Ardennes limestone,but how such identification might be used to indicate the location of brass workshops. Stone dressing was an important allied industry to brass production, though whether the two arts were always carried out by the same individuals is uncertain.

In the second of his valuable volumes on *The Lost Monumental Brasses of Sussex* (1970), Mr A. G. Sadler also pays special attention to the stone used for the slabs of local brasses. At least two, at Chichester Cathedral and Winchelsea, appear to be of Ardennes limestone, the brasses probably being of Flemish or French origin. The ever reliable Herbert Haines did not miss the above point either, as in a footnote in his *Manual* (Intro. p. xxiii) he notes that some incised limestone slabs in Boston church, Lincolnshire, that were partly inlaid with brass, probably came from the area around Liège, Belgium, or the banks of the River Meuse. The equally astute Waller brothers, in the introduction to their magnificient book of engravings, also make some valuable comments on this matter.[17] The link between incised stone slabs and brasses has already been mentioned above, by such authorities as R. H. Edelston, Rev. W. F. Creeny,[18] W. E. Gawthorp,[19] F. A. Greenhill,[20] and very briefly in my *Beginners' Guide*, so I need not expand on it further. A comparison between the illustrations in the above works and any well illustrated work on brasses, makes the latter abundantly clear. Dr Greenhill's work in this field is especially valuable and readers are advised to study it closely, since it may result in some radical changes in our ideas on the origins of brasses.

The Woodworker

Wooden tombs are rare in England and most of those which survive are almost identical to their stone counterparts. 'Poppy-head' pews, pulpits and rood-screens also present features copied from stone though virtually no complete original roods survive. It is therefore difficult, perhaps, to see any direct link with the designs of monumental brasses. One important type of carving not mentioned so far, however, is the curious and fascinating misericorde seat, of which many examples still survive in Britain and western Europe. The carvers of such seats were fortunate in not being confined to traditional motifs and were thus able to express themselves freely. Apart from being able to draw or caricature their subjects from real life, they could also create or copy mythological beasts, just as the engravers of Flemish brasses like that of Abbot Thomas de la Mare (c. 1360) St Albans Abbey, Hertfordshire, did at a similar date. Biblical scenes, especially from the Old Testament, were not forgotten by any means, but several authorities mention other manuscript and printed sources of designs as well.

The 'family likenesses' between groups of misericorde carvings have long been recognised, just as certain designs of brasses present strong similarities in style. Rev J. S. Purvis has shown clearly how the 'Ripon School' of early sixteenth century carvers copied prints in the *Biblia Pauperum* and the *Speculum Humanae Salvationis*.[21] Others may have used a Bestiary, or *Physiologus;* still others, some of the famous engravings of Israel van Meckenen, the Master E. S.[22] or Martin Schongauer. Mr J. L. Barnard states that carvings on some of the stalls in King Henry VII's Chapel, Westminster Abbey, are based on prints by Dürer and van Meckenen, engraved at the end of the fifteenth century; the latter's designs were also copied at Hoogstraten, Belgium.[23] Another carver at Bristol Cathedral, copied four of his designs from decorative borders in a book published in Paris in c. 1500, designed by Thielmann Kerver and others. This is the same book mentioned above in the note on a stone mason at Boxgrove Priory, Sussex (p. 54).

Much of this may seem irrelevant to the student of brasses, but collectively it was all part of the same movement, and although brasses may lack the freedom of expression visible on many stone and wood carvings, their engravers and/or designers could not fail to be influenced by these allied branches of Gothic art and architecture. Some of the curious beasts or devices between letters on early marginal inscriptions e.g. Northleach, Gloucestershire (1447); the two battling dogs at the feet of Lawrence de St. Maur (1337), Higham Ferrers, Northamptonshire; the strange, twisted creatures in the elaborate diapered background of Albrecht Hovener's brass (1357) at Straslund and de la Mare's brass (c. 1360) at St Albans Abbey, Hertfordshire, must surely reflect the influence mentioned above, or be copied from similar sources.

The Manuscript, the Drawing and the Printed Book

Byzantine and early Italian manuscripts were other important influences on west European artists and designers, and extensive copying from such work is all too evident. Later, towns like Cologne, Bruges and Paris became famous for their illuminated manuscripts and miniatures, men like Gerard David of Bruges being as famous in the field of miniatures as Matthew Paris of St Albans had been earlier amongst manuscript artists and painters. Much work has been done in recent years on determining what is generally called the 'iconography' of medieval drawings and illuminated work. Illuminated prayer books, homiles, Books of Hours, psalters and Bibles offer ample scope for such exacting work. The "iconography of monumental brasses" has received little such attention to date, and more will be said about this subject later in this chapter.

As an example to illustrate the above point, plate 56 of a recent book by Michael W. Evans [24] shows a copy of a fine drawing of an archbishop, taken from the famous thirteenth century Lambeth Apocolypse in the British Museum. This figure exhibits many similarities in style to the mutilated figure of Archbishop Grenefeld (1315) in York Minster, and to the two early German brasses of bishops at Verden (1231) and Hildesheim (1279), (*vide* illus f.p. 48) and may well have been the kind of model from which the engravers worked; all show clear Byzantine influence. Similarly, the two drawings of St Christopher in Plate 123 of the same work, could equally well have been designs (or cartoons) for funeral sculpture in metal or stone.

The drawing has always tended to take second place to illuminated work, but Mr Evans states that in some areas, notable England, southern Germany (especially around

Regensburg) and in Austria, the 'drawing was the predominant technique for manuscript illustrations' during the twelfth and thirteenth centuries. The fact that the earliest extant brasses are recorded in two of these areas may possibly be of some significance. Regrettably no medieval artists have left any personal sketch-boks, but a number of 'model-books' containing standard types and designs have survived. Earlier books were similar to those of men like Villard de Honnecourt (*q.v.*) but the later ones were more like those associated with artists like Leonardo da Vinci, Giotto and da Fabriano. Many of the latter type contain lively drawings and sketches of animals and flowers.

The strong traditions of religious and funeral art, and the way in which the artists and engravers adhered to them is shown well on brasses. Few examples exist from before the Reformation of brasses showing anything like what we now call 'free expression' (and even these are fairly rare)—it was only the skill of some engravers that brought the figure or subject 'to life.'

Such tradition was not, however, confined only to funeral art, but to most of the allied arts mentioned in this chapter, even the early printed books. Symbols of the Evangelists such as those in Plate 10, the Holy Trinity seated in majesty, (both clearly of Byzantine origin); representations of popular saints like SS Christopher, Catherine and Mary Magdelene; the Blessed Virgin Mary, etc., are nearly always drawn to the same pattern whatever the medium. A good example is the figure of St Christopher in the side shaft of the canopy of the brass of Lady Joan Cromwell (c. 1470) at Tattershall, Lincolnshire, whose counterpart can be seen in many contemporary prints and woodcuts. Scenes showing the Crucifixion and the Annunciation have rarely survived on brasses, but continental examples such as that at Nivelles, (c. 1600)[25] and Froyennes[26] (1574), Belgium, showing Jerusalem in the background, is a Renaissance adaptation copied from paintings or engravings by earlier artists like Grünewald, Memling, Dürer and Cranach.[27] The well-known brass of George Rede (1500) at Fovant,

Wiltshire, is a good example of a type which could just as easily have been an engraved printing plate or printer's mark, and might well have been made by the engraver of such a work.

Printing Plates and Printer's Marks

The Rev Herbert Haines was one of the first writers about brasses to draw attention to the similarity between the latten memorial and the engraved metal printing plate (*Manual of Monumental Brasses*, Pt. I, pp. xxxv-vi especially). Although the original idea was not his own (he acknowledges Joseph Strutt's famous *Dictionary of Engravers*[28] as his source), Haines' additional comment is worth quoting in full:—

'. . . if the makers of monumental brasses did not invent the art of printing from engraved metal plates, the most skilful of them, no doubt, when the discovery was made, relinquished their former occupation, and directed their energies to a higher branch of the art . . .'.

He concludes, succinctly, that this may explain the deterioration in the design and execution of brasses following the invention of printing. This would appear to be borne out in practice by the noticeable rise in the skill of the engravers and designers of title pages and printer's marks in the early sixteenth century.[29]

Haines' theory was strangely ignored by succeeding writers on brasses until more recent times, though reference to it is made in many books on the history of the woodcut. Mr Henry Trivick has recently given attention to the subject (with illustrations) in his book, *The Craft and Design of Monumental Brasses* (*c.f.* Further Reading (page 77)), with special reference to a type of engraving known as manière criblée, or, dotted prints. An earlier authority, A. M. Hind, in his *Introduction to the History of the Woodcut*, illustrates another example of a dotted print, reproducing it in both relief and intaglio. The latter bears a striking resemblance both in appearance and design to what might have been a typical Annunciation scene on a brass, but also seen in many contemporary paintings throughout western Europe. In this particular instance, Hind suggests that the plate came from Cologne, because of its great resemblance to the Annunciation by Stephen Lochner (ob. 1451) on the "wings of his Altarpiece in Cologne Cathedral" (p. 180).

Strutt (*op. cit.*) and Hind both support the theory that the early engravers of printing plates may also have been goldsmiths, largely because of the fineness and detail of the engraving. I have already made reference to this fact above in respect to brasses (p. 30) noteably those at Great Berkhamsted, Hertfordshire (c. 1500) and St Giles' Cathedral, Edinburgh (1569). At Herne, Kent, the curiously designed brass of the wife of Sir Matthew Philip (1470), Mayor of London and himself a famous goldsmith, is thought to be the work of a craftsman more used to engraving precious metal.[30] The antiquaries John Weever and John Stow both record several memorials, probably brasses but now lost, of other London goldsmiths in the City and surrounding London churches. Amongst the names in Weever are those of Sir Nicholas Farington (or Farenton) (ob. 1361); John Sutton, Sheriff, (1450); William Breakspeare (1461): William Holland (1525); William Lowth(e) (1528). All but Holland are mentioned in Sir Charles Jackson's famous book, *English Goldsmiths and their Marks*, pp. 237-9 (Dover: Constable. repr. 1964). Regrettably, little other evidence remains.

Albert Way appears to have been the first writer to mention the work of the niellests in respect to brasses.[31] 'Niello' was actually a branch of goldsmith's work, adapted to other metals. Nearly one hundred years later a great authority on the history of wood-engraving, Douglas Percy Bliss, commenting on the 'manière criblée' metal cuts, suggests that they derived from 'the practice of mediaeval metalsmiths, particularly the niellests' (p. 24).[32] Certainly, the latter's technique was similar to that used for monumental brasses, in that the engraved design on a plate or other metal object, had the incised lines filled up with black enamel powder, which was then heated until it melted and hardened. The plate was then polished to make the black lines stand out. Bliss considers the technique to be of German of Flemish origin—further suggesting a link with the technique of making and engraving latten plates for brasses. Finally, Bliss says that the metallurgist would 'naturally take an impression' of his work before giving it to his client, either by printing the plate or 'even by rubbing a sheet of paper stretched over it as one might take a rubbing of a monumental brass . . . ' (p. 25). Certainly the technique Bliss describes corresponds closely to that for brasses described by the Waller brothers, who carried out practical experiments in this field as well as being makers of brasses.[33]

Before concluding the section on printing techniques and their relation to the engraved latten plate, brief mention should be made of the device known as the printer's mark. The earliest marks were almost certainly copied from those used by merchants to stamp their goods, of which many examples survive on brasses.[34] Compare the simple mark of the St Alban's printer (c. 1485) with any contemporary merchant's mark on a brass. (*vide* illus. Pl. 4*a*). As printing and engraving techniques improved, so the marks became more elaborate, until we find examples like that illustrated in Plate 00 from France. This has obvious similarities in style to engraved brasses of the period, especially those of English manufacture. It is only regrettable that so few French brasses have survived with which comparison can also be made.

William Roberts in his admirable book, *Printers' Marks*, says that the marks and title pages were designed by artists as famous as Dürer, Holbein, Cranach and Schauffelein, exhibiting their best designs in the early sixteenth century (pp. 47-8); this substantiates Herbert Haines' comment quoted on p. 59 above.

Enamelling

Enamelling of metal, first in cloisonné and later in champlevé, was another art learned from Byzantium, and many years later adapted for use on brasses and other funeral monuments. It has been suggested by a number of writers that when the art of copper enamelling was introduced, enamelling became the main vehicle of the medieval artist's expression. This could also be applied, to a lesser extent, to brasses (as many writers have been at pains to point out), Limoges enamels being the most quoted example in this context. Although very few brasses survive which retain much of their original enamel (many more have coloured pigment which is not the same), those like the enamelled copper shield of Sir John D'Abernon the Elder (1277), Stoke D'Abernon, Surrey; the figures of Sir John Say and his wife Elizabeth (1473), Broxbourne, Hertfordshire; Sir William Fynderne (1444), Childry, Berkshire, and Sir Thomas and Lady Bourchier, Little Easton, Essex (1483), present good examples.

Enamelling by the two methods first named above was both highly skilled and expensive, and was largely reserved for more decorative and valuable items of domestic and ecclesiastical metalwork, e.g. pyxes; chalices; crosses; tryptyches; reliquaries. Another method more suited to flat latten plates was known as *basse-taille*, where the enamel was 'floated' on the surface of the metal, as in the poorer Limoges work. The often quoted link between brasses and Limoges enamels, though perhaps exaggerated, has several points in its favour. As distinct from the fine Rhenish and Lorraine work, Limoges was, according to one authority, largely carried out in a 'commercial spirit by uncultured artisans',[35] though this has been disputed in more recent times. The enamelling of flat surfaces, requiring little decoration or ornament, the constant use of blue colouring, stiff and conventional figures and 'want of originality and initiative', makes Limoges work quite distinctive. Like engravers of brasses, and artists in most of the other media named above, the enamellers copied the designs of Dürer and other artists, chiefly working on ecclesiastical goods including, without doubt, monumental brasses when clients could afford the high cost.

The use of enamel on brasses appears, from surviving evidence, to have been adopted in England from very early years. Not only do we have the enamelled shield of 1277 mentioned above, but in 1908 during excavations on the site of Leez Priory, Essex, a complete enamel shield dating from about 1275-1300 belonging to a brass or tomb chest (and the fragment of a second showing part of a lion, c. 1410-20), was discovered. Despite being buried for so long, the enamel was in good condition.[36]

The use of coloured pigments or other compounds, as distinct from the costly process of enamelling, was more common, and almost every brass had the incised lines filled with a black compound. On many brasses blazons of arms; the edging of robes and vestments; academical colours; decorative borders; roundels and sword belts of knights in armour, were coloured to heighten the effect. At Avila Cathedral in Spain, is one of the very rare examples of a Flemish brass in almost perfect condition, with green, red, white, blue and black colouring in the incised lines. The whole surface of the metal is also gilded and varnished, as were the metal plates of the niellists mentioned earlier. The fine brass of Sir Hugh Hastings (1347), Elsing, Norfolk, would have presented the same splendid appearance, and was further embellished according to one authority, with coloured glass in part of the head of the canopy.[37]

One unusual English example of the use of pigment that is of great interest, was recorded by the late H. F. Owen Evans on the reverse of a palimpsest brass at Easton Neston, Northamptonshire.[38] Four pieces of the marginal inscription from the brass of Richard Fermer and his wife (1552), join to form a Crucifixion scene in which the blood is represented by red pigment. The reverse is illustrated, with the colour added, in the article quoted in the chapter footnote at the end of this book.

Lecterns

It is again to the incredible industry of the late H. F. Owen Evans that we owe the only article on the link between the engraved brass and the latten lectern.[39] As the author points out at the end of his article, only one of the four he describes and illustrates was previously noted in any of the lists of brasses published. There seems little doubt that brasses and latten lecterns of the type described came from a common source. Many points in the style of the decoration and lettering on the lecterns are identical to similar work on brasses, especially the Evangelistic symbols on the Eton College Chapel example. The four described are at Merton College, Oxford; King's College Chapel, Cambridge; Eton College Chapel, Berkshire, and Yeovil, Somerset. The first three date from the early sixteenth century and the last from c. 1460; the second and third were made in the same workshop. Only the Yeovil lectern is not illustrated, but an illustration may be seen in the late A. B. Connor's *Monumental Brasses in Somerset*;[40] it is the only example with a figure of the donor as part of the design. No continental lecterns of the above type appear to have survived.

Stall-plates

Brief mention only need be made here of the latten and copper stall-plate, since their connection with brasses is a rather tenuous one. The finest collection of the old stall-plates is the famous series of those of the Knights of the Garter in St. George's Chapel, Windsor. Each plate bears the Achievement of Arms of the Knight concerned, many bearing close resemblance to similar devices on contemporary monumental brasses. The plates date from the early fifteenth century onwards.

At the end of the nineteenth century an authority on stall-plates, W. H. St. John Hope, was given permission to remove them for photographing for a book he proposed writing.[41] During their removal, those of Sir Nigel or Neel Loryng; Sir Richard Grey; Sir Hugh Stafford and Sir John le Scrope (all dating from the fifteenth century) were found to be palimpsest. In the case of the first three the design had simply been corrected or altered in some way, but in the latter case another blazon altogether was discovered on the reverse, suggesting a 'waster' from the workshop similar to those found on brasses. Many of the plates are also gilded and/or enamelled, again suggesting at least an affinity with the monumental brass or even a similar source.[42]

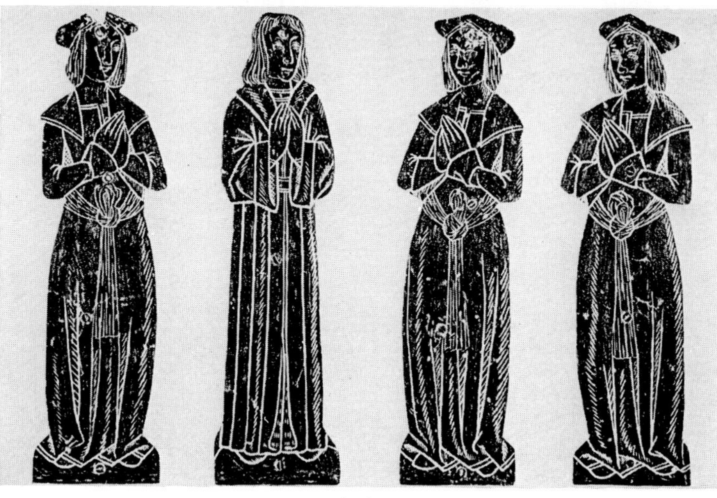

(*a*)

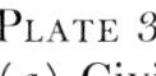

PLATE 3

(*a*) Civilian & 3 wives (c. 1530), Offley, Herts. (*d*) Civilian & 3 wives (c. 1535), Hitchin (St Mary's Church), Herts. Two almost identical brasses from what Mr J. R. Greenwood has recently designated 'Haines's Cambridge School of Brasses' (see *MBS Trans* XI,1 (Dec 1969; [pub. Dec. 1971], 2–12). The two churches are only a few miles apart and Offley has a second similar brass of 1529 (see p. 66 below). All figures are 45.7 cm (18 ins) high. (*b*) John Gill (1546), Wyddial, Herts [detail]. (*c*) Richard Thornton (1544), formerly at Gt Greenford, Middx., now in private possession. Another example of almost identical designs from a London workshop. Both are palimpsest and several other similar examples survive in the Home Counties. Size: (*b*) 51.5 cm ($20\frac{7}{8}$ ins); (*c*) 47.75 cm ($18\frac{7}{8}$ ins). Rubbings by the author (except (*c*)). Photos Peter Marshall.

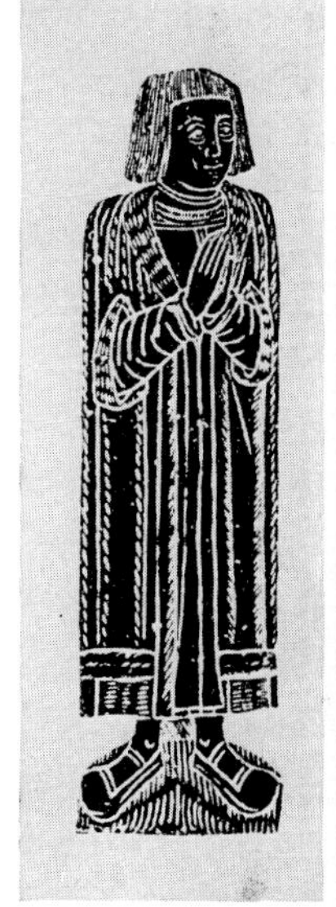

(*c*)

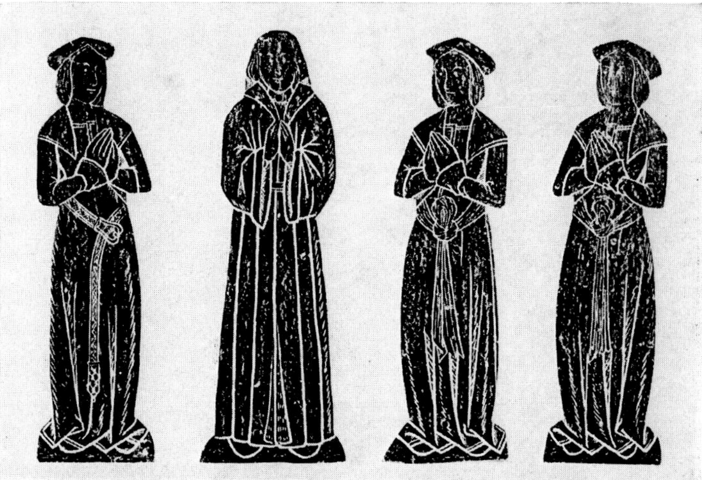

(*d*)

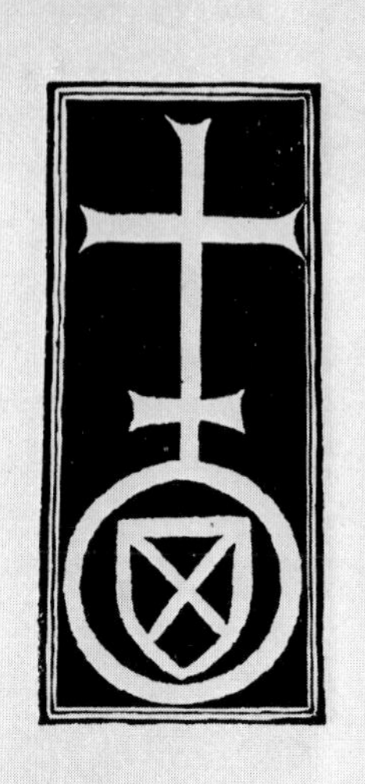

(a)

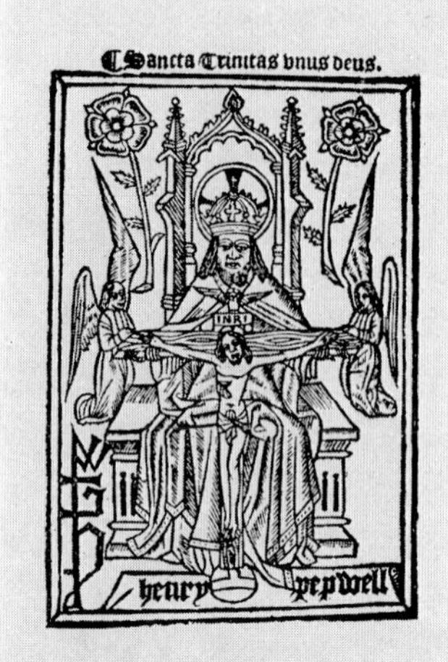

(b)

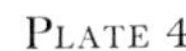

PLATE 4
(*a*) Mark of the St Alban's Printer (c. 1485); (*b*) Printer's Mark of Henry Pepwell (1521); (*c*) & (*d*) French printer's mark of c. 1520 – these marks all have some affinity with brasses and may possibly have been designed or engraved by makers, or former engravers, of brasses. To highlight the similarity (*c*) & (*d*) is shown as a 'positive' and 'negative' print. (*e*) shows an anonymous woodcut of c.1490 bearing a strong resemblance to Crucifixion scenes on contemporary brasses and other works of art (see p. 71). Photos: Peter Marshall.

(c)

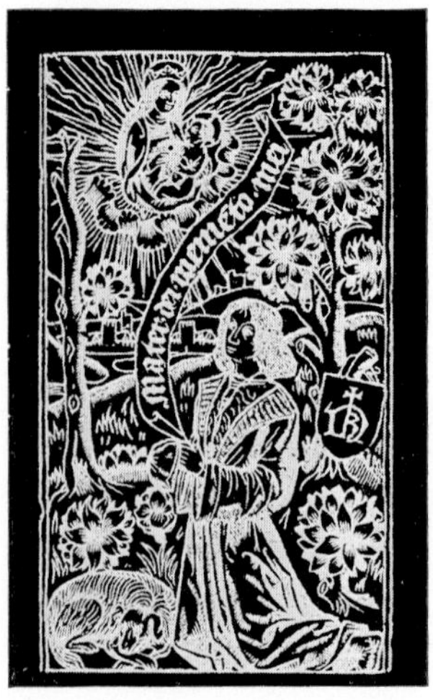

(d)

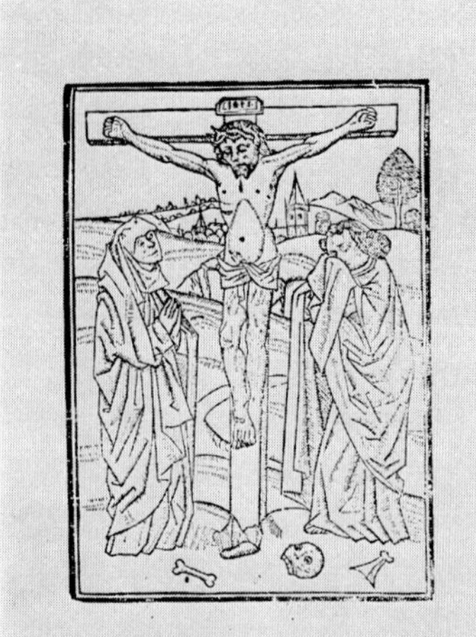

(e)

The Iconography of Monumental Brasses

I hope I have shown by the above examples something of the influences surrounding craftsmen of every description, all of which must be considered by any student of monumental brasses. A great deal of research will be necessary to make a more complete study of the iconography of monumental brass designs, and space does not permit me to do more than make some very general observations.

Certain common factors emerge from most of the allied arts described above, notably the close link between the engravers of brasses and the goldsmiths, the enamellers, the masons, the niellests and famous artists like Albrech Dürer (whose name is associated with nearly every branch of Gothic art) and Lucas Cranach. Malcolm Norris has noted two striking examples of figures on brasses copied direct from works by the above artists.[43] Indeed, continental brasses generally offer the most fruitful area for such work. Two figures on the brass of Cardinal Casmiri in Cracow Cathedral, Poland (1510), engraved by Hermann Vischer the Younger (*op. cit.* p. 28), were copied direct from a Dürer woodcut. In another example quoted by Mr Norris, Lucas Cranach's portrait of Henry, Duke of Saxony (1541), is copied on the Duke's brass at Freiberg. It should be noted here that many fifteenth and sixteenth century drawings and paintings were actually made to be copied by engravers and sculptors.[44]

Probably the greatest single influence on designers and engravers of brasses was the advent of the printed book, and it is from this source that the clearest comparisons can be made. I have already shown how it influenced artists in media like wood, stained glass and stone. The spread of printing to England at the end of the fifteenth century also marked both a deterioration in, and the beginning of mass production of, brasses.

With the coming of the printed page and the rise of 'popular literature', came the first mass distribution of crudely drawn illustrations of Fables, Biblical scenes, Lives of the Saints, Bestiaries, etc., many in a form similar to the eighteenth century broadsheets, ballads and chap-books.[45] The commonest form was the block-book, in which text and illustration appeared on one sheet; these were first printed by a method similar to that used many years later by Sir John Cullum and Craven Ord to take impressions of brasses. Books like the *Ars Morendi*, the *Biblia Pauperum* and the *Cantica Canticorum* eventually became printed in hundreds and were available to all able to afford a copy. There can be little doubt that brass workshops, especially those employing local, and often unskilled artists, used such sources for patterns, particularly where Biblical figures, Saints, mythical beasts, etc., were required.[46]

As printing and blockmaking techniques improved, the use of decorative borders, heavy and elaborate canopy and scroll work (showing a strong Renaissance influence) became fashionable, especially on title pages. Many brasses (and stone monuments), particularly those of the sixteenth and early seventeenth centuries, exhibit similar designs again suggesting direct copying or common artists. The west and north of England, notably Somerset and Yorkshire, provide many such examples. On the continent, where perhaps even more, covering a longer period, can be seen; examples can be found at Meissen (1534–39); Freiberg (1607); Brussels (1567) and Lübeck (1561). An earlier form, without effigy, is the curious decorative border inscription at Ypres (Hospital Notre Dame, 1489), which not only looks like a contemporary printed title page, but is used as such to good effect by the Rev Creeny on the title page of his invaluable book on continental brasses. A similar example from Nieuport Ville, Belgium, 1468, in memory of Jan Clays and his wife was destroyed during the last war.[47]

Apart from that peculiarly English invention, the 'pictographic' brass (*c.f.* p. 70), the clearest links with the printing industry in England are of seventeenth and eighteenth century date. The strong influence of Renaissance and Jacobean design in funeral sculpture, architecture and art is very evident on the later brasses on which the lettering is often far superior to any figures or decoration. The rectangular brass plate still remained the most common form, but by the end of the eighteenth century oval, shield-shaped, lozenges and other designs appeared, copying their stone counterparts; the cadaver, 'skull and cross-bones', hour-glass and figure of Time were also frequently used, again copying (often very badly) contemporary stonework, title pages, funeral cards and broadsheets.[48] Typical examples of the above type can be seen at Shepton Mallet (1649); Taunton, St. Mary Magdalene (1696-1716) and Bishops Lydeard (1733), Somerset; Dronfield, Derbyshire (1675); Mawgan in Meneage, Cornwall (1709) and Colne, Lancashire (1670). Another fashion popular at the same time was the bust in a medallion, oval or lozenge of which the most famous series are at Llanwrest, Denbighshire. Although the half-effigy had been used earlier in both Britain and abroad, e.g. Halvergate, Norfolk (1540, rev. c. 1440); Chinnor, Oxfordshire (1385); Wyddial, Hertfordshire (1575);[49] Freiberg, Germany (1541), it reached the height of its vogue in the eighteenth century, possibly following the contemporary fashion for miniatures and silhouettes. Some were undoubtedly portraits, a good example being that of Peter the Wild Boy (1785) at Northchurch, Hertfordshire.

Another curious, and co-incidental link with the printing industry occurs at Steeple Ashton, Wiltshire, where the reverse of a late inscription to Deborah Marks (1730), shows it to have been cut from a copper printing plate (21.59 × 15.87 cm)* of c. 1713 from a Bristol printing house. The drawing on the latter has a strong satirical flavour and may well have been disposed of for this reason.[50] Of a similar design, but undoubtedly made as a memorial and not a printing plate, is the earlier brass of Humfey Willis in Wells Cathedral, Somerset (1618). It is conceivable that the latter was, however, engraved by a book-plate engraver rather than a funeral artist.[51] At Mulbarton, Norfolk (1680) is a unique form of 'brass',

* $8\frac{1}{2} \times 6\frac{1}{4}$ ins

where the inscription is composed of two hinged copper plates in the form of a book; this was probably intended as a copy of similar work in stone.[52]

As a final example in this section, may be mentioned a series of nearly identical plates at Arlesey, Bedfordshire (1761, 1768 and 1769) and Lowick, Northamptonshire (1769) which suggest to the writer of an article in the Monumental Brass Society's *Transactions*, the work of a 'book plate engraver'.[53] Many such inscriptions at this time also resembled contemporary coffin plates like those illustrated in Plate 6 below. Those shown are from Warsop and Teversal, Nottinghamshire and required special techniques like those used by the late A. B. Connor to make the rubbings suitable for reproduction. That from Warsop could equally well have been the design of a simple book or stall plate.[54]

'Comparative' Monumental Brasses

Just as comparative studies can be made of religion, education and linguistics, so, in a smaller way, can the student compare designs of monumental brasses with each other to find common links. These may be similarities in the method of drawing; the type of costume; the method of engraving, e.g. of chain mail; diaper work; classification by similarities in the depiction of armour, or parts of a suit of armour, as Dr. J. P. C. Kent has suggested, and so on. More recently, special attention has been given to an idea begun, as far as I can tell, by the Waller brothers in the 1850s, of what is now called the science of 'palimpsest links'. This 'link' occurs when positive identification of, say, parts of the same Flemish brass, can be seen on the reverse of later brasses in several different churches. Even as long ago as 1898 Mr T. E. Sedgwick was asking for such rubbings, or examples, 'especially fragments . . . '.[35] Mr John Page-Phillips (who recently revised and re-wrote Herbert Macklin's *Monumental Brasses*) is one of the leading English authorities on this subject, and readers are referred to the above work or to his articles in recent MBS *Trans.* for details.

To even the newest student of brasses, it soon becomes apparent that there are a great many brasses which, if not actually identical, are so similar as to suggest a common source. I have already mentioned above how the designs of some continental brasses are known to be direct copies of earlier memorials, since they were requested in the will of the deceased. Those about which only visible (as distinct from documentary) evidence can be used as a means of comparison, offer one of the best methods of determining either the existence or approximate location of a particular workshop, or the work of a single engraver.[56]

I have used two examples above to illustrate direct evidence of almost identical designs. Those in plate 3 from Great Greenford, Middlesex (stolen c. 1918,[57] later recovered and now in private possession) and Wyddial, Hertfordshire, are clearly copies, made either from a rubbing, print or template. Both figures are palimpsest. Other figures of this distinctive design can be seen at churches including Pottesgrove, Bedfordshire (1535);[58] Stanstead Abbotts, Hertfordshire (c. 1540);[59] Bletchingly, Surrey (1541).[60] Thame, Oxfordshire (1543);[61] Upminster (1545) and Lambourne (1546), Essex,[62] and Banwell, Somerset (1554).[63] The female effigy accompanying some of these figures also exhibit similarities to each other, and the fragment of such a figure at Bayford, Hertfordshire (c. 1540)[64] has a counterpart in the Upminster brass (1545) noted above.[65] Similarly, a very interesting feature of the above groups are the number of plates known to be palimpsest, some of which 'link' together to form part of the same brass. It would seem that this workshop 'specialised' in re-using imported Flemish brasses plundered from Holland and Belgium, probably being based in London.

The other illustration (Plate 3) shows identical brasses from Hitchin and Offley churches (Hertfordshire) dating from c. 1530. These are thought to have come from a local workshop at or near Cambridge, and can be seen in a number of churches north and east of London.[66] Other random examples of brasses displaying strong similarities in design can be seen at the following churches (for reasons of space no more than three are given):—

(*a*) St. Paul's, Bedford (1573. *Illus.* Pl. 9); Kingsnorth Kent (c. 1577) and Churchill, Somerset (c. 1577).
(*b*) Cople, Bedfordshire (1556) and Fordingbridge, Hampshire (1568)—both to members of the Bulkeley family and either made together and the date posthumously/later inserted, or the latter copied from a 'rubbing' of the former.
(*c*) Wormley, Hertfordshire (1479); Quethiock, Cornwall (1471); Great Chart, Kent (1485).
(*d*) Beckington, Somerset (1485); Harpwell, Lincolnshire (c. 1480) and Strelley, Nottinghamshire (1487)—all Knights and their wives.
(*e*) Watton-at-Stone, Hertfordshire (c. 1370); Cottingham, Yorkshire (1383)—both priests in plain choral copes.

The distance between some of the places suggests the following possibilities, (a) the existence of 'pattern books' or templates sent into the provinces for engravers to copy (or adapt); (b) that certain workshops in, say London, were of sufficient reputation in the provinces for an order to be made regardless of distance and without seeing the designs first; (c) that 'stock' designs were re-used time and again when no type was specified by the customer, or were displayed at the workshop and chosen "off-the-peg". It seems almost certain that many groups of children were ordered in this way, being cut off 'by number' from a strip of pre-engraved identical figures.

If a guide to 'comparative brasses' were produced or a distribution map made, it would be an extremely interesting, not to say painstaking, task. Not only might it verify the sites of the major workshops, but might also indicate their distribution patterns and output, or even, in rarer cases suggest the movements of a particular engraver.[67]

'Pictographic' Brasses

Before concluding the present survey of allied arts, I would like to add a few notes on this rather special type of brass. I would define these brasses as those showing either an event or subject directly associated with the deceased, or, showing a religious subject in which the deceased figures. The examples below will indicate the difference in the two types.

Of the latter type but few examples have survived, and those which have are mainly continental examples. Among those may be mentioned the *Crucifixion* scenes at Moyvillers (1604); Trier Museum (c. 1500); Nivelles (c. 1600); Nouans (1517) and Templeuve (1615). At Aachen (1487, 1534 and 1560); Amiens (1456); Termonde (1560) and Nivelles (c. 1460), the *Virgin and Child* figures prominently, either in rays of glory or enthroned.[68] In England examples of this type are rarer as few have survived the Reformation or Commonwealth periods. Examples can be seen at Fovant, Wiltshire (c. 1500) and March, Cambridgeshire (1507)[69] – *Annunciation* scenes, very similar to contemporary woodcuts and paintings; Cranley, Surrey (1503)[70] – *Resurrection;* St. George's Chapel, Windsor (1522) – *St. Katherine* and the *B.V.M. and Child.*[71] It is worth noting that these brasses usually show the figures in reverse just as they would be printed, suggesting that the engravers of brasses, *per se*, makers of printing blocks, were used to working in this way and may well have been one and the same individual.

The first type of 'pictographic' brass usually deals with a secular, as distinct from a religious subject, and seems to be a peculiarly English invention. Continental examples do however exist, a fine one being that of Dr Jacob Schelewaerts (1483) in St. Saveur's Church in Bruges, Belgium, who is shown addressing a class of academics.[72] Most of the surviving English examples are Elizabethan and Jacobean. Good examples can be found at the following places:—

(*a*) Hunsdon, Hertfordshire (1591) – Park-keeper shooting at stag, with figure of 'death' (as a skeleton) between.

(*b*) Lower Halling, Kent (1587); Wormington, Gloucestershire (1605); Marden, Herefordshire (1614) – bedroom scenes.

(*c*) Walton-upon-Thames, Surrey (1587) – park-keeper capturing stag (palimpsest; curious).[73]
(*d*) Boxford, Suffolk (1606) – child in cot, died aged 22 weeks.
(*e*) Margate, Kent (1615)—fully-rigged sailing ship.
(*f*) St. George's Chapel, Windsor (1630) Little Ilford, London (c. 1630). } 'cradle-brass'
(*g*) Bishop Henry Robinson (1616) Queen's College, Oxford and Carlisle Cathedral – identical; eccles. bldgs., etc . . .
(*h*) Barwell, Leicestershire (1614); Hackney, Middlesex (1618); Buntingford Hertfordshire (1620) – priests in pulpits; latter example still hangs in its original wooden frame.

Finally, mention must be made of the curious and little-known brass at Llandinbo, Herefordshire, showing the figure of a little boy standing in a pond, with a cross hanging from a chord round his neck; the inscription tells us that, tragically, he was drowned at an early age. The brass is illustrated (I think for the first time) in Mr J. C. Page-Phillips' fascinating and unusual book *Children on Brasses* (Allen & Unwin. £1.75. 1971)[74].

By the end of the eighteenth century the wheel had turned full circle, and the engraved latten plate with effigy was replaced by the stone monument and tomb. The increased use of white and veined marble became fashionable, and the 'new' stone monuments, often taking up far more room than the importance of their owners warranted, had a fresh, but short lived revival. Although the brass plate continued in use in various forms, memorials sometimes consisting solely of small brass shields like those from Southwell Minster Nottinghamshire (Illus. Pl. 6), the figure brass was soon to see a revival during the wave of Victorian Gothic interest which swept the country during the nineteenth century. With this, came new manufacturing processes and the first serious studies of the medieval brass as an art form.

FURTHER READING OR REFERENCE

Architects

COLVIN, H. M. – *Biographical dictionary of English Architects 1660–1840* (John Murray. £4.20. 1954)

Craft guilds

KNOOP, D. & JONES, G. P. *Medieval mason* 3rd edn. (Manchester University Press. £2.52. 1967), First pub. 1933.

KNOWLES, John A. 'Artistic craft guilds of the Middle Ages' *RIBA Jnl.*, 3 Ser., 34, viii (1927), 265–71.

PHYTHIAN-ADAMS, C. 'Records of the Craft guilds' (Pt. 3 of Sources for Urban History) *Local Hist.* 9, vi (May 1971) 267–74.

UNWIN, George. *Guilds and Companies of London.* 4th edn. (Frank Cass. £2.50. 1963).

Enamels

BURLINGTON FINE ARTS CLUB. *Catalogue of a collection of European enamels from the earliest date to the end of the XVIIth century.* Compiled by J. S. Gardner; intro. by Alfred Higgins (Pub. by the Club. 1897. xxxi pages; 72 plates (some coloured))

Higgins' introduction is especially useful as a general summary, although one or two of his theories have been questioned by recent writers. This very large volume is well illustrated throughout.

WESSEL, Klaus. *Byzantine enamels; from the 5th to the 16th century.* Trans. by I. R. Gibbons (Irish U.P. £8.40. 1969. First pub. Germany, 1967; in U.S.A. by N.Y. Graphic Soc. 1968).

Engraving

HIND, A. M. *Engraving In England in the 16th and 17th centuries. 3 vols.* (Camb. U.P. £36.50 set. 1952, 1955 and 1964).

Part III is by M. Corbett and M. Norton and covers 'The reign of Charles I'. The whole series is very fine and repays close attention, the clarity and size of the illustrations make them excellent for 'iconographic' work.

Ibid An Introduction to the History of the Woodcut . . . 2 vols. (Dover: Constable. £2.65 set (pbk. edn.) 1963).

HODNETT, E. *English Woodcuts 1480–1535* (Oxford U.P. for the Bibliographical Soc. 1935).

JACKSON, John & CHATTO, W. A. *Treatise on wood engraving* (1839)

SCHRETLEN, M. J. *Dutch and Flemish woodcuts of the 15th century.* (Benn. 1925).

Glass – painted and stained

ARMYTAGE, L. *Stained glass* (L. Hill. 1960)

BAKER, John. *English Stained Glass;* with intro. by Sir Herbert Read. (Thames & H. £6.30. 1960).
Esp. pp. 27–32 'Sources of design'; 34 illus. in colour.

HARRISON, F. 'Medieval pictorial art' *Master Glass Painters Jnl.,* VIII (Apr. 1941), 85–95.
Makes special reference to York and the subject matter of the pictures.

HOGAN, J. H. 'Stained glass' *Jnl. Roy. Soc. Arts* LXXXVIII (May 1940), 569–85.

WOODFORDE, C. *English stained and painted glass* (Oxford U.P. £3.00. 1954).

Grafitti

PRITCHARD, V. *English Medieval grafitti* (Camb. U.P. £3.50. 1967).
Espec. illus. and reference (p. 144) to small segmenta which appears both on the brass of (?) John Lydgate and on a pillar in the south arcade of St Mary's Church, Lydgate, Suffolk. Good bibliog.

Iconography: Manuscripts and drawings

HENDERSON, George. 'Studies in English in English Manuscript Illumination'. Pts. I–III. *J. Warburg and Courtauld Inst.* 30 (1967), 71–137; 31 (1968), 103–47.
Espec. useful for the illus. and for showing how designs were used and re-used by artists like Matthew Paris and Villard de Honnecourt.

KURTH, B. 'Matthew Paris and Villard de Honnecourt' *Burlington Mag.* LXXXI (1942), 227–8.

Misericords

ANDERSON, M. D. *Misericords: Medieval life in English wood carving.* (Penguin [King Penguin.] 1954).

REMNANT, G. L. (ed.) *A Catalogue of Misericords in Great Britain.* (Oxford U.P. £3.15. 1969).
Esp. pp. xxiii–xl 'Iconography of misericords' by M. D. Anderson; pp. 203–5 'Bibliography' and pp. 209–16 'Iconographical Index'. Copiously illustrated.

ROE, Fred. 'Some old English Misericords' *Conn.* lxxvii, 302 (Oct. 1926), 81–9; 'More about Misericords' *ibid,* 306 (Feb. 1927), 77–80; 'Misericords again' *ibid* lxxviii, 309 (May 1927), 18–24. Illus.

Printing

HUMPHREYS, H. N. *Masterpieces of the Early Printers and engravers . . .* (Henry Southeran. 1870).

Espec. plates 9 (2), 21, 24, 41 and 42, all of which have strong iconographic similarities to continental brasses in particular.

McKERROW, R. B. *Printers' and publishers' devices in England and Scotland 1485–1640*. (Oxford U.P. for Bibliographical Society. £3.00. 1894, 1913; repr. 1949).
ROBERTS, William. *Printers' Marks: a chapter in the history of typography*. (G. Bell. 1893).

Sculpture

GUNNIS, Rupert. *Directory of British Sculptors. 1660-1815* (Odams P. 1953; rev. edn. Murray's Bk. Sales [Abbey Library] £1.50. 1968).
WHINNEY, Margaret. *Sculpture in Britain 1530 to 1830*. (Penguin; Pelican Hist. of Art. £4.50. 1964).

Books illustrating the works of a few of the European artists cited
The following are valuable. With the five-hundredth anniversary of Dürer's birth being commemorated in 1971, more books have appeared recently than would normally have been cited; those below are a small selection only.
(i) *Albrech Dürer* (1471–1528)

ANZELEWSKY, F. (editor). *Drawings and graphic works of Dürer* (Hamlyn. £3.00. 1970).

KNAPPE, K. A. *Dürer: the complete engravings, etchings and woodcuts* (Thames & Hudson. £4.50. 1965).

WHITE, Christopher. *Dürer, the artist and his drawings*. (Phaidon P. £5.00. 1971).

WOLFFLIN, H. (editor). *Drawings of Albrecht Dürer*, selected and with introductory essay by Heinrich Wolfflin, trans. by S. Appelbaum . . . (Dover: Constable. £1.40 (pbk.) 1970).
First pub. in Germany 1923. The same author has also just had re-published his *Art of Albrecht Dürer;* ed. by K. Gerstenberz, first pub. 1905. (Phaidon P. £5.25. Oct. 1971).
From 15 October 1971 to 27 February 1972, the British Museum also held a very fine exhibition of Dürer's work; a valuable catalogue (price £1.00) was published to accompany the exhibits.
(ii) *Grünewald* (c. 1462–1528)

PEVSNER, N. & MEIER, M. *Grünewald* (Thames & Hudson. 1958).

RUHMER, E. (editor) *Grünewald drawings: complete edition* (Phaidon P. £3.75. 1970).
(iii) *The Master E.S.* (early 15th cent.)

VALENTINER, W. R. 'The name of the Master E.S.' *Art Q.* XI (Winter 1948), 218–48.
Cited by the author as 'the greatest engraver, north of the Alps,

before Schongauer and Dürer . . . who never copied others while he himself was copied by an endless number of artists; including engravers, miniaturists, panel and mural painters, glass painters and enamel workers, goldsmiths and especially sculptors'. The writer favours Erwin Von Sterge of Frankfurt (1426–?) as the probable identity of the Master.

(iv) *Lucas Cranach* Snr. (1472–1553)

KUENZEL, H. *Cranach;* trans. by A. Ross. (Uffici: Clematis Press. £0.37½. 1968).

RUHMER, E. *Cranach.* (Phaidon Press. 1963.)

Other general works

Reference has been made to these, many of value for their illustrations, including some recent books on brasses to which passing reference is made in the text or other footnotes, notably the following:—

ANDERSON, M. D. *History and Imagery in British Churches.* (John Murray. £4.25. Oct. 1971).

Combining and enlarging on the author's two earlier books on this theme, this is the first recent general treatise including the history and iconography of sculpture, monuments, painting, etc.; some notes on, and examples from, brasses are also included, a few with illustrations. There is a long bibliography, regretably marred in a few instances by errors or poor proof-reading (e.g. varients of C. J. P. Cave's initials; date of pubn. of same book given differently when quoted twice).

BERTRAM, Jerome. *Brasses and brass rubbing in England* (David & Charles. £2.75. 1971).

CROSSLEY, F. H. *English church Monuments A.D. 1150–1550 . . .* (Batsford. 1921).

HARVEY, John. *Master builders . . .* (Thames & Hudson. £1.95. (£1.00 pbk.) Nov. 1971).

HAUSSIG, H. W. *History of Byzantine Civilisation* (Thames & Hudson. £6.30. 1971).

PAGE-PHILLIPS, J. C. *Macklin's Monumental Brasses* (Allen & Unwin. £2.10. (£1.25 pbk. edn.) 1970, repr. with corrections 1972).

POOLE, A. L. (ed.) *Medieval England* 2 vols. (Oxford U.P. £4.20. 1958).

Esp. vol. II Ch. 2, pp. 439–514 by C. F. Webb and T. S. R. Boase.

TALBOT-RICE, D. *Byzantine art* (Penguin. £1.50. rev. edn. 1968).

TRIVICK, H. H. *Craft and Design of Monumental Brasses* (John Baker. £10.50. (1969): Readers Union edn. £8.40. 1970).
Ibid. Picture Book of Brasses in Gilt (John Baker. £3.25. 1971)

WHINNEY, M. *Early Flemish paintings* (Faber. £3.00. 1968).

At the time of writing a fine new work of which only the first volume had appeared, was issued. This is Gertrud Schiller's well illustrated and fine study *The Iconography of Medieval Art* (Lund Humphries. £10.50. 1971). It has all the appearances of becoming a standard work in this field.

CHAPTER THREE

Reproduction of Brasses— Past and Present

To those who have been studying the history of brasses for some time, whether on a national or local basis, the fascination and variety of old prints, drawings, lithographs, engravings and other reproductions of brasses and indents soon manifests itself. The search for these amongst the vast number of published and manuscript books, notes and documents can be both rewarding and absorbing—not to say time consuming. In the following chapter I can mention only a few of the engravers, artistis, antiquaries, publishers and works worthy of attention; some more are listed in Appendix II, at the end of the book. For the discovery of others, I can but leave this pleasure to the personal satisfaction of the searcher himself.

Early methods: Impressions and Rubbings

I mentioned in Chapter 2 (p. 70) the possibility that the engravers of monumental brassses took impressions or 'rubbings' from their plates for future reference or for use as pattern books for the benefit of prospective clients. Although no 'rubbings' have been discovered to date which are more than about two hundred years old, mention was also made of the original sketches for the design of the Gage brasses at West Firle, Sussex (p. 35), made by Gerard Johnson and dating from the early 1580s. It seems unlikely that any original design of earlier date is likely to be discovered in England.

The above examples represent what are two of the best known and earliest methods of copying brasses—rubbings and drawings—the others are comparative newcomers, namely, the lithograph and photograph and adaptations of them. I have already described in outline in my *Beginner's Guide* the general history of the traditional brass rubbing, but I would like to draw reader's attention to one or two other details. My reference to a painting showing brass or stone rubbings in progress in the New Church at Delft should be enlarged upon by reference to Mr J. C. Page-Phillips' revised and rewritten edition of *Macklin's Monumental Brasses*, on the cover of which is a reproduction of the above painting. It was made by the Dutch artist Hendrik Cornelisz Van Der Vliet (1612-75), and another painting by the same artist of 1656 is reproduced in part on p. 108 of the same book. Also, some interesting information on the history of rubbings is given by Mr Henry H. Trivick in his first book, especially pp. 101-2, in which the author traces the 'rubbing' back to ancient China and other Far Eastern countries.[1]

As far as I know, no examples of the above types of rubbing have survived, but what is thought to be the earliest surviving English 'rubbing' was made in c. 1754 by Thomas Martin (1697-1771). It was made in pencil on rough paper and is of a now lost inscription of 1526 from St Peter's Church, Kirkley, Lowestoft, Suffolk.[2] This is a rare survival, predating the various methods of taking impressions and dabbings devised by Sir John Cullum, Craven Ord, Thomas Fisher and others.[3]

Brass Rubbing 1830-1930

Although I have been unable to establish the exact date at which the first rubbings were made with black heel-ball, it would seem to be the late 1830s or early 1840s. The painstaking but somewhat messy process used by the contemporaries of Richard Gough (*q.v.*) mentioned above, and the delicate and unsatisfactory nature of the early dabbings, no doubt inspired its adoption. The credit for the marketing and exclusive manufacture of the first heel-ball for brass rubbing seems to belong to Messrs Ullathorne of Long Acre, London, (near neighbours, incidentally, of the Waller brothers). It superseded other methods then in use, including the piece of black shoe leather, graphite, the carpenter's pencil and the lithographic crayon and paper. Heel-ball was certainly in use by 1844, as it is mentioned by Albert Way in an excellent paper of that date as one of the most suitable materials available, together with other methods then in use.[4] Although Ullathornes produced a yellow coloured heel-ball shortly afterwards, it never attained the popularity or perfection of the black on white paper. To my mind, this fact still remains true, despite competition in recent years from the advocates of gold heel-ball on black paper.

Mention of the latter brings me to the next invention which attained considerable popularity for a time—the metallic rubber. This was the idea of the master-printer and bookseller Henry S. Richardson (*q.v.*) of Stockwell St., Greenwich, became known commercially as 'Richardson's Metallic Rubber', and was used with a dark grey or black 'Prepared Paper'. An interesting advertisement for the materials appears at the end of some editions of Rev Charles Boutell's *Monumental Brasses and Slabs* (1847). First marketed in about 1844, it was widely reviewed in journals of the day, and, said *The Athenaeum* 'gives almost a perfect fac-simile of the original.'[5] A number of Richardson's own rubbings have survived (as well as others made using his materials), many of them cut out and mounted as recommended by the manufacturer, though some have tarnished almost to the point of being black. Whether this will happen to the modern gold and bronze coloured rubbings now in fashion remains to be seen.

Inspired by the wide interest in Gothic architecture and art, brass rubbing soon reached remarkable popularity, especially amongst young students at Oxford and Cambridge Universities, though as a hobby was somewhat frowned upon by archaeologists of the time for a number of years to come. Evidence of the enthusiasm of the early Oxford Architectural Society's members is proved by their publication in 1848 of the *Manual for the Study of Monumental Brasses . . .*, in which the young Herbert Haines catalogued and described 450 of the rubbings then in the Society's possession. It was a fitting basis for his own *Manual* (1861) which was to become the finest book on brasses ever to be written, and was to raise the study of the brasses from a hobby into a science. Friends and contemporaries of Haines, some to become even more prominent in their own fields, including Rev. Charles Boutell, Albert Way, Sir Augustus Franks, Sir Henry Dryden, Rev. C. R. Manning, Rev. C. H. Hartshorne and J. D. T. Niblett nearly all began brass rubbings while at university, retaining their interest throughout their life. Their enthusiasm was paramount. Many of their rubbings and/or notes have survived in our national collections, of which details are given in Appendices I and II below.

However, the enthusiasm for brass rubbing was not long shared by everyone, not least some of the church authorities. Just as to-day certain churches have forbidden or restricted rubbing because of excessive demand, or worse because of malpractices by unskilled enthusiasts, so by the mid-1840s the same circumstances had arisen. The malpractices were not, however, all perpetrated by the brass rubbers. The reviewer of Richardson's metallic rubber in *The Athenaeum* is seen to remark: 'When every parish clerk . . . is busily engaged in providing rubbings, or impressions for the instruction of young architectural students—ladies, we are glad to say, especially—an improved process of taking rubbings will be generally acceptable.'[6].

Not many years later, however, these same clerks were adding to 'their scanty income by supplying visitors with "rubbings" ', according to the reviewer of Boutell's first book (*op. cit.*).[7] Boutell himself in a footnote, remarks that the practice had become so popular that 'an exorbitant fee for *their permission* to make rubbings' was also being charged.[8] The same 'discouragements', though now used more to combat commercial exploitation, have been forced on church authorities again especially during the last five years. By 1852 permission to rub the famous brass of Lodweyc de Corteville, then in the Museum of Practical Geology, Jermyn St., London, was refused in 'consequence of the number of applications for that purpose',[9] by what one reviewer a year before had scornfully called 'our new super-abundant brass-rubbers'.[10]

Exhibitions are dealt with in a separate chapter, but passing reference needs to be made here to one unusual public (as distinct from those held at Society's and Institute's members' meetings) exhibition in 1847, at which the first display of coloured rubbings were shown. Held at the Cosmorama in Regent Street, London, it appears to be an isolated case as the general use of colour on a wide scale is of fairly recent origin. Formal and informal displays of collections of single rubbings at meetings of interested societies has long been practised, and are usually noted in the publication of the society concerned. Not least amongst these are the Society of Antiquaries of London, Scotland and Newcastle-upon-Tyne; British Archaeological Association; Archaeological Institute; Cambridge Camden and Cambridge Antiquarian Societies; the Oxford Architectural Society and many local archaeological societies like the London and Middlesex, Surrey, Norfolk, Kent and Yorkshire. Considerable interest was also shown in the then new study of continental brasses, and the work of Albert Way, W. H. J. Weale, A. W. Franks and Rev. W. F. Creeny was only just beginning.

Despite much good work, brass rubbing itself remained to many people the domain of the amateur enthusiast. Boutell had summarised this attitude well in the Preface of his first book which had the stated aim of reducing 'the prevalent amusement of brass-rubbing into something of a system . . .'.[11] He later qualifies this with the following comment:—'There is an association, or rather an inherent quality, in the engraven plate, the object of the brass-rubber's research, which calls forth feelings and sentiments far worthier than those of the most refined curiosity' (p. 2).

By the end of the nineteenth century the study of brasses had certainly attained something of 'the system' Boutell had hoped for, and had witnessed the publication of the fine works by Creeny (1884), E. H. W. Dunkin (1882) and the first edition of Rev. H. W. Macklin's concise and useful handbook (*Monumental Brasses*, 1890). In addition, and equally important, was the foundation in 1887 of the Cambridge University Association of Brass Collectors (usually referred to for convenience as C.U.A.B.C.). Their first recorded meeting was at Cambridge on 3rd June, 1887, and amongst its first members was the young Mill Stephenson. In 1894 the C.U.A.B.C. was dissolved and was extended in scope to form the present Monumental Brass Society, with Rev. H. W. Macklin as its first President and Mill Stephenson as Honorary Secretary and Treasurer (and, incidentally, first General Editor of a new list of brasses based on that of Rev. Herbert Haines). The Oxford University Brass Rubbing Society was also founded at this time, but remained, as it does to-day, a separate publishing society from M.B.S. It was founded, appropriately enough, by the youngest son of Rev. Herbert Haines, Rev. Harry Fowler Haines, M.A. (1869-99) in May, 1893; their first journal appeared in 1897.

The impetus given by the above has continued (with a few lapses mostly resulting from the two world wars) unabated ever since, and as well as giving rise to an enormous and very scattered literary and pictorial output, has captured the attention of some of the distinguished names that frequently occur in these pages or in the 'Who's Who' in Appendix II below.

Other benefits often forgotten in the general history of the subject, were the first systematic attempts to form complete collections of brass rubbings for historical and reference purposes. Much of the early credit for this must go to Sir Augustus Franks, who gave to the Society of Antiquaries of London, not only his own fine collections of rubbings, but others of great hisorical value which he had acquired, including some by Thomas Fisher, John Gough Nichols and his friend Rev. Herbert Haines. Help in sorting the collection was given him by Mill Stephenson. Notes on many of these collections are given in Appendix I below, but special mention must be made of the very fine one at the Museum of Archaeology and Ethnology at Cambridge. Cared for from 1920 until his death in 1941 by that industrious scholar Ralph Griffin, the high standards he set for the quality of the rubbings included, make this one of the finest and most complete series in the country.[12]

Brass Rubbing To-day

As I have shown above, traditional techniques have changed little during the last one hundred and thirty years. Black heel-ball on white paper still remains the most suitable medium, despite the re-introduction of gold and other colours in recent years. For the purpose of direct reproduction (other than by photography of the brass *in situ* mentioned below) I do not think black heel-ball will ever be bettered for the clarity and accuracy required for historical purposes. The question of rubbings for decoration and display are dealt with in a later chapter. The use of various colours is described in my *Beginner's Guide.*

In my first book, I attempted both to inform and to set down some level of standard for those beginning, or already learning, the techniques of brass rubbing in various forms. It is essential that, with the unprecedented upsurge in the popularity of brass rubbing that standards should be set and adhered to, but regrettably there will always be those who will not conform. Almost every issue of the Monumental Brass Society's *Newsletter* to members, lists churches where rubbing has been prohibited or severely restricted. On January 9th, 1968 (p. 8d) the vicar of Edlesborough, Buckinghamshire was reported in *The Times* as having strongly criticized brass rubbers, who, he feared, might damage the valuable brasses in his church. He described some of the abuses he had witnessed, including the use of 'graphite pencils and other abrasive materials . . . playing of transistor radios while they took rubbings . . . , standing on the pews to reach mural brasses [and] smoking while working.' Regrettably, this is not an isolated case, and it is this kind of abuse which has been the cause of numerous bans on rubbing, even to serious students. It has also been partly responsible for the high fees for brass rubbing now levied in many churches—another cause being the unfortunate rise in 'commercialisation' of brasses, particularly the sale of rubbings themselves for exorbitant prices (notably to the United States).

Of the senseless and deliberate theft of, or damage to, the brass itself little but serious concern can be expressed; examples like that from Sedgefield, Durham (c. 1320) which was reported stolen (and is illustrated) in *The Times* of 11th July, 1969 (p. 11e) is only one such instance. In my own county, Hertfordshire, the brass of a friar (c. 1440) was stolen from Great Amwell church in 1968 and is still (Nov. 1971) missing; and at Sawbridgeworth, the interesting figure of Lady Joan Leventhorpe (1527), was badly damaged by vandals in 1969, in an effort to prise the figure from the slab.[13] Regrettably, such people are rarely caught, but the implications of all the above examples could eventually have far wider repercussions than hitherto. The pity is that those responsible will probably never read the above, or realise the effects of their actions. Although I had not begun this section with the idea of decrying this unfortunate trend, I think it is none the less necessary to repeat it if only to bring home the seriousness of the situation to those who may be in a position to be able to aleviate it. I would make a special appeal to all those who have contact with children and young people, who although they are not the only offenders, probably receive the most adverse publicity in this respect. From those who choose to make commercial gain from the sale of rubbings there seems to be little protection at present.[14]

Rubbings of Modern Brasses

With the greatly increased interest now being shown in this hitherto neglected category of brasses, some brief notes on the difficult process of taking rubbings of modern brasses does not seem out of place as a conclusion to this section. By 'modern' I mean any plate dating from the late eighteenth century onwards, though quite a number of brasses of any date from about one hundred years previously, might require such techniques.

The chief credit for the discovery of the process below seems to go to the late A. B. Connor, and is described in the new preface to the reprint of Mr Connor's fine series of articles on the *Monumental Brasses of Somerset* (p. *ix*).[15] Basically, he took a pencil rubbing of the plate first, then carefully marked in the 'detail of the engraving with indian ink and chinese white'. It requires little imagination to appreciate how long larger brasses copied in this way must have taken. For the purposes of copying modern brasses for reproduction, this, or the similar process described below, is almost essential to make the detail stand out. In a strictly historical sense one might criticize the process in the same way as cutting out and mounting rubbings, for however careful one is, very slight alterations to the design seem inevitable during the 'touching-up'.

I used a somewhat similar process to make the rubbing of the shield-shaped coffin plate illustrated in Pl. 6. In this instance, however, I made a light rubbing with a hard heel-ball on detail paper first. Then, using a small bottle of Winsor & Newton's Art Masking Fluid, I painted over the white parts of the rubbing very carefully using a small camel-hair brush. Once dry, the masking fluid forms a thin, impervious film over the areas painted, after which a wash of indian ink can be applied over the whole surface of the rubbing. Once the ink is dry, the masking fluid can be removed using a *soft* rubber (or by rubbing very lightly with a finger), leaving the white areas appearing considerably heightened in tone. The rubbing was then ready for reproduction by direct photography with a process camera (*q.v.*). I might add that even this small shield took about four hours of concentrated work! Any brass in which the engraving is shallow or still coloured with enamel or pigment, will require such treatment to obtain a satisfactory rubbing. The use of the 'dabber' I have described in my *Beginner's Guide* (pp. 51-2), and notes on its use also appear in several of the early standard works on brasses, in Malcolm Norris' *Brass Rubbing* (pp. 15-16) and in a useful article by J. A. Humphries in the M.B.S. *Trans.* VII, 6, (1939) 290-93 called 'Use of the Dabber and how to make it'.[16]

A Footnote on Stone Rubbings

Although the taking of heel-ball or crayon rubbings from

stone slabs should not be practised by any but the very expert, I would just like to draw reader's attention to one or two points in this connection. For recording indents of brasses the 'dabber' is certainly the least harmful and most satisfactory in terms of clarity. Similarly, old incised stone slabs should be treated in the same way, as rubbing with heel-ball can result in irreparable damage to the delicate edges of the engraved lines. I cannot stress this point too strongly. Recently, however, a book has appeared in one of the excellent Dover: Constable paperback series called *Early New England Gravestone Rubbings*, by Edmund V. Gillon, jnr.,[17] in which the author describes briefly how he made many of the rubbings illustrated, which are mostly of eighteenth and early nineteenth century examples. The designs of some of the headstones are both curious and interesting and reflect very clearly a strong non-conformist influence, though quite a large number have counterparts in both metal and stone in Great Britain as well. Although, again, I cannot recommend the practice of rubbing headstones, the method described is not without interest and appears to cause no damage to the stone itself.

The taking of rubbings from stone memorials is not, I hasten to add, a recent practice, or peculiar to the United States. In *Notes & Queries* (7 Ser., VI, Sept. 1, 1888, p. 172) are a number of letters relative to this subject, in which various methods are suggested. The most favoured method was the use of a tough white paper, or wall paper, which was then 'rubbed' with grass or vegetation, e.g. dock leaves. An alternative was to use powdered black-lead rubbed on to thin paper with a piece of soft leather or 'small piece of linen rag'. 'The letters can afterwards', states Andrew Oliver (*q.v.*) 'be filled in with indian ink'. Heel-ball was fortunately not advocated![18]

Bell rubbings

A very brief note only need be added here on the method of taking rubbings of inscriptions and makers' marks etc. on church bells. The shape of the bell-rim presents obvious problems, necessitating making the rubbing or dabbing in small lengths which can afterwards be joined or mounted in tiers. In one of the letters in the issue of *Notes & Queries* mentioned above, passing reference is made to this practice, the 'black side of a bit of new shoe leather (as used by Mr. Ellacombe) . . . ' being recommended. The work referred to is a leaflet published c. 1875, called, *Instructions for taking rubbings of Inscriptions on Bells, or other raised letters*, signed 'H.T.E.' [i.e. Henry Thomas Ellacombe, author of a number of standard works on bells and bellringing]. An original copy of the leaflet is in the British Museum Library. Difficulty of access, problems of getting permission and a certain degree of risk to the individual concerned, make this practice a minority one. Rubbings can be made using black heel-ball or crayon on many bells, but satisfactory results are difficult to obtain without a good deal of touching-up afterwards. Dabbings give quite good results, but are no use, except for re-copying, if only done on the tissue-type paper usually recommended. If a suitable mould or other impression can be made without damage to the bell itself, a cast might be made from which future 'rubbings' could be done, e.g. in a school or college where the history of a local bell-foundry was being studied, by a whole class.

Coal Plates

Personally, I have not yet had the courage to make rubbings of coal-hole covers in a busy London street, but for those so inclined there are still in existence (though fast disappearing) large numbers of pleasing, geometrical cover designs. One sometimes sees rubbings of them offered for sale in large stores.

One of the very few books dealing with the subject first published in 1929, was reprinted again a few years ago, and has an introduction by Raymond Lister. Written under the pseudonym of "Aesulapius Junior", it was called *Opercula: London coal plates* (Cambridge: Golden Head Pr. £0.75. 1965), and was based on a series of drawings made in 1863 by Dr Shepherd Taylor. The only recent treatment of the subject I have seen is an excellent article by Anthony Robinson,

'Design Underfoot' (*Typographica*, 7, (May, 1963), 33-45), which is not only well illustrated, but includes several designs not in '*Opercula*' above. Traditional heel-ball rubbings generally give the best results, though a 'cake' is preferable to a stick where there are deep gaps between parts of the design.[19]

Drawings and Engravings

(1) Drawings:— A remarkable number of drawings of brasses have survived and are to be found in a widely scattered selection of public and private collections throughout the western world. In England, for example, students investigating the history of the brasses of a particular county, town or region will probably find relevant drawings (of both existing and lost examples) located in the numerous manuscripts in the British Museum, in other national or local museums and libraries; libraries of private societies and institutes; his local record office, and so on. To see all those relevant to his own interests may mean considerable travel and expense, and the rewards or disappointments can only be understood by those seriously interested in such research.

Original sketches or drawings, many of them often crude in the extreme, may, however, prove to be the only surviving source of information about a particular brass, so must never be dismissed out of hand. A large number were made, for example, by the various Heralds, particularly during the seventeenth century, while making their Visitations of the English counties, e.g. John Philipot, Somerset Herald. Others are in notebooks kept by officers of the Cromwellian or Royalist armies, made either for patrons or from personal interest; men like Gervase Holles, or Richard Symonds (*q.v.*) a keen amateur archaeologist, Royalist soldier and collector, whose original diary of the years 1643-45 in the B.M., is full of notes and sketches about brasses, monuments and stained glass. Many of the early antiquaries like John Weever, Richard Gough, Dr William Stukeley, Thomas Dingley (or Dinely), Wenceslus Hollar, Sir Wm. Dugdale and Sir Edward Dering made and collected sketches and notes of brasses, large numbers of them since lost or mutilated; the majority are made with pen and ink.

Drawings or engravings of more competence were made later by professional artists like John Carter, Thomas Fisher, John Sell Cotman, John Chessell Buckler and Charles Alfred Stothard; others of varying quality by amateur artists like Thomas Sugden Talbot, Craven Ord, George Shepherd, Henry Geo. Oldfield and Edward Steele. Most of the above are detailed in the '*Who's Who*' at the end of this book.

(2) Engravings:—Many of the above artists' work was later transferred to printing plates to illustrate works on brasses and funeral monuments, or quite often were commissioned for the great eighteenth and nineteenth century county histories, e.g. Nichol's Leicestershire; Hasted's Kent; Cussan's Hertfordshire. Richard Gough the antiquary in his fine work *Sepulchral Monuments of Great Britain* . . . (3 vols. 1786-99) included many illustrations of brasses (mainly by fellow members of the Society of Antiquaries of London) by artists like the Basires, John Carter and amateur friends such as Michael Tyson, Craven Ord Rev. Thomas Kerrich and Jacob Schnebbelie. Although not all of these are artistically good and lack a scale, many are of great historical interest, as indeed are the small series of impressions in Volume 2 (i), 'rolled' off original brasses, and thus appearing in reverse.

Two artists of considerable ability whose work was soon after copied onto engraving plates (in the former's case to their detriment as the example in Pl. 9 shows) were Thomas Fisher of Hoxton (?1771-1836) and John Sell Cotman (1782-1842). Fisher's original drawings (of which the Bedfordshire and Kentish examples are best known) were exacting in their detail, drawn to scale and made mainly during the first quarter of the nineteenth century. Fisher made many of his drawings from his own 'dabbings' or rubbings, a number of which still survive at the Society of Antiquaries. Apart from their obvious artistic merit, many were of brasses which have subsequently perished or been mutilated; added to this is his valuable practice of including indents and/or small sketches of the entire brass and slab as an inset to the main drawing. The extent of his work can be gauged by examination of the sale catalogues of his drawings in the B.M., which include a large number of other topographical views.[20]

John Sell Cotman's drawings of Norfolk and Suffolk brasses were also drawn to scale, though they do not always have quite the quality of Fisher's. It has been stated by one authority that Cotman's *Sepulchral Brasses* . . . , largely undertaken at the instigation of his friend Dawson Turner, was produced mainly for 'financial reasons', which may account for some lack of attention to detail in some of the plates.[21] Other detail may have been lost during Cotman's difficult task of transferring the copies of the original sketches to printing plates. A copy of the original pencil sketch (60.96 × 35.56 cm.) of the Braunche brass, King's Lynn, Norfolk, is shown (very reduced in size) in Plate 69 of Mr Rienaecker's book (note 21 below). Like Fisher, Cotman made his originals from 'dabbings' and impressions of the brasses, in many cases, lent to him by his friends. Amongst these may be noted Rev. Thomas Sugden Talbot, whose own collection of excellent drawings of Norfolk brasses, made in 1793-94, and more faithful than Cotman's own, is now in the possession of the Norfolk and Norwich Archaeological Society.[22] It seems likely that the idea of using a light yellow wash over the finished drawing may have been copied by Cotman from Talbot. In the West Suffolk Record Office is a proof copy of the text and index of Cotman's *Suffolk Brasses* (1838).

Other topographical artists of the time often carried out work for private benefactors, and their drawings sometimes found their way into annotated or, 'grangerised', editions of county histories. Amongst those I have seen are an interleaved set of Lysons *Environs of London* (1796 edn.) at the Guildhall Library, London, with drawings or engravings of brasses, monuments, etc. by J. P. Malcolm (1767-1815) and T. Cadell; a 'grangerised' edition of Clutterbuck's *History of Hertfordshire* (pub. 1815-27), compiled by J. W. Jones and including drawings of brasses by Fisher and other artists (B.M.

Add. MSS 32348-52); another copy of the same work with sketches of brasses by J. C. Buckler (1793-1894) in the Hertfordshire C.R.O.; in the Crace Collection in the B.M. (Add MSS 169666-67) a number of coloured drawings by George Shepherd (fl. 1800-30). So diverse and scattered are the sources that it is impossible to list them in one volume, though a union list would be invaluable. With the advent of photography the original drawing has now become obsolete, but it must be remembered that most of the above were made before either heel-ball rubbings or photolithography had been invented.

Prints and Lithographs

Following the perfection of printing and photographic processes during the first half of the nineteenth century, methods of illustrating brasses greatly improved. Before then the wood engraving and lithographic stone were almost the only materials used. Etchings on steel and copper plates quickly followed, in which artists like John Carter (1748-1817), J. S. Cotman (*op. cit.*), Charles Alfred Stothard (1786-1821; who fell to an early death while copying a stained glass window) and the two Waller brothers were pre-eminent in our context. In the mid-1850s however, the revolutionary process known as photo-lithography was developed, and gave rise to a completely new concept in book illustration.[23]

For illustrations of brasses the traditional wood engraving, used since the discovery of printing, and the lithographic stone were the cheapest and most common materials in use up to the 1850s. Following the practice of contemporary book and periodical illustration, works about brasses in journals like *Archaeologia*, the *Gentleman's Magazine*, and the pioneering books by Boutell and Haines used wood cuts. These tended to follow the lead of the house style of the Archaeological Institute and John Henry and James Parker the publishers. Robert B. Utting, T. O. S. Jewitt, J. R. Jobbins and J. S. Heavyside were some of the specialists in wood engraving who were used to good effect in most of the above publications. Herbert Haines apparently purchased the blocks used in his 1848 *Manual* from the Oxford Architectural Society (in addition to those he had already paid for himself) for use in his famous 1861 edition. Publishing at this time was mainly done by subscription (as lists in Waller, Haines, Boutell, Kite, etc. show) helping to defray both author's and publisher's costs. Indeed, Haines was even accused by a reviewer of his 1861 *Manual* of using some of Boutell's engravings without acknowledgement![24]

Lithographs were used in the curious publication by the Cambridge Camden Society, *Illustrations of Monumental Brasses*, edited by Rev. J. M. Neale (1846);[25] twenty four are included, though not all are of high standard. Gradually, however, the heavy lithographic stone was replaced by zinc plates, making handling easier and great improvements in execution possible. Rev. Edward Kite's book, *Monumental Brasses of Wiltshire* (1860 repr. 1969), for which the author made his own drawings, employed this method. The drawings were transferred to zinc plates and printed in relief by what was then called the 'anastatic process', but Kite does add that "the more difficult subjects were reduced photographically". An interleaved and annotated copy of his book is in the library of the Wiltshire Archaeological Society at Devizes Museum, edited by J. E. Jackson in 1862. Kite also illustrated the enlarged edition of John Aubrey's *Wiltshire*.[26] The enthusiasm for the anastatic process was such, that in 1854 the Rev. J. M. Gresley, M.A., founded the Anastatic Drawing Society, whose declared object was to 'delineate the remains of Antiquity . . . ', including, sepulchral monuments, brasses, etc. The first issue of their journal was published in 1859, and one early volume states that the process depended greatly for its success on the skill of the plate maker. In the Suffolk Institute's *Proceedings* 'Cowell's Anastatic Process' was used for a number of years; Cowell had a business in Ipswich.

One early writer on brasses who produced a unique, though somewhat misguided work, was Franklin Hudson, a young surgeon from Braunston, Northamptonshire. His book, *Brasses of Northamptonshire* (1853) contains over ninety bronze coloured lithographs made on zinc plates and copied from the author's own rubbings. Publication was carried out in four parts (one for each Deanery), but was not quite complete at the time of Hudson's premature death. Thomas McLean, the publisher, completed the work for Hudson and wrote some notes for the small paper edition. Issued in both a large and small paper edition, the work has many faults and inaccuracies, but is of some aesthetic interest as the only one of its kind to be attempted on such a scale. It bears no comparison at all to Mr Trivick's excellent work of recent times, and was presumably produced to follow the then fashionable interest in Richardson's 'Metallic' rubbings (*op. cit.*).

Before passing to the photo-lithographic methods, brief mention must be made of an interesting process of obtaining ordinary lithographic 'rubbings'. In the *Procs. Society of Antiquaries* (2. Ser. I, 21 March, 1865, p. 365) is an article by John Williams, F.S.A., 'Methods of obtaining lithographs from brasses'. Basically, it uses yellow soap mixed with water, to which powdered black lead is added to make a paste. This is spread evenly on a sheet of strong paper, allowed to dry, after which it can be scraped off leaving a thin film of the mixture. A sheet of white paper is then fixed over the object to be copied, the prepared paper laid on it face down, and the whole rubbed with a piece oı wood. The surface of the white paper will thus be blackened and a copy made, which if properly prepared can be further darkened by continued rubbing. The process was awarded the Silver Medal of the Society of Arts in 1832. The process can also be adapted using lithographic compound and paper to prepare a lithographic stone from which many prints could be made. By now, readers of my *Beginner's Guide* will recognise the similarity between the above and the silk screen printing process I described on pages 60-64 of my book.

Photographic processes

Apart from the illustrations of brasses in the numerous county histories of the time, most of the writers on brasses after Haines used photo-lithographic processes for their illustrations.

This had the advantage of being an exact copy of the original rubbing as well as being able to enlarge or reduced to any size required with little difficulty. It also excluded any small errors inevitable in even the most exacting artist's drawing or engraving. It was used to excellent effect by writers like Creeny, E. M. Beloe, Jnr., in the Transactions and Portfolios of the various Monumental Brass Societies and in journals like *The Builder*, which produced some excellent reproductions of brasses, many from rubbings by Andrew Oliver, in the last quarter of the nineteenth century. These were mainly printed by the firms of Sprague & Co. (fd. c. 1880) and William Griggs & Son (fd. 1848), specialists in photo-lithography.[27]

Direct photography

The only departure from the above methods was another application of the camera, namely the direct photography of brasses and indents *in situ*. This was the subject of an interesting paper read before the Oxford University Brass Rubbing Society in 1899 by Rev. W. Marshall, M.A., of King's College, and a Minor Canon of Windsor (it was fully reported in *Amateur Photographer*, Nov. 17th, 1899, 384-5). Technical details of the procedure are given, using a simple box camera, on a tripod, with fixed focus lens. The speed and accuracy of the process were indicated, pointing out how easily the results could be transferred to slides. These could then be readily stored and used for reference or lecture purposes.

Not many years later, in 1907, the late R. H. Pearson spoke at the Annual General Meeting of the Monumental Brass Society about two methods of 'duplicating' rubbings by photo-printing. The first method was by using ferro-prussiate paper to obtain a 'sun print'; the second was to take a negative by printing the rubbing face downwards, on to specially prepared paper, and taking a print from the former. This gave a dark sepia 'duplicate' of the original rubbing, which then required 'fixing' to prevent further darkening, and could be touched-up with diluted sulphuric acid to "bring up the white parts, if not quite perfect".[28]

To return, however, to direct photography, Herbert Druitt in his scholarly *Manual of Costume on Brasses* (1906, reprinted 1970), includes many such photographs of brasses *in situ*—some, admittedly of poor quality. In more recent times, the volumes of *Reports of the Royal Commission on Historical Monuments*, have included in many cases, direct photographs of brasses. Similarly collections of rubbings and photographs of brasses are being collected by the various offices of the Victoria County Histories that are still in progress, e.g. Shropshire; the National Monuments Record and similar bodies. Lastly, special mention should be made of the Berkshire Archaeological Society who have been collecting slides and photographs for a number of years as a means of recording brasses *in situ*. This is not only to obtain accurate records, but to alleviate the storage problems inevitable with full size rubbings.[29] In the *Home Counties Magazine* (VIII, (1906), p. 211) is mentioned a collection of similar photographs of brasses *in situ* then being collected by the Architectural Section of the Surrey Photographic Survey and Record Society.

Modern methods

With the ever increasing number of books and articles about brasses currently appearing (including reprints of older works by Haines, Kite, Davis, Druitt and Suffling) it is important for all writers on the subject to understand the modern methods at their disposal. Cost is usually the only prohibiting factor in producing work of high standard.

Most works still use the traditional, and I think superior, black on white reproduction made from a photograph of a rubbing. To obtain results comparable to those of the photolithographers mentioned above, modern printers and photographic laboratories use a sophisticated and expensive machine known as a process camera. To get the same result with an ordinary camera by the method described in my *Beginner's Guide* (pp. 58-60) is extremely difficult.

The modern photo-printer with large studios where the biggest brasses can be photographed in one process are

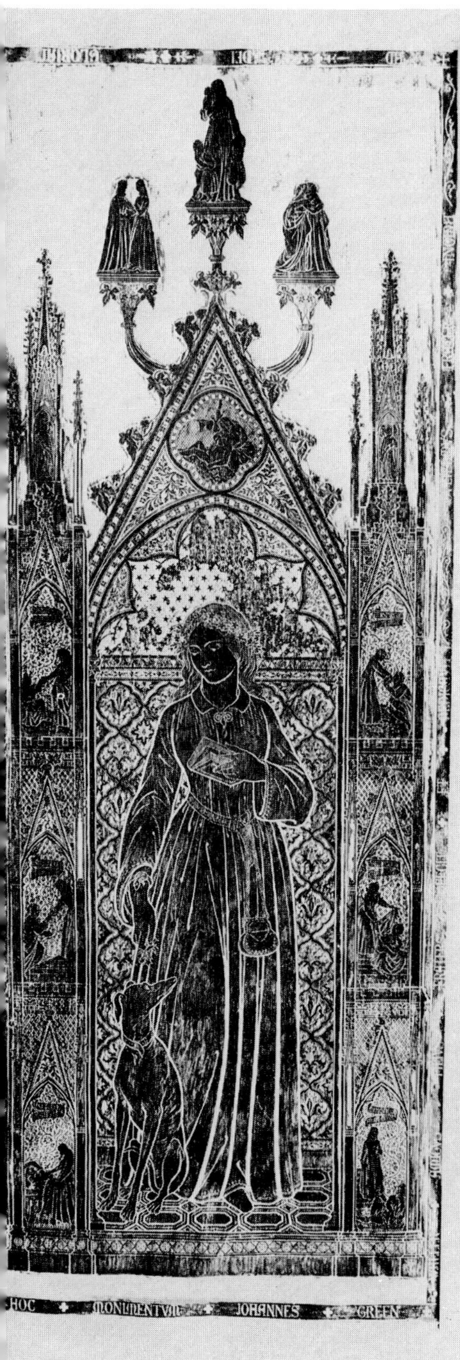

PLATE 5

Sara Hornby, Suzanne and Mary Waller; this magnificent, enamelled brass was made for the Great Exhibition of 1851 by John Green Waller (1813–1905), and was later re-used as a memorial to the above. A photograph cannot do justice to the original; note the canopy which is based on a restored version of that on the Hastings brass (1347), Elsing, Norfolk. The brass is now in the Chapel of Pitt House Schools, Torquay, Devon. Overall size 269 by 101 cm (106 by 40 ins). Rubbing Sally Morris. Photo Peter Marshall. Courtesy, Pitt House Schools Ltd.

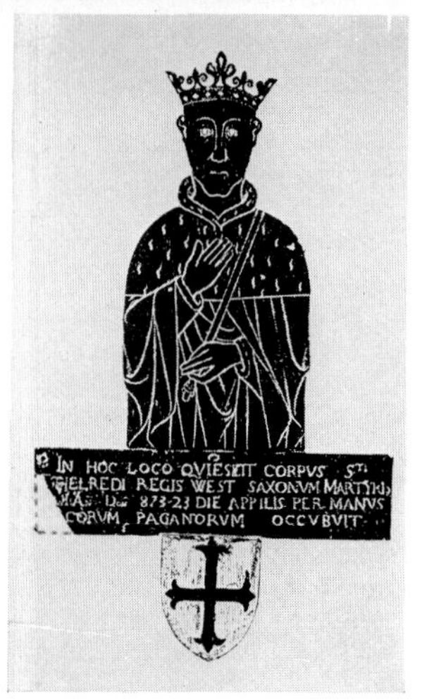
IN HOC LOCO QUIESCIT CORPUS S.TI
HELREDI REGIS WEST SAXONUM MARTYRIS
873 23 DIE APRILIS PER MANUS
CORUM PAGANORUM OCCUBUIT

(a)

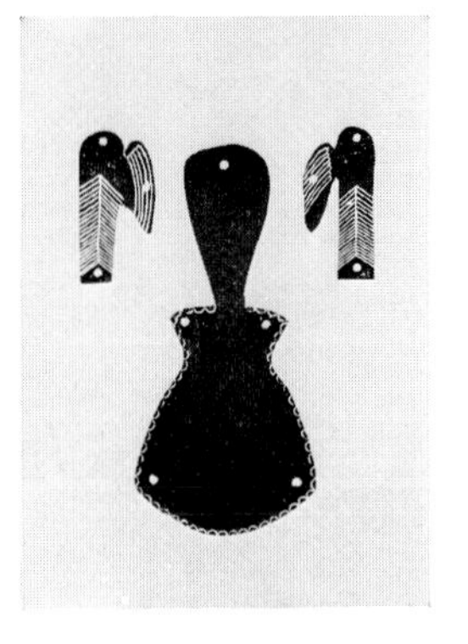

(b)

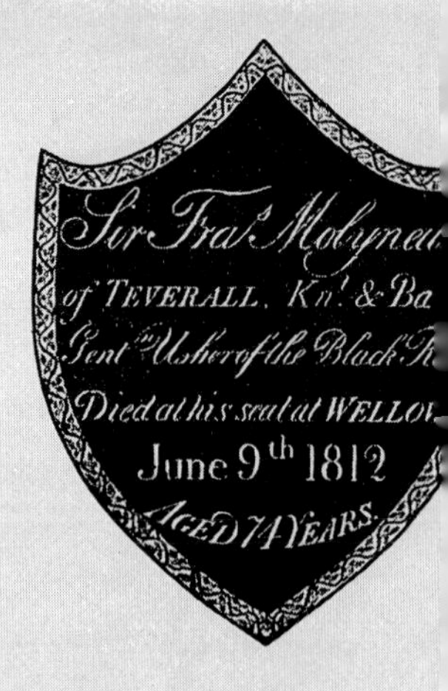
Sir Fra.s Molyneu
of TEVERALL. Kn.t & Ba
Gent.n Usher of the Black R
Died at his seat at WELLOW
June 9th 1812
AGED 74 YEARS.

(c)

WILLIAM CLAY
Died December 23.rd
1812
Aged 80
Years.

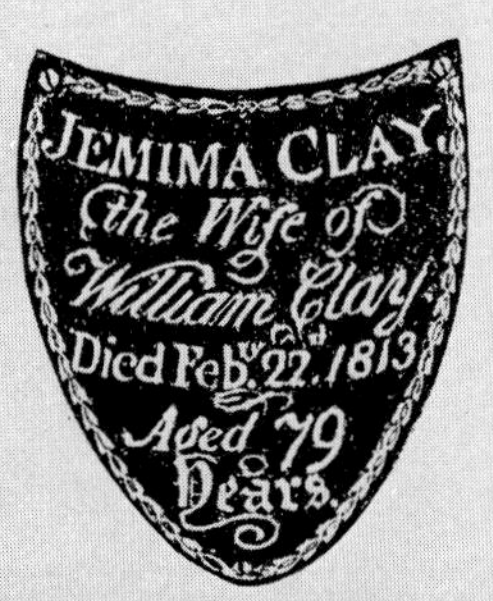
Benjamin Clay Esq.r
Elizabeth his wife
daughter of
John Grundy Esq.
OF BLEASBY.
DIED 1781.
JEMIMA CLAY
the Wife of
William Clay
Died Feb.y 22. 1813
Aged 79
Years.

(d)

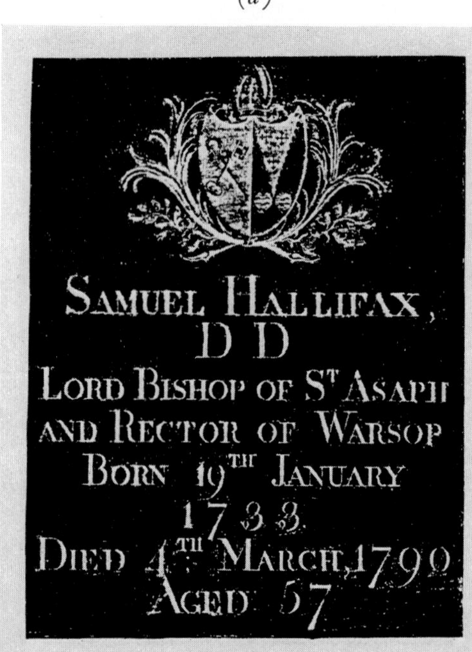
SAMUEL HALLIFAX,
D D
LORD BISHOP OF S.T ASAPH
AND RECTOR OF WARSOP
BORN 19.TH JANUARY
1733.
DIED 4.TH MARCH, 1790
AGED 57

(e)

difficult to find. The process-camera needs less space and is mounted on a sliding frame with graduated scale attached, and can be adjusted horizontally and vertically to enlarge or reduce a brass in part or whole (if small enough) in exact proportion. Very large brasses can be photographed in sections first, printed, joined together and a master negative made on which joins, creases and blemishes can be touched out. From this the finished print can be made on a high contrast photographic paper ready for further reproduction. With small brasses (or details) copied in one process the intermediate work can be omitted. Most of the illustrations in this book were made in this way, which is not in any way the same as the direct photography of rubbings described in my earlier book, since it pre-supposes access to expensive equipment not generally available outside specialist photographic laboratories or printers. I think comparison of my two books will indicate the difference quite clearly. Prints for reproduction should normally have a gloss finish, as this facilitates a far better result for block-making purposes.[30]

All the time improved methods of printing and copying are being discovered. Apart from several attempts over the last

PLATE 6
(*a*) King Ethelred (dated 873 engr. c. 1440), Wimborne Minster, Dorset. Only surviving 'Royal' brass in England, incorrectly dated 873 (he was slain by the Danes in 871); the copper inscription is a 17th cent. restoration; another dd. 872 being in the Minster library. Figure 36 cm (14⅛ ins). (*b*) Curious devices from slab in All Hallows, Barking, London for which no satisfactory explanation has been found. They were originally in the slab (incised) of Thos. Vyrly, vicar (ob. 1454), a notorious 'miracle worker'. (*c*) Coffin plate of Sir Francis Molyneux (1812), Teversal, Notts. Finely engraved plate rubbed by author 1970 when Molyneux vault opened for repairs (see note p. 86); the plate is now sealed up again in the vault. Height 47 cm (18⅜ ins); (*d*) Three small shields from stones in Southwell Minster, Notts. Possibly brass coffin plates, they now mark the vault where the family lie buried (from rubbing by W. Clay Dove); (*e*) Brass coffin plate of Bishop Samuel Hallifax (ob. 1790), Warsop, Notts. Typical simple design which might well have been a book-plate; a fine stone monument to the Bishop and his family is in the north aisle of the church. Size: 40 by 31 cm (15⅝ by 12¼ ins). Rubbing W. Clay Dove. Other rubbings by the author. Photos Peter Marshall.

one hundred years or so to produce good coloured reproductions, e.g. Heraldry Society—*Colour of Heraldry* (1958), the most recent break with traditional methods is that I have already mentioned by Mr Henry Trivick. Not only has he made full size 'autographic gilt facsimiles' in gold on black, but recently wrote an authorative book on brasses. In this work are many smaller illustrations in the same medium which, in the author's opinion, make clearer reproductions of the original than the conventional black on white, and are also nearer the way in which the engravers originally conceived their designs. For general use, however, this method is too expensive (as the price of the book indicates), but the same author has now published a second book of reproductions, some line drawings, but most of them in gold and black, at a much more attractive price.[31] At a talk I gave recently I was also shown somewhat similar work produced photographically and screen printed onto black and red card. The photographer had experimented with them as a relief from his normal industrial photographic work and was preparing some for use in a book in preparation in the United States.

Facsimiles

On a larger scale, the type of facsimiles I mentioned in my *Beginner's Guide* (pp. 66-67) made by Laurent Designs Ltd. (now at The Mill, Watton-at-Stone, near Hertford) are now made to scale in small and large sizes*. If it were not for the somewhat high cost, the casting method used could prove very valuable as a means of taking facsimiles of, say, palimpsest brasses or those in private possession, museums, etc.[32] There is no chance of experts confusing them with the originals, though 'counterfeit' brasses were produced early in this century, and in one case were on general sale by antique dealers in Bruges, Belgium (see interesting note on an illustrated article by Dr Frans Van Molle, 'Counterfeit Brasses', in MBS *Trans.* 9, ix (Nov. 1962), 525-6).[33]

*Since writing the above, production and marketing of these facsimiles has been taken over by Holland Warnock Ltd., 4, Market Pl., Chalfont St. Peter, Bucks. (R.B. 5.11.72).

Small scale facsimiles, like those first made by Mr. S. A. Illsley, etched into a metal plate (similar to a printing plate) and mounted on a wooden base, are still produced in large numbers. Most have a copper finish, others have a matt silver surface. Most of them are made on the same principle used for producing printed circuit boards for electronic equipment. I even saw one such plate mounted into the base of a battery clock.[34]

'Commercial' and other reproductions

Apart from screen printed designs on a large range of household products, e.g. tea-trays, table-tops, door plates, ash-trays, etc. (usually on plastic laminates) those printed on wall hangings or other fabrics, a number of prints of varying quality are also available. Firms like the Black Knight Art Co. and the 14th Century Art Studios are producing a large range of quite pleasing book marks, greeting cards, sheets of wrapping paper and unframed prints of brasses, including some in colour or embossed in gold. Another firm 'Golden Knights', produces twenty-two carat gold prints on coloured suedes. These bear no similarity to Mr Henry Trivick's fine facsimiles (*op. cit*). A number of American firms also produce similar products, and I even have a press-cutting sent to me from Melbourne, Australia, advertising 'Old English Brass Rubbings . . . re-created on a scroll of moon-stone parchment, 28″ × 19″, with traditional Teak Rods . . . '.

Some excellent prints, postcards and other reproductions can be obtained, from the Victoria and Albert Museum (exceptional value), the British Museum (mostly postcards only) and places like the Westminster Abbey Bookshop in London. Phillips and Page in Kensington (suppliers of brass rubbing materials) also stock a limited range of cards. An enterprising and well produced portfolio of reproductions of their brasses, has recently been produced by the Church of St Helen's, Bishopsgate, London (price £0.25). A number of churches and cathedrals also sell postcards or prints, of varying size, quality and price. Many others include photographs of rubbings of their brasses in their guide book, together with varying amounts of detail about each brass (one or two even sell slides with brasses on them). One excellent guide I obtained some years ago of very high standard, was from Felbrigg Church, Norfolk, which has a fine series of brasses despite its somewhat isolated position in a park.[35] Most of the illustrations are taken from the rubbings of Mr R. H. Clark, made in the 1920s or early 1930s.

One use of a brass of which I have only found one example to date, was on a Finnish stamp of 1933, issued to commemorate the Finnish Red Cross, on which the kneeling figure from the brass commissioned by Magnus Olsson Tawast, Bishop of Abo (1421-50) is reproduced. A description of the stamp (with illustration) and brass is given by the late H. F. Owen Evans in M.B.S. *Trans.*, VII (2), Dec. 1935, p. 86.[36]

In the above survey much has been omitted, but I hope it will stimulate or interest at least some of its readers to delve further into this fascinating and still relatively unexplored aspect of brasses. If topographical lists of reproductions were produced (adequately documented) for even a few counties an invaluable service would be performed.[37] Although it would be impossible to obtain absolute completeness, I hope one day such a work might be produced. Collections of rubbings and book illustrations are generally well known, but many prints, manuscripts, sketches and drawings, etc., remain almost forgotten in libraries, museums and record offices throughout Europe (and to a lesser extent in America) as well as scattered throughout countless periodicals of every description. By knowing how, when and where they were reproduced, the searcher can find untold pleasure and satisfaction.

CHAPTER FOUR

Brasses and Brass Rubbings for Education

Nearly every book or journal article dealing with the general history of this subject tells, in varying amounts of detail, how one can learn about other disciplines through the study of monumental brasses. These include the arts of heraldry, costume, arms and armour, genealogy, calligraphy, architecture, engraving and so on. Few books, however, can go much beyond fitting brasses into the general history of art, except where the whole book is devoted to one particular aspect, e.g. costume, and in the following chapter I hope to suggest some alternative applications or expand further on some of the established lines of enquiry. This has special significance for those working with children and young people and those studying local history and art.

Some General Principles

I have shown in an earlier chapter how the first groups of students most closely associating themselves with brasses, at the universities of Oxford and Cambridge especially, were those studying Gothic architecture and art. Indeed, the Universities have traditionally remained the most active bodies associated with both academic and technical research into the history, manufacture and repair of brasses since the foundation of the Oxford and Cambridge Brass Rubbing Societies. Today, for example, under the guidance of Dr H. K. Cameron, Dr G. H. S. Bushnell, Mr. Brian S. H. Egan and others, much invaluable work of repair and restoration is carried out at Cambridge and in the 'Egan workshop' at Stoney Stratford.[1] In more recent years also, a number of museums, traditionally keepers of 'stray' monumental brasses, have taken more than just the role of 'conservationist' and have actively encouraged the study of the brasses and rubbings in their care, e.g. Ashmolean, Manchester, National Museum of Wales, V. & A. Museum.

Historically speaking, the Universities have also been the traditional 'recruiting' grounds for membership (and later foundation) of the principal Monumental Brass Societies, the Church, the legal and teaching professions forming a high percentage of the interested parties. Most of the older standard works on brasses, both books and periodical articles, have come from student or practicing clergy and barristers, notably those of Boutell, Haines, Creeny, Macklin, Beloe, Griffin and Mill Stephenson. Today, membership of the Monumental Brass Society is drawn from a much wider selection of people and is essential to those seriously concerned with the study and preservation of brasses of all ages. In addition, to cater for local interests, Brass Rubbing or Monumental Brass Societies like those of Sussex and Gloucester have, or are, being formed.

Every brass, however large or small, old or new, well or badly engraved, should be of potential interest and must never be dismissed out of hand. The interest may, in many cases, 'be in the eye of the beholder', and will vary according to those of the individual concerned and his/her motive in rubbing or looking at a particular brass. For example, points of interest may arise because the style of engraving suggests a brass of local origin, or may well resemble a design in a neighbouring church. Alternatively, the brass may be to an ancestor, or member of a family, connected with the person studying it and the work he is engaged on; there may be a mistake in the engraving of the dress or vestments (e.g. at Clothall, Hertfordshire, the brass of John Vynter, rector, 1404 (M.S.I.) has the stole omitted; at Wixford, Warwickshire, Sir Thomas Crewe, 1411, has no sword belt although otherwise armed).[2]

To many people, the various animals and devices shown at the feet of figures or on shields are of interest. Most of these are heraldic or mythological in origin, and although the lion and the dog are the most frequently used, others of every variety can also be seen. These mostly occur on military and civilian brasses, but two unusual ecclesiastical examples at Battle, Sussex (c. 1430) and Watton-at-Stone, Hertfordshire, (c. 1370) also survive. The former depicts a priest with a dog at his feet, whilst the latter has the unusual combination of a priest with his feet resting on a lion. Amongst the more unusual animals to be seen are the following:—

Elephant: Wivenhoe, Essex, 1507.
Dragon: Tong, Shropshire, 1467.
Sheep: Northleach, Gloucestershire, c. 1485.
Eagle: Little Easton, Essex, 1483.
Hedgehog: Digswell, Hertfordshire, 1415.
Leopard: Digswell, Hertfordshire, 1415.
Unicorn: Ewelme, Oxfordshire, 1436
Wyvern: Sawley, Derbyshire, (1467).
Boar: Sawley, Derbyshire, (1467).
Griffin: Sawley, Derbyshire, (1467).
Pelican: Saffron Walden, Essex, c. 1430.
Stork: Old Buckenham, Norfolk, c. 1500.

Mr. C. T. Davis (author of *Monumental Brasses of Gloucestershire* (1899, repr. 1969-), wrote an article called "Zoology on brasses, chiefly from Gloucestershire Examples", which those interested will find absorbing;[3] an equally erudite paper by the late H. F. Owen Evans called 'The Elephant on Brasses', appeared in a recent issue of the M.B.S. *Transactions*.[4]

Teaching History with Brasses

One of the most popular teaching methods at present in use in schools is the topic or project, and here brasses offer considerable scope. This use can, of course, also be extended to older students in colleges of education and art, though the emphasis may be different. What has become known as 'field study', especially in the teaching of local history is one obvious application.[5]

In this respect, the Cotswold wool trade has become an established and excellent example, and has inspired a number of projects often begun by making rubbings of the famous brasses in the 'wool churches' at Northleach, Cirencester and Fairford. From learning about the brasses and the people they commemorate, from their 'merchant's marks' and the tools of their trade, the study can enlarge to the church itself and its records, to the town, the history of the wool trade, social conditions at the time and so, depending largely on the age of the students. In a large class, each group can be given a different aspect to study. One group may find, for example, that the church was enlarged and the famous south porch at Northleach built by John Fortey, whose fine brass of 1458 still remains in the nave. The same brass also exhibits other interesting features including the sheep and woolsack at John's feet, well-drawn costume and the ornate merchant's mark with which his goods were branded.

Another group studying the town itself may find houses or other buildings associated with the trade still in existance, while others now lost may be seen on old prints or drawings in the local Record Office or Library. Sketches or photographs can be made of these, or photocopies supplied by the Record Office, Library, etc. concerned. The scope for enlargement is endless, and should take in both surviving and documentary evidence. One Gloucestershire school some years ago developed a project similar to the above which arose from the interest created by the class reading Cynthia Harnett's excellent historical novel *The Woolpack* (Methuen, 1951; Penguin, 1961). A similar study could be made of the wool trade in East Anglia, where not only are there many similar 'wool' churches, brasses of merchants, etc., but much documentary and visible evidence of sea-trade with the sister ports on the North German, Dutch and Belgian coasts. On some of the brasses, either at the feet of the figures or on shields, are shown tools associated with the trade of the person commemorated.

Those studying history along more traditional lines may choose to select persons whose name(s) appear in some historical event or period, and whose brass (or tomb) has survived. Those like the inscription to Anne Hathaway (ob. 1623), wife of William Shakespeare, in the parish church at Stratford-on-Avon, Warwickshire, or the brass of King Ethelred (dated incorrectly 873, engraved c. 1440) at Wimborne Minster, Dorset, are well-known examples. Lesser known persons of importance abound, especially officers of the Royal Household, but many more brasses of historical importance were lost from churches like Old St. Paul's[6]; many more have been deliberately stolen or destroyed at various times in history, a number of which are recorded in the works of the great antiquaries like Stow, Weever, Leland and others.

Of existing examples may be mentioned brasses like that of Sir Arnald Savage (ob. 1410), Speaker of the House of Commons and held in high favour by Henry IV. Ralph Griffin called him "one of the great men of the realm",[7] and the remains of his brass (engraved c. 1420) is doubly interesting as it was produced at the direction of his son (ob. 1420) in the latter's will[8]. This immediately gives any prospective project two centre-points around which to build, but could well embrace such topics as the duties of the Speaker, other positions held by Sir Arnald; the Kentish manorial system; the domestic goods and chattels most important to the family (as noted in the will); making a map of the village and manor, comparing it with modern maps to see what features, if any, still remain; investigating the origin and blazon of the Savage family's Coat of Arms; visiting Bobbing and neighbouring churches to see if any other memorials to the family survive; making or obtaining copies of any surviving documents of importance in local or national archive collections, e.g. Public Record Office, British Museum, College of Arms; making a plan or model of the village and manor of Bobbing and following more conventional lines of enquiry like costume, armour, as outlined in the first example.

Amongst other surviving brasses, taken at random, which might offer equal scope are the following examples:—

(a) Sir John Peryent and wife Joan (1415). Digswell, Hertfordshire.
Sir John was Esquire to Kings Richard II, Henry IV and Henry V; pennon-bearer to Richard II; Master of the Horse to Queen Joan of Navarre. His wife was chief lady-in-waiting to Joan of Navarre. Thefamily was of Breton descent, held several manors in Hertfordshire and Sir John mustered three men-at-arms and nine foot archers for King Henry V's first expedition to France i n 1415, and fought at Agincourt. (M.S.I.).[9]

(b) Sir William Sydney (1552/3), Penshurst, Kent—Chamberlain and Steward to King Edward VI; tutor to the same Edward when Prince of Wales; Commander of the English right flank at Flodden Field, 1513; attended Henry VIII at the Field of the Cloth of Gold; lord of the manor of Penshurst. There is no figure on the tomb itself, but tremendous scope for an historical project (M.S.V.).[10]

(c) Rowland Taillor, (ob. 1555, br. engr. c. 1560), Hadleigh, Suffolk—
Inscription (palimpsest) with twenty verses in frame attached to north chancel arch where it was placed in 1594. Taillor was the local parson and was martyred on 9th February 1555. (M.S.I.). An account of his tragic death appears in John Foxe's famous *Book of Martyrs*.

(d) Sir John Beton (1570), Edensor, Derbyshire—Sir John had aided the unfortunate Mary Queen of Scots in her escape from Lochleven Castle. The Latin inscription (probably composed by his brother Andrew Breton, whose initials appear in the lower sinister corner of the plate) state the sympathies of the deceased (who died at Chatsworth) quite clearly. The whole brass is interesting and unusual in itself, and abounds in scrollwork, leaves and fruit in the border decoration (M.S.I.).[11]

(e) Joan Harvey (1605), Folkestone, Kent – Mother of William Harvey, discoverer of the circulation of the blood. (M.S.II.).

I think the above examples should give some idea of the kind of examples surviving on brasses, and which may well give the impetus to a class of students to pursue the matter further. Any brass rubbing undertaken by younger children must, of course, be done under adequate supervision.

At a more advanced level, such as L.E.A., Worker's Educational Association or university extra-mural classes, brass rubbings can be used not only to illustrate local examples, but additionally as evidence of manorial descent; incumbancies of local churches; genealogical work or to supplement details where the person commemorated is mentioned in contemporary documents on display, e.g. wills; inventories; leases and so on*. In Nottinghamshire, for example, the work of Mr. W. Clay Dove in this field is typical of the best use of brasses in this context, and I have included a photograph of an 'end of term' exhibition of his students' work (Plate 14 (b) f.p. 193. From 18th-20th July, 1969, Staffordshire County Council held a week-end course on Monumental Brasses and Brass Rubbing under the able guidance of Drs. J. R. Bishop and C. E. Cope. Practical as well as factual lectures were included and proved successful enough for a second course entitled 'Heraldry, Arms, Armour and Brasses' to be announced at the same place. (Pendrill Hall College of Residential Education) from July 24th to 31st, 1971. An annual week-end conference is also now a regular feature of the M.B.S.'s programme for members and provides an excellent forum for free discussion and exchange of ideas and information.[12] While I am writing this I see that the April 1971 M.B.S. *Newsletter* mentions that the Youth Hostels Association are hoping to organise three one-week courses on brasses and brass rubbing at three different centres.

Genealogy

Mention has already been made of the use of wills as both a

*Since writing the above the valuable paper below has appeared by Miss Nancy Briggs, M.A., in MBS 10,vi (Dec 1968 [pub. Dec 1970]), 472–82, 'Chapter and Verse; Documentary Sources for the Study of Monumental Brasses', which the present writer somehow overlooked.

source of information about a particular person and his family and friends, and as a possible source of direction for the making of the brass itself. Where they have survived they can also help to 'bring alive', particularly to children, someone who might otherwise seem of little interest. In a typical will may be found bequests to the church, to the immediate family and friends, to the town or village; to neighbouring or distant places associated with the deceased; names of lands and/or estates held by the deceased and to whom they are to pass; household goods and chattels of value, e.g. bedding, cutlery, plates, cooking utensils, clothes, other valuable commodities such as horses, cows, sheep, plus, in rarer cases, directions as to the type of memorial required (perhaps with costings).

The will may be in Legal Latin or English, and if no transcript or translation survives (say in one of the published guides or in the local Record Office), some difficulty in reading may be incurred, It is best. therefore, where possible, to choose your example according to the relevant age of the class, unless you are fortunate enough to be able to read or translate the original beforehand yourself.

Space does not permit me to record examples at length, though many of the standard works on brasses give examples or extracts. The field still offers scope for a great deal of original research, as known references to brasses in wills are still comparatively few. In many other cases it is not certain that a brass is required, unless it is fortunate enough to have survived. A typical example in this respect is the will of Thomas Leventhorpe of Albury, Hertfordshire, who requested that 'some decent and convenient marble stone withe oure armes uppon our tombes with the pictures of me and my saide wife and oure children as commonly the manner is in that behalfe . . . ' (P.C.C. 26 Leicester).

Thomas died in 1588 and in this instance the request was carried out, as the brass survives (M.S.3); but Thomas may equally well have meant a stone monument or slab.[13]

Apart from those brasses laid down before decease, it would seem that, generally speaking, the choice of a latten or stone monument was left to the executors. Cost would also enter into the decision, as would other factors such as room in the church itself, any verbal request made before decease, availability of materials and so on. Most wills seem to go little beyond mention of the part of the church requested for burial, but may go a little further and request, like Rev. Willam Lucas (ob. 1602) of Clothall, Hertfordshire, to be interred "Nere unto the place where Doctor Dollisoune was buried . . ." (P.C.C. 37 Bullein). Thomas Dallison (ob. 1541) also has a brass in Clothall Church, and appears, from his will to have been a man of some substance despite his position as priest of a small parish. Doubtless his degree in civil law brought him additional income beyond his modest stipend!

Many extracts and guides to wills have been published, and it must be remembered that the earlier examples were proved in courts often many miles from the parish concerned e.g. Perogative Court of Canterbury (usually refered to as P.C.C.). Use of the invaluable published extracts, or the transcripts in local or diocesan record offices, is a great help, but for serious historical research, reference to the original is often necessary both to check accuracy and expand on detail. For general guidance on this subject I would recommend students to consult a copy of *Wills and their whereabouts* by A. J. Camp (Phillimore & Co. for the Society of Genealogists 3rd edn. 1963) or any good general genealogical hand book such as G. E. Gardner and Frank Smith's *Genealogical Research in England & Wales* (Bookcraft Publishers: Bailey Bros. 3 vols. 1964-66); *Genealogist's Handbook* (Soc. of Genealogists. 5th edn. 1969); A. J. Willis. *Genealogy for Beginners* (Phillimore; rev. edn. 1970); A. J. Camp. *Tracing your ancestors* (Gifford. £0.62½. r.e. 1970).

In a few rare cases, genealogical information is recorded on the brass itself, with relevant information about several generations of a family. Good examples are at Ilmington, Warwickshire, (1531-1666); Newton Flotman, Norfolk (1490-1571) and Westall, Suffolk (14th cent.—1602).[14] The most famous example is the curious brass of Thomas Beale and his wife, 1594, at Maidstone, Kent, showing seven generations of the family. This was once used in a legal case to prove ownership of a parcel of land![15]

Heraldry

This is a field traditionally associated with brasses and monuments and into which considerable research has already been done. Nearly all the standard works on brasses, of Visitations, and on heraldry illustrate such examples, since brasses are one of the most accessible and tangible *contemporary* records available. Errors in engraving do, however, occur from time to time making double-checking necessary in some cases (e.g. the shields on the Flemish brasses of Andrew Evyngar and Thomas Pownder (*op cit.* p. 00) have heraldic errors, probably accounted for by their foreign origin). For the general enquirer capable of backing his work with suitable reference books to check tinctures, ownership, etc., the field is unlimited.

Arms are found displayed on brasses on shields, roundels, lozenges, jupons, tabards,[16] mantles, scabbards, sword belts, canopies, vestments, etc., many originally being coloured with enamel(s) or pigment(s). The base metals were often represented by different hatching or metal inlays, e.g. lead. Colour was paramount in medieval churches and brasses were no exception. Sadly, little of either has survived the rigours of time and weather, and a new brass, complete with colouring, inlays, gilding and lacquering must have presented a magnificent sight. In one or two early examples other materials were added, around the brass itself, e.g. that of Margaret de Valence; Westminster Abbey (1276), where the slab between the stem of the cross (now lost) and the border inscription, cut in separate letters of brass, was inlaid with coloured mosaic.[17] A much ealier monument in memory of Pope Benedict V. (ob. 965), formerly in Hamburg Cathedral, was made entirely of coloured faience tiles very much in the pattern of the earliest brasses, but with effigy and canopy instead of a cross or figure alone.[18]

Only one brass showing a herald has survived, but at least

three others are lost. At Broughton Gifford, Wiltshire, is a curious rectangular plate on which the figure of a herald (upper half only) is shown facing the figure of death.[19] This brass, in memory of Robert Longe (ob. 1620), is not quite so useful heraldically as the lost examples would appear to have been. Illustrations of each have survived in early manuscripts and details are given in M.B.S. *Trans.* IX (6) 1958, pp. 301-3 in a valuable article by Mr H. S. London.[20]

Finally, other aspects which might be studied under this heading include the heraldic devices and animals themselves; the Arms of the various livery or trading companies, e.g. Haberdashers; Merchant Adventurers; Mercers' Company. At Great Saxham, Suffolk, is a tomb bearing Arms, very rare on brasses, of the East India Company, and the Russia and Turkey Merchants. In memory of John Eldred (1632) there is a curious woodcut of the brass by James Basire the Younger (*q.v*) made in 1806 from an impression by Craven Ord (*q.v*) who exhibited the same to the Society of Antiquaries (*vide: Archaeologia,* XV (1806), Appendix pp. 403-4).

Those wishing to conduct experiments with, say a class of older children, will find ample scope for introducing colour to the traditional rubbing. This could mean, either making a very light rubbing using the technique described earlier for modern brasses (pp. 00 above) or taking some sort of tracing from a normal rubbing. This will give a 'reverse' rubbing in outline which can then be coloured with the correct heraldic tinctures in paints or coloured inks, materials (collage fashion) or paper, depending on the accuracy or detail required. A good 'tabard' brass such as that of Sir Ralph Verney (1547) at Aldbury, Hertfordshire, or Sir William Gascoigne and his two wives (1540), Cardington, Bedfordshire, are ideal in size and scope for such an excercise. For real enthusiasts, or large groups, the twenty-seven shields on the brass of Margaret Lambert (1608) at Pinchbeck, Lincolnshire, offer a wonderful challenge! (M.S.I.).

Making rubbings directly with coloured crayons or heel-ball is a very skilled and painstaking art, and is not often practised.

For those wishing to understand something of the possibilities of using colour, the delicate work of C. A. Stothard (*Monumental Effigies of G.B.* 1817), the frontispieces of Cotman's *Brasses of Norfolk and Suffolk*, or the more recent publication of the Heraldry Society – *The Colour of Heraldry* . . . (1958) offer excellent examples. Mr H. H. Trivick's recently published *Picture Book of Brasses in Gilt* (*op. cit.*), has mainly gold on black illustrations, but the dust-jacket has a pleasing coloured design. Standard works on heraldry by Boutell, Fox-Davies, etc., noteably the latest revision of Fox-Davies (1969), make many references to brasses.[21] For less detailed work the *Observer's Book of Heraldry* by Charles Mackinnon (Warne. 1966) is ideal.[22]

Costume and Armour

Here, perhaps more than in any other field, brasses offer one of the finest and most accessible evidence of contemporary armour and fashion. Few books on these subjects do not, in part at least, use brasses as illustrations. Although over the years a number of misnomers have crept in with respect to the terminology of armour in particular, the brasses themselves are, generally speaking, accurate within the limits of the medium and the skill of the engraver. The most usual complaints against brasses, compared, say, to effigies in the round, are that they do not often show figures sideways, or that the back of the costume or armour cannot be shown. To experts this can be frustrating if, for example, the method of fastening a particular piece of armour or dress is being investigated and no manuscript illustration or original piece survives.

Military: Although there is no single book on armour in which only brasses have been used as illustrations, nearly all the standard works on the subject naturally make good use of them. Claude Blair's excellent handbook *European Armour* (Batsford. 1958) happily now back in print, or the earlier work of Charles H. Ashdown – *British and Continental Armour* (First pub. 1909. Repr. Dover: Constable. £1.75 (pbk), 1970) contain many examples based on existing brasses.

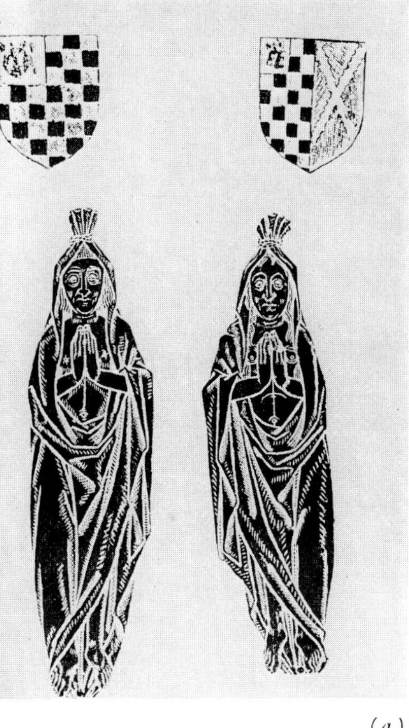

(*a*)

PLATE 7

(*a*) John Reynes & wife Agnes (c. 1500), Clifton Reynes, Bucks. Curiously drawn shroud brass of local school to members of prominent local family; F.I. missing. Figures: Man 49.2 cm ($19\frac{3}{8}$ ins). Lady 45 cm ($17\frac{5}{8}$ ins); (*b*) Academic (c. 1500), St Mary the Less, Cambridge. Well drawn $\frac{3}{4}$ length figure in Doctor's cap and gown; inscription lost. Academic dress has a considerable literature of its own (see pp. 116–7). Figure 60.5 cm ($23\frac{7}{8}$ ins); (*c*) Wm. Taylard, LLD, Rector (c. 1530), Offard D'Arcy, Hunts. Another brass of the 'Cambridge School' showing quite different method of depicting academical dress. Note the economy of line and shading characteristic of this 'school'. Figure 57.8 cm ($22\frac{3}{4}$ ins). Rubbings by the author. Photos Peter Marshall.

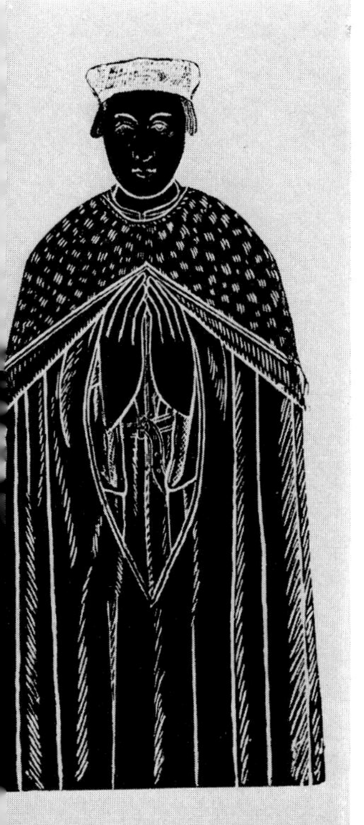

(*c*)

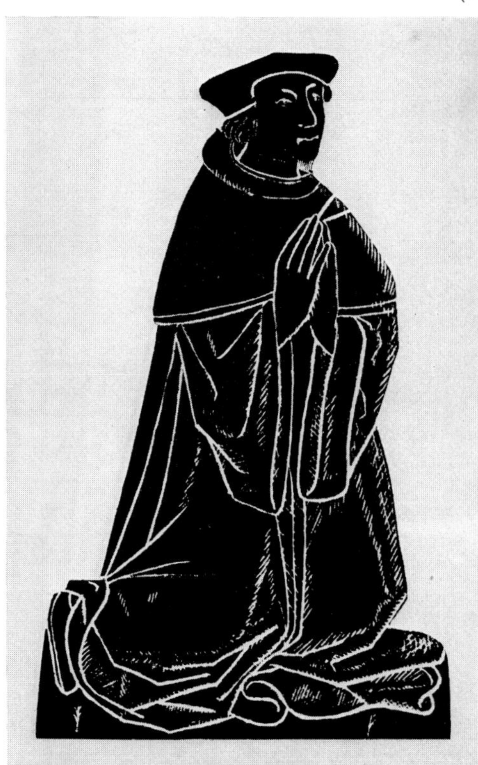

(*a*)

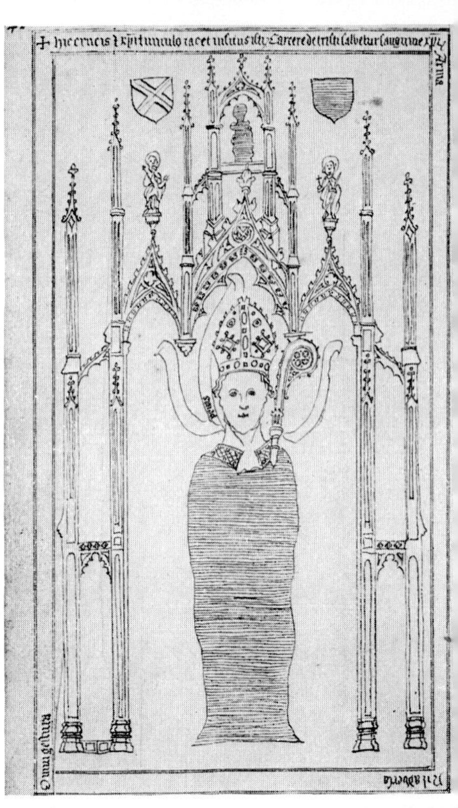

PLATE 8

(*a*) Sketch by Dr Wm. Stukeley (1687–1765) the famous antiquary; now among the Gough mss at the Bodleian, it shows missing parts of the brass of Abbot John Stoke (ob. 1451), St Albans Abbey, Herts. Photo: *Copyright Bodleian Library, Oxford;* (*b*) Two lost brasses from Gt. Gaddesden church, Herts from sketch by Edward Steele made c. 1714. Typical 'amateur' drawing, inaccurate but the only surviving record of the designs; the indents only remain (see note p. 231). Photo James Brown. Reproduced from original by courtesy St Albans City Library.

(*b*)

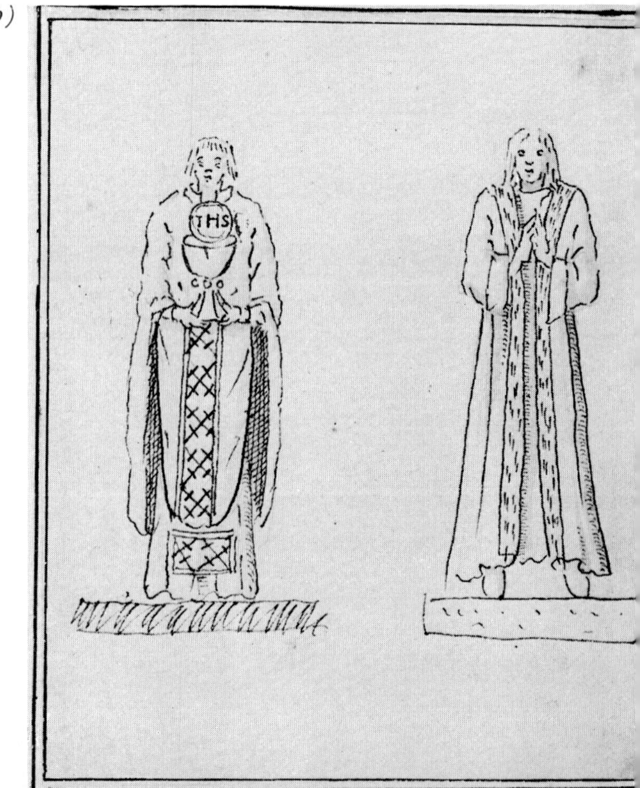

Ashdown also wrote an interesting article 'English Medieval Armour as exemplified by Hertfordshire Brasses . . . ', for an illustrated lecture he gave in 1901 (*St. Albans & Hertfordshire Archit. & Archaeol. Soc. Trans.* (N.S.) 1901, & 1902, 388-95).[23] The work in this field of the late Sir James Mann (*q.v.*), Keeper of the Armouries at the Tower of London, is already well known to most students, and he has done much to correct the errors of terminology, evident in many of the older works on brasses and armour. His researches in the field of brasses are summarised in the article quoted on p. 102 of my *Beginner's Guide* and in his excellent handbook, *Monumental Brasses* (King Penguin. 1957). The sections on military brasses in the older works of Druitt (see below) and E. R. Suffling's *English Church Brasses* (1910 repr. 1970), especially the latter, are examples of the dangers of not fully understanding the terminology of the subject.

For those who wish to study armour in closer detail they can find no more stimulating articles than those named below. First of these specialised articles to appear was the prize winning one by Dr. J. P. C. Kent 'Monumental Brasses: a new classification of Military Effigies'. (*J. Brit. Archaeol. Assn.*, XII (1949), 70-97. iillus.). In this, the author groups individual pieces of armour, e.g. elbow, shoulder, breast-plates, and places them in classes according to their various design features, i.e. shape, date, etc., More recently Dr. Lawrence E. James of Oxford wrote an article in which he compared the cost of armour like that shown on the brasses of Sir Nicholas Dagworth (1401) Blickling, Norfolk and Sir John Erpingham (1415), Erpingham, Norfolk. He based his estimate of 45 *livres* on contemporary wills and contracts (see: *M.B.S. Trans.*, X (iv) Dec. 1966 (1967), 226-31 – 'The Cost and Distribution of Armour in the 14th century').

Lastly, for the many enthusiasts, both young and old, of the military arms themselves, the most useful works of R. E. Oakeshott are recommended. His classic work *The Sword in the Age of Chivalry* (Lutterworth Press. 1965) repeatedly uses examples on brasses to illustrate the various classes and designs of pommel or handle. Mr. Oakeshott has also written a series of simpler works for children for the same publishers. Ideas using military (and other) brasses for decorative work are given in the succeeding chapter.[24]

In the field of costume, both civilian and ecclesiastical brasses offer one of the best continuous series of contemporary illustrations available. Not only do they include every class and profession, but all but the most extravagant fashions of the day. This is certianly one of the most attractive aspects of brasses for young people. Few books on the history of costume from J. R. Planché's famous *Cyclopaedia of Costume* . . . (Chatto. 1876, 1879. 2 vols.) to the modern works of writers like James Laver are without illustrations of brasses. Especially valuable are the following:—

CLINCH, George—*English Costume* (Methuen. 1909.).

HOUSTON, Mary G.—*Medieval costume in England and France during the 13th, 14th and 15th centuries.* (A. & C. Black. 1939).

CUNNINGTON, C. Willet & Phyllis— *Handbook of Medieval English Costume* (Faber. 2nd edn. 1969). Also their companion volumes on the sixteenth and seventeenth centuries.

The only book devoted entirely to brasses in this context is Herbert Druitt's excellent *Manual of Costume as Illustrated by Monumental Brasses* (1906 repr. Kingsmead Reprints. 1970). This has over one hundred illustrations, many of brasses *in situ*, and has a text well powdered with useful footnotes and references. At the time of writing there were few other more complete sources of information.

Ladies: Some of the best works dealing with the many specialised studies possible with costume on brasses are regretably hidden in older periodicals. For civilian costume, of which female head dresses are a popular topic, the best article I have seen to date lies buried in Vol. XVI (1902-3) of the *Surrey Archaeological Collections* pp. 35-54. By J. Lewis André—'Female Head-dresses exemplified by Surrey Brasses', shows quite clearly the scope of such a study, and is well complemented with line drawings made to scale.[25] A less detailed article of a more general kind by A. L Laishley—'Ladies fashions on church brasses', can be seen in *East Anglian Magazine*, July 1956, pp. 522-27.

If a particular period only is being studied, apart from the general works on brasses or costume, some of the best illustrated works are from the pens of the industrious Miller Christy and W. W. Porteous. Their many articles on Essex brasses include two of special interest in our context:—See (1) *Antiquary*, 38 (1902) 6-10, 44-47. 'Some Essex Brasses Illustrative of Elizabethan Costume', (2) *Ibid* 39 (1903), 113-18, 175-78, 233-38. 'Some Essex Brasses Illustrative of Stuart Costume', Both are amply illustrated to their usual excellent quality.

Legal: Other aspects which might be studied are different professions where costume is other than the normal civilian dress. Some can only be identified by the tools of their trade e.g. notaries, gamekeepers; others, like Yeoman of the Crown, by their distinct dress or badge, e.g. John Kent, Aston, Hertfordshire (1592). One of the best represented professions, however, is the legal profession, and brasses of judges in their robes are fairly numerous. e.g. Watford, Hertfordshire (1415), Cople, Bedfordshire (1544); Deerhurst, Gloucestershire (1400). The late Lewis Edwards wrote a detailed article on this subject for those wishing to study this aspect. (*J. Brit. Archaeol. Assn.*, XL (1934), 135-54; Repr. *M.B.S. Trans.* VII (3) Nov. 1936, 97-108; VII (4) Nov. 1937, 145-64. 'Professional costume of lawyers illustrated chiefly by Monumental Brasses'), which complements and enlarges on the general articles in Macklin, Druitt, etc.[26] Another good general article, again relating to Essex, appeared in *Essex Rev.* XLVIII (Apr. 1939), 69-78; *Ibid* Addenda XLVIII (Oct. 1939), 222-3 (Hills, Alfred—'Legal Brasses of Essex'). This makes special reference to the famous brasses at Dagenham, Latton and Witham.

Ecclesiastical: Other costume which has received special attention are those of ecclesiastics and academics, not only in general books on brasses, but also in separate books and articles. In the case of ecclesiastics, brasses depict almost every office in the Church and Monastic hierarchy from deacon to Abbot and Archbishop. Many of the best modern brasses are of ecclesiastical dignitaries. The articles in periodicals are too numerous and diverse to record, but as a general introduction E. M. White's 'Ecclesiastical Costume on Brasses' (*Sussex County Mag.* 5 (1931), 545-9) is useful, even if rather cursory; it has seven illustrations.

The only book entirely illustrated with examples from brasses is that specially written for the Alcuin Club by Rev. H. J. Clayton with the rather off-putting title of *The Ornaments of the Ministers as shown on English Monumental Brasses* (1919). Long out of print, it lacks the detailed descriptions of vestments found in the works of Macklin, Druitt and Haines, but has some useful illustrations. As the title suggests, it does not include monastic dress on which I have found no specialised work to date specifically related to brasses (beyond the general works already mentioned above).[27]

Academic: Academic dress has always had an extensive literature of its own, and brasses offer one of the few tangible pieces of surviving evidence of the earliest habit worn.[28] The only specialised study related to brasses I have seen is that by Mr E. T. Beaumont (q.v. author of *Ancient Memorial Brasses* (1913) – a well intentioned but misguided book). His later work, printed in typescript and now largely forgotten, is rarely seen outside libraries but deserves attention. Called *Academical Habit; illustrated by ancient armorial brasses*, it was privately printed for the author shortly before his death. The earliest academic brass surviving is usually stated to be that of John Hotham (1361) Chinnor, Oxfordshire, but Beaumont, in the work quoted above (fp. 5) illustrates a figure of c. 1350 in the mutilated head of an octofoil cross in Merton College Chapel, Oxford. This, he considers to be the earliest surviving example which, despite the 'curtain-like' dress (similar to that of Richard Torrington (1356) Great Berkhamsted, Hertfordshire) is of a graduate because of 'the fact that the tonsure is shown. We may also infer that at this time it was not customary for graduates to wear a distinctive habit' (p. 5). Mill Stephenson, however, dates this example as c. 1370 (too late in my opinion), but Beaumont is wrong in thinking the Merton College example to be the earliest as there is one of c. 1340 at Great Brington, Northants. (M.S.I.).

Beyond indicating some of the, perhaps, lesser-known sources of information, there is little point in my repeating what has been said many times before in other works on brasses.[29] No book can completely ignore the evidence of costume and armour afforded by brasses, though it would be nice to see a more general work to complement and up-date that of Druitt more on the lines of the Miller and Porteous articles, but with the additional benefits of modern colour printing techniques.[30]

Finally, many schools of art, colleges of education, museums and similar bodies are taking an appreciably greater interest in rubbings for use in the graphic and commercial arts, as well as for the value described above. The City of Manchester Art Galleries, for example, now have a Gallery of English Costume, with mounted and unmounted brass (and rock), dyeline and screen prints of rubbings, original rubbings, etc., both for reference and loan to educational organisations, groups, etc. This enterprising venture makes a welcome departure from the 'commercialisation' more commonly found to-day. Display stands are provided for exhibiting the rubbings. It is also no coincidence that the Costume Society have their headquarters at the Victoria and Albert Museum, well known for its excellent collection of brass rubbings and original costumes.[31]

Inscriptions

Inscriptions on brasses offer three facets for study – calligraphy, etymology and versification. For example, some contain obsolete words and curious turns of phrases; (e.g. the rector of Great Billing, Northamptonshire (1625) who gave £1,200 "to nourish Oxford artes"); others, humorous references to the deceased, usually in verse (see below).

The use of Middle/Old English from the late fourteenth

century onwards (Brightwell Baldwin, Oxfordshire c. 1370), contemporary with Chaucer's *Canterbury Tales* and sometimes equally humorous, has a particular fascination. Many inscriptions, however, merely conform to traditional phraseology in Norman-French, Latin or English, which once the contractions are mastered, present little difficulty in reading. Macklin (new and old editions), the late J. Franklyn[32] and others give notes both on reading inscriptions, plus lists of Latin words or vocational texts, both common and uncommon on brasses, to assist the unskilled. At Usk, Monmouthshire, is the earliest Welsh rhyming inscription found on brasses (1421).

In addition to the guidance given by the above works, the books below will be found very handy for reference purposes:—

STRATMANN'S Middle English Dictionary . . . rev. edn. (Oxford U.P. 1891 repr. 1951).
LATHAM, R. E. (ed) Revised Medieval Latin word-list (Oxford U.P. for British Academy. 1965).
LEWIS & SHORT'S Latin Dictionary (Oxford U.P. rev. edn. 1966).

To take a few random examples to conclude this chapter will give readers a better idea than any explanation:—

At Kelshall, Hertfordshire (1435) is the following curious inscription (now regrettably almost too worn for rubbing due to the brass being polished at some time):—

"Her lyth the bones of Rychard Adane't Maryon his Wyff. God G'ant/
Ther soules ev'lasting lyff. The which Rychard dyed—/
In ye yer of our Lord M.CCCC—The which Rychard Adane as/
Y now say, Leyd here his ston in his lyff day.[33] The yer of our Lord was/
yan trulie M.CCCC. fyve 't thyrtty: Man yt behoveth ofte to have in/
mynde That you gevest wt yun honde yat shalt you fynde, for Women/

ben slowful 't chyldren bey unkynde. Executors bey coveytous 't kepe all/
yt yey fynde For our bothe soules unto ye t' nyte seyeth a patur for charite,"
[/Denotes end of line on original plate]

Weever gives an almost identical inscription formerly in the church of St. Edmund, Lombard St., London which ends alternatively with:—

'If eny body esk wher ye deddys goodys becam yey ansqueare
So GOD me help, and halidam*, he died a pore man.
Yink on Yis.'

Note in the above the then common transposition of 'y' for the modern 'th' in 'yis', 'yink', etc.

Another verse of comparable date is given by Weever from Edmonton, Middlesex:—

'Erth goyth upon erth as mold upon mold
Erth goyth upon erth al glysteryng gold
As thogh erth to erth ner turne shold
And yet must erth to erth soner then he wold'

At Holme-next-the-Sea, Norfolk (c. 1405) the brass of Henry Nottingham and his wife has the following foot inscription concluding with the traditional 'Pater Noster':—

'Henry Notingham 't his Wyffe lyne here/
Yat Moden this Chirche Stepull 't quere/
two Vestmentz 't bellez they made also/
Christ hen gave therefore ffro Wo/
and to bringe her soules to blis of heven/
sayth pater 't ave with mylde steven'

One of the most popular rhyming inscriptions of late fourteenth century date is recorded by Weever (1631) as formerly being in St. Martin's, Ludgate Hill; St. Michael's, Fish St., (1487); Romford and Malden, Essex and Baldock, Hertford-

*Holy Virgin

shire. Surviving examples are few; Northleach, Gloucestershire, (c. 1485; Davis, p. 89) has one variant on a marginal inscription, while the one below is from Royston, Hertfordshire (c. 1490):—

'Now farewell my frendys all/The tyde abydethe no man/
I am depted hens and so ye shall/Yn thys passage ye best
song^e that I can/Requie eternan now Jhu graunte yt me/
When I have endyd all myne adversite/Graunte me yn
paradyse to have a macion/That shed they blod for my
redemcion'

Extolling the virtues of the deceased was commonly practised from the simple "Good William Maynwaryng" at Ightfield, Shropshire (1497) to a laudatory array of verses or couplets, like some of these below, usually comparing wordly and heavenly virtues amidst a host of metaphors and predicatives. Some are very moving and competent and may well have been borrowed from contemporary verse of the time. Much research could be done on the sources of such verses though the task is a forbidding one. Typical examples, chosen at random, are as follows:—

The inscription in memory of Frideswide Johnson (1626) St. Maurice, Winchester, Hampshire (1626) ends:—

'Her virtues and her Husbands have contende/
With this hard brasse, which shall have the last end'.

More touching is the inscription at Shenley, Hertfordshire (1618) in memory of the infant daughter of Ralph Alwaye and his wife, which describes her as,

'A jewell of rich prise/Who natvre in the worlds
disdayne/Bvt showd and pvt it vp againe',

whilst the two young wives of Francis Rowley (Brent Pelham, Hertfordshire, 1627) who died within a year of each other, are thus mourned by their bereaved husband:—

'Thy sting on death most sharply here appeares/
To take them both away in their prime of yeares . . . '

Finally, in this class is the inscription to Susanna Pyckering (1641), Guisborough, Yorkshire (N.R.), who is praised *par excellence*:—

'A vertvovs wife, this marble stone doth hide,/
Assvredly – , a saint in heaven shee's tryde;/
Religiovs was her life, the like her end,/
In seeking Christ, she most her time did spend . . ./

Cause of death is sometimes given and may vary from dying of 'the grete swetyng syknesse' (Great Berkhamsted, Hertfordshire, 1485) to the unfortunate Isaac Allen of Lindfield, Sussex (1656) who died in prison for issuing 'false and malicious words'.

Some inscriptions make very specific reference to the day of death, as in the case of Ffulke Onslowe (Hatfield, Hertfordshire) who died " . . . on Sunday, beinge the viiith day of Aug. 1602". More curious still is the inscription on the lost brass of Edward Mackwilliams and Henry and Anne Spelman which offers passers-by "300 dayes of pardon".[34] At Adderbury, Oxfordshire, is the brass of Jane Smyth (1508), who died on the now defunct day of 30 February (M.S.II),[35] while a small plate on the brass of John Sedley and his wife (c. 1520), Southfleet, Kent, directs categorically 'Dyg not wtyn too ffote of this tombe'. (M.S. VII).

Punning, comic and curious verses (mostly of post-Reformation date) are an established part of monumental art, and are a useful means of winding up a not too serious talk on that subject or on brass rubbing. Most of those usually quoted come from stone memorials, others from now lost or unknown sources quoted in works by the old antiquaries. Camden, for one, was especially fond of quoting them. Three examples typical of this type are quoted in Dingley's *History of Marble* . . . (2 vols. repr. 1867–8), only one of which is definitely from a brass; the first one is also quoted by William Camden in his *Remains Concerning Britain* . . . (1674) p. 535, which states that it was probably composed by John Hoskins [1566-1638]:—

'Here lieth John Craker* maker of Bellows
Who was his Crafts maker and king of Good fellows
But when it came to the hour of Death
He that made Bellows could not make breth'.
(Dingley, I. p. cxxxi).

On the brass inscription (now lost) of Thomas Weeks, then† loose in the Cathedral Library at Hereford, Dingley records the following punning verses:—

'His labours lost how hither comes and seeks/
For months or Dayes or Yeers heers none but weeks/
Can weekes be without Dayes? Yes, be not offended/
For here you see that this Weeks days are ended'
(Dingley, I clxv).

Finally, most unkind of all, is the following amusing inscription formerly on the grave of one 'Gammer Trewman' of Oxford. Dingley says she died 'of a Dropsie having her right leg tap't whence its foot went all wayes wett shod'.

'Here lyeth one disprove it if you can
Who lived a woman yett dy'd a True man/
Amongst all her skill, this was her cunning/
Whilst one legg stood still, the other was running'.
(Dingley, I. cxxxi).

Calligraphy

For following up the different types of lettering used on brasses from the single lombardic or longobardic letters used on the early coffin slabs, incised slabs and brasses, to the black letters or Gothic and capital letter of later years, the following will be found useful:—

M. Christy and W. W. Porteous. 'Some interesting Essex brasses'. *Essex Rev.* 10 (Apr. 1901), 84–100 Illus.
Deals mainly with various types of lettering in use between c. 1315 and 1638.

* Camden says 'Cruker'
† Mid 17th century

H. T. Morley 'Lettering on some Monumental Brasses of Berkshire' *Berks. Archaeol. J.* 48 (1944-5), 43-6; 110 letters are illus., with date and location under.

Ibid. 'Notes on Arabic numerals in Medieval England' *Berks. Archaeol. J.* 50 (1947), 81-6 Illus.

Includes a number of examples from brasses.

Useful notes on lettering, reading inscriptions, etc. giving examples like the above are given in most works, but especially Boutell. *Mon. Brs. and Slabs* (1847. Appx. F. pp. 198-206); 'little Macklin' 1890 *et seq.* and in Mr. Page-Phillips revised edn. of same (*op. cit.* pp. 97-102), the late Julian Franklyn's *Brasses* (*op. cit.*); Dr. Bouquet's *Church Brasses* (1956), pp. 151 ff.; J. Bertram. *Brasses and Brass Rubbing in England* (1971), pp. 142-51; M. Norris *Brass Rubbing* (1965), pp. 83-5. Haines' *Manual* (1861 repr. 1970) gives many examples of inscriptions, but little comment on the lettering itself or its uses.

Finally, a short but unique note by the late Major H. F. O. Evans 'Faces on Brasses' (*M.B.S.* 9, IV (1954), 206), illustrated with examples of capital letters into which the engraver has incorporated a human 'face', is worthy of attention.

FURTHER READING

The books below are recommended in addition to those named in the text for supplementing the above or for reference purposes.

BRIGGS, Geoffrey. *Civic and Corporate Heraldry: a Dictionary of Impersonal Arms of England, Wales and Northern Ireland.* (Heraldry To-day. £9.00. Sept. 1971). 1000 illus.; 432 pages. Largely supersedes A. C. Fox-Davies' *Book of Public Arms* (T. C. & E. C. Jack. 1915). For those interested in civic heraldry reference should also be made to C. W. Scott-Giles *Civic Heraldry of England and Wales.* (Dent. 1953) and F. E. Evans' concise *Civic Heraldry* (Shire Pubns. £0.25. 1968). For those wishing to keep abreast of current thought and research the Heraldry Society's quarterly journal *Coat of Arms* is essential. Lesser known, perhaps is *The Armorial,* published quarterly since 1959.

CHILD, Heather. *Heraldic design*. (Bell. £3.50. 1965)
A valuable handbook for all students, especially those wishing to understand the ancient and modern art of designing and Achievement. Well illustrated; including several of brasses.

CORFE, Tom (Editor). *History in the Field*. (Blond. £1.50. 1970).
A series of papers by practising teachers and lecturers on practical ways of stimulating interest in local history, especially in schools, by work in the field. Esp. pp. 33–5, 127–8.

DOUCH, Robert. *Local History and the Teacher*. (Routledge & K. Paul. £0.65. 1967).
Includes useful guide to sources of information and several examples of projects undertaken.

EMMISON, F. G. *Introduction to archives* rev. edn. (Phillimore. £0.50. (pbk). Dec. 1971).

HOPE, W. H. St John. *Heraldry for craftsmen and designers*. (Pitman 1913).
Invaluable for its illustrative material, though regrettably difficult to obtain.

HOSKINS, W. G. *Fieldwork in local history*. (Faber. £1.50. 1967. Pbk. edn. £0.65. 1969).

MERTON, K. C. *Medieval local records: a reading guide*. (Historical Assn.; Helps for Students of History Series, No. 38. £0.30 (pbk). 1971).

PLUCKROSE, Harold (ed). *Let's use the locality: a handbook for teachers*. (Mills & Boon. £2.50. 1971).
Includes notes on brass and gravestone rubbing; or the same editor's *Art and craft to-day* (Evans Bros. £2.50. 1971).

PUTTOCK, A. G. *A Dictionary of Heraldry and related subjects*. (John Gifford. £2.10. 1970).
Attractively produced, though oversimplified in places and the small entry for brasses has a bad mistake in it relating to the 'Brass' (*sic*) of Thomas de Berkeley, 1242, in Bristol Cathedral!

TATE, W. E. *Parish Chest*. 3rd rev. edn. (Camb. U.P. £3.75. 1969)

WEST, John. *Village records*. (Macmillan. £1.90. 1962).

CHAPTER FIVE

Brass Rubbings for Decoration and Display

Throughout this book the emphasis has been largely historical, but in this final chapter it will be mainly on modern techniques. Much of its content must be read in conjunction with the preceding chapter and the relevant sections in my earlier book.

Decoration

I have already touched briefly on the decorative use of rubbings, both in my *Beginner's Guide* and in Chapter 3 above. In this respect rubbings have much to offer, both to the individual and, regrettably, to some commercial organisations. Most of the notes below will, therefore, be confined to complementing those in my previous book, with only a modicum of new ideas added.

The fine facsimiles produced for Laurent Designs Ltd, by Mr S. A. Illesley, or the gold on black 'autographic gilt' rubbings of Mr Henry H. Trivick are already well known to most enthusiasts and collectors. Another method of producing gold on black 'rubbings', using a different technique, is that devised by Lady Elizabeth Montague and Mr Michael Papirnak. Known appropriately as the *Beaulieu Brass Rubbings*, they can be seen on display at Beaulieu Abbey, Hampshire, and occasionally outside. Using pulverised old brass worked into the backs of rubbings, prints are made from the 'master'. When first produced in 1966, demand greatly out-stripped the supply of the first 'rubbings' offered for sale. (See, *The Times*, 16th September, 1966, p. 11).

'Do-it-Yourself' methods (for home or school)

For the less ambitious, I would like to draw reader's attention to an illustrated article in the magazine *Do-it-Yourself* of

August, 1969, pp. 940–41, 969. By Ralph Matthews, it is entitled 'Decorextrusion', and suggests making a simplified pencil enlargement of a rubbing on a piece of board, round the main lines of which is piped instant 'Polyfilla'. When completely dry, the 'highlights' are smoothed off, and the whole composition painted with matt black emulsion or poster paint; once dry, the 'highlights' are dabbed with a pad dipped in gold paint to make the outline stand out. The complete work can then be framed and hung. Although the effect may appear a little heavy, I think the idea deserves more credit and publicity then hitherto, and would certainly appeal to children. Fuller details are contained in the original article of which the above is only an extract.

Since the publication of my *Beginner's Guide*, I have received a number of letters suggesting alternative methods of using rubbings. One of the most helpful letters, for which I am very grateful, came from a junior school teacher, Mrs T. E. Skiffington of Herne Bay, Kent, and her notes are used here with her consent. Two methods are described, one using a crayon resist technique, the other a modification of the same process.

In the first method, the children made rubbings, using coloured wax crayon on coloured frieze paper, under the teacher's supervision. The rubbings were later washed over with a solution of Indian ink and water, and once dry the wax was removed with turpentine. The resulting 'tinted' effect gives a pleasant texture, and any outlines that are indistinct can be 'lined-in' with a fibre pen. The figure is then cut out and pasted on to a coloured background of frieze paper chosen to contrast with or complement the colour of the rubbing. Essentially, the method is a simplified adaptation of the 'reverse' method described in my *Beginner's Guide* (pp. 50–51).

The second method tried by Mrs Skiffington was again using coloured wax and paper for the rubbing, but this time the white lines were painted in various colours to emphasise the different garments, etc.; Elizabethan brasses of ladies are particularly useful in this respect. I have used a similar technique (though not using coloured crayon or papers) for tabard brasses.

Various other adaptations are possible on both the above methods. The 'Brass Rubbing Book-Cloth' sold in various colours by Phillips & Page Ltd. (50 Kensington Church St, London W8 4DA) though expensive, lends itself readily to a number of different techniques.

Commercial and other uses

Although, as I have said, I am basically against commercial exploitation of brasses, I have come across a few enterprising ideas not *directly* done for profit, or more tastefully carried out than many that are so produced.

One of the more unusual uses of brass rubbings which deserves mention is that by Mr and Mrs Peter Scott, licencees of the 'King's Head' public house at Pebmarsh, Essex. Pebmarsh is well known to brass rubbers as the home of the famous military brass of Sir William Fitzralph (1323). This fact has been utilised by Mr and Mrs Scott not only by their using original rubbings as wall hangings in the main dining room of the King's Head (appropriately named the Fitzralph Room), but on their menu and wine covers which have a gold on black reproduction of the Fitzralph brass on the cover. The latter is the excellent work of Mr S. A. Illesley (*op. cit.*) and I am very grateful to Mr and Mrs Scott for their supplying me with specimens of the above covers and the photograph in Plate 16. (f.p. 209). Another public house near my home, 'The Hedgehog' in Welwyn Garden City, takes its name and sign from the famous Peryent brass in St John's Church, Digswell nearby (*vide* illus. Plate I of my *Beginner's Guide*). The hedgehog is seen at the feet of Lady Peryent (1415) and is a pun on her maiden name of Rizain, Risain or Arisain (from the French *Hérisson* – hedgehog or *Oursin* – sea-hedgehog); Lady Joan was like her husband, a Breton by birth.

Apart from the occasional use on book jackets or posters, brasses have not been much used in graphic arts. London Transport uses them on its posters occasionally, and have also produced a small (free) leaflet *Brasses and Brass Rubbing*, listing 'Churches with Good Brasses', in the London area within their sphere of operation and giving brief notes on making a rubbing[1]. The Monumental Brass Society produces its own Christmas card each year, suitably illustrated with a motif from a brass. In 1970 the leaflet issued to accompany the events held in connection with the Bramfield Becket Festival at Bramfield, Hertfordshire, skilfully incorporated the figure from a brass in its cover design (see illus. Pl. 15). The result is simple but very effective and a credit to its designer Dr René Pudifoot.

Exhibition and Display

It is not stretching creditability too far to say that the first 'exhibitions' of rubbings or impressions were in the workshops of the engravers themselves. These were the templates and 'pattern books' of standard designs mentioned earlier (see pp. 69–70 above). As the art of engraving brasses died out, so the impressions of brasses produced by Craven Ord, Sir John Cullum and others appeared as a natural outcome of the beginnings of improved printing and engraving techniques then receiving attention. A number of their impressions were exhibited at the time before the Society of Antiquaries of London and other bodies. From about 1800 onwards the display of impressions, dabbings and then rubbings became a regular feature at meetings and lectures of archaeological, art and antiquarian societies both in England and abroad.

The early authorities on brasses like Boutell, the Wallers, Haines, Sir A. W. Franks, Albert Way, Creeny and W. H. J. Weale regularly spoke about and/or exhibited their rubbings. One of the earliest public exhibitions seems to be that one already mentioned (p. 00 above) at the Cosmorama, Regent St, London, in the Spring of 1847. Described as 'Illuminated Monumental Brass Rubbings'; a full description can be seen in the M.B.S. *Trans.* 3, (1897–9), p. 270, based on a surviving copy of the original catalogue. Regrettably the name of the organiser or exhibitor(s) is not stated in the catalogue.

Rather than attempt to speak about each public exhibition individually, I am listing below a selection of them for which I have found (in most cases) detailed notices or catalogues.

Anyone interested can then consult these for full details. Members of the Monumental Brass Society regularly arrange exhibitions, many of which are noted in the Society's *Newsletter*, or, in some cases in the *Transactions* of the Society:

WEALE, W. H. J. – *Catalogue de frottures de tombes plates, en cuivre et pierre, exposées par W. H. J. Weale.* Bruges. 1862. 16 p. (Copy in V. & A.; Soc. of Antiq.)

MASON, Rev. F. R. Hawkes.
Arranged a large exhibition in Cambridge in 1890 under patronage of C.U.A.B.C. Some had shields coloured.

HASTINGS. Science and Art Schools and Museum – *Catalogue of the Loan Exhibition at the Brassey Institute, March 16th, 1896* . . . by F. R. Fairbank, F.S.A. 132 page catalogue with 72 page intro. on history of brasses, incl. notes and extracts from wills, glossary of armour, etc. Note on 'Peacock Feast' on Braunche brass at King's Lynn, Norfolk by J. G. Waller (pp. 76–7). Rubbings lent by E. M. Beloe (jnr.); Revs. Creeny and H. N. Fowler; R. A. S. Macalister; Mill Stephenson; Dr F. R. Fairbank and others.

HASTINGS MUSEUM – *Catalogue of local Antiquities Loan Exhibition . . . 1909.*
Incl. 'A Brief Description of 25 Sussex Monumental Brasses' (with illus.) by Rupert K. W. Owen.

VICTORIA & ALBERT MUSEUM, LONDON. – Notes on an Exhibition of Rubbings of Monumental Brasses . . . 1918.

BROOKLYN INSTITUTE OF ARTS & SCIENCES MUSEUM, NEW YORK. *English Brass Rubbings. Brooklyn Museum, Nov. 29th, 1935 – Jan. 28th, 1936. Catalogue . . .*
Based on collection of H. W. Williams. 28 plates. (Copy Brit. Museum; Soc. of Antiq.)

VICTORIA & ALBERT MUSEUM, LONDON. – 'Costume through the Ages'.
An exhibition held in the Autumn of 1946 in which the first two and a half centuries were represented by brass rubbings;

exhibits shown as reversed or positive photos. in style adopted by Sussex Archaeological Society.

HOME ART MUSEUM, BLACKPOOL, LANCS.
Exhibition by Mr G. Burren of Blackpool (M.B.S. Member). February, 1959. (*see* Notes and illus., *M.B.S. Trans.* IX (ix). Nov. 1962, f.p. 528).

ST JAMES' PARISH HOUSE, NEW YORK.
About 400 rubbings (many linen backed) exhibited and offered for sale, May 8th–21st, 1960.
(see *American Artist*, 24 (Oct. 1960), 46–9. Illus.)

ALL HALLOWS, LONDON WALL. – *People from the Past: An Exhibition of English Brasses . . . sponsored by the Historic Churches Preservation Trust and the Monumental Brass Society. Organised and selected with an introduction and notes by V. J. Torr. 24 September—13 October, 1962.* 24 pages. 101 numbered items; a model of its kind.

CALIFORNIA Palace of the Legion of Honour, Lincoln Park. 1962. Exhibition by Mr & Mrs K. Garner.
(see photo. & note *M.B.S. Trans.*, X (ii) 1964, 106–7).

BRITISH MUSEUM, LONDON. Greville Library. 1963. Small display of early 19th cent. rubbings by Rev. Henry Addington [ob. 1882], Vicar of Langford, Bedfordshire (*q.v.*)

DURBAN Museum & Art Gallery, S. Africa. 1965. 'Monumental Brass Rubbings'. (Catalogue in V. & A.)

BRISTOL CATHEDRAL. – Exhibition by Miss J. D. C. Proctor, R. K. Morris and other M.B.S. Members, 14–24, July, 1965. (see M.B.S. T*rans.* X (iv) Dec. 1966, 322. photo.)

ALL HALLOWS, LONDON WALL. 1966. 'Monumental Brasses': an Exhibition of gilt and black 'positive' full size facsimiles [by Henry H. Trivick].

MALTWOOD MUSEUM OF HISTORIC ART, VICTORIA, BRITISH COLUMBIA. 'Mediaeval Brass Rubbings'. June 2 – Aug. 30, 1970. (Catalogue published).

TREVELYAN COLLEGE, DURHAM. 'Exhibition of Monumental Brasses by C. R. A. Davies', [M.B.S. Member]. 2 Sept. – 27 Nov. 1970. Catalogue (typescript) with useful notes on each rubbing staged for meeting of British Association at Durham.

ROYAL ALBERT MUSEUM, EXETER, DEVON. Exhibition of Rubbings organised by Rev. J. B. Pack. [M.B.S. Member]. 4–29 May, 1971.

The above represent but a small, random selection of some of the larger public exhibitions; there have been (and will be) others of equal interest and the writer can only apologise to those whose work has been omitted. The fault is mine and not theirs.

There seems little I can usefully add to the above notes which I have not already discussed in my *Beginner's Guide* (pp. 64–66 esp.).[2] Similarly, for those giving illustrated lectures, the photographic slide is undoubtedly one of the most practical methods of showing rubbings, since it saves much preparatory work (often in poor display conditions) before the talk, as well as saving valued rubbings from damage and deterioration inevitably resulting from constant handling.[3] When I give talks where I know display facilitates to be inadequate or non-existant, I have a set of smaller rubbings mounted directly on to sheets of white card of varying sizes (up to about 36 inches (91.44 cm.) high – the largest size available and readily manageable). Although these get marked through constant use, and the corners damaged, they can be cleaned fairly well with a soft rubber. During the talk they can be hung or held up as space and conditions decree.[4]

Methods of storage are discussed in my earlier book, and there seems little I can usefully add to what I have already said. To conclude, I am adding a few additional notes on mounting rubbings for those who still, like myself, find this a constant problem.

Mounting – some further thoughts

The question of a suitable method of mounting rubbings, either with an adhesive which is (a) not so wet that the paper stretches or tears, (b) does not make the paper 'pucker' or 'crinkle' as it dries, or, (c) is not too expansive, remains a perennial problem.

One method which I did not mention in my *Beginner's Guide* which avoids the use of a liquid adhesive is using *photographic dry mounting tissue*. Not too expensive, this can be bought in sheet or roll form and is simple and quick to apply. It does present some problems with larger compositions, but for smaller figures or compositions such as one might use as a wall hanging or for exhibition, it has much to offer.[5] Carefully applied, a domestic electric iron can be used for the heat required. My only advice on large rubbings is simply not to mount them unless absolutely necessary. If they are for reproduction, any really bad blemishes can be scraped off or 'inked-out' of the master negative during the art-work stage.

A *simple mounting table* can be made by anyone with a basic tool-kit and a little skill in working with wood. Most important is a long, flat work-top (measuring about 4 ft. (121.92 c.m.) long by 2 ft. 8 in. (81.28 c.m.) wide, to allow for the average width of paper, i.e. 30 in. (76.2 c.m.) At each end, and preferably attached below the work-top, a roller should be fixed, to which the two surplus ends of the mounting paper can be firmly attached with masking tape (*not* drawing pins as these will tear the paper as it is tightened). The surface of the work-top can either be laminated with an off-cut of formica or with a self-adhesive material like 'Fablon' or 'Contact'. This ensures easy removal of adhesive, dirt and so on. The rollers will have to have some kind of locking or holding device to keep them in position once the paper is stretched tight, or alternatively, the whole roll of paper can be placed at one end and the 'take-up' roller wound on until no movement takes place (on the principle of the roll-film in a camera).

The idea of the 'mounting table' is to keep the paper or material on which the mounting is being done as taut as possible during and after the work is carried out. This will stop, or at the very least, minimise the risk of uneven shrinkage of the two papers or materials as they dry. The size and shape of the 'table' can be altered to suit the space available or the skill of the person concerned. If a folding 'table' can be made for easy storage, so much the better. Use of the 'table' is obviously most suited to smaller rubbings. If the sides of the work top are cut absolutely square, a draughtsman's T-square, set square, etc., can be used for 'lining out', to assist correct and straight mounting. For those unskilled in woodwork, a ready-made paperhanger's pasting table might be adapted as an alternative.

Finally, for those displaying large rubbings, the addition of round wooden batons at each end is recommended. Although rather clumsy to handle, they do ensure that the rubbing hangs well, provided the size of the baton gives sufficient weight. Batons with cord or chain attached make quick mounting of display material possible and require, in most cases, little in the way of hooks or pins to hang them on. Exposed ends of wooden rollers are best painted to give a pleasing finish. For small rubbings, the triangular-shaped plastic rod for protecting saw blades is a quick and easy alternative end attachment by which to hang rubbings. Because of its light weight, the latter may require a metal rod or other weight added to the lower baton, preferably inserted inside where it is hidden.[6]

Chapter Notes

Chapter 1 (1) The Brasses

1. 'Testamentary brasses' *Antiq. J.* 30, iii & iv (1949), 183–91.
2. *Sussex Wills,* IV, p. 185. At Thorpe, Surrey, an inscription and achievement to Wm. Denham (1583) – mentions his 'picture in ye Wall Ingraved in Brasse' *SAC,* xxxiii, 7.
3. See also, B. Dutton 'Latten: an etymological note' *MBS* 10, iii (Dec. 1965), 167–8.
4. 'Scottish Notes. I' *MBS* 8, v (Dec. 1947), 170. How many French brasses of this design existed it is no longer possible to tell due to the catastrophic losses sustained during the Revolution and during the two world wars. Some idea of the magnificence of French brasses can be gained from examination of the eighteenth century drawings by Francois-Roger de Gaignieres in the Gough colln. at the Bodleian Lib., Oxford and the Bibliothèque Nationale in Paris. As a result of the above little study has been possible of French brasses or indents. New research by Dr M. Norris is to be pub (d). shortly.
5. 'Flemish Monumental brasses in Portugal'. *MBS* 10, iii (Dec. 1965) 151–66.
6. At Fivehead Somerset, part of the reverse of the palimpsest figure of Jane Seymour (1565) is cut from a fragment of Flemish brass with marginal inscr. in Spanish. This could be a workshop waster, but might well have come from a Spanish church or abbey. See: *MBS 5* (1904–9), 219–20.
7. *List of Monumental Brasses on the Continent of Europe* (Mon. Brass Soc. 1970), p. 69.
8. *Brass Rubbing* (Studio Vista. 1965), p. 69.
9. *Monastic Craftsmen* (Heffer. 1932). Esp. table on pp. 101–7.
10. See: John A. Knowles 'Artistic craft gilds of the Middle Ages' *R.I.B.A. Jnl.* 3 Ser., 34 (8) 1927, 265–71 (esp. p. 270).
11. Knowles – *op. cit.* p. 269.
12. See: W. SWANN. *Gothic Cathedral* (Elek. 1969) (esp. 90–101).
13. *vide* illus: Haines, p. xxxii; Gawthorp (*op. cit.*), frontis.; Bouquet – *Church Brasses* (1956), f.p. 17; Greenhill, F. A. *Incised Slabs of Leicestershire and Rutland* (1958), Pl. I, f.p. 14; in the same work (Pl. II, f.p. 15) a similar contemporary drawing, not yet reproduced in any book on brasses, is shown. Both illustrations are shown actual size.
14. Haedeke (see note on p. 48 for details), p. 57 who says Apengeter was in Lübeck during these years; 'an important metal-producing centre specialising in brass'.

15. Although several of the above are cited on very tenuous grounds, little contrary evidence is available to make positive identification possible.
16. *MBS* 4 (1900–3), 216.
17. See note and illus. (Fig. I) *MBS* 9, vi (Apr. 1958), 292–3.
18. *op. cit.*, pp. 65–70.
19. A curious reference occurs in a will, to a brass erected by a widow to the memory of her son John Revell (1524), in which she enjoins that the figure is to be as nearly as possible like that of her son. This is one of the few documented English examples requesting a 'portrait' brass that I have seen (see note in *Antiquary*, 31 (Apr. 1895) 122, referring to paper given at Brit. Archaeol. Assn. meeting by Rev. J. Cave Brown on 'church and Manor of Offham' [Kent]).
20. A. de la Grange & L. Clouquet. *Études sur l'Art à Tournai et des anciens artistes de cette ville.* 2 vols. (1887) esp. pp. 125, 131 & 321.
21. *op. cit.* note 4 above.
22. *Brasses of England* (Methuen. 1907), p. 35.
23. See: W. Watkins-Pitchford. 'Baldwin memorial brass in Munslow Church' *Shrop. Archaeol. Soc. Trans.* 50 (1939–40), 95–104. Illus. f.p. 95. Brass made 1689 is described as ' a curious blend of Christian and Cabalistine motifs, signed "Geo. Baldwin Sculp." '
24. *MBS* 7, ii (1935), 49–56, *Ibid* 8, ii (Dec. 1944), 47–8. Illus. *MBS Port.* IX, pl. 6.
25. Greenhill, F. A. 'Late 17th cent. brass in Dorset' *MBS* 10, iv (Dec. 1966), 274–5 *and* Prideaux, W. de C. 'Ancient Memorial brs. of Dorset. Pt. 7' *Procs Dorset N.H.A.F.C.* XXIV (1913). 162–3.
26. *Monumental Brasses of Somerset* (Kingsmead Reprints. 1970) pp. 82, 360 and 366.
27. *ibid* p. 59, and, *MBS* 8, ii (Dec. 1944), 38 and Pl. I ff.
28. *MBS* 8, ii (Dec. 1944), 40–1 and Pl. 2. Also illus. *MBS Port. IV* (Dec. 1913), Pl. 20. A number of Eighteenth century signed plates in the Midlands are also noted by Dr G. A. E. Ruck in the article cited in footnote 53 of Chap. 2 below, many never before noted. Those named include '*S. Peacock*" (Tilbrook, Beds., 1781), '*Parry Sculpsit*' (E. Farridon, Northants 1787); *J. Thompson sculp.*' (Stow-nine-churches, Northants, 1777) and sev. by William Wright (also in Northants).
29. *Craft and Design of Monumental Brasses* (John Baker. 1970) Pls. 174–7.
30. For example see F. W. Kuhlicke. 'Waller brasses in St Paul's Bedford'. *MBS* 7, viii (Sept. 1942), 355–6, describing an early seventeenth century inscr. bearing a monogram (followed by 'SCULP') which the author identifies as an engraver called Matthews.
31. F. A. Greenhill 'Sandys Contract' *MBS* 9, vii (Oct. 1960), 354–61.
32. *ibid* 'Ledger of Andrew Halyburton' *MBS* 9, iv (Nov. 1954), 184–90.
33. (i) F. A. Greenhill 'Scottish Notes III Aberdeen (St Nicholas). *MBS* 9, ii (1952), 92–5; (ii) C. T. DAVIS 'Mon. brs. in the Old or

West Church, Aberdeen' *MBS* 3 (1897–9), 183–6. The brass itself was based on an original portrait (see. *Procs. Soc. of Antiq. of Scot.* XI (1875), 458).

34. R. H. Pearson. 'A palimpsest brass in St Giles', Cathedral, Edinburgh'. *MBS* 7, iii (Nov. 1936), 130–5. Illus.
35. See (a) K. A. Esdaile *English Church Monuments* (1946), pp. 87–8; (b) *ibid, MBS* 8, ii (Dec. 1944), 43–4 and Pls. III and IV; (c) *Sussex N and Q* 2 (1928–9), 175–7. Illus.; (d) J. Bertram. *Brasses and Brass Rubbing in England* (David & Charles. May 1971) p. 21 and 67; Fig. 3 (p. 22).
36. P. Bell. *Bedfordshire Wills 1480–1519* (Beds. Hist. Rec. Soc. Pubns. XLV (1966), 29–30).
37. See also Ch. 4, p. 105 below.
38. *Gesta Abbatum, I,* 149, 158.
39. Chronica Monasteri de Melsa; ed. by E. A. Bond (Rolls Ser. 3. (1868), p. 223. Repr. by Kraus Reprint Corp., Rolls Ser. Vol. 43 (1964).
40. P.C.C. 78 St John; see also V. J. B. Torr. 'Chigwell and its Brasses' *MBS* 10, iv (Dec. 1966), 238–9.
41. For other examples of wills see (i) CUABC No. 8 (Sept. 1890), 18, John Argentein, Kings Coll., Camb.; (ii) *Som. and Dorset N and Q;* I (1890), 241–6, D'Aubeney brasses at S. Petherton; (iii) *MBS* 4 (1900–3), 136–7, Thos. Salter, priest, 1558; (iv) *ibid* 7, ii (Dec. 1935), 77, John Annsell, Southwark Cath.; *ibid* 7, iv (Nov. 1937) 173, Edw. Pulter, Hitchin, Herts., 1626.
42. T. E. Sedgwick. 'Notes on the Poley monument in Rochester Cathedral' *Home Counties Mag.*, V (1903), 55–8. Illus. f.p. 55.
43. 'Monumental Brasses in the United States' (i) *MBS* 10, v (Dec. 1967), 369–75. Illus f.p. 369; (ii) 'A lost brass in Jamestown, Virginia' *Family History,* Nos. 8–9 (Aug. 1970), 270–71.
44. W. B. Jones 'An American brass' *MBS* 10, i (Dec. 1963), 29. Illus.
45. M. G. T. Harris 'A Canadian brass' *ibid,* iv (Dec. 1966), 269.
46. Made by Hardman – see note and illus. *Gent. Mag.* May 1851, I, p. 514.
47. *ibid* 1864, II, pp. 762–3.
48. *ibid* May 1851, I, p. 514.
49. Now a private school where the brass still exists in good preservation. Through the kindness of the Headmaster, Mr M. C. Spedding, and his staff, and with the generous help of Mrs Sally Morris of the M.B.S., I was able to obtain a fine rubbing of this superb Victorian brass.
50. Rev. Charles Boutell speaking in 1854 remarks that 'Restoration, however, at best must be taken in hand continuously, and amounts to no more than a tribute to the past . . . To be true to its proper position, monumental art ought to have the lead in these days of Gothic revival . . . we have able artists who have engraved many excellent examples.' As examples he quotes Messrs. Waller, Hardman and Mr Archer *(q.v.)* Some 'restorers' took the words too literally, others, to their shame, ignored them! (*see Builder* XII, No.

614, 11 Nov. 1854, p. 580). Also, Dr Paul Thompson in his recently published definitive biography *William Butterfield* (Routledge. 1971) mentions two brasses designed by Butterfield (i) at Babbacombe (1877), in memory of Anna Maria Hanbury; (2) to Cuthbert Dawnay (1889), Sessay, Yorkshire (p. 457 note 2).

51. e.g. *MBS* 6 (1910–14), 202–13 'Additional notes on repairs to brasses (by Messrs. Gawthorp of Long Acre, mainly by T. J. Gawthorp]'. This notes repaired and relaid brasses at Charwelton, Northamptonshire; Tattershall, Lincolnshire; Harlington, Middlesex; Cowley, Middlesex; Fawley, Berkshire; Edgemond, Shropshire; and Audley, Clifton Campville and Norbury, Staffordshire.

52. King was a well known local antiquary in Sussex; in *Pigot & Co's Royal, National & Commercial Directory* (1839) he is cited as 'Drawing Master; antiquary, medallist, artist and engraver. East St'. He made a number of engravings of Sussex brs. for *Cartright's Hist. of the Rape of Bramber (See: Sussex A.C.,* 23 (1871), 130, 141). He was dead by 1853.

53. The brass regretably suffered when the church was closed following bomb damage during the 1939–45 war, and shows the effects of corrosion.

54. Since writing the above, I have come across the following names in addition (1) '*Forsyth Sc., London*' (St Mary's, Chislehurst, Kent 1878), (2) Jones and Willis (St John the Evan., Digswell, Hertfordshire, 1888); (3) '*Moring. London*' (St Nicholas, Harpenden, Hertfordshire, 1881); (4) F. Osborne & Co. Ltd, London (All Saints, Datchworth, Hertfordshire, 1929). (5) T. Pratt & Sons, Tavistock St, London (St Mary, Chislehurst, Kent, 1893), (6) Ramsden & Carr (ibid, 1908); (7) 'Thomas & Son, (?) 9, Clipstone St, London W.' (Digswell, Hertfordshire, 1876). Of earlier date but of great interest is the brass by J. H. Muntz (1727–98) formerly at Strawberry Hill (for details see article 6 under R. H. D'Elboux in Appx. II); at Abbotsbury; Dorset I saw an inscr., with hour glass and skull above, to Rev. Jas. Harris, vicar, (ob. 1773) signed 'C. Sherborn, Gutter Lane, London'. Finally, in the now closed chapel of St Saviour's, Shrewsbury, Shropshire, are a series of 23 inscr. of mainly 18th century date, removed from the Meeting House at Dodington nearby in January 1898 by G. E. Evans. One of these is signed 'W. Bowley Shrewsbury'. See G. E. Evans *Midland Churches* . . . (1899), pp. 240–45 and *ibid* 'Non-Conformist Brasses in Shropshire' *MBS* 2 vi (1897–9), 326–9. (see also note in Appx. I, p. 165).

55. Not all Victorian or later brasses received approval when first made. A writer in the *Athenaeum* No. 1920 (13 Aug. 1864), p. 217, commenting on a new brass in Westminster Abbey refers favourably to the brass of Bishop Monk (i.e. James Henry Monk, ob. 6 June 1856) but not to that of Robert Stephenson the engineer. 'Fanatical mediaevalism' is seen in the brass of Sir Robert and Lady Wilson i.e. Sir Robert Thomas Wilson (1777–1849) and wife Jemima (1777–1823). Finally the writer comes to the main point of the article, Sir

Charles Barry's brass bearing a representation of the Houses of Parliament', altered, 'we presume, in protest on behalf of the deceased that his design was meddled with'.

Chapter 2(2) The Allied Arts.

1. Since writing the above, a general work which in some part covers the above field without special reference to brasses, has been published by M. D. Anderson (See '*other wks.*' in Further Reading at end of chapter for details).
2. See also: L. James 'Brasses and medieval piety' *MBS* 10, v, (Dec. 1967), 328–34.
3. See: 'Observations on some medieval glass in York Minster' by T. W. French, F.S.A. *Antiq. J.* 51, 1 (1971), 86–93×Pls. XIII–XX; for more general treatment see A. L. Laishley *Stained glass of York* (W. & L. A. Oldfield, 25, Stockton Lane, York. £0.36. Aug. 1971. Pbk.)
4. *op. cit* Ch. I, p. 46 above.
5. F. S. Eden. 'Ancient painted glass in the Conventual Buildings, other then the Church, of Westminster Abbey' *Conn.* LXXVII, 306 (Feb. 1927), 81–8, esp. p. 87.
6. For some fine illustrations of Gothic stonework see W. Swann. *The Gothic Cathedral* (Elek Books. 1969).
7. H. H. TRIVICK. *Craft and design of Mon. Brs.*, p. 229. The author also has some interesting comments on the origins of brasses in the pages following the above.
8. 'Education of the mediaeval architect' *RIBA. Jnl.* 52 (June 1945), 230–34.
9. See letter from K. A. Esdaile 'Engraving of monumental Brasses' *Country Life* C111 (20 Feb. 1948), 388.
10. W. L. Hilburgh. 'Group of Medieval English alabaster carvings at Nantes' *J. Brit. Archaeol. Assn.* (NS) x1 (1948) 1–12: descr. 12 panels of mid-15th cent. date, prob. from York school.
11. T. Bodkin. 'Medieval English alabaster – work in Portugal' *Boletin de Museu Nacional de Arte Antiga* (Lisbon), I, Jan. – Dec. 1945, 70–4.
12. *op cit.*, p. 35. In *MBS* 3 (1897–9), 114, a note by H. K. St J. Sanderson also mentions a brass to John Caterick (1419), Rector of Crick, Northants., in 'S. Lawrence Church, Florence'. It is not noted by Dr Cameron and I can find no other reference to it. The basilica of S. Lorenzo is one of the oldest churches in Florence. In 1418 a plan for a new church was made, and between 1419 and 1428 Brunellescho designed a new sacristy for the Mecici family. Possibly Caterick was in Florence in some connection with the above when he died.
13. *Brasses* (Camb. University Press 1912, pp. 87–99).
14. See Appx. II, p. 240 for details.
15. A curious indent at Pleshey, Essex, c. 1490 shows a priest and a knight standing on either side of a tall shaft or column – the only such example I have seen. It is described and illus. by C. Miller and W. W. Porteous, *Essex Archaeol. Soc. Trans.* (NS.) 7 (1900),29–30.
16. *MBS* 10, iv (Dec. 1966), 285–6.

17. *A series of Monumental Brasses* . . . (1842–64), Intro. p. iv.
18. *Illustrations of Incised Slabs on the Continent of Europe* . . . (1891).
19. 'Some remarks on Stones used for Ancient Brasses and Incised Slabs' (Read at Meeting of Nat. Assn. of Monumental Masons & Sculptors, 24 Jan. 1912). *Builder,* C11 (16 Feb. 1912), 185–6.
20. *Incised Slabs of Leicestershire and Rutland* (1958), esp. pp. 13–14 and Pl. 17.
21. 'Use of continental wood cuts and prints by the 'Ripon School' of wood carvers in the early 16th century' *Archaeologia* LXXXV (2 Ser. XXXV), 1935, 105–28. Illus.
22. W. R. Valentiner 'The name of the Master E.S.' *Art Q.* X1 (1948), 218–48. Illus.
23. See article by J. L. Barnard *The Sacristy,* I (1871), 266 ff.
24. *Medieval Drawings* (P. Hamlyn. 1970).
25. Illus. Creeny (*op. cit*), p. 70.
26. Illus. *MBS* 9, ix (Nov. 1962), f.p. 495.
27. See also: Rev. J. E. Field 'The Resurrection: as represented on monumental brasses' *OUBRS* I, iv (May 1898), 130–6.
28. *Biographical Dictionary* . . . *of* . . . *Engravers* . . . 2 vols. (R. Faulder. 1785, 1786). Speaking of one English print Strutt remarks: 'The figures are executed entirely with the graver, in a very slight and skilful manner, which seems evidently to prove the inability of the artist, who, perhaps being used to the execution of large figures on monumental brass plates, met with no little difficulty in contracting his designs, and expressing it in so small a compass.' (Vol. I, p. 18).
29. See note p. 61.
30. *vide illus.* W. D. Belcher – *Kentish Brasses,* I, p. 66.
31. *Glossary of terms used* . . . *in Architecture.* 5th edn. 1850, p. 83.
32. *History of Wood Engraving.* (Dent. 1928).
33. *op. cit.* note 17 above; Introduction, p. iii especially.
34. See e.g. (1) DAVIS, C. T. 'Merchants' Marks' *BAA Jnl.* 49 (1893), 45–54. (2) ELMHIRST, Edw. M. – *Merchant's Marks,* ed. by L. Dow (Harleian Soc. Pubns. Vol. 108. 1959. o/p.) (3) F. W. Kuhlicke. 'Merchant Marks and the like . . .' *MBS* 9, ii (Oct. 1952), 60–71; (4) H. K. St J. Sandeson 'Merchants Marks . . .' *OUBRS* I, ii (June 1897), 30–41.
35. Alfred Higgins, p. xvi of intro. to item in notes on 'Further Reading' at end of chapter.
36. First shield bears Arms of Gernan, poss. for Sir Ralph Gernan (ob. 1274) or his son William (ob. 1327). See note by W. H. St J. Hope *SAP,* 2 Ser., XXII (1907–9), 117–9. Coloured illus. f.p. 118. Fragt. of second sh. exhibit. by M. E. Hughes and descr. by Hope, *ibid* 317–8, illus. f.p. 318 and by Christy, Porteous & Smith *EAST* (N.S.) XI, ii (1909), 130–32. illus. The exact dating of the first shield is still undecided, Mill Stephenson says c. 1300 in his *List* (p. 577, under list of Brasses in British Museum; Sect. IV, No. I); Christy, Porteous & Smith (*EAST* (N.S.) 10, iii (1907), 211–14, coloured illus. f.p. 212), think it may be anything up to fifty years earlier.

37. W. H. St J. Hope's note on the discovery of fragments *SAP*, 2 Ser., 21, (5 Apr. 1906), 146–7. *See also:* A. R. Wagner & J. G. Mann, 'A 15th century description of the Brass of Sir Hugh Hastings at Elsing, Norfolk'. *Antiq. J.* 10, iv (Oct. 1939), 421–8. An undated letter from Mr Lawrence Stone in the University Museum of Archaeology and Ethnology, Cambridge, referring to Sir Wm. St J. Hope's note above says that in 1952, when Mr Stone examined the brass and slab for evidence of the glass fragments, 'less than a dozen tiny particles none larger than a pin' could be found. These appeared to be of different colours. 'blue, red and perhaps green' Referring to the origin of the glass, which appeared to be thinner than window glass, Mr Stone points out that it might have got there during the 'Reformation or Commonwealth iconoclasm' when many windows were smashed. In favour of Sir William's theory however is the fact that it was not uncommon for glass to be used on what Mr Stone calls a 'court product', citing as examples the tombs of Edmund Crouchback and Queen Philippa in Westminster Abbey. He concludes by saying that no trace of the glass could be found in the missing shields borne by the figures in the side shafts of the canopy as Sir William and the medieval description quoted above suggest; these, states Mr Stone were 'more probably enamel'. I think this lengthy sidelight sheds an interesting and important aspect on this famous brass, now happily protected by being recessed in the chancel floor with wooden, hinged covers to protect it from wear and 'casual' brass rubbers.
38. H. F. O. Evans 'Easton Neston, Northants.' *MBS* 9, ii (Oct. 1952) 50–59. (the article includes notes on a chemical analysis of the metal by Dr H. K. Cameron). The late Major Evans also describes an almost identical example to the brother of the above, similarly illustrated, in Oxfordshire (see : *MBS* 9, iii (July 1954), 98–104).
39. 'Latten Lecterns' *MBS* 9, vii (Oct. 1960), 375–8.
40. *op. cit* Ch. I, note 26 above. See also (a) H. Druitt. *Manual of Costume . . . on Brasses* (1906 repr. 1970), f.p.97; (b) H. H. Rogers.' The Lectern, Yeovil Church' *Som. & Dorset N & Q.* IX (1905), 71.
41. Finally published in large folio as: *Stall plates of the Knights of the Order of the Garter 1348–1485: a series of Ninety full-sized coloured facsimiles with descriptive notes and historical introduction.* (Constable: 1901) 25p+90 plates. *See also:* article by Hope 'On the early Stall-plates of the Knights of the Garter in St George's Chapel, Windsor' *Archaeologia,* 54 (1895), 399–418.
42. *ibid* 'Palimpsest stall plates of Knights of the Garter at Windsor' *SAP*. 2 Ser., XVIII (1902), 148–51.
43. *Brass Rubbing*, p. 69.
44. e.g. (1) Van Dyck's series of engraved portraits for the *Iconography;* (2) Thomas Howard, 2nd Earl of Arundel and Surrey (1586–1646) sent a painting to Rome and Florence to be copied in marble bas-relief. See these and other examples in *Flemish Art,* 1300–1700 (Catalogue of Roy. Acad, of Arts Winter Exhibn. 1953–4).
45. For good selection of illus. from chap-books see: John Ashton.

Chapbooks of the Eighteenth Century (1882 repr. Seven Dials Press. 1969).

46. Facsimile reprints of several of the above are available in late nineteenth century and later editions.
47. *vide* illus. *Oxford Port. of M.B.* Pt. 3 (5).
48. There are some bearing resemblance to scientific trade cards of which many are illustrated in *Scientific Trade Cards in the Science Museum Collection* by H. R. Calvert (H.M.S.O. £1.90. Oct. 1971). This fact is especially noticeable on eighteenth century brasses and coffin-plates, some of which have strong similarities to the trade cards illus. in plates 48 and 56 of the above work. The curious designs on the Baldwin brass, Munslow, Salop. (see details Ch. I, n. 23 above) could well have been engraved by a trade card or book-plate engraver.
49. H. C. Andrews. 'The brass of Dame Margaret Plumbe in Wyddial Church (1575)' *EHAS* 7, ii (1924–5), 140-7. *Illus.*
50. See illus. of rev. and details, E. P. KNUBLEY 'Notes on a palimpsest br. from Steeple Ashton Church', *Wilts. AHNS Mag.* XLII (1922–4), 438–41. The latter fact could mean that the plate maker/printer also engraved brasses, or more likely, the scrap metal was bought from him by the brass workshop concerned.
51. Illus. in Rev. A. C. Bouquet's *Church Brasses* (Batsford. 1956) Pl. 18, f.p. 114; the late Major H. F. O. Evans states that the Willis brass is by the same engraver as a rect. plate at St Cross, Holywell, Oxon. (1622). See, *MBS* 7, v (June 1938), 222–4 where both brs. are illus.
52. *Vide* illus. and description by Rev. C. L. S. Linnell 'Scargill memorial, Mulbarton Ch., Norf.' *MBS* 8, iii (Dec. 1945), 91–3. At Longston, Derbyshire is the curious brass of Rowland Eyre (1624) engr. on an oblong plate of copper ($25\frac{1}{2} \times 19\frac{1}{2}$ ins.)* See (1) Rev. H. E. Field 'Mon. Brs. of Derbys. Pt. VI.' *MBS* 5 (1904–9), 137–8, and (2) H. F. O. Evans 'The "Brass" of Rowland Eyre and his wife . . .' *MBS* 10, v (Dec. 1967), 393–6. Illus.
53. Dr G. A. E. Ruck – 'Additions to the List, from Beds., Northants., Oxon., Rutland and Shropshire' *MBS* 9, i (Feb. 1952), 27, 36; Illus. of Lowick br., Fig. 3, f.p. 30.
54. In completely different fields of metalwork, direct borrowing and copying of designs of earlier work was frequently practised by even the best craftsman. An example occurs graphically in the work of the ironworker Tijou, who copied designs for his '*New Booke of Drawings*' (1693) directly from earlier French engravings by Jean de Martin of c. 1640. See article by G. Jackson-Stops. 'English Baroque Ironwork – I. The sources of Tijou's designs'. *Country Life,* CXLIX, No. 3842, (28 Jan. 1971), 182–3. As another example where 'iconography' has been applied to metalwork, see article by Anabell Harris, 'Romanesque candlestick in London' *BAA Jnl.*, 3 Ser., XXVII (1964), 32–52 and Pls. I–X.
55. *MBS* 3 (1897–9), 202.

* 64.77 ~ 49.53 cm

56. For an interesting and valuable example, see article by H. Eichler 'A Flemish brass of 1398' [Whichbold von Dobilstein, Bishop of Kulm, at Altenberg, Germany] which is similar to brass of Bishop Gottfried von Bülow (1375) Schwerin and others. *Burlington Mag.* 61 (July–Dec. 1932), 84–6.
57. *Conn.* LVIII, No. 231 (Nov. 1920), 164 (letter and illus. by C. R. Beard). For recent history of figure since re-discovery see J. C. Page-Phillips 'A Palimpset in private possession' *MBS*. 9, iv (Nov. 1954), 195–7. Illus.
58. Illus. *MBS* 4 (1900–3), 124.
59. N. Wright and H. K. Cameron 'Notes on the palimpsest brass at Stanstead Abbots, Herts.' *MBS* 9, ix (Nov. 1962) 475–6. Illus. p. 476. obv. and rev.
60. Mill Stephenson. *List of m.b. in Surrey;* New edn. repr. in one vol. with preface and appendix by Dr J. M. Blatchly (Kingsmead Reprints. 1970), pp. 49–51, 567, Illus. p. 50.
61. H. F. O. Evans 'A palimpsest at Thame, Oxon.' *MBS* 10, vi (Dec. 1968), 492–3. Illus.
62. Illus. *MBS* 4 (1900–3), 54.
63. A. B. Connor. *Mon. Brs. of Somerset.* (Kingsmead Reprints. 1970) pp. 328–30. Illus. p. 329.
64. See details and illus. of obv. and rev. *Home C. Mag.* VIII (1906), 272–3 Mill Stephenson. 'List of Palimpsest brasses in Hertfordshire'.
65. *MBS* 4 (1900–3) 115 (obv. and rev.)
66. E.g. (1) Elmdon, Essex (c. 1530), civ. and 2 ws. (Illus.: *EAST* (N.S.) 7, iii (1900), 214; (ii) Saffron Walden, Essex (c. 1530), civ. and w. (Illus. *ibid*, 242); (iii) Toppesfield, Essex (1534) civ. and w. (Illus. and descr. *ibid*, i (1898), 23).
67. For some valuable notes on the distribution of English brasses see: (i) C. J. P. Cave. 'Notes on the distribution of Brasses in England' *MBS* 3 (1897–9), 109–11 – these are largely based on totals in Haines' List of 1861; (ii) Margaret L. Gadd 'English M.B.'s of the fifteenth and early sixteenth centuries – with special reference, (a) to their manufacture, and (b) to their distribution' *BAA*, 3 ser, 2, (1937), 17–46 – includes maps; (iii) J. C. Page-Phillips *Macklin's Monumental Brasses*. rev. edn. *(op. cit)* p. 126 (map showing 'Present Distribution of pre-A.D. 1700 Brasses'). This indicates that Norfolk, London and the Home Counties have one brass per 2000 acres.
68. See Dr Cameron's *List (op. cit)* for sources of illus. of these and other continental brasses cited.
69. Illus.: Dr A. C. Bouquet. *Church Brasses*. Plates 71 and 99.
70. Illus.: M. Norris – *Brass Rubbing*, Fig. 114 (p. 93).
71. *ibid*. Fig. 113.
72. *ibid* Fig. 69, p. 59; Dr A. C. Bouquet and M. Waring *European Brasses* (Batsford. 1967) p. 53.
73. A good direct photograph of this brass accompanies an article by John Patten in *Country Life*, CL, No. 3875 (16 Sept. 1971), 660.
74. Since writing this, illus. have also appeared in (i) Clare Gittings'

Brasses and Brass Rubbing (Blandford Press. 1970) [1971], p. 63, Pl. 69, and (ii) Jerome Bertram *Brasses and Brass Rubbing in England* (David & Charles. May, 1971), p. 47, Fig. 18.

Chapter 3 Reproductions of brasses – past and present.

1. *Craft and Design of Monumental Brasses.* (John Baker. 1969).
2. C. P. H. Wilson 'An eighteenth cent. rubbing' *MBS* 10, ii (Dec. 1964), 93–4. Illus.
3. Miller Christy and W. W. Porteous in one of their fine series of articles 'On some interesting Essex brasses' (*EAST* (N.S.) 7, i (1898–9), 4) mention a rubbing of a brass at Aveley, Essex formerly in the possession of 'the late Mr H. W. King' made c. 1726 (*sic*).
4. 'Sepulchral Brasses and Incised Slabs' *Archaeol. J.*, I, (Sept. 1844.) 197–212. It is also mentioned in general articles on brasses in *Penny Magazine*, 13, No. 812 (23 Nov. 1844) 457–9, *and*, No. 814 (7 Dec. 1844), 476–8. 'Old English Tombs, Effigies and Mon. Brs.' esp. p, 477. For an interesting note on the original uses of heel-ball see letter from 'J.T.F.', of Durham 'Heel-ball or "cobbler's wax" ' *N and Q* 9 Ser., V (3 Mar. 1900), 166. In reply to the above Mr Thomas Ratcliffe says the cobbler's wax was used by many people as a 'heal-all for sores, wounds and boils . . .'! According to a report on a talk by J. W. Archer (*q.v.*) the writer states that the study of brasses began in this country 'about ten years since . . .' If brass rubbing is what is inferred as well, this would date its origin to c. 1836–8.
5. No. 888 (2 Nov. 1844), 1004. The 'metallic rubber' was apparently still available in the 1880s or early 1890s as Andrew Oliver (*q.v.*) mentions it in a paper he gave at the time, remarking that it was 'too dark' to recommend for general use (*Salisbury Field Club., Trans.* I (1890–93), 57). Richardson himself died in 1905. Mounting criticism of the above lead in c. 1900 to the marketing of the 'Delamare Brass Rubber', which used white paper and a cake of yellow composition used like heel-ball. The finished rubbing was washed over with liquid black which was then wiped off leaving black for the incised lines of the brass. It was available from Messrs. Parker of Oxford (see details *OUBRS* 2, i (Feb. 1900), 10).
6. *op. cit.* Note 5 above.
7. *Athen*, 1026 (26 June 1847), 680.
8. *Monumental Brasses and Slabs* (1847), pp. 165–6, note z.
9. Letter, *N and Q* VI, 150 (11 Sept. 1852), 254.
10. *ibid* III, 62 (4 Jan. 1851), 14.
11. *op. cit.* note 8 above, p. vii.
12. For full details see Appx. I, p. 154.
13. Shortly after writing this it was reported that the historic brass of Lady Catherine Howard, great grandmother of Henry VIII's fifth wife, had been stolen from Stoke-by-Nayland Church, Suffolk. Luckily, in this instance the brass was soon recovered by the police (see: *Daily Telegraph* 15 May 1971).
14. The direct sale of rubbings in the United States is probably one of the

most serious cases, since they fetch exhorbitant prices for which the church concerned sees little or no return in proportion. The whole question of the sale of rubbings and the 'commercialisation' of brasses is under serious consideration by the Council of the Monumental Brass Society. While it would seem impossible to stop the sale of rubbings themselves by private individuals, it might be possible to find a point of law forbidding the commercial sale of reproductions made from rubbings without a 'royalty' of some kind being made to the church concerned, and/or only with the incumbant's express permission in writing.

15. See Appendix II, p. 186 for details.
16. See also letter from Drs G. H. S. Bushnell and G. A. E. Ruck (*MBS* 7, viii (Sept. 1942), 371) giving additional notes. They recommend 'best salad oil' in preference to linseed oil for mixing with the powdered graphite, as it gives a less greasy finish. Many fine dabbings made by Dr Ruck are in collection of rubbings at the University Museum of Archaeol. and Ethnol., Cambridge. See Appx. I below.
17. Published 1966, price £1.42½. 207 pages + 95 plates.
18. For a fascinating history of English headstones, etc. see F. Burgess *English Churchyard Memorials* (Lutterworth Press. 1964). As a useful supplement to the above the Rt Rev. K. Healey's paper of the same title in *Roy. Soc. Arts J.* No. 5128, Vol. CXV (March 1967), 260–9, is valuable and also adds notes on legal aspects of maintenance, removal, etc.
19. Since writing the above, an exhibition of rubbings of 'Opercula', sponsored by the London Museum where the rubbings were displayed, has been held (see note p. 161). Mr J. R. Greenwood of the MBS is making a special study and collection of these items.
20. Press mark 10368. e. 3, Nos. 26 and 27. For useful list of drawings of one country see J. H. Busby 'Hertfordshire drawings of Thomas Fisher (1771?–1836)'. *Herts. Archaeol.* I (1968), 110–16. The late Ralph Griffin and R. H. D'Elboux also reproduce many Fisher drawings or sketches in their series of articles on Kentish brasses. (See Appx. II).

PLATE 9

(*a*) & (*d*) Rubbing, and engraving of drawing by Thomas Fisher (dd Nov 19, 1813), of the figures of priest and St John the Baptist, Apsley Guise, Beds (c. 1410). Note the different positions of the hand of St John on the engraving; a cross between the figures is lost. Figures 45 cm (17⅝ ins); (*b*) & (*c*) A similar example of brass of Sir William Harper & his wife Margaret (1573), St Paul's Church, Bedford. Fisher's drawing has, as was so often the case, suffered for its transference to a printing plate; the brass was originally on a tomb. The shield is omitted from the rubbing. (see note p. 70). Figures 51.8 cm (20⅜ ins). Rubbings by the author. Photos Peter Marshall

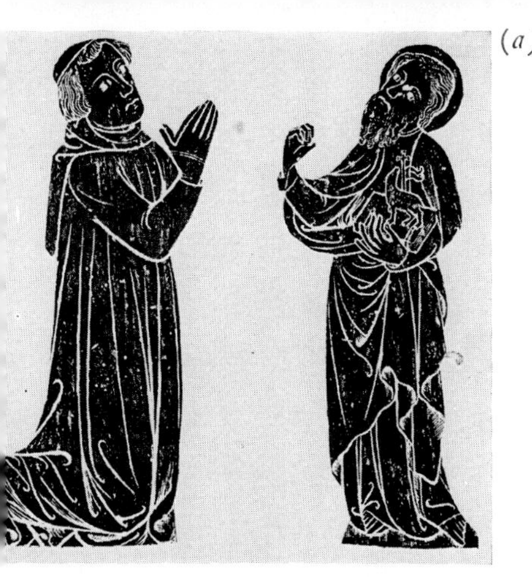

(a)

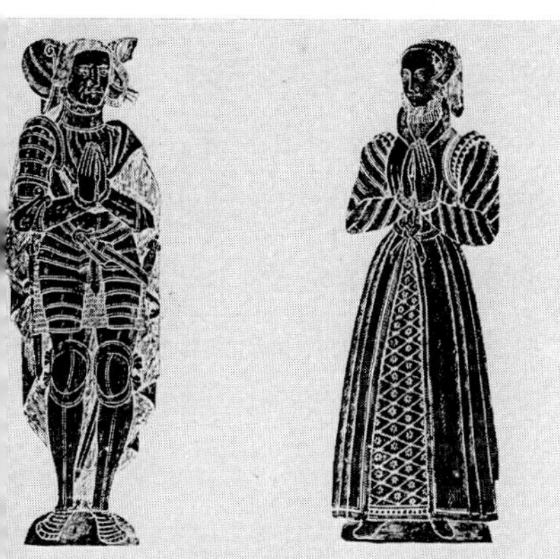

(b)

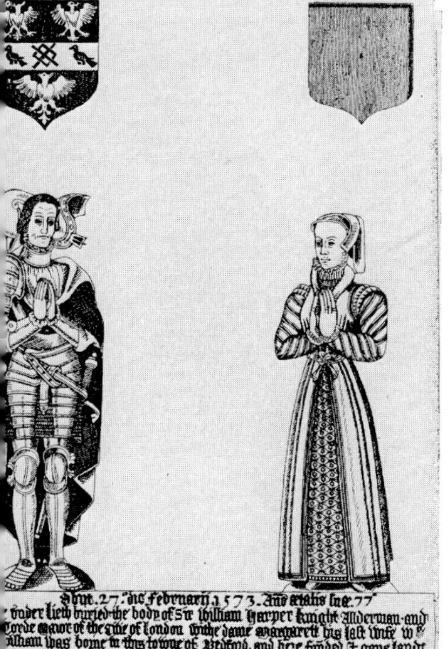
Obijt. 27. die Februarij 1573. Ano ætatis sue 77
vnder lieth buried the body of Sir William Harper knight Alderman and
Lorde Maior of the Citie of London with dame Margarett his last wife w
William was borne in this towne of Bedford, and here founded & gave landes
maintenance of a Gramer schoole.

(c)

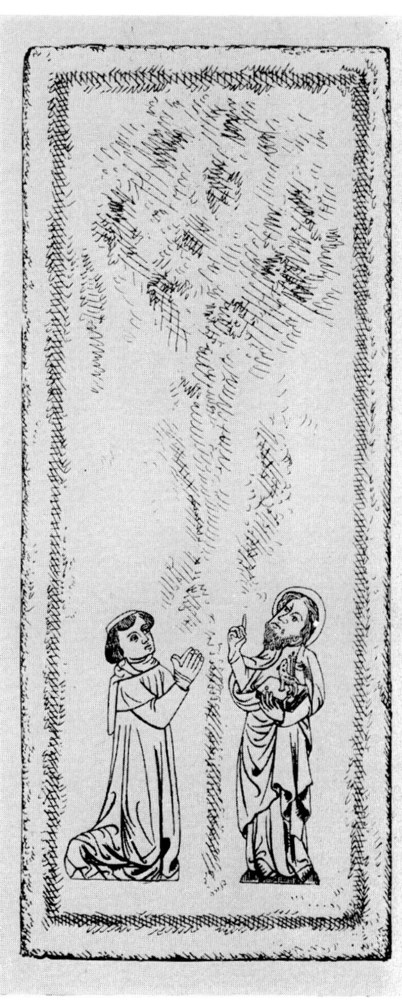

(d)

PLATE 10
(*a*) Henry Denton, Priest (1498), Higham Ferrers, Northants; (*b*) John Bloxham, priest (1519), Gt Addington, Northants; (*c*) John Wright, priest, (1519), Clothall, nr. Baldock, Herts. Three 'stock' designs all probably drawn from templates or 'rubbings' in the workshop's pattern books. Note the similarity between (*b*) and (*c*) especially, particularly the large chalice and the hands of the figures. Figures: (*a*) 48.9 cm (19$\frac{1}{4}$ ins); (*b*) 61 cm (24 ins); (*c*), as (*a*). Rubbings by the author. Photos (*a*) & (*b*) Peter Marshall; (*c*) Henry W. Gray

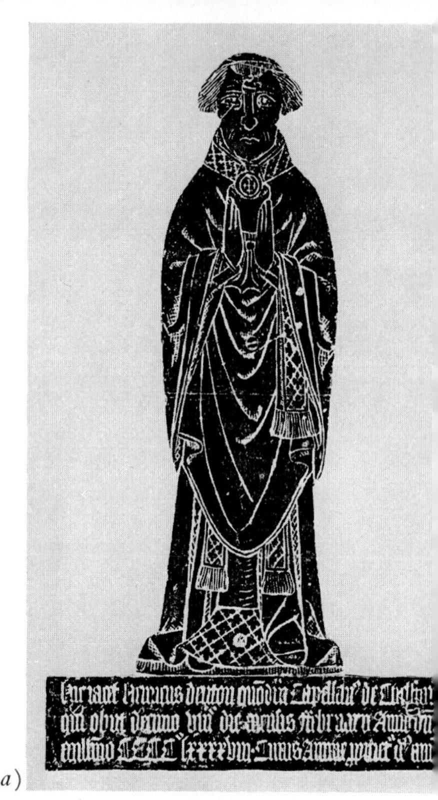

(*a*)

(*b*)

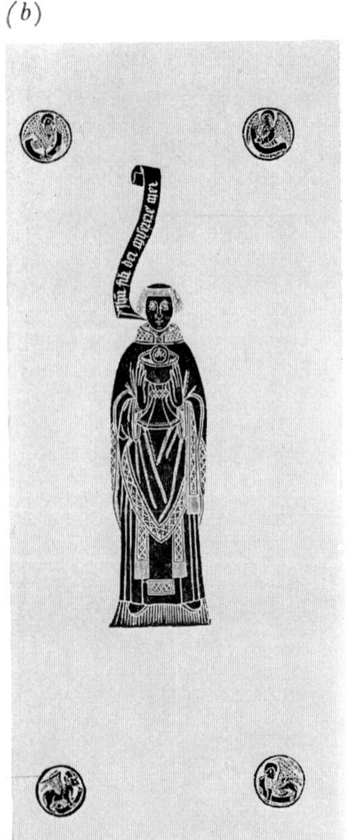

(*c*)

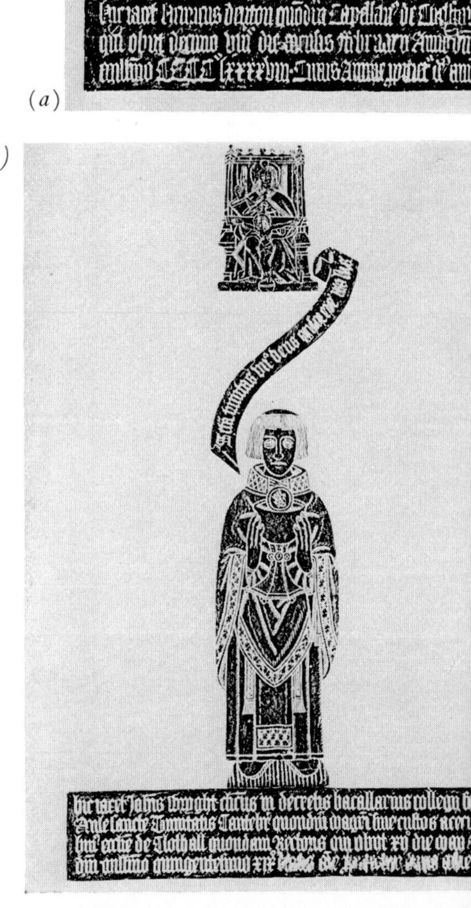

21. V. Rienaecker. *John Sell Cotman, 1782–1842.* (F. Lewis. £7.35. 1953).
22. For details see entry for Talbot in Appx. II below.
23. See also entry under C. Hullmandel in Appx. II below.
24. See my new intro. to the repr. of Haines' *Manual* (Adams & Dart. 1970), p. 10.
25. The reviewer of Boutell's first book (*op. cit.* note 7 above) calls the Society's publication. 'a puerile work . . . a wonderful exhibition of ignorance and assumption on the part of people who aimed to be teachers in such matters'.
26. Published 1862.
27. Griggs was the inventor of the superior photo-chrome lithography and an improved method of photo-lithographic transfer (see Appx. II).
28. *MBS* 5 (1904–9), 212.
29. See some examples, *Berks. Bucks. & Oxon. Archaeol. J.* 19, i (1912–13) figs. 5–10 and *ibid* ii, figs. 43–7.
30. A word of warning. If the work is for publication in reduced format, especially in normal book size, the choice of paper for printing the reproductions is vitally important. Use of a paper that is too soft or 'chalky' can result in poor or patchy finishes and can ruin the considerable work necessary to collect, choose and caption material for publication. Quality reproductions like those in Bouquet and Waring's *European Brasses* (Batsford. 1967), made to a larger scale, require the best paper but do not suffer the added problem of loss of small details that reproductions in books of the present size exhibit.
31. *Picture Book of Brasses in Gilt* (John Baker. £3.25. July 1971).
32. Similar moulds (made of one of the plastic polymers) are also used to make electro types, but again these are very expensive. Facsimiles do, however, offer alternatives to brass rubbers where protection of the original brass from damage or wear is necessary. At churches like Trumpington, Cambridgeshire the famous brass of Sir Roger de Trumpington, which may be rubbed anything up to 800 times a year is showing definite signs of wear and may actually fracture because the stonework under the metal is crumbling with the frequent pressure of rubbing. As a result of this the metal has also 'bowed' slightly and stresses set up in it by the action of rubbing may soon crack the metal right across at this point. Such occurrence would, of course, be disastrous, and the possibility of making an electro-type may be the only alternative to prohibiting rubbing altogether. A similar situation is occurring at St John's, Digswell, Hertfordshire with the famous brass of Sir John Peryent and his wife (1415), illustrated in my *Beginner's Guide,* especially with the female figure, which Mr B. S. H. Egan is now (Jan. 1972) repairing.
33. For example of copying of ancient brasses for use in a church, see: A. Chadwick 'Pseudo-antique brasses of St Chad's, Rochdale' *MBS* 10, iv (Dec. 1966), 287–93. Illus.

34. In *Connoisseur* XCII (July–Dec. 1933), 199–200 is a note about two inventors calles Messrs. R. Tyler and J. Murphy, who were then producing metal facsimiles of brasses in miniature, about one quarter of the original size. At the time of writing five had been produced viz. Eliz. Bohun (1399), Westminster Abbey; male eff. of Wm. Lord Willoughby (1410), Spilsby, Lincs.; Sir Philip Courtenay, Exeter Cath., Devon. (1409); John Hadresham. Lingfield, Surrey (1417) and Samuel Harsnett, Chigwell, Essex (1631), which is also illustrated. I would be interested to hear from anyone still possessing one of these.
35. *The Church of St Margaret, Felbrigg* . . . (Norwich: Gosse & Son. n.d.) 36 pages. illus. (pp. 9–25 'The Brasses', mainly written by R. H. Clark).
36. The Third Annual Weekend Conference of the *M.B.S.* at Canterbury from September 3–5, 1971 had its own 'conference' one day cover available to delegates for use with a special envelope. The post mark bears an illustration of the upper-half of the Septvans brass at Chartham, Kent.
37. Mill Stephenson indicates many sources of his *List and Appendix*, but this needs substantial revision. Recently published lists of brasses like those compiled by the Cambridge City Libraries '*Mon. Brs. of Cambs. and the Isle of Ely*' 4th rev. edn. 1970, and two volumes on the *Lost Monumental Brasses of Sussexs* by Mr A. G. Sadler (*op. cit*), indicate some sources of illustration where located (see fuller details in note 1 to Ch. 5 below).

Chapter 4. Brasses and Brass Rubbings for Education

1. For excellent example of the type of work undertaken see article by B. S. H. Egan and R. K. Morris, 'A restoration at Fletching, Sussex', well illustrated and showing well what good results the M.B.S. team can achieve; *MBS* 10, vi (Dec. 1968), 436–44.
2. See also H. A. Dillon 'Some peculiarities and omission on brasses' *OUBRS* I (1897–9), 2–3.
3. *BAA Jnl.* (N.S.) 7 (1901), 189–204; repr. *MBS* 4 (1901–3) 79–92. Illus.
4. *MBS* 10, iii (Dec. 1965), 128–35. Illus.
5. See Further Reading at end of chapter.
6. Many are mentioned by Weever (1631); in John Stow's *Survey of London* (1598) and Dugdale's *Old St Pauls*. For destruction of brasses in other cathedrals see e.g. (a) William Page 'Brasses and indents in St Albans Abbey'. *Home Counties Mag.* I (1899), 19–25, 140–61, 241–7, 329–32. Illus.

   (b) H. K. St J. Sanderson 'Lincoln Cathedral' *MBS* 2 (1893–6) 314–25; 3 (1897–9), 67–87, 119–42 incl. plan;

   (c) T. E. Sedgwick 'Indents of the despoiled slabs in Rochester Cathedral' *Home Counties Mag.* V (1903), 136–41; 294–30; VI (1904), 307–15. Illus.
7. 'Kentish Items'. *MBS* 6 (1910–14), 361–7.

8. See also: (i) H. K. Cameron 'Speakers of the House of Commons Commemorated by brasses' *MBS* 7, viii (Sept. 1942), 331–41, and 8, i Dec. 1943), 23 [additional note]. Apart from the Savage brass Dr Cameron makes special reference to the brass of Thos. Chaucer and w. (1436), Ewelme, Oxon. (reputedly son of the poet Geoffrey Chaucer) Speaker of the House of Commons in 1407, 1411, 1421 and two other occasions; (2) 'Sir Arnald Savage of Bobbing' *Archaeol. Cant.* LXX (1956), 68–83; (3) J. S. Roskell. *The Commons and their speakers in English Parliaments 1376–1523* (Manchester U.P. 1965).
9. For full details of Peryent family see valuable article by Henry W. Gray 'The Peryents of Hertfordshire' *Herts. Archaeol.* I (1968) 76–88. Illus.; geneal. tree; bibliog.
10. For details of this and other tombs at Penshurst see, R. Griffin 'The Sidney Tombs at Penshurst and Ludlow' *MBS* 5 (1904–9), 391–408. Illus.
11. For description and full text of inscription see, Rev. H. E. Field 'Monumental brasses of Derbyshire, Pt. VI' *MBS* 5 (1904–9), 135–6.
12. The 3rd Annual Conference at Canterbury from 3–5 Sept. 1971, not only had its own special postmark and envelope, but had a brass rubbing programme in local churches, several lectures including one of great significance – by Dr H. K. Cameron, President, on the 'Future of the Monumental Brass Society'.
13. See: *EHAS* 7, ii (1930–31) 162–70. Andrews, H. C. – 'Sidelights on Brasses in Herts. Churches (Pt. I).
14. For a specialised study relating to Irish genealogy see B. M. Lott 'English Memorial Brasses of Irish interest' *Ulster J. of Archaeol.*, 3 Ser., 4, ii (July 1941), 128–39. Illus.
15. At St. Mary's Hall, Coventry, Warwickshire, is a good example of a 'brass lease' recording the recovery of a parcel of land for the City. It is illus. and described in full by H. W. Jones and F. A. Greenhill in an article 'A brass lease in St Mary's Hall, Coventry' *MBS* 10, ii (Dec. 1964), 63–6. (illus. f.p. 63).
16. e.g. Alfred Hills 'The Tabard Period' *Essex Rev.* July 1938, 115–20.
17. See (1) E. M. Beloe, *jnr. Photolithographs of Brasses in Westminster Abbey* (1898) Plate I; (2) J. S. N. Wright, *Brasses of Westminster Abbey* (J. Baker. 1969), pp. 8–9.
18. *vide* illus.: Anne Berendson *Tiles: a general history.* (Faber. £8.00. 1967), p. 60.

    The tomb was destroyed in 1806, but an old print of 1661 is reproduced on the page quoted.
19. Illus. E. Kite *Mon. Brs. of Wilts.* (1861 repr. 1969.), Pl. XXIX.
20. 'Lost brass of John Clarenceaux, 1428'.
21. See A. C. Fox-Davies' *Complete Guide to Heraldry* 3rd rev. edn. by J. P. Brooke-Little (Nelson. £10.50. 1969), esp. illus. article by W. J. Kaye (jnr). 'Heraldic Brasses', pp. 40–44. The above work is based on Fox-Davies' magnificent and now rare volume *The Art of Heraldry* (T. C. & E. C. Jack. 1904. 504 pages, copiously illus., many

in colour), in which the above paper by Kaye first appeared. I have been fortunate enough to borrow from a good friend of mine Kaye's own copy of the work, presented to him by Fox-Davies from whom a letter dd. January 18, 1904 is pasted in the front. Kaye was then at Pembroke College, Harrogate.

22. The M.B.S. has had its own Hon. Heraldic Adviser for many years, of which the present holder is Mr A. C. Cole, O. StJ ., B.C.L., M.A., F.S.A., Windsor Herald. Earlier holders of the position include Sir Anthony Richard Wagner, K.C.V.O., D.Litt., F.S.A., present Garter King of Arms, and Sir Alfred Scott Scott-Gatty (*q.v.*)

23. For another general study based on local examples see the late Mrs C. E. D. Davidson-Houston's article 'Military costume on Monumental Brasses' *Sussex Co. Mag.* 3 (1929), 560–64. Illus.

24. For specialised studies of military brasses see also: John A. Porter 'Garter brasses' *Antiquary* 14 (Nov. 1886), 197–9, H. K. St J. Sanderson 'On the S.S. collar, and others' *CUABC* No. 7 (Feb. 1890), 6–11;

    For two important and well documented articles questioning the designation and/or date of two of the earliest military brasses at Trumpington (Cambridgeshire) and Acton (Suffolk), the following are essential reading:

    S. D. T. Spittle 'The Trumpington Brass' *Archaeol J.* CXXVII (1971), 223–7. Illus.

    This questions the designation of the brass to Roger de Trumpington I (ob. 1289), suggesting it was made for his son Giles I (ob. betw. 1327 and 1332) prior to the latter's death, but that it was then appropriated to commemorate Roger II in c. 1326. This would date the brass to the first quarter of the Fourteenth century.

    Jennifer C. Ward. 'Sir Robert de Bures' *MBS* 10, iii (Dec. 1965), 144–50.

    Corrects the long held belief that this is a brass of 1302 and shows by documentary evidence that Sir Robert did not die until 1331 (probably in September).

25. The same author has also produced a similar paper relating to Norfolk brasses (see bibliog. under Mr Andrè's name in Appx. II for details). One of the earliest articles on this subject to appear was one by L. H. Cooley 'Brasses of Ladies' *CUABC.* No. 5 (May 1888), 26–32. Another useful article, with 21 good illustrations, by the late Mrs C. E. D. Davidson-Houston, 'Female dress on Sussex Brasses', appeared in *Sussex Co. Mag.* 6 (1932), 216–23.

26. See also a very full study by W. N. Hargreaves-Mawdsley *A History of Legal dress in Europe until the end of the eighteenth century* (Oxford U.P. £1.75. 1963).

27. Two articles in the early issues of the Oxford Univ. Brass Rubbing Soc's. Journal are worthy of note; viz:

    (i) H. C. P. Dobrée 'Ecclesiastical brasses, their classification, general features, and Peculiarities' *OUBRS* I, iii (Dec. 1897), 86–98. Illus., (ii) R. A. Raven 'Brasses of Ecclesiastics in the 14th century' Pt. I, *OUBRS* 2, iii (March 1912), 116–35. No further parts issued.

For two specialised studies see (i) H. F. O. Evans 'Brasses to Canons of Windsor' *Oxon. Archaeol. Soc. Repts.*, LXXXII (1937), 21–2. (with special reference to brasses at North Stoke, Magdalen College, Eton College). (ii) Rev. Hugh S. Lawlor 'The Monuments [tombs and brasses] of the pre-Reformation Archbishops of Dublin' *J. Roy. Soc. of Antiq. of Ireland,* 6 Ser., 7 (1917) [Vol. XLVII, Pt. ii concec. series], 109–38 (12 plates).

28. Two recent studies of importance giving very full descriptions of academical dress are the following: (1) W. N. Hargreaves – Mawdsley's *History of Academical Dress in Europe until the end of the Eighteenth Century* (Oxford U.P. £2.25. 1963). This is carefully documented and includes quite a number of examples from brasses (incl. some illus.); (2) A new work of great authority based on many years of research is Rev. Dr C. A. H. Franklyn's privately printed, limited edn. (200 copies) of his *Academical Dress from the Middle Ages to the present day, including Lambeth Degrees.* (Privately printed for the author by W. E. Baxter Ltd, Lewis, Sx. £5.00. 1970). The book includes long extracts from Prof. E. C. Clarke's classic papers. 'English Academical Costume' *Archaeol. J.* 50 (1893) 73–104, 137–49, 183–209 (the last two papers covering the medieval period include many examples drawn from brasses, regrettably the work is not illustrated); from Edw. Beaumont's two works (q.v. p. 177 below) and shorter extracts from Druitt (q.v.). Dr Franklyn's work has several illus. (though none from brasses) and a full bibliography (pp. 245–8).
29. Little mention has been made of civilian brasses in the above notes as all the standard works on the subject cover them in detail. A useful article, using both brasses and stone monuments as examples, might be added to the basic list, viz., M. E. Bagnell-Oakley 'The dress of civilians in the Middle Ages from Monumental Effigies'. *Bristol & Gloucs. Archaeol. Soc. Trans.* XVIII (1893–4), 252–70. Unfortunately it is inadequately illustrated.
30. For another specialised and little explored type of brass see H. T. Morley 'Shroud brasses of Berkshire' *Berks. Archaeol. J.* 33, 8 (Spring 1929), 34–9. Illus.
31. The Costume Society's Offices are still (Nov. 1971) at the V. & A. c/o The Textile Dept.; the Society's Publications Dept., is c/o 24, Burghley Rd., London, S.W.19.
32. Julian Franklyn. *Brasses* (Arco. 2nd edn. 1970).
33. The reference to the fact that the brass was laid down during Richard's 'Lyff day' actually being stated on the inscription is unusual. The absence of his date of death not only confirms this, but as was so often the case, evidences the laxness of his executors in completing their work either.
34. Given by Weever at 'Stanbridge', Essex.
35. H. F. O. Evans 'Lady who died on the 30th February' *MBS* 9, vii (Oct. 1960), 362–3. Illus.

Chapter 5: Brass rubbings for Exhibition

1. For fuller guide giving locations, fees for rubbing and many other details see '*Where to go brass rubbing in the Greater London Area*' (Phillips & Page Ltd. £0.15. Rev. edn. Dec. 1971. 10 pages. Typescript). For guides of a similar type to other areas see:
   (a) J. Bertram. *Brass Rubbing in Sussex;* 2nd rev. edn., June 1971. £0.12½. Typescript. (sold in aid of Chichester Cathedral Restoration Fund; also available, as are all those quoted while stocks last, from Phillips & Page Ltd., postage extra – inclusive prices on application).
   (b) Cambridge City Libraries. *Monumental Brasses in Cambs. and the Isle of Ely*. 4th comp. rev. edn. Nov. 1970 (Camb. City Libraries. £0.15 (+ postage). 30 pages. typescript).
   (c) Paul Corbould. 'Monumental Brasses of Devon' *Devonshire Assn. . . . Rpts. and Trans.*, 100 (1968), 29–43. Illus. (Off-prints available from the Registrar, Devonshire Assn., 7 The Close, Exeter, EX1 1ET, price £0.37½+postage. Also available from Phillips & Page Ltd. under title '*Where and how to find church brasses in Devon*' price £0.25.
   (d) R. Grimes. *Brief guide to the Monumental Figure Brasses in Essex . . . and info. on where to go brass rubbing*. (The Author, 13 Foxall Rd., Upminster, Essex, RM14 2DD. £0.25. (+postage). 42 pages. typescript).
   (e) Sally Morris *Brass Rubbing in Devon Churches*. (Privately printed and available from Mrs Q. Morris, Chancery Cottage, Harberton, Totnes, Devon. £0.36. (+5p. postage). Pbk. 1967 3rd rev. edn. 1970 14 pages. illus.) No prices given and in narrative rather than tabular form; very readable. The author is hoping to publish a similar guide called 'Brass Rubbing in Cornish Churches' in the near future.
   (f) T. G. and N. Wood. *A brief guide to figure brasses in Devon in chronological order . . . and information of where to go brass rubbing*. (Available from: The Authors, 'Summerhill' Pathfields, Dartmouth, Devon. Price £0.15+postage. 1969).
2. For good general hints on exhibiting see: (1) Norman Cook. *Local History Exhibitions: how to plan and present them*. (Nat. Council for Social Service [N.C.S.S.] 1970. 12 pages, illus. £0.16 (pbk.); (2) Ronald Crawley. *Simple guide to Designing an Exhibition*. (N.C.S.S. 1971. 23 pages. illus. £0.30 (pbk.))
3. As early as 1897 Ethert Brand, addressing the M.B.S. favoured the 'lantern slide' as the best method of exhibiting brasses for lecture purposes. He proposed three methods, viz. (1) photographs taken directly from brasses; (2) photos, taken direct from rubbings; (3) Photolithographs taken from rubbings. By reversing the last process Brand remarks, a good effect is produced if transferred to slides.
4. For a humorous and practical approach to giving public talks or lectures see Avril Exham's handy little booklet *Public Speaking without Tears* (Available from the Author, Eagle Lodge, Mile Path, Woking, Surrey. £0.20 (pbk.) 1970).
5. For further details see *Focal Encyclopaedia of Photography*. Vol. 2. pp.

977–9. (Focal Press. £11.00 set. 1965) which also suggests the use of a rubber gum solution as an alternative adhesive, e.g. 'cow' gum.

6. For an original work showing rubbings of all types from a variety of different objects see L. Andrew's excellent *Creative Rubbings* (Batsford. £1.50. 1967). Among recent materials for brass rubbing is a small kit produced by Finart, containing two gold, two silver, two white and two black crayons of thick wax, with explanatory booklet on their use. The Kit costs £0.80 (incl. post) and can be bought from John Dobbie, 79 High St., Wimbledon, S.W.19 or 32 Putney High St., S.W.15 (see note *The Times*, Wed. 7 Apr. 1971, p. 10. col. (g)).

Another work, of American origin, similar to Mr Andrew's is John J. Boder's excellent *Rubbings and textures: a graphic Technique* (Van Nostrand: Reinhold. £3.00. 1968).

Appendix I

A Survey of Historical and other Collections of Brass Rubbings in the United Kingdom (1971)

The list below was compiled mainly from answers to over 250 questionnaires sent out by the author to Museums, Record Offices, Societies and Libraries in the U.K. Many were only able to give a 'NIL' or small return – the remainder are itemised below.

The list includes not only fuller notes than in my *Beginner's Guide* on the main national collections, but a large number of smaller but historically or aesthetically valuable collections in other locations. The survey is accurate within the limits of the answers received to the original questionnaire or from personal observation. I would be more than pleased to hear of serious omissions either in the U.K. or abroad.

Many of the collections included will already be well known to serious students of brasses, and it must be stressed that few of them can be made accessible to any but *bona fide* enquirers. Those containing historically valuable rubbings are a special case in point. A rubbing on paper is fragile by definition and must only be handled with the greatest of care and respect. When that rubbing is over 100 years old it deserves more than ordinary care and cannot be made available to the 'casual' enquirer. Unless otherwise stated, prior permission to see the rubbings, in writing, is necessary. Right of access is reserved by the authority housing or responsible for the collection.

The value of old rubbings for historical research is self evident, since they are often the only surviving record of many brasses. For others, the rubbings show parts since lost or mutilated. They can be especially useful to those making a study of the brasses of one particular county, area or type. *As yet*, there are few collections of any size containing rubbings of continental brasses, though a number of private individuals have extensive collections as their published works indicate. The information in the list below was obtained between July 1970 and September 1971.

In closing these notes I wish to add a special word of thanks to all those many busy archivists, curators, librarians and officers of archaeological societies who gave up valuable time to completing what must have been one of many questionnaires they receive. I am pleased to record that nearly Ninety per cent of those sent out were answered. Without their help this survey would have been impossible.

In compiling these notes reference has also been made to the following works:

Directory of British Associations. 3rd edn. 1971–2. (C.B.D. Research Ltd., Beckenham, Kent. £6.00. 1971).

Historical, archaeological and Kindred Societies in the British Isles: a list. (Univ. of London, Inst. of Historical Research. rev. edn. 1968).

Libraries Museums and Art Galleries Year Book 1971; ed. E. V. Corbett. (James Clarke. £6.30. rev. edn. Dec. 1971).

Museums' Calendar 1971 (Museums' Assn. £1.30. 1971).

Record Repositories in Great Britain. 4th rev. edn. (HMSO (for Royal Commn. on Hist. MSS), 1971).

BEDFORDSHIRE

The Social History Assistant, Luton Museum, Wardown Park, Luton. 100–200 rs., poss. made abt. 1930, donor unknown. Mainly Beds. examples. Stored in folders on Archive Room. No Catalogue.

Available (by appointment): 0930–1700 hrs. Mon.–Fri.

Books, MSS, etc: Drwgs. of brasses in Luton parish church – prob. made for Austin's *History of Luton* (1928).

BERKSHIRE

The Hon. Sec., Berkshire Archaeological Society, 'Turstins', High St., Upton, Didcot.

100–200 rs., made late 19th and early 20th cent. by Rev. J. E. Field, H. T. Morley. (author of *Monumental Brasses of Berkshire* (1924)). Donated by latter. Stored rolled in Society's store at Reading. Arr. and catd. under county and by type. Includes abt. 6 rs. of incised slabs and sev. of palimps. No further adds. proposed at present.

Available: by prior arr. only.

Books, MSS., etc.: Oxford Univ. Br. Rubbing Soc. pubns.

See additional note on P. 96.

BUCKINGHAMSHIRE

The Curator, Buckinghamshire County Museum, Church St., Aylesbury.

Several hundred rs. (exact number unknown), made between c. 1880 and 1960, arr. under parish. Stored in folders in Museum store. Not catalogued. Rs. still being added.

Available: (only by appointment and under supervision). Mon.–Fri. 0930–1700; Sats. 0930–1230; 1330–1700 hrs.

CAMBRIDGESHIRE

The Curator, University Museum of Archaeology and Ethnology, Downing St., Cambridge.

6–7000 rs. under care of Hon. Curator, made betw. 1840s and present day to which examples are still added from time to time; the basic colln. is that of the Camb. Antiqn. Soc., begun 1847–8 and therefore of enormous historical importance; at present confined to English brs. it incl. rs. by Revs. Herbert Haines and H. W. Macklin, Sir Augustus Franks, the Bramble Colln, C. E. O. Griffith, C. D. Buchanan and many others; betw. 1926 and 1938 alone, 4,230 rs were added from 1,760 churches at instigation of Ralph Griffin, then Hon Curator, bringing total held to 6,370 by the latter date; dabbings of entire slabs showing indents, etc. or late brs (mainly 17th cent.) not prev colld, made by or for Dr G. A. E. Ruck, until recently Mr Griffin's successor as Hon. Curator; sev of these made by the late A. B. Connor. The present Hon. Curator is Dr H. K. Cameron, President of the M.B.S., and a teaching officer in the University's Dept of Engineering.

Arrangement: Topographically by counties and parishes; stored in folders in wooden cabinets specially made for them in 1889 and 1924; there are over 70 folios. Rubbings vary in quality and condition, some being very fine (with colours added), others poor but of great hist. value; there are two or more copies of many brs, usually a second is made for comparative purposes if losses have occured, palimpsests discovered, etc.

Books, MSS, etc.: Fine colln of books and bound vols of pamphlets, cont. all imp. works on brs/incised slabs pub(d) since 1820s; many given by M. Stephenson who helped Mr Griffin reorganise colln; incl. good edn of T. Fisher's *Bedfordshire Brasses* given by author to Rev T. Raffles dd. 1 Dec. 1828. Also sev. ms. notebooks of Rev H. W. Macklin, (given by his widow) incl 'Chronological List of Monumental Figure Brasses' from 1277–1773, plus County Lists (as in his pub(d) works); several files of unbound pamphlets and some ms letters and notes by various hands. Card index of books.

Catalogue: based on annotated copy of Mill Stephenson's *List* and *Appendix*, with separate vol for brasses in museums, private possession, etc. based on above; these have been cut up and inserted into bound vols with ancillary vol. as index. The index up to 1925 was comp by Mr H. F. Bird and was based on Haines' *List*, but was superseded in 1926 by the above. A 'Book of Wants' is also maintained.

Special note: This fine colln is of great historical importance and is probably the most complete in the country. Housed in a room far from adequate it is open only to serious students of brasses by prior arrangement with, and at the discretion of, the Curator of the Museum or Hon Curator of the collection; it cannot be made accessible to 'casual' visitors. The Museum is open to the public from 1400–1600 hrs Mon–Fri. For historical and statistical account of colln see RUCK, G. A. E. 'Monumental Brasses; with special reference to the Cambridge Antiquarian Society's Collection . . .' *Procs Camb. Antiq Soc*, XXXVII (1938), *50–59*; XLIV (1950), *33–46* Plates VII–XII (Pl. VII is a copy of a portrait of Ralph Griffin painted by the late A. B. Connor (*q.v.*) in 1935). The latter article first appeared under the title 'Centenary of a Collection' in *MBS* 8, v (Mar. 1949), 220–33. In the *Procs Camb. Antiq Soc* it appeared under the title 'An Account of the University Collection of Brass Rubbings in the Museum of Archaeology and Ethnology'. Both are well illustrated.

CORNWALL

The Curator, Royal Institution of Cornwall, County Museum and Art Gallery, Truro.
Rubbings formerly belonging to Institution appear to have perished in the floods of 1956, and only some of early Christian inscribed stones remain.

DEVONSHIRE

The Director, Royal Albert Memorial Museum, Queen St, Exeter.
'Copeland Collection' 113 rs of Devonshire br made by the late G. W. Copeland during the second quarter of this cent. Given by his widow to the Devonshire Association who subsequently deposited them here in 1968. Stored folded in boxes at Rougement Hse Museum, Castle St, Exeter. Cat. for use in building only.
Available: (by prior arrangement) to *bona fide* students 0900–1700 hrs Mon.–Fri.
Books, MSS. etc: MSS notes and some distribution maps of Devon br made by G. W. Copeland.

DORSET

The Curator, Dorset County Museum, High St West, Dorchester.
100–200 rs, arr. under counties (mainly Dorset), made in 1920s and '30s by W. de C. Prideaux and G. DruDrury of the Dorset Natural History and Archaeol Soc. Donated by them. Stored rolled. No cat. Adds still being made.
Available: (by prior application) Mon.–Sat. 0900–1300, 1400–1700 hrs.

DURHAM

The School Museum Officer, Bowes Museum, Barnard Castle.
Less than 50 rs from various locations, mostly made 1966, mounted

for display and loan to schools; a catalogue is held in above office for use by Durham schools only; rs still being added. They are available for public inspection during school holidays. Incl some of incised slabs.

ESSEX

CHELMSFORD

Borough Librarian and Curator, Chelmsford and Essex Museum, Oaklands Park, Chelmsford.

100–200 rs mostly late 19th cent.; donors unknown. Arr under counties or boroughs (18 represented). Some continental examples. Stored in portfolios in cupboards. No cat.

Available for inspection on written appn to above (1000–1700 hrs daily).

Books, MSS etc: M.B.S. Portfolio Vol. 1, No. 1 (1894) – Vol III, Pt 10 (Dec. 1910).

An exhibition of some of the Museum's colln was held from 11 Dec. 1971 to 9 Jan. 1972 and a cat. issued.

COLCHESTER

Hon Sec, Essex Archaeological Society, 'Hollytrees', High St, Colchester (or to Hon Librn).

200–250 rs made at various dates betw. 1890 and 1965 by several donors, incl. many by A. H. Brown (*q.v.*); arr. under parishes (mainly Essex and E. Anglian examples). Stored rolled at above address (belonging to the Colchester and Essex Museum) but remaining the property of the Society to whom all enquiries should be addressed. Rubbings still being added. Cat. for use in building only.

Available: by appointment only.

Books, MSS., etc: Selection available in Museum Library, mainly *Archaeol Soc Trans* articles by Miller Christy, W. W. Porteous and E. Bertram Smith; these articles make frequent references to early rubbings made by Messrs. Procter, H. W. King and others.

SAFFRON WALDEN

The Curator, The Museum, Saffron Walden.

100–200 rs made prior to c 1915 when most acqd. Mostly made by students of Saffron Walden Training College and commissioned by the Museum. Arr by area; stored rolled in cabinets in Museum. Cat. available for use in building. No further additions.

Available: for inspection on prior appn to the Curator: 1100–1300, 1400–1700 May–Sept. incl. Sundays; 1100–1300; 1400–1600 Mon.–Sat., Oct.–Apr.

GLOUCESTERSHIRE

CHELTENHAM

The Curator, Art Gallery and Museum, Clarence St, Cheltenham.

A few (under 10) rs made 1900–1930 by F. J. Thacker, W. L. Mellersh, A. A. Hunter and H. B. Stevens (the donors). Kept rolled in Museum's store room.
Available: by previous appt 1000–1300, 1415–1700 weekdays and Sats.

GLOUCESTER

City Librarian, City Library, Brunswick Rd, Gloucester.
100–200 rs mostly mid- and late-19th cent, some by Rev Herbert Haines and C. T. Davis (author of a book on Gloucs. br). Not arr. in any order at present. Some fragile condition. Stored in box. It is hoped the newly formed Gloucester Brass Rubbing Society will undertake the task of cataloguing and rolling the rs. Inspection by appointment during Library hours (0900–2000 hrs. Mon.–Fri.; 0900–1700 hrs Sats.)
Books, MSS., etc. In The Gloucester Colln includes:

(1) original drwgs and M.S. notes illustrating C. T. Davis' book *The Monumental Brasses of Gloucestershire* (1899), as well as the author's annotated copy of this book (Ref. No. 16588) and several offprints of articles written by Davis for *Gloucester J., Archaeol. J., MBS Tran., J. Brit. Archaeol. Assn.*, etc.
(2) Haines' *Manual* (2 copies) 1861.
(3) Boutell, C. *Monumental Brasses and Slabs* . . . (1847)
(4) Manning, C. R. *List of Monumental Brasses* . . . (1846)
(5) Stephenson, Mill. *List of mon br. in Brit. Isles* (1926)
(6) Macklin, H. – *Monumental Brasses* 7th edn (1952)
(7) Druitt, Herbert – *Gloucestershire Notes* (repr from *M.B.S.* 5 (1906) 159–60.)

HAMPSHIRE

The County Archivist, Hampshire C.R.O., The Castle, Winchester.
Under 50 rs made c 1900–1920 and acqd 1970. Owner unknown; arr. under place name. Includes one of incised slab. Kept rolled in strong room. No cat. No additions contemplated.
Available on prior appn. 0915–1300, 1400–1630 hrs any weekday.
Books, MSS. etc.:

(1) *Trans C.U.A.B.C.* 1892 (for Havant). Ref. No. H9/1
(2) Typescript notes on brasses at Itchen Stoke. Ref. No. 2M65/25
(3) Article on brasses at Brown Candover. Ref. No. B18/2
(4) *Hants. Field Club. Procs.* Vols. 2, 3, 6, 7, 8, 9, and 10 which have references to brasses.

HERTFORDSHIRE

(1) The County Archivist, Hertfordshire C.R.O., County Hall, Hertford.

Abt. 800 rs (all Herts. examples) made by William Blyth Gerish and forming part of the Gerish Colln late 19th/early 20th cent date. Mostly re-mounted. Stored, folded in large pamphlet boxes in main search room. Arr. under parishes.

Books, MSS., etc.

(1) ANDREWS, W. F. *Memorial Brasses in Hertfordshire Churches.* 2nd edn. Large paper edn with loose notes inserted giving refs to articles or notes on Herts. brs in *Herts. Mercury* betw. 1899–1906 by W. F. Andrews and W. B. Gerish.

(2) A copy of sm. paper edn of above bound in one vol with G. Isherwood's *Memorial Brasses in Bedfordshire Churches.*

(3) Fine colln of topographical drwgs by H. G. Oldfield (*q.v.*) bound in vols. incl many of brs since lost or mutilated.

(4) 'Grangerised' edn of Clutterbuck's *History of Hertfordshire,* interleaved with topog views by J. C. Buckler (*q.v.*) and Thos. Fisher (*q.v.*);

(5) Haines' *Manual of M.Bs.* (repr of 1861 edn 1970)

Available 1000–1300, 1400–1730 hrs. Mon.–Fri.

(2) The Curator, Hertford Museum. Bull Plain, Hertford.

Abt. 1000 rs made betw. c 1846 and 1947 by W. F., R. T. and H. C. Andrews, incl sev of brs since lost. Mainly Herts. examples only. Most unmounted and stored in large folders alphab. by parish; some are in poor repair; additions made only occasionally; some are the property of the East Herts. Archaeol Soc. of which the three men were co-founders and/or members.

Books, MSS, etc: The Museum has a fine colln of topographical and historical books, drwgs, newspapers, press-cuttings and archaeological periodicals of varying date colld by the Andrews and the E. Herts. Archaeol Soc. whose Library is housed at the Museum. Most valuable in the present-context are the MSS. notes and drwgs of the Andrews made over nearly 100 yrs on Herts. brs, notably those of H. C. Andrews, FSA (*q.v.*) for his uncompleted series of articles in the *E.H.A.S. Trans* betw. 1930–47. There are also an almost complete set of the *MBS Trans* from Vols 1–7 and a few CUBAC Trans, annotated editions of W. F. Andrews' *Memorial Brasses in Hertfordshire Churches* (*q.v.*), Mill Stephenson's *List* and *Appx.* and off-prints of other of M.S.'s works in periodicals; and a good original copy of Weever's *Funeral Monuments* (1631).

Available: (pref, by prior arrangement) 1000–1700 hrs. Mon.–Sat.

KENT

CANTERBURY

The Hon Sec, Canterbury Archaeol Soc, 3 Queen's Ave, Canterbury.

Under 50 rs made c 1900 and donated by executors of Mrs Livett (wife of Canon Livett). Arr. by type. Stored rolled at Sudbury Tower, Pound Lane, Canterbury (key from Mr A. J. McFarlane, 53 St Peters St, Canterbury).
Available: by prior appt only.

MAIDSTONE

The Curator, Maidstone Museum, St Faith's St, Maidstone.
A very valuable colln of abt. 500 rs belonging jointly to the Museum and Kent Archaeol Soc mostly made in the last century. All Kentish brasses arr. under parishes. Stored rolled in chest at Museum. Card index. Rubbings still being added.
Available for inspection on prior application to above 1000–1700 hrs Mon.–Fri.

LANCASHIRE

LIVERPOOL

The Keeper, Dept of Ceramics and Applied Art, City of Liverpool Museums, William Brown St, Liverpool.
Under 50 rs of unknown origin, including 4 of incised slabs; some in gold finish. Arr. under parish. Stored rolled in Museum's warehouse. Additions still being made. No cat.
Available by prior appn. only.

MANCHESTER

The Keeper, Gallery of English Costume, Platt Hall, Rusholme, Manchester.
Over 550 rs of various dates, mainly given by Mr Hugh Kingsford, plus 94 from the Mon Brass Soc. The former are on loan from the Manchester Museum, and used mainly for their value in showing costume and armour. Manuscript cat. (2 vols) made by Mr Kingsford of his own collection, but no official cat. otherwise.
Available: (pref. by prior appn.) during normal Museum hours. 1000–1600 Mon.–Sat., 1400–1600 hrs Sun. (Nov.–Feb.); 1000–2000 Mon.–Sat., 1400–2000 Sun. (May–Aug.); 1000–1800 Mon.–Sat., 1400–1800 Sun. (Mar., Apr., Sept., Oct.)

LEICESTERSHIRE

The Keeper of Antiquities, Museum and Art Gallery, New Walk, Leicester.
Abt. 100 rs, mainly of local brasses.
Available on prior appl. at Newarke Homes Museum, Mon.–Sat. 1000–1900 hrs Apr. and Sept., 1000–1700 hrs Oct.–Mar., 1000–1900 hrs May–Aug. Sundays, all year, 1400–1700 hrs.
No further details supplied.

LINCOLNSHIRE

(1) The County Archivist, The Castle, Lincoln.
200–500 rs made c 1900 onwards, and most acquired during 1950s. Abt 300 rs from Mr G. Nussey of Boston, Lincs. Stored rolled. Well indexed and cross referenced; cat. for use in bldg. No additions proposed.
Available: (by prior appt) 1000–1300 hrs, 1400–1700 hrs weekdays. 1000–1300 hrs Sats. Closed public holidays and *first 2 weeks* of October.
Books, MSS., etc: Some odd vols of *M.B.S. Trans*, plus a few other general histories of brasses.
(2) Director, Lincoln City Libraries, Central Library. Free School Lane, Lincoln.
100–200 rs of unknown date and origin; arr. alphabetically under counties. Stored flat in drawers in local collection library; catd.
Available: 0900–1930 hrs daily; 0900–1800 Sats.
Books, MSS. etc: some in Local Collection on Lincs. brasses *e.g.* Rev G. E. Jeans' *List* (1895).

LONDON

(1) The Keeper, Dept of Manuscripts, British Museum, London, W.C.1.
Sev 1000 rubbings incl the historical Douce Colln of 'Impressions' of brs by Sir John Cullum and Craven Ord (Add. MSS. 32478/9) and other large 19th cent collns of rs by Rev Henry Addington (Add. MS. 32490); Rev W. F. Creeny and Rev G. Rowe (Add MSSS. 32481 A–X); all of the above are arr. topographically in folders except Addington's. There are other smaller collns to which ref. can be found in the printed cats. of MSS. The vast colln of original MSS themselves are far too numerous to mention, some being made by or for antiquaries like John Philipot and Wm Cole, incl sketches or drawgs of brasses, indents, etc of varying quality, with notes on each item; some are contained in 'Grangerised' editions of County histories. Nearly all can only be found by ref. to the many cats. available. The Rev D. T. Powell's mss., drawgs and books (Add MSS. 17456–63) and those of the artist George Shepherd, made mostly in 1820s (Add MSS. 16966–7) are typical examples.
Available: Admission only by reader's ticket on completion of necessary formalities. Details on appl.
Note: The large size of the folios of rubbings and the handling problems involved in fetching them, suggests that inspection of them simply to look at one rubbing (unless it is the only one extant) should not be undertaken lightly or without recourse to more accessible collections.

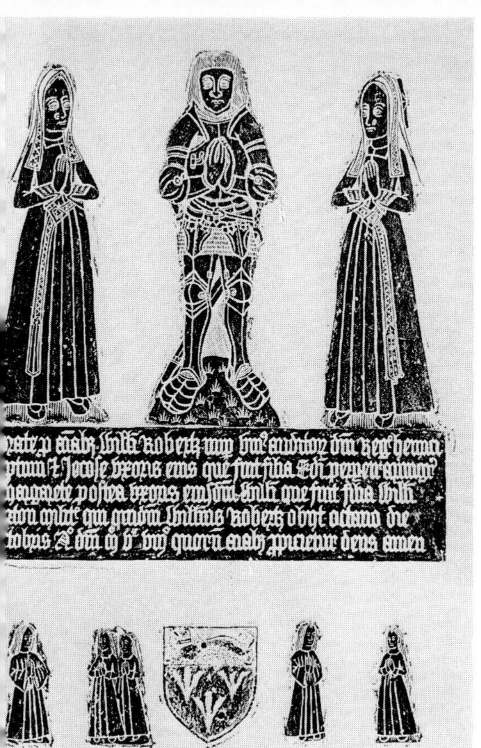

(*a*)

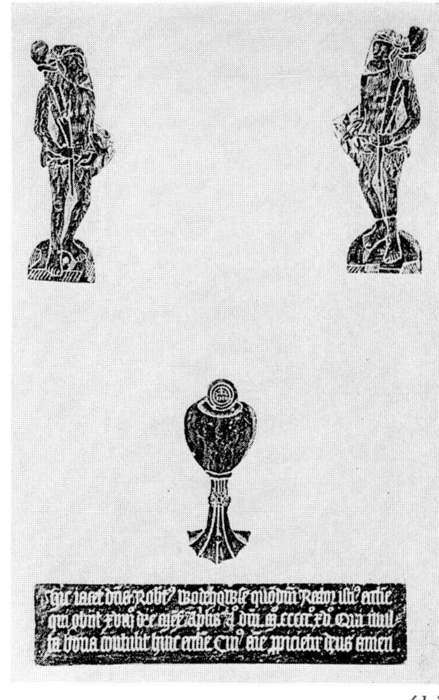

(*b*)

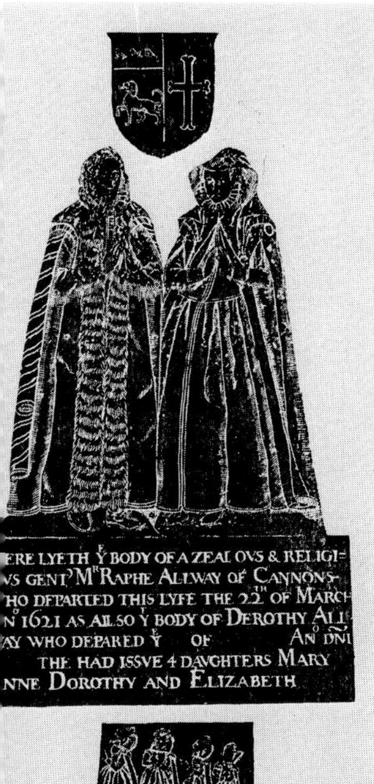

(*c*)

PLATE 11

(*a*) Wm. Roberts & 2 wives, Jocosa (ob. 1484) and Margaret, Little Braxted, Essex (1508). William and Jocosa have an earlier brass, with figures in shrouds (1484) in St John's Church, Digswell, Herts. 3 shields above the figures are omitted on this illus. Figures 48 cm ($18\frac{7}{8}$ ins); (*b*) Robert Wodehouse, rector (1515) Holwell, nr. Hitchin, Herts. A unique brass showing two 'wodehouses' or wild men with clubs and shields – a pun on the name of the deceased. The engraver may well have copied the figures from a contemporary woodcut or print; each figure is 27.8 cm (11 ins) high. (*c*) Raphe Allway and wife Dorothy (1621), St Botolph's Church, Shenley, Herts. Only recently fully uncovered, this unusual brass, probably of local design, is reproduced here for the first time; the engraver has apparently attempted a perspective drawing. The strange shape of the plate suggests a palimpsest, also the metal is thick for a late brass. Note the incorrect spelling of the wife's name. Approx. overall size: 94.5 by 45 cm ($37\frac{1}{4}$ by $17\frac{3}{4}$ ins). Rubbings by the author. Photos: Henry W. Gray (*a* & *b*); Peter Marshall (*c*)

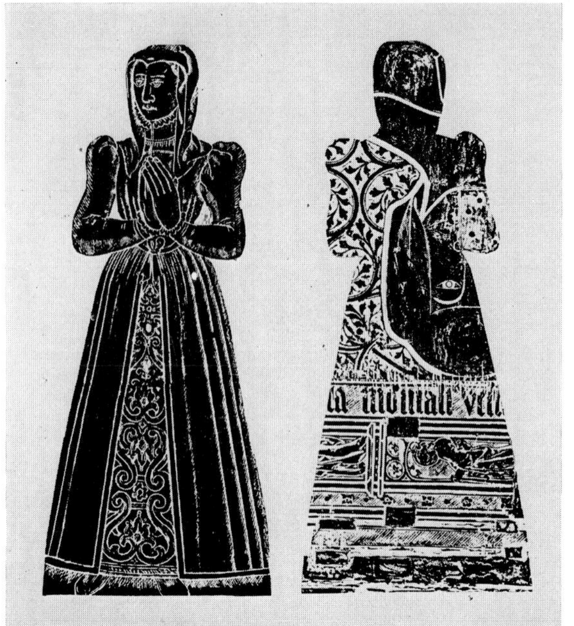

(*a*)

PLATE 12

(*a*) Margaret Cheyne (1578), King's Langley (All SS Church), Herts. *Obverse* Ty Elizabethan female figure; F.I., 5 children & original slab lost. *Reverse* Portions of Flemish brasses showing part of head of female figure (c. 1350) and part of canopy M.I. from same brass. Figure 58.8 cm (23 ins); (*b*) Lady (c. 1535), Aldenham Watford, Herts. A very competently drawn figure in unusual costume rarely seen brasses, probably East Anglian School; F.I. and children lost. Figure: 41.5 cm (16$\frac{3}{8}$ (*c*)—Collys, lady, with young son (c. 1510), Dunton, Bucks. A typical female figure 'informalised' by the addition of a small boy peering round his mother's skirt; the half of the F.I. is missing. Figure: 30.5 cm (12 ins). Rubbings by the author. Photos I Marshall (*a* & *b*), Henry W. Gray (*c*)

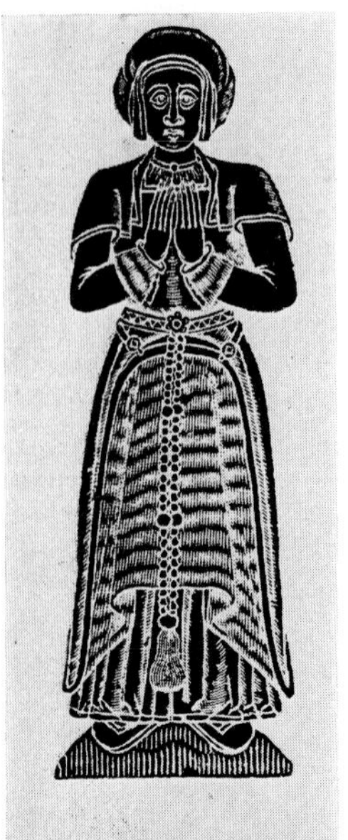

(*b*)

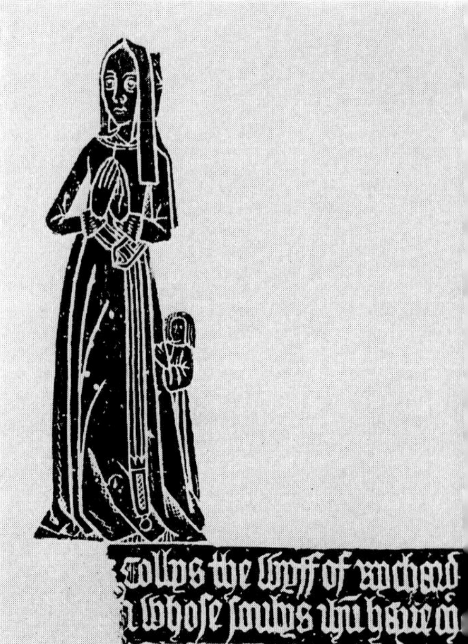

(*c*)

(2) The Librarian, Central School of Art and Design Library, Southampton Row, W.C.1.
Small colln of less than 50 rs mounted on linen and from various locations, not catd. at moment.
Available only by prior arrangement.
(3) The Director, The London Museum, Kensington Palace, London, W.8.
50–100 rs arr. under County (i.e. London and Middx.) made in late 19th cent and acquired 1961 from Castle Museum, Norwich. Stored rolled at Museum. No cat. or additions.
Available: (pref. giving three days notice) weekdays (incl Sats.) 1000–1700 hrs.
Other materials: Rubbings of 'opercula', London coal-hole covers, made by London schoolchildren at invitation of Museum to preserve a record of those fast disappearing phenomena. An exhibition of the rubbings was held, ending on 10 Oct. 1971.
(4) The Secretary, Society of Antiquaries of London, Burlington House, Piccadilly, W.1.
Several thousand rs dating from early 19th cent onwards and forming finest historical colln in the U.K.; includes examples of dabbings and black lead rubbings from earliest period of br rubbing, incl some by Thomas Fisher (*q.v.*) and Wm. Alexander (*q.v.*); rs made by many hands, but largest single colln of over 3000 rs given by Sir Augustus Franks (*q.v.*) in late 19th cent which incl those of his contemporaries Rev Herbert Haines, J. G. Nichols, Albert Way and Rev E. Farrar, as well as his own extensive colln. Franks and Mill Stephenson did a great deal to organise and cat. the colln. (see: *SAP* 2 Ser. XVIII (1899–1901), 170–71). Arr. topographically, the main part of the colln is stored in folders in special cabinets in the inner library and on a landing off the same room. The Society's journals record many individual gifts of rubbings apart from the above; from 1944–61 the late R. H. Pearson (*q.v.*) was Hon Curator.
Available: This colln is that of a private, learned society principally for the use of its members. *Bona fide* students may be admitted at the discretion of the Secretary to who any appls must be addressed stating the reason they wish to use the Library. The historical value of the whole collection cannot be stressed too strongly and the greatesr care must be exercised when handling MSS. and rubbings in particular. The Library is open from 1000–1700 hrs daily (except during annual stocktaking).
(5) The Keeper, Dept of Prints and Drawings, Victoria and Albert Museum, S.W.7.
Over 3000 rs of brs and incised slabs, incl many continental examples; made from the late 19th cent onwards by various persons and incl

2,154 rs given by Soc of Antiq in 1911; 375 by J. S. M. Ward (*q.v.*) and others given by Mill Stephenson, M. Huish, E. W. Morley and Miss Frances Weale; there is also a separate colln of rs of heraldic medallions from incised stone slabs of 17th cent date onwards. Rs kept in folders or rolled in Print Room Store; a cat. is available apart from the printed list named below. Rs are still being added. To obtain good idea of extent of colln see: *Catalogue of Rubbings of Brasses and Incised Slabs* comp by Muriel Clayton. 2nd edn 1929 repr 1968. (H.M.S.O. £0.62½ and excellent value for money).
Available: 1000–1630 hrs weekdays.
Add note: There is also a fine library (National Art Library) of books and ms notes etc in the Museum, containing most of the imp printed works on brs and incised slabs in Britain and the continent, incl original material by W. H. J. Weale (*q.v.*), Rev W. Sparrow Simpson and cats. of manufacturers of 'modern' brasses like Hardman; Hart, Son, Peard & Co., etc.

NORFOLK
(1) The Assistant Director, Castle Museum, Norwich.
Over 1000 rs made from c 1840 onwards by various donors incl some by Rev W. F. Creeny. Abt. 40 are of continental br and incised slabs, otherwise mainly E. Anglian. Mostly rolled, but on removal to new premises in Bridewell Museum, Bridewell Alley, Norwich will be stored flat in purpose built stands. Card index of Norfolk rubbings only. Rs arr. under counties then alphab. by place.
Available: (by prior arrangement with Assist Director) 1000–1700 weekdays only.
(2) Norfolk and Norwich Archaeological Soc – c/o Hon Librarian, Garsett House, St Andrew's Hall plain, Norwich.
Rubbings formerly in possession of society now passed to the Norwich Castle Museum (above)
Books, MSS:

(1) 2 vols drwgs of Norfolk brasses by Rev Thomas Sugden Talbot (*q.v.*) made in ink 1793–4. Presented to Soc 1932 by A. M. Talbot, grandson of artist. Vol I: 32 *illus* Vol II: 68 *illus*.
(2) MS account by Benjamin Mackerell comp 1737 'Brief historical account of all the Parish churches in the City of Norwich, with all the Monumental Grave-Stones, Inscriptions and Brass Plates . . .' *2 vols.*

(3) FRERE MS. cont descr of brs at Cley-next-the-Sea, Norfolk made Jan. 25th, 1715/16, incl exg and lost brs (*see MBS Tran.* VIII (5), 1947, 196–7).

(4) Cotman's Norfolk and Suffolk Brasses.
(5) Vols 2 and 3 *MBS Trans* and odd pts of later vols.
(6) V&A Catalogue of Brasses.

Viewing by prior arr. only.
(3) City and County Archivist, Central. Library, Norwich.
6 unidentified rs only (MS. 20530/Z/IA) and of St Ethelred, King of W. Saxons, Wimborne Minster, Dorset (PD/4/45). Available by prior notice during normal hours.
Available: Mon.–Fri. 0900–1700; Sat. 0900–1200.
Books, MSS, etc.

(1) Description of rubbings of m.b. in colln of Arthur Wright. Vol I. 1900–1. (MS 4254).
(2) Notes on brs in Norwich and Norfolk by Fred Hunt. 1861 (MS 4612).
(3) Brass rubbings in two Oxford College chapels (Magdalen and New Coll) and in five Welsh churches. (by Arthur Wright). (MS 4255).
(4) List of foreign mon brs (MS 10991. 34EI).

NORTHAMPTONSHIRE
(1) Chief Archivist, Northamptonshire Record Office, Delapre Abbey, Northampton.
c 20 rubbings of local brs only, unclassified.
Available: (pref. by prior arrangement) Mon., Tues., Wed. 0915–1300, 1400–1645, Thurs., 0915–1300, 1400–1945, Sat. 0915–1215.
(2) The Curator, Central Museum and Art Gallery, Guildhall Rd, Northampton.
50–100 rs made before 1960 but not catd or indexed. Stored in chest. Origin unknown. *Viewing* by prior appt only.

OXFORDSHIRE
(1) The Keeper of Western MSS, Bodleian Library, Oxford.
Over 1000 rs of many dates, made by a variety of persons from the late 18th cent onwards. Collns vary in size from just a few rs or notes to large series of over 700. Among the more interesting or important are those in (1) the *Gough Colln* of MSS. amongst material he colld for ms addns to his *Sepulchral Monuments* (e.g. MSS Gough Maps 221–228, 228, Summary Catalogue Nos. 17579–87; (2) in the *MSS Rubbings* group are three good series (a) by R. Proctor (given by his mother in 1904); (b) 44 rs by *J. Gray* made in 19th cent – given by Rev E. A. Gray and Mrs Decima Sturges in 1904; (c) 33 rs given by Miss Ramsey in 1956; (3) *MSS Rubbings Evans* comprise over 700

rs made by or for the late Major H. F. Owen Evans (*q.v.*) and given in 1966; this colln also includes Major Owen Evans' notes, descr. of brasses, photos of rubbings, etc.

Books, MSS etc: Being a copyright library the Bodleian holds copies of nearly all major English publications, and all the important works on brasses and allied subjects will be held. Apart from these there is a vast amount of MS. material relating to brasses, not only in the Gough colln, but in those of other antiquaries like Richard Rawlinson and Anthony Wood: only by use of the numerous cats. and indexes can these be located. All rubbings of English brasses are recorded in an annoted copy of Mill Stephenson's *List*, kept in the Duke Humphrey, the MSS Reading Room (R.6.484). Rubbings in most of the above collns are arranged under counties and parishes.

Available: The Library is open to all serious students who must complete the necessary form of appln, which must be signed by a suitable referee. All members of the University are admitted upon Registration. For full details see pamphlet issued by Library *General Notes for Readers* (rev April, 1970).

(2) Mr D. A. Hinton, Dept of Antiquities, Ashmolean Museum, Beaumont St, Oxford.

Over 1000 rs, made from early 20th cent onwards by various individuals; largest colln is that of Mr F. A. Greenhill F.S.A. 'loaned' by the Oxford Archit and Hist Soc with some other rs; also three by Lawrence of Arabia made when he was a youth (see KIRBY, H. T. 'Lawrence of Arabia – Brass Rubber' *Apollo.* XXVIII (163), July 1938, 18–19; illus); others by Dr H. W. Catling, editor of the 6th edn of the Museum's invaluable *Notes on Brass Rubbing* (1969). Colln at present having some repairs carried out to rs. There is *no* cat. Stored folded in drawers in the Museum basement. No more rubbings are being added at present.

Books, MSS. etc: The Museum's extensive Library contains most of the imp work on brs/incised slabs and also houses the archives of the Oxford Architectural and Historical Society (Hon Librn Dr H. Colvin); amongst these are an original copy of Haines' *Manual* of 1861 donated by the author, and a series of letters to and from Haines written while his *Manual* was in preparation (for details, see my intro to the repr of Haines' *Manual* (Adams & Dart. 1970), esp pp 7–8, 10–11 and 16).

Available: At time of writing the work being carried out on the colln makes it necessary to restrict use to all but specialist scholars.

(3) Clerk of the Council, County Hall, Oxford.

Under 50 rs mainly made in 19th cent (poss by Mrs J. M. Davenport) bound in one volume (Cat. No. DL V/i/28); poor condition; incl one of incised slab.

Available: 0900–1300, 1415–1700 hrs by prior appointment. Cat. for use in CRO only where colln is housed.

SHROPSHIRE

(1) Shropshire Archaeological Soc c/o Librarian and Curator, Shrewsbury Borough Library, Castle Gates, Shrewsbury.
50–100 rs made c 1940–46; mainly Shropshire examples; no special arr. or cat.; stored at Riggs Hall Museun in polythene bags.
Available: (pref by prior appt). Weekdays 1000–1800 hrs; Sats. 1000–1700 hrs.
Books, MSS. etc.

(1) Stephenson, Mill 'Mon Brs of Shropshire' (repr from *Trans Shrop. Archaeol Soc* 2 ser, 7, iii (1895), 384–440);
(2) Evans, George Eyre 'Non-Conformist Church Brasses in Shropshire' This was pubd in (a) *Church Chronicle* No. 35 (1896); (b) *MBS* 2, vi (N.S.), Jan. 1897, 326–9 (c) EVANS, G. E. *Midland Churches* . . . (pub 1899). pp 240–45 under 'Whitchurch, Salop., Dodington Presbyterian Chapel'. Evans moved the brasses to St Saviour's Unitarian Church, Whitchurch in 1898; this church is now (1971) also closed.

(2) Victoria County History of Shropshire, Shirehall, Abbey Foregate, Shrewsbury.
The staff of the above office have collected a complete set of rubbings of Salop. brasses, which in July 1970 were going to be photographed for the V.C.H. and a second set deposited at the Shropshire C.R.O. who have no rubbings at present. (I am grateful to Mr D. T. W. Price, formerly Asst editor Shropshire V.C.H. for the above information and other help.)

SOMERSET

BRISTOL

The Curator, Dept of Archaeology and History, City Museum, Queens Rd, Bristol.
50–100 rs of various dates, some 19th cent of brasses since lost or damaged, at present (1971) being re-arranged; incl 5 of continental brs; 2 incised slabs. Many damaged during war or by natural decay. Stored rolled and on boards. Cat. for use in building.
Details (a) W101–290 *Master's Colln* made by Rev George Streynsham Master (ob 1900). Loaned to Museum 1927 by Mr C. Onslow Master; (b) N577–636, N734–767. *Brackenbridge Colln;* presented 1908–10 by Mr Matthew Hale; (c) N637–733 *Ellacombe Colln,* collected by Canon Ellacombe of Bitton (see p 88 above), Presented

Aug. 1910; (d) N748–51 *Downside Colln*, presented 1908 by Downside College; (e) N753–69 Bundle of unknown origin, (f) N770–71 given by V&A Museum 1934.

Available: by prior appt. 1000–1730 Mon.–Fri.; occasionally Sats.

TAUNTON

The Secretary, Somerset Archaeol and Nat Hist Soc, Taunton Castle. c 50 assorted rs of unknown provenance and origin; No cat. or special arrangement. Un-used for at least last 12 years. *Viewing* can be arranged for serious students by prior appt.

Books, MSS. etc. Society's library includes pubd works by Cotman, Dunkin, Belcher, Thornely, Druitt, H. E. Field, Kite, Creeny, R. Griffin and others.

STAFFORDSHIRE

The Librarian. William Salt Library, 19 Eastgate St, Stafford.

100–200 rs made c 1840–50 for William Salt, incl some of mural tablets and bell inscr; mostly of Staffs memorials/bells. Stored rolled and cared for jointly by Wm. Salt Lib. and Staffs. C.R.O.; a cat. is available in the bldg; colln arr by location.

Available: (pref. by prior arrgt) Tues.–Sat. 1000–1245, 1345–1700.

SUFFOLK

BURY ST EDMUNDS

County Archivist, Bury St Edmunds and West Suffolk Record Office, 8 Angel Hill, Bury St Edmunds.

24 rs mainly of Suffolk brs, some endorsed 'Mr F. Ford, Bury St Edmunds'. Prob 19th cent: given by Moyses Hall Museum, Bury (Acc 1689).

Available: Mon.–Fri. 0900–1300; 1400–1700 hrs.

Books, MSS. etc:

(1) FARRER, Rev E. – *A List of Monumental Brasses remaining in Suffolk* (1903);

(2) Folder cont prints (Mainly pub 1817) and few drwgs of brs, mostly from Suffolk churches (26 items). Acc 1546B;

(3) 3 portfolios of drwgs of painted glass, brasses, etc in Suffolk by H. Watling, c 1865–75 (Acc 1527);

(4) Proof copy of J. S. Cotman's *Engravings of Sepulchral Brasses in Suffolk* (1838) – text and index only. (Acc 449/5/31.9).

IPSWICH

The Curator, The Museum, High St, Ipswich.

Abt. 500 rs made from c 1870 onwards and donated by Rev W. Holland (112 rs), Rev C. G. Betham, Rev G. H. Porter, Mr H. T. Belcher and others. Stored rolled in racks and boxes at the Branch

Museum, Christchurch Mansion, arr. under county and town, with location and subject index. No complete cat., some index cards, some MS. notebooks. Rubbings still added occasionally. The Museum also houses the famous Pownder brass (1525) from the destroyed church of St Mary Quay, Ipswich.
Available: to serious researchers by prior appt only.

SURREY

The Hon Sec, Surrey Archaeol Soc, Castle Arch, Guildford.
A major colln (number unknown) mainly rs of Surrey brs made from 1854 onwards by numerous persons, and at present being overhauled and recatd.; rs are still being added, a card cat. to most of colln exists. No further details available at time of writing.*

SUSSEX

BRIGHTON

The Chief Librarian, Public Library, Church St, Brighton.
30 rs of Sussex brs made c 1920, 6 acqd 1969 (3 in gold finish), occasional additions still made. Stored in folders in Reference Library Local Colln. No cat.
Available: 1000–1900 hrs Mon.–Fri.; 1000–1600 hrs Sats.
Books, MSS., etc. Abt. 28 books/articles indexed in cat., mainly from *Sussex Archaeol Collns.*

CHICHESTER

The County Archivist, West Sussex Record Office, County Hall, West St, Chichester.
66 rs of indents of brs in Sussex made and given 1968–70 by Mr A. G. Sadler when coll material for his recent books *Lost m.b. of West Sussex* (pub 1969) and *Lost m.b. of East Sussex* (pub 1970); the books act as a cat. to the colln. Rs stored rolled and arr. under locations.
Available: Mon.–Fri. 0915–1230; 1330–1700 hrs.

LEWES

The Hon Librarian, Sussex Archaeological Society, Barbican Hse, Lewes.
Over 200 rs made at various dates, mainly Sussex examples, but some other counties also; arr. under location, some in bad repair. Two largest collns made by E. H. W. Dunkin (*q.v.*) and Mr Brown; others by various donors. Stored in portfolios at Lewes and at time of writing (Sept. 1971) being re-arranged and catd by Mrs V. B. Lamb, recently appt Hon Librarian, Other rs at Michelham Priory (near Hailsham), some on display.

*Work now (Oct. 1972) almost complete. See valuable article by Dr J. M. Blatchly SAC. LXVIII (1971 [1972]), 31–8. Illus.

Available: (by prior appointment only) most weekdays (but not weekends).

Books, MSS., etc. Society's library contains a number of books on brs, incl those by the Wallers and Rev W. F. Creeny.

WORTHING

The Curator, The Museum, Chapel Rd, Worthing.

Under 50 rs of Sussex brs made 1960s (acqd. 1965) rolled and in folders; acquired for exhib. of rs from West Sussex Churches held in 1965.

Available: 1000–1900 hrs daily in Summer, 1000–1700 hrs in Winter, Mon.–Sat.

WARWICKSHIRE

BIRMINGHAM

Reference Librarian, Birmingham Public Libraries, Birmingham.

Betw. 100–200 rs made betw. 1889 and 1923 by Francis James Thacker (*op. cit.* p 157 above) and acqd 17/4/1923; mostly stored rolled but some flat in map cabinet; arr. under county and location; ms. index of places and names; mostly Warwicks. and Worcs. examples.

Available: any time during Library hours in Local Studies Library. Weekdays 0900–2100 hrs; Sats. 0900–1700 hrs.

Dept of Archaeology, City Museum and Art Gallery, Congreve St, Birmingham.

136 rs presented by W. Bonser and Sir William Cornewall (through F. C. Morgan), all from locations outside the Midlands. At the time of writing the rubbings are being offered to various record offices and museums within the areas concerned.

Museum hours: 1000–1800 Mon.–Sat.; 1400–1730 Sun.

WARWICK

The County Archivist, Shire Hall, Warwick.

30 rs of Warwicks. brs made by Mr C. M. C. Armstrong, of Warwick and deposited 1942 (Cat. No. HR 95); one of Beauchamp brass, St Mary's, Warwick in gold finish, stored rolled; cat. for use in building.

Available: Mon.–Fri. 0900–1300, 1400–1730; Sats. 0900–1230.

Books, MSS., etc. (1) Badger, Rev E. W. *Monumental Brasses of Warwickshire.* (2) Macklin, Rev. H. W. *Monumental Brasses.*

WORCESTERSHIRE

The Keeper, County Museum, Hartlebury Castle, Kidderminster.

102 rs of Worcs. and other locations, 4 of incised stone slabs of 17th/18th cent date, 1 of br of Bishop Bocholt (1341). Lübeck; made by a Mr J. F. Parker mainly before 1930, some in 1968 given by Trustees of Tickenhill Colln at this time; others still being added. Stored rolled

or flat; inventory available on request: Museum also possesses four actual brasses of unknown origin.
Available: By prior appt only every day except Friday. 1000–1800 hrs; Sats. and Sundays 1400–1800 hrs.

SCOTLAND
The Keeper, Dept of Arts and Archaeology, Royal Scottish Museum, Chambers St, Edinburgh.
c 750 rs mostly acqd 1884 from unknown source, incl 3 of early incised slabs; arr. under county; stored rolled, cat. for use in building.
Available: (by prior appt only) 1000–1700 hrs; Mon.–Thurs., 1000–1630 hrs Fri.

WALES
Keeper of Archaeology, National Museum of Wales, Cathays Pk, Cardiff.
Over 200 rs made c 1880–1920, incl some 10 of incised slabs, no special arrangement; made by W. J. Hemp, T. A. Glenn, J. A. Bradney and others, acqd betwn. 1910 and 1935, stored rolled in wooden crates; no cat., no additions.
Available: (by prior arrangement): 1000–1700 Mon.–Sat. (1000–1800 Apr.–Sept. and Bank Holidays and Tues. following); 1430–1700 Sun.
Note: A loan exhibition, prepared by Miss J. K. Evans, Development Officer for the Council of Museums in Wales, of 40 rubbings from the above colln and some from the Newport (Mon.) Museum, is being displayed for the first time during late 1971 at the County Museum, The Castle, Haverfordwest, Pembroke. The latter Museum also sells a high quality screen-print of the 'modern' brass in St David's Cathedral (price £0.50 (plus post.)), rubbing of which is now banned. I am very grateful to Mr R. A. Kennedy, B.Litt, N.D.A., A.M.A., F.S.A.Scot., Curator of Pembroke County Museum, for the above information. The rubbing was screen printed by a local firm, owned by Mr T. C. Senior, called Visual Art Studio, 67a, Pembroke Rd, Canton, Cardiff.

Appendix II

Who was Who in Brasses and Brass Rubbing:
a Bio-bibliographical Guide.

The Appendix below has been added in order to collect together just a few of the people who have made important written or personal contributions to the history and study of monumental brasses. This includes not only the private individuals whose names frequently occur throughout this and other books, but also a few societies, institutions or manufacturers intimately connected with the preservation or manufacture of brasses during the last two hundred years or so.

I have purposely restricted my list of persons now dead in order to save embarrassing omissions of living persons. There are, of course, omissions from the list below which should, or might, have been added – the fault here is mine and not theirs. Space has also restricted the size of the list, as has the amount of information I have been able to discover about the person concerned. Some doubtless have more space than the importance of their work justifies, others far too little.

In compiling the list I have tried to set down each entry consistently, and in the references to publications to give as fuller information as possible. I have examined almost every obituary notice quoted personally (indeed of necessity) as well as trying to see or check every written work quoted under each name to ensure bibliographical accuracy. Probate and other records at Somerset House have also been consulted where possible to verify dates of death, next-of-kin, etc., in particular.

Some may question the need for such a list as this, but I hope that those seriously interested in the study of brasses will become as interested in this unexplored area of study as I have. If, at the same time, it contributes in some small way to the bibliography of monumental brasses (at which so many attempts have been made but never came to fruition) then it well be more pleasing to its compiler. There are inevitably omissions (but I hope few errors) and I shall be more than pleased to receive notes of these. Abbreviations used are as cited at the beginning of this book (pages 13 to 17).

In compiling this list it is impossible to name the many colleagues in libraries, officers and individuals of societies and institutions, as well as private individuals, who have assisted in various ways. To all those with whom I have corresponded, or from who I have requested help, I tender my sincere thanks – many of them are named in the preliminaries at the beginning of this book. The task has been a very difficult, but I sincerely hope, worthwhile one.

ADDINGTON, Rev Henry (1821–83)
Antiquary: b (?) Goldington, Beds. *s* Capt. Wm. Silvester A., R.N. *Educ* Bedford G.S.; Lincoln Coll., Oxon.; Matric 26.3.1840. BA 1843. MA 1860. Ord 1844.; C Castle Ashby, Northants. 1844–5, Harpenden, Herts. 1845–50. V Langford, Beds. 1850–53, where he built vicarage and ch sch *m* (1850) Matilda Frances, e.d. General Thomas Alex. Raynsford of Henlow Grangs, Beds. (ob. 1871), to which Henry succ. 1869; 1 *s* (*b* 1855). Early member Oxford Archit Soc where he met J. H. Parker the publisher (*q.v.*), for whom he wrote two works (nos. 1 and 2 below). Asst Boutell (1847); subscr to Haines' *Manual* (1861). Member Royal Archaeol Inst (and exhib vol of rs before their 1881 meeting at Bedford); Beds. Archit and Archaeol Soc, V.P. Archit Sectn. Early int. in brs, now chiefly remembd for his fine colln of rs, formerly in 54 large folio vols in BM (Add MS. 32490) but recently repaired and rolled; some have Arms coloured, others are cut to fit folders dest. some of value. Spec. gd. colln of rs and drwgs of Beds brs up to 1700; keen student her and geneal (see *AASRP, 34th Ann Rpt* Archit Sectn, Beds AAS, 1881–2, lxxvii) *Pubns incl* (1) Parker, J. H. (publs). *Ecclesiastical and Architectural Topography of England*, 7 pts Pt I. Beds, intro. by Rev H.A. . . . (1848) (2) *Some account of the Abbey Church of St Peter and St Paul at Dorchester, Oxford.* (Parker. 1845; later edn with add notes, 1860). (3) 'Monumental Brasses of Bedfordshire'. *AASRP*, xvii, I, 1883, 77–92 (repr *Archaeol* J, 40 (1883) 303–15).
Died: 17 Aug. 1883 at Henlow Grange, aet 63
Obit. AASRP, xvii, I, 1883, xxxv–vi (repr from *Beds Times and Indep.*, 25.8.1883).

ALEXANDER, William (1767–1816)
Artist: b Maidstone, Kent 10 Apr. *Educ* privately; RA Schools (from 1784); travelled in Far East and made reputation for drwgs of antiquities; Prof. of Drwg, Military Coll, Gt Marlow 1802–8; Keeper Prints and Drwgs BM 1806–16; apart from official commissions, he made fine pte colln of drwgs of ancient crosses and antiquities in Eng.; FRS; in Phillipp's MS 34481 at Soc of Antiq, Lond., are a series of 'dabbings' of m.b.s made by A. in black lead, and now of some historical importance. See also, SAC, XL (1932), 107.

Died: 23 July 1816 at Maidstone, Kent; *obit Gent. Mag* 86, Pt. II (July–Dec. 1816) 94, 369–71.

ANASTATIC DRAWING SOCIETY (later ILAM Anastatic Drawing Society)
Fd 1854 by Rev J. M. Gresley, MA (1816–66) who was its first editor 1854–9 when it was incorporated as above. First Hon Sec ILAM Anast. Drwg Soc Rev G. R. Mackarness, Ilam Vicarage, Ashbourne, Derbys. First issue of Journal 1859. *Object:* 'to delineate the remains of antiquity . . .' (e.g. sepulchral monuments, brasses, etc). Anastatic process was used to good effect in a number of works illus brs, incl those by Camb Camden Soc, Kite, Dunkin, Suffolk Inst. Procs; the latter two works used S. H. Cowell's Anastatic Press, Ipswich, one of best known early presses. M.S.'s *List* records issues of above Journal where illus of brs occur.

ANDRE, James Lewis (1833–1901)
Ecclesiologist and antiquary: b London. *Educ* (?) St Paul's Sch; trained as architect; a keen antiquary he contrib in later years to several journals on various matters; FSA; member Surrey and Sussex Archaeol Socs; occasional contrib to *Archaeol J and St Paul's Eccles Soc Trans; m* (c 1862), Lucy Marian (née Hartwell) who survived him; 2 *s*, 6 *dau.* He had a special interest in Sussex local history (he lived for many years at Horsham) and a number of his books of press cuttings and ms notes remain in the family. His interest in brasses appears to have begun late in life. *Pubns incl* (1) 'Notes on three Sussex brasses' *Sussex A.C.* xxxvi (1888), 172–9; (2) 'Female head-dresses exemplified by Norfolk brasses' *Norfolk Archaeol* 14 (1901), 241–62; (3) 'Female head-dresses exemplified by Surrey brasses' *Surrey A.C.* xvi (1902–3), 35–54. Both latter articles illus with line drwgs, mostly to scale, by author.
Died: Sorcelles, Horsham 9 Aug. 1901 aet 68.

ANDREWS, Herbert Caleb (1874–1947)
Ecclesiologist: b Hertford 4 Oct. *s* Robt Thornton A., architect and builder. *Educ* St Catherine's Sch, Broxbourne (Herts); S. John's Coll, Camb, adm 13/10/92. BA 1892; MA 1900. Asst Master St Cath. Sch above and Oliver's Mt. Sch, Scarboro', Yorks. Asst Keeper V&A 1899–1935 (A/Libn i/c Photo Dept). Early devotion to archaeol and allied arts; Coun. and Hon Sec (1922–47) EHAS and freq contrib to *Trans;* FSA 1931; Dir Hertford Mus., 1928–47 where he cont. research into Herts. brs begun by his uncle (W. F. Andrews) and father; most of H.C.A.'s orig. notes and rs now at Hertford Mus.;

married, he left a son and dau.; contrib to sev archaeol jnls incl *Berks A.J.*; *Walpole Soc* 8, etc and author of sev books. Member M.B.S. 1934–47. *Pubns incl* (1) 'On Lockleys and some of the Peryents' [incl notes on brs in Digswell ch Herts.] *EHAS* 7, i (1923), 56–61; (2) 'On brass of Dame Mgt. Plumbe in Wyddial Ch' [Herts] *ibid*, ii (1924–5), 140–7; (3) 'Notes on some families and brs at Gt Thurlow and Lit. Bradley, Suff.' *Suffolk Inst Procs* xx, i (1928), 43–7; (4) 'Sidelights on brs in Herts. chs' *EHAS* 8, ii (1930–31), 155 [Albury] to 13, ii (1952–4), 165 [Eastwick]; cont since latter date by R. J. Busby; (5) 'Geo. Canon, Wyddial' [Herts], *MBS* 7, ii (Dec. '35), 66–8; (6) '16th cent br in St Mary Overy (Southwark Cathedral)' *ibid*, 77; (7) 'Broxbourne Ch, Herts.; recovery of lost portion of the John Borrell br, 1531' *MBS* 7, iii (Nov. '36), 121–2; *ibid EHAS* 9, iii (1936), 356–7; (8) 'Fitz Geffrey br in Sandon Ch, Herts.' *MBS* 7, iii (Nov. '36), 136–7; *ibid* EHAS 9, iii (1936), 366–7; (9) 'Pulter family brs in Hitchin Ch, Herts.' *MBS* 7, iv (Nov. '37), 1–4; (10) 'Braughing Ch, Herts.' note only *ibid*, 169; (11) 'Layston Ch, Herts.' *ibid* 192; (12) 'Brass in Furneaux Pelham Ch, Herts.' *ibid*, vi (May '39), 279–80; (13) 'Chaworth br formerly in the Savoy Chapel, London.' *ibid* 281–3; (14) 'Lost brass at Broxbourne Ch, Herts.' *ibid* viii (Sept. '42), 353; (15) 'Saxaye br Stanstead Abbots, Herts.' *MBS* 8, ii (Dec. '44), 64; (16) 'Bostock br Wheathampstead, Herts.' *ibid*, 65. (17) 'Two altar tombs at Hitchin Church' *MBS* 8, v (Dec. '47), 192–5.
Died: Hertford 21 Dec. 1947; *obits* (1) *EHAS* 12, ii (1947–9), 20–2; (2) *Antiq J* 28 (1948), 224.

ANDREWS, William Frampton (1838–1918)
Ecclesiologist and antiquary: b Hertford 2 *s* Sam A., timber merchant (ob. 1866) and *w* Marie Anne (née Thornton). *Educ* Hertf. G.S.; Burford Hse, Hoddesdon, (Herts.) and Brighton with his brother Robert Thornton A.; joined brother in timber business on death of father. Great benefactor Hertf. town.; fd Museum '05; memb Boro. Coun. nearly 25 years; Alderman '04; Mayor '99, '03, '13; member many other committees; freq contrib to *Herts Mercury* on archaeol and other matters. Co-founder, with his brother, EHAS '98. Married, 1 *s*, 1 *dau.* Member M.B.S. '90–'14; coll valuable series rs Herts. brs now in Hertf. Mus.; his written work on brs generally lacked scholarship of his nephew Herbert C. Andrews *above*. *Pubns incl* (1) *Memorial Brasses in Hertfordshire Churches*. 1886 (rev *MBS* 2, iv, (Sept. '94), 137). 2nd rev edn (incl limited edn 50 copies on large paper), 1903 (review *MBS* 4, iv ('03), 342). (2) 'Topog collns of a Herts. archaeologist', EHAS I, ii (1900), 159–67. (3) 'Mon brs in Herts. churches; addns, etc to Haines' *List*'. *Antiq* 14 (Aug. 1886), 49–51;

(4) 'Notes on some of the memorial brs in Herts. churches'. *J Nat Soc for Pres. Memorials of the Dead*, I (1892), 19–25 [Read at 10th Ann meeting at Bishop's Stortford High Sch; exhib of rs also on view].
Died: 30 Nov. 1918 at Hertford. *Obit:*(i) EHAS VI, ii ('16–'18), 232–3 (note); (ii) *Herts Mercury* 7/12/'18, 7 (photo) (iii) *Times* 2/12/'18, 5 (f).

ARCHER, John Wykeham (1808–64)
Antiquary, engraver and artist: b Newcastle, 2 Aug. and showed early promise in drwg; apprenticed 1820 to John Scott, engr of Clerkenwell. After sev jobs with different firms, he changed from steel to wood engr, incl series of illus of old London for Wm. Twopenny (now in BM) and for Wm. Beatie's *Castles and Abbeys of England* (1844). Towards end of 1847, A. gave talk to Soc of Arts on 'Sepulchral Brasses and Incised Slabs'. Mr (later Sir) Henry Cole remarking on the talk on 8 Dec. 1847 states that 'it is about ten years since the study of brasses recommenced in this country' (the year of Queen Victoria's ascension to the throne). Archer, according to Bryan (Vol I, p 50) claimed 'to have revived the ancient practice of engraving on monumental brasses and produced several large monuments of this description from his own designs'. Boutell (*Brasses of England*, 1847) also mentions A's work as noted in n.46, Chap I above. The *DNB* says A. designed a brass for India for Lord Hastings, to commemorate the officers who fell in the battles of the Punjab; the 'Oxford' *Manual* (1848) Appx B, p 186 cites four brs designed by A. and on p 113 of intro (note q) says that A's brasses 'have a peculiar merit, although they are less like the old examples'.
Died: Kentish Town, London, 25 May 1864; *Obits:* (1) *Builder* 4/6/1864, 409; (2) *Art J* (NS)3 (1864), 243.

BADGER, Rev Edward William (1854–1921)
Teacher and author: b 25 Dec. *e.s.* E. W. Badger of Moseley, Warwicks. *Educ* privately; Univ Coll. Oxford 1874–79, BA 1878, MA 1881. Assistant Classics Master, King Edward's Sch, New St, Birmingham 1880–1912, where he was favourably remembered by all the boys for his kindly, genial manner mixed with firm discipline. Master 8th and 9th classes and later Matriculation Classes. Ordained 1893. C Acock's Green 1893–1912. R. Bradenham, Bucks. 1912–21 where he produced a number of miracle plays. Keen amateur botonist and member Assoc. Nat. Hist, Philos. and Archaeol Socs and Field Club of Midland Counties whose journal, *Midland Naturalist* he edited jointly from 1878–93; *m* Charlotte Mary who survived him.
Pubns incl (1) *Monumental Brasses of Warwickshire. Midland Natural-*

ist IX (1886) 8–11, 50–53, 78–84, 106–110, 123–26, 156–60; 183–87, 212–18, 244–49, 271–75, 298–304, 324–330. These formed the basis of his book of the same title, pub in limited edn of 100 copies (each signed and numbered) by Cornish Bros, Birmingham, 1895; regrettably it is not illus. (2) 'Our Schools. XXX: King Edward's School, Birmingham'. *School*, July, 1908. Details of his work and writings are in the Birmingham Public Libraries.
Died: 19 Jan. 1921 at Bradenham aet 66. *Obit:* (1) *Birmingham Post* 22/1/1921 (2) *King Edw. Sch Chronicle*, March, 1921, pp 62–3.

BARKENTIN & KRALL, 291, REGENT STREET, LONDON (fl. 1870–1920)
Ecclesiastical metalworkers: Specialists in silver gilt chalices and patens, but makers of many memorial brass tablets, usually cast in relief. For example of former see *Connoisseur* 165 (663), May 1967, 36–8; in 1902. Carl Krall made a fine silver gilt morse, designed by Sir John Ninian Comper (see note and illus in Peter Howell's *Victorian Churches*. R.I.B.A. 1968, pp 56–7). In the field of brasses, perhaps their most famous work is the brass of Sir Geo. Gilbert Scott (1811–78), made posthumously and exhibited at the Architectural Museum, Tufton St, Deans Yd, Westminster in May 1881. Consisting mainly of a large ornamented cross with Agnus Dei in head, within a border inscr, it has allegorical figures at the corners representing the painter, sculptor, smith and carpenter, as well as shields and other devices. In a slab of black marble 8 ft × 4½ ft, supplied by Messrs Farmer and Brindley, the brass is now in Westm. Abbey (see: *Builder* XL, No. 1999 (28 May 1881) 681). More typical examples of their work is seen in the wall plaques at St Nicholas' ch, Harpenden, Herts. (Sir John Bennet-Lawes, ob. 1900; Mary Vaughan, ob. 1901); St Mary's Chislehurst, Kent (L. W. McArthur, M.C., ob. 27 May, 1917) signed 'BARKENTIN & KRALL. LONDON. 1918'. The original co-fdr of the firm was George Slater Barkentin.

BARNARD, Ettwell Augustine Bracher (1874–1953)
Ecclesiologist, palaeographer and antiquary: b Evesham, Worcs. *Educ* privately; St Cath. Coll, Camb.; took special interest in local hist of Worcs., esp Vale of Evesham on which subj. he contrib long series of articles to *Evesham J.* betw. 1906–53; Member Worcs. Archaeol Soc from 1913; FSA 1912, serving once on Council (1925) but best known for his work on the Prattinton Colln of Worcs. Hist (1931) for the Society. His interest in palaeography was widespread and he transcribed several registers incl the *Records of K. Edward's Sch, Birmingham* (jt editor) for Vol 3 of Dugdale Soc Pubns; deputy

editor *Alumni Cantab.* (1939): also appt Keeper of Records of his old college and of Episcop. Records of Dioc. of Ely (1942). V.P. Camb. and County Folk Museum and Royal Archaeol Inst (1937–40). His interest in brs did not show itself in print until 1934 when he took over (with J. F. Parker) the series of articles below, from F. J. Thacker (q.v.) He also contrib to other antiqn journals incl SAP; Y Cymmrador; Camb. Antiq Soc Procs; Birmingham and Midland Inst Trans and Procs and Bristol and Gloucs. Archaeol Soc Trans *Pubns incl* 'Monumental Brasses of Worcs.' (with J. F. Parker) Pts III–V (1934–40) *Worcs Archaeol Soc Trans* (N.S.) IX (1934–5), 139–43, XV (1938–9), 1–9 XVI (1939–40), 1–13.
Died: 16 Feb. 1953; *obits:* (1) *Antiq J.* 33 (1953), 271, 273 (2) Trans Worcs. Archaeol Soc (N.S.) XXIX (1952), 1.

BASIRE, James, *the Elder* (1730–1802)
Wood Engraver: b 1730 *s* Isaac Basire (1704–68); Engraver to Soc of Antiquaries c 1760–1802; to Royal Soc from c 1770. Drew royal portraits and some illus of brasses for Gough's *Sepulchral Monuments* (q.v.); work freq appeared in *Archaeologia* and other archaeol pubns. His son James (see below) held a similar position. *s.a.* DNB.

BASIRE, James, *the Younger* (1769–1822)
Wood Engraver: s James Basire (above) and like him engraver to Soc of Antiq and Royal Society by whom most of his work was published. Also worked for John Carter (q.v.) His son James III (1797–1869) was the fourth holder of the above offices and also assisted Gough. An example of the work of the above is in *Archaeologia,* XV (1806), Appendix, 403–4, Plate XXXIX, showing engr of brass at Gt Saxham, Suffolk (1632) copied from impression by Craven Ord (q.v.)

BEAUMONT, Edward Thomas (1851–1931)
Author: b Oxford. Keen student of archaeol, archit and brs; at Oxford, where he spent most of his life, he devoted much of his energy to working for the George St Congregational Ch, for whom he was treasurer, teacher and later superintendent of the Sunday School at various times; curator Oxford YMCA; member Oxf. Philatelic Soc, Oxf. Archit and Hist Soc; J.P. At age of 71 entered Univ as student, but never took degree. His first book on brs. was not well received, being based too heavily on Macklin's work (pub 1907); his study of academical costume is of more value. His wide interests lead to his giving a series of talks on brasses and other matters to the Oxford Ladies Archit and Brass Rubbing Soc, incl one on 'Mediaeval Academical Habit', illus with some of his many rs (see *Berks A.J.* 24 (1918),

44) Married, he left a widow son and dau. *Pubns incl* (1) *Ancient Memorial Brasses* (1913). (2) 'Three Interesting Hants. brs'. *Hants F.C.A.S.* Vol 7 (1914) 75–80 (3) *Academical Habit illustrated by Ancient Memorial Brasses* (privately printed. 1928). Typescript; illus, photo of author on frontis.
Died: Acland Nursing Home, Oxf., 18 April 1931 aet 80.
Obit: Oxf. Times 24.4.31 p 13.

BELCHER, William Douglas (1844–1911)
Unable to discover much abt. Mr Belcher whose main work in the present context was the publication of the two works below. Unfortunately neither volume was very favourably received. Notice of intending pubn of Vol 2, appeared in *MBS* 3 (1897–9), 201, and Vol I was reviewed by Mill Stephenson (MBS 2, iv (Sept. 1894), 137) who says 'Here was a grand opportunity for the student, but of letter-press there is next to nothing, and even what there is is disfigured in places by the grossest mistakes. Many of the illustrations are unreliable, children and shields-of-arms being inserted in the wrong places and in many instances omitted altogether'. There is a second long and useful review (anonymous) in *The Builder* LV (2375), 11 Aug. 1888, 95–6; Vol II (1905) is reviewed in *MBS* 5, ii (1905), 95. Mr Belcher was a member of the Kent Archaeol Soc and the Harleian Soc. His help is acknowledged by Macklin in the intro to his *Brasses of England* (1907). When he died, probate was granted to his widow Edith Anna Belcher. *Pubns incl Kentish Brasses* Vol I, (1888), 119 p incl 109 pp of plates; Vol II (1905), vii, 148 p incl. 480 numbered plates. (Pub by Sprague & Co.)
Died: 22 June 1911 at Herne Hill.

BELOE, Edward Milligan, jnr (1871–1932)
Solicitor and antiquary: b S. Ann's Hse, Kings Lynn, Norf. *e.s.* Edw. Milligan Beloe, FSA (1826–1907) and Lydia (née Dickinson). *Educ* Privately at Hunstanton, Rugby Sch; Keen sportsman. Entered father's firm in Lynn; adm to Bar 1894; succeeded to father's large solicitor's business 1907, plus sev public offices incl Coroner for Borough. Was also Notary Public, perpetual Comm. for Oaths, Clerk to Cleave's Charity and Educ Fdn; Clerk to Trustees of Sugar's Almshouses; Hon Solicitor to Hunstanton Convalescent Home. Bought Elizabethan hse in Lynn (1911) which he restored and opened as Greenland Fishery Museum a year later; housed large colln of local antiquities, maps, mss, etc. Served short time on Town Council; declined Mayorality. Early int. in archaeol inherited from father; pubd item (1) below while at Rugby. *Member:* CUABC/MBS;

Norwich and Norf. A.S.; Camb. Antiq Soc; Royal Archaeol Inst; Brit Numismatic Soc; Hon Corr Member Brit. Archaeol Assn frequent contrib to journals of above. Served 3rd V.B.N.R. 20 yrs attg rank of Capt; T.D.; FSA; (elec 1908) and local sec for Norfolk. Pres Kings Lynn Soc of Arts and sciences. His tinted lithos of brs (and local views) were chiefly printed at own expense; see early issues *CUABC Trans* (1890's) for adverts. Married, his widow, Edith Ann, son (Stephen Edward) and dau. (Lydia) survived him. *Pubns incl:* (1) *Series of Photolithos of M.B. in Westminster Abbey . . .* (Elliot Stock. May 1898). 8 pp of Plates (one tinted) scale drwgs. (2) *Series of Photolithos. of M.B. and Matrices in Norfolk.* (Privately printed in 3 pts 1890–91). 25 plates. (3) 'Notes of some early matrices in the Eastern Counties'. *OUBRS* I,; (Feb. 1900), 35–9. (4) 'List of brs existing in the churches of St Margt. and St Nich., Kings Lynn, in the year 1724'. *CUABC* II (1893–6), 57–9.
Died: Kings Lynn Nursing Home, Friday 12 Feb. 1932.
Obit: (1) *Eastern Daily Press* 16.2.32 (2) *Times* 16.2.32, p 17e (3) *Antiq J* XII, 3, (July 1932) 350, 351. (4) *Norfolk Archaeol* 25 (1933–35), p i (note).

BIRCH, Rev Charles George Roberts (1839–1903)
Ecclesiologist; President MBS: b Sawtry, Hunts *o.s. Rev* Charles B.; Rector Sawtry All Sts (1863), Stroxton, Lincs.; Conington, Hunts.; R. Brancaster, Norf. 1868. *m* Martha Jane, *d* Rev F. Johnson of Hernington, Northants. 1 dau. Studied brs for over 40 yrs becoming great authority on subj.; often paid for restor. of brs himself. Had fine annotated edn of Haines' *Manual* (to which he was an orig subscr). Also amongst subscr to Creeny (1884); Davis, C.T. (1899); suffered much ill-health during last years of life; helped prepare and select illus for Rev Farrar's List of Norfolk brasses (1890); Member Brit. Archaeol Assn. 1879–1903, and local member of Council for Norfolk and Norfolk & Norwich Archaeol Soc. Despite the fact that he was considered to possess a knowledge of brasses 'probably greater than that of any man in England . . .' (obit, p 344), he rarely displayed it in print. *Pubns incl* (1) 'On certain brs at Necton and Gt Cressingham'. *Norf Archaeol* XII (1895), 298–303 (2) 'Brs at Scrivelsby, Lincs.' *MBS* 2 (1893–6), 107–9. (3) 'Necton and Gt Cressington brasses'. *ibid,* 179–81 (4) 'Note on the br of Dr Walter Hewke, Trinity Hall, Cambridge' *ibid,* 223–4; (5) There are several letters and notes on brasses by Rev Birch in early vols of *The Antiquary.*
Died: 8 June 1903. *Obit:* (1) MBS 4, iv (1903), 343–4 (by W.A.C.) (2) Norfolk Archaeol XV, iii (1904), p iii (note only).

BLOXAM, Matthew Holbeche (1805–88)
Solicitor, ecclesiologist and author. b Rugby, 12 May; 5 *s* Rev Richard Rouse B. (asst master Rugby Sch) and Anne (née Lawrence). *Educ* in Prep. Schs. and Grammar Sch in Rugby; Adm to Bar 1827. Clerk to Justices at Rugby 1831–71. Pubd first work on Gothic archit 1829 (which was to pass thro. 11 edns before his death) having first become interested in subject about 10 yrs before. His work was to become an important influence in the Victorian Gothic revival; he was also a keen student of local history, publishing some 200 pamphlets on this and allied subjects, incl occasionally brasses. He was a member and Hon V.P. Royal Archaeol Inst; Hon Sec (and later Pres) Warwicks. Archaeol and Nat. Hist Soc; Hon Member Yorks. Archit Soc; V.P. Worcs. Diocesan Archit and Archaeol Soc; B's help is acknowledged by Boutell (1847) and F. Hudson (1853); subscr to Waller's *Series*... (1864 ff.); FSA 1863. *Pubns incl* (1) *Principles of Gothic Architecture* (1829 *et seq*); (2) *A Glimpse at the Monumental Architecture and Sculpture of G.B., from the Earliest Period to the Eighteenth Century* (1834; rare); (3) *Notices of the Churches of Warwickshire* with Wm. Stainton 2 vols. (1847–8); (4) B. also began work on another large antiquarian work which, regrettably, was never published, viz. *Fragmenta Sepulchralia, a Glimpse at the Sepulchral and early Monumental Remains of G.B.* I have also seen references to a (?) pamphlet on 'Monumental Brasses of Warwickshire', details of which I have been unable to trace.
Died: St Matthew's Pl., Rugby 24 April 1888. *Obits: SAP.* 2 Ser XII (1887–9) 387–8; (2) *AASRP* XIX (1887–8), lxxvii, xcii; (3) *Ann Reg.* (1888), 145 (4) *B.A.A.* 44 (1888), *s.a.* Kirkby, H. T. 'Some notes on Bloxam's *Principles*'. *Archit Rev,* CIII (Jan. 292–4, 1948), 27–8 (with port, illus, brief biog and bibliog notes).

BOUTELL, Rev Charles (1812–77)
Antiquary: b St Mary Pulham, Norf. Aug. 1. *Educ* St John's Coll, Camb., BA 1834. Incorp. Trinity Coll, Oxf. 1836, MA 1836; Curate Sandridge, Herts. 1837–46. R Downham Market, Norf. 1847–50. V Wiggenhall St Mary, Norf. 1847–55; Reader St Luke's, Lower Norwood (Sy), 1860–67; Asst Minister St Stephen's, Portland Town, London. 1872–3; London Chap R.N.A.V. First joint Hon Sec St Albans Archit Soc (fd 21.10.1845) 1845–7; prepd sev papers and reports for them, incl the 3 talks which formed the basis of his famous work (No. (1) below); Member Oxf. Archaeol Soc (adm 30.4.1845), Archaeol Inst, Prov Committee (1855) to form Lond. and Middx. Archaeol Soc (Hon Sec 23.7.1857, but dismissed at 9th General (Special) Meeting 27.11.1857 in storm of protest over his handling of

financial affairs of society, to whom he had to refund moneys owing (see; *LAMAS Procs* I, 203)). Edited journal connected with Navy in 1870's. *Pubns incl* (1) *M.B. and Slabs* . . . (1847); first issued in parts. (2) *M.B. of England* . . . (1849); first issued in 12 pts. (3) 'On Sepulchral Brs and their Art-Manufacture' [Pts 1–111] *Builder* XII (611), 21.10.1854, 542–3; (613), 4.11.54, 568–70; (614), 11.11.54, 578–80. [repr of lecture given 18.9.54]. (4) 'M.B. of London and Middx.' *LAMAS* I (1855–9), 67–112. (5) 'On M.B. with special notice of that at Stoke D'Abernon . . .' *SAC* I (1858) 213–35. Many illus (some coloured); also pub sev bks on heraldry, archaeology; contrib to most of impt archaeol and art jnls of time. For contemp reviews of (1) above see: (a) *A.J.* VI (1847), 91 (b) *Athen,* 1026 (26.6.47), 680 (c) *J Design & Manuf* I (Mar. Aug. 1849), 125–6. *Died:* 18 Portsdown Rd, London 31 July 1877, aet 64. *Obit:* (1) *LAMAS* N.S. I (1877), 209, 316. (2) *Art J* (N.S.) 16 (1877), 309; (3) *B.A.A.* 34 (1878), 264 (4) *Athen* 11 Aug. 1877.

BRISCOE, John Potter (1848–1926)
Librarian and antiquary: b Lever Bridge (Nr Bolton), Lancs. 20 July. *e.s.* John Daly B. *Educ* privately by his father, Bolton Church Inst; pupil teacher St George's Nat Sch, Bolton. Asst Librn Bolton P.L. 10.12.1866–69. City Librn Nottingham P.L. 1869 – Dec. 1916 (being selected out of 153 candidates!); Consulting Librn 1917; Council Member Lib Assn, Vice-Pres. 1891–1920; co-founder N Midland Lib Assn; fd first public lending lib for children 1882.; fd *Notthm. Lib Bull,* July 1896. Council Member Thoroton Soc; FRS Lit, F.R Hist Soc, Hon FLA; active Freemason. Author of several books on local history, folklore, freq contrib to journals of above societies and editor *Notts. and Derbys. N. &.Q.;* antiqn editor *Notts. Guardian.* Married. his son, Walter Alwyn, succeeded him as Chief Librn of Nott'gh'm *Pubns incl* (1) *M.B. of Nottinghamshire* (with Rev H. E. Field). Pt I 1904. No further parts pubd; review in *MBS Trans* 5 (1904–9), p 99, criticises its 'misleading and irritating headings and lack of titles to illus'. (2) 'Peckham Mon br. in Ossington Church' [Paper read . . . 4th Sept. 1902]. *Thoroton Soc Trans* VI, 65–8. Illus.
Died: Addison St, Nott' ghm., 7.1.1926 aet 78. *Obit:* (1) *LAR* (N.S.) XXVIII, iv, March 1926, 5–6 (by L.S.J.[ast]) *port.* (2) *Notthm. J.,* 8.1.1926, p 9 (with photo.)

BROWN, Arthur Henry (1830–1926)
Musician and ecclesiologist. b Brentwood, Essex 24 July. *Educ* privately, he became an accomplished church musician and a keen student of poetry, local history and antiquities. Interest in brs began c 1848 and

continued all his life; his last rubbing was made 16.7.1924. After his death his colln of some 800 rubbings, mounted and rolled (mostly of Essex and E Anglican brs) with catalogue and ms notes, given to Essex Archaeol Soc of which B. had long been a member; most of the rs dated. He married Hilda Mary Agnes (née Cook) who survived him. *Pubns incl* 'Some curious brasses in Essex' *Churchwoman*, 16 Dec. 1898.
Died: 12 Crown St, Brentwood, 15 Feb. 1926; *Obits:* (1) EAST (NS) 19, iv (1929), 321–3 (by G. Montague Benton); (2) *Church Times* 19.2.1926.

BUCKLER, John Chessell (1793–1894)
Architect and topographical artist: b Bermondsey *e.s.* John Buckler, FSA (1770–1851); Exhib Roy Acad betw 1810–44; did much work on colleges at Oxford and helped in restoration of Lincoln and Norwich Cath.; second to Sir Charles Barry in competition for design of Houses of Parliament after fire of 1834. Many of his topog sketches in BM, Bodleian. The Herts. C.R.O. have a set of drwgs of Herts. Churches etc (given 1932), incl a number showing brasses, slabs or monuments. Some of B's letters of 1821–36 in Lewisham Central Lib. Died with effects of only £28 3*s* 10*d* which were granted to Charles Alban Buckler, Surrey Herald extraordinary.
Died: 5.1.1894 aet 100, Melbury, Cowley St John, Oxon. *Obits:* (1) *Athen*, 3456, 20.1.1894, 91. (2) *Ann Reg* (NS) 1894, 139 (note).

BURRELL, Sir William (1732–96)
Antiquary. b Leadenhall St, London 10 Oct.; 3 *s* Peter B. of Beckenham, Kent; *Educ* Privately; St John's Coll, Camb., LLB (1755); LLD (1760); Commissioner of Excise from 1774, practising chiefly in Admiralty courts; *m* (1773) Sophia (née Raymond). 2 *s*, 2 *dau*; Bart. 1789. FSA, FRS. Compiled valuable ms history of Sussex, and commissioned drwgs by S. H. Grimm (q.v.) and others, of monuments, brasses, etc. Huge folios incl Bodiam and other Sussex ch now in BM Add M.S. 5697, f. 25; some of his notes transcribed for Sussex Archaeol Soc by E. H. W. Dunkin (*q.v.*)
Died: Deepdene, Surrey 20 Jan. 1796. *Obit. Ann. Reg.* 38 (1796), p 56. *See also:* (1) DNB. (2) Lower, MA – *Worthies of Sussex* (pub 1865), pp 131–3.

CAMBRIDGE CAMDEN SOCIETY (Later The Ecclesiological Society)
Fd 1839 as 'a small association of mutual friends resident in the University', it was soon to become, chiefly through its Journal the

Ecclesiologist, a short lived but powerful arbiter over the design of Anglican churches. One of its first secretaries was Rev Benjamin Webb (1819–85), who, with his friend John Mason Neale (1816–66), was largely responsible for founding the Society; its first president was Archdeacon Thorpe. In 1848 it became the Ecclesiological Society; other close associates were A. J. Beresford-Hope (1820–87) and F. A. Paley (1815–88); Webb remained as secretary both at Cambridge and later when the Soc moved to London. In the present context the Society is best known for its publication betw 1840 and 1846 of the curious work *Illustrations of the Monumental Brasses of Great Britain.* Issued in six parts between abt May 1840 and Feb. 1846 its 24 illustrations vary in quality and production the best being those engraved by C. Hullmandel (q.v.) eg. Abp. Harsnett (1631), Chigwell, Essex; Prior Nelond (1433), Cowfold, Sx.; edited by J. M. Neale, contributors incl C. H. Hartshorne (q.v.), the letterpress being of varying usefulness. For useful account of work see 'Bibliographical Notes' by Ralph Griffin (*MBS* 5 (1904–9), 180–5).

CAMBRIDGE UNIVERSITY ASSOCIATION OF BRASS COLLECTORS (CUABC)

According to Stewart Fiske (see below) the Society was apparently the result of 'the unorganised efforts of a small body of undergraduates', who issued their first printed notice in March 1887, which is recorded in *The Antiquary* of that month. The first recorded general meeting was held on 3 June, 1887, and the following November the first issue of the *Transactions* was published. Life Membership (for corresponding membs) in 1888 cost 5/– p.a., plus *6d* for each of papers issued to members (see: 'A Brass Society' letter from Andrew Oliver dd 12.3.1888 *Archit Assn Notes* II, 13 (Apr. 1888), 248). Full ann membp cost 2/*6d.* p.a. Amongst prominent early members were Mill Stephenson, Rev H. W. Macklin, Rev R. W. M. Lewis, Rev W. F. Creeny (first President), Rev C. G. R. Birch, H. K. St J. Sanderson, and Sir Alfred Scott-Gatty (Consulting Herald). One of their chief aims was to draw up a revised list of brs to up-date Haines, for which Rev H. W. Macklin (1887–94) and later Mill Stephenson (from 1894) were General Editors. The Society also offered advice to clergy and others on the care of brasses (sometimes with amusing results as the *Trans* show), as well as issuing pamphlets and notes incl *Hints for the Discovery and Description of M.B.'s.* Their unfortunate choice of name gave rise to some ribald comment and prompted widening their activities and membership in 1893 to form the present Monumental Brass Society in 1894. For further info see: (A) 'A Bibliographical Note' by Stewart Fiske of Mobile, Alabama, U.S.A. (written c 1907).

Unpublished ms written for *Notes and Queries* now in Univ Museum of Archaeol and Ethnology, Cambridge; (B) Rev R. W. M. Lewis 'The early days of our Society' *MBS* 8, v (Dec. 1947), 161–4; (C) Stephenson, Mill. 'A Society for the better preservation of m.b.'s' *MBS* 2, iv (Sept. 1894), 138–40; (D) V. J. B. Torr 'Brasses and the Mon Br Soc' *Amateur Hist* I, v (Apr.–May 1953), 159–62.

CARTER, John (1748–1817)
Architectural draughtsman; engraver. b London 22 June. *s* Benjamin Carter; *Educ* privately in Battersea; Kenington Lane. Aged abt 12 he was apprenticed to his father (who died 1764); from 1764–c 1774 worked for surveyor and mason named Dixon; 1780 appt draughtsman and engr to Soc of Antiq; FSA March 1795; worked for number of years for Rich. Gough (q.v.). Pubd first imp works betw 1780 and 1794. Made fierce attack on those destroying ancient monuments and sculpture in *Gent Mag.* Ill health during last year of life ended his activities; he was unmarried. His pubd drwgs of brs are generally of excellent quality, though many more are unpublished in the 26 vols of sketches and drwgs sold at his death. He exhib many works at the RA, Soc of Artists and Free Soc of Artists betw 1765 and 1794. *Pubns incl:* (1) *Specimens of English Ecclesiastical Costume from the earliest period down to the sixteenth century, selected from sculpture, painting, and brasses* . . . (1817); (2) *Specimens of Gothic architecture and Ancient Buildings in England* . . . 4 vols (1824); (3) *Specimens of Ancient sculpture and Painting* . . . 2 vols (1780–94); (4) *Views of Ancient Buildings in England* . . . 6 vols (1786–93).
Died: Pimlico, London. 8 Sept. 1817 aet 69.

CAVE, Charles John Philip (1871–1950)
Meteorologist and author; Vice-Pres. MBS: b London 1 May. *e.s.* L. T. Cave and *w* Lucy (née Greenwood). *Educ* Oratory Sch Edgbaston, Bhm.; Trinity Coll Camb. BA 1893. MA 1896. *m* (1895) Wilhelmine (née Kerr) ob. 1944. 4 *s.* 1 *dau.* (who married P. W. Kerr); FSA (1926), J.P. (Hants.) 1906; FRMetS. (Pres 1913–15; 1924–6); FRAstronS; Royal Photo Soc; V.P., R.N.L.I., Temp. Capt R.E.; V.P., MBS.Wrote many books and articles on roof bosses, and some on meteorology. Early member MBS (from 1891) and close friend of O. J. Charlton (q.v.). *Pubns incl* (1) 'Brasses of Cambs.' with O. J. Charlton and R. A. S. Macalister. *MBS* 2 (1893–6), 174–9, 237–75, 307–14; 3 (1897–9), 2–30, 88–106; 4 (1900–3), 60–78, 176–84; 5 (1904–9), 8–16, 39–48 (not completed). (2) 'List of Hants. brasses' *MBS* 5, 247–91, 295–325, 343–71; 6 (1910–13), 1–39, 121–57. (3) 'Note on the distribution of m.b. in England'. *MBS* 3, 109–111, (4)

'A Winchester Indent' *ibid* 8, *v* (Dec. 1947) 207; (5) 'A recovered brass at Itchen Stoke, Hants'. *MBS* 9, i (Feb. 1952), 44.
Died: 8 Dec. 1950; *Obit:* (1) (note) *MBS* 8 viii (Feb. 1951), 388 (2) *Antiq J* 31 (1951) 253–4.

CHARLTON, Oswin John (1871–1941)
Solicitor and antiquary: b Newcastle-upon-Tyne 20 Aug.; 3 *s.* Dr Edw. Charlton, MD. *Educ* Oratory Sch, Edgbaston; Gonville and Caius Coll, Camb. 1890–94; BA (1894), MA and LL.M (1925). Articled with Dees and Thompson of Newcastle; later estab own solicitor's office in town. *m* (1919) Mary Ellen (née O'Keefe). 2 *s*, 1 *dau;* began collect. rs while graduate with C. J. P. Cave and R. A. S. Macalister; early member CUABC (1890); Hon Managing Sec and Treas. 1891–3. V.P. MBS 1893 to death. Helped produce list of Cambs. br; many of his rs used to illus *MBS Trans* and *Portfolio.* When he died, his fine colln of rs and books on br given to Newcastle Univ by brother G. V. Charlton. (Cat pub 1967). Active member Soc of Antiq Newcastle-upon-Tyne (elec 24.2.1892); Hon Sec 1925–34; V.P. 1935; FSA London. (elec 14.1.1926); Member Law Soc Newcastle-upon Tyne; V.P. 1924–5, Pres 1931–2. Council Member Kings Coll, Newcastle. *Pubns:* see mostly under CAVE, C. J. P., but also: (1) 'Notes on a matrix in the Church of St Andrew, Newcastle-upon-Tyne'. *MBS* 2, v (Aug. 1895), 182–3. (2) 'Trinity brass at Newcastle-upon-Tyne'. *MBS* VII, i (Dec. 1934), 33–4.
Died: 10 May 1941. *Obit:* (1) *MBS Trans* VII (viii) Sept. 1942, 373–4 (by C. J. P. Cave). (2) *Archaeol Aeliana* (4th Ser) XX, 1942, 8–10. (by C. J. P. Cave; portrait f.p. 8).

CHRISTY, Robert Miller (1861–1928)
Antiquary and ecclesiologist: b Chignall St James, Essex 24 May. *Educ* Epping; Bootham Sch, York.; 1880–87 went to Canada where he pubd first book (1885); on return to Eng., devoted himself to study of Essex history; early member Essex Archaeol Soc and Council Member 1898–1928, Pres 1905–6, one of fdrs Essex Field Club; 1889, joined firm of printers Hayman, Christy & Lilley, where he met W. W. Porteous with whom he is most closely associated; classfd. Bryant & May's Match Museum at Bow and produced catalogue. Freq contrib to DNB, Essex VCH and journals below. Joined CUABC 1891; F.L.S. A proof copy of Vols I and II of the complete edn of Christy and Porteous' work on Essex brs is in Soc of Antiq Library. Of his many works on brs the following are amongst the most important. All are in conj. with Porteous. *Pubns incl:* (1) 'On some interesting Essex brasses' *EAST* (N.S.) 6 (1897), 146–70; 7

(1898–9), 1–31; 207–48; 8 (1900–2), 15–54, 249–85; 9 (1903) 22–67; 10, i (1907), 181–227; 11, ii (1909), 101–46, iv (1910), 321–34; 12 (1912), 225–53. (all these articles are well illustrated and referenced); (4) 'Some Essex brasses recently refixed' *EAST* (N.S.) 8, iv (1902), 363–8 (5) 'Some interesting Essex brasses'. *Essex Rev* 10 (Apr.1910), 84–100 [deals mainly with lettering used betw. c 1315 and 1638]. (6) 'Some Essex brs illustrative of Elizabethan Costume'. *Antiquary* 38 (1902), 6–10, 44–7. (7) 'Some Essex brs illus of Stuart Costume'. *Antiquary* 39 (1903), 113–8, 175–8, 233–8. (All the above articles are well illustrated) (8) 'Mon Brs of Essex' with W. W. Porteous and E. B. Smith. Cont in: A. C. Kelway (ed) *Memorials of Old Essex* (G. Allen. 1909) pp 118–37. Illus; (9) 'Mon brs of Colchester' *EAST* (N.S.) 13 (1915), 38–52.
Died: 25 Jan. 1928 *Obits:* (1) *Essex Rev* 37 (1928), 58–62 (with photo.) (2) *Essex Nat* 22 (1926–9), 110 (1) *EAST*, (N.S.) 19 (1927–8) 138 (4) *Times* 1.2.28 p 9 (d).

CLAYTON, Rev Henry James (fl 1890–1920)
Ecclesiologist: Educ privately; King's Coll, London, winning Trench and Barry Prizes; Theological Associate (1st class), 1897; *Ord* Deacon 1897; priest 1898 (Rochester); curate Aylesford 1897–9; Stone, 1900–02; Sub-Warden, St Mary's Stone 1900–02; Curate St John Evan., E. Dulwich 1902–4; Lecturer Ch Comm for Ch. Defence and Ch Instruction 1904. He was living in Mulgrove Rd Croydon 1907–9. He was Vicar of Bognor, Sx. in 1919. Author of sev books on Church Defence and dogma, and two on eccles. dress for Alcuin Club (fd 1897). He joined MBS 1898 being Hon Auditor 1906–14; his book (No. 1 below)acknowledges help from sev MBS members incl C. J. P. Cave, M. Christy, Cecil Davis, W. E. Gawthorp, Rev R. W. M. Lewis and Mill Stephenson. *Pubns incl* (1) *Ornaments of the Ministers as shown on English Monumental Brasses.* (Alcuin Club Collns No. 22. 1919); (2) 'Cassock and gown' [a survey of clerical dress] *ed* R. M. Woolley (Alciun Club Tract. No. 18 1929).

CLINCH, George (1860–1921)
Antiquary: b Borden, Kent 9 Feb. *Educ* privately, showing early interest in archaeol. Worked for time in BM Lib; Clerk to Council of Soc of Antiq from 9.12.1895 and from 1910 Librarian as well. Spec. int. in prehist archaeol, Kentish and London hist; ecclesiology and costume. FGeolSoc, FSAScot.; Member Surrey and Kent Archaeol Socs. Regular contrib to Croydon N.H. and Sc. Soc Procs and Trans; Archaeol Cant.; J. Roy Anthrop. Inst; Surrey A.C. *Pubns incl* (1) *Old English Churches* (1900. 2nd edn 1903) – cont. good general hist

of brs (pp 196–241), though some of illus poor. See note and list of illus. *MBS* 4 (1900–3), 94–5. (2) *English Costume* . . . (1909). Valuable general history, cont many illus from brs of good quality. *Died:* 2 Feb. 1921 *Obits:* (1) *Times* 7.2.1921, 12 (b) (2) *Antiq J* I (1921), 145, 165, 266, 269.

CONNOR, Arthur Bentley (1880–1960)
Artist, ecclesiologist and teacher. President MBS: b 21 Sept., Clapham, London. *s* J. H. T. Connor, MRCS. *Educ* privately; Haileybury 1894–96; Heatherley Sch 1896–1900; Royal Acad Schs. 1900 *ff.* Exhib RA many times. Teacher 1914–38 Petergate Sch, Weston-super-Mare (H/M 1921–38) where he met his wife Kathleen (née Wilkins). Int. in brs began when schoolboy, made special study of Somerset brs; devised special method of making rs of 'modern' brs; V.P. MBS. '46–55; Pres '55–60; member Somerset Archaeol and N.H. Soc from 1922. His dau Miss I. K. Connor married 1959. *Pubns incl* (1) 'M.B. of Somerset'. *Procs Som. A.N.H.S.* 72 (1931) – 98 (1955) in 22 pts. with *Index*, 103 (1958–9), 72–5. (Reprinted in one vol with new biog intro by Paul Corbould. Kingsmead Reprints. 1970). (2) 'A plea for late inscriptions' *MBS* VII, i (Dec. 1934), 37; (3) 'Half-effigy in Academical Costume at W. Monkton, Som.' *MBS* 8, ii (Dec. 1944), 67–8; (4) 'Half-effigy at W. Monkton, Som.' [add note] *ibid,* iii (Dec. '45), 102; (5) 'An 18th cent brass' *MBS* 8, vi (Dec. 1948), 299.
Died: Kingswood, Sy., 28 March 1960 aet 79; *Obits:* (1) *MBS* 9, viii (Dec. 1961) 409–10 (by G. H. S. B[ushnell]), with photo.; (2) *Procs Som. ANHS* 104 (1959–60), 147. *s.a.* (1) P. Corbould's biog intro to repr of Mr Connor's articles above, pp vii–x. (2) *Haileybury Register 1862–1961*), pp 113–4.

COTMAN, John Sell (1782–1842)
Artist: b 16th May the son of a wealthy silk merchant. *Educ* Norwich G.S.; came to London c 1799; exhib RA 1800, Brit Inst, Old Water Colour Soc etc. Member Norwich Soc of Artists; strongly influenced by his friend Dawson Turner, a Yarmouth banker and antiquary of note, at whose instigation C undertook his now famous drwgs of Norfolk and Suffolk brasses between 1812–22; according to Rienaecker (No. 2 in list of sources below) Cotman undertook this work for purely financial reasons, making the original drwgs in pencil then transferring them to printing plates. Add notes in Turner's own copy of the Norfolk volume of drwgs are descr. by late Rev C. L. S. Linnell (q.v.) By his wife Ann (née Miles) C. had 5 children, incl Edmund Miles Cotman who himself to become an artist of note. *Pubns incl*

Engravings of the most remarkable of the Sepulchral Brasses of Norfolk . . . (1819); (2) *ibid, Suffolk Brasses* . . . (1819); (3) Engravings of sepulchral brasses in Norfolk and Suffolk . . . 2nd edn 2 vols (1838–9). *s.a.* GRIFFIN, R. H. – *Cotman's Suffolk Brasses, 1819* (Privately printed. 1937).
Died: 24 July 1842. *See* (1) KITSON, S. O. – *Life of John Sell Cotman* (1937); (2) RIENAECKER, V. – *John Sell Cotman 1782–1842* (F. Lewis. 1953); (3) COOPER, F. C. 'Norwich School of Artists' *E Anglian Mag* Feb. 1948, 278–85; Mar. 1948, 347–51.

COX, SONS, BUCKLEY & CO. LTD, LONDON. (fl c 1860–1915)
Ecclesiastical metalworkers: Fd mid-19th cent as Messrs Cox & Sons, ecclesiastical furnishers of 28 Southampton St, London by Edw. Young Cox. Later took over supply of materials for decoration of churches, incl church plate designed by such well known artists as Butterfield, Street, Burgess and Keith. Also made many memorial brasses and plaques, examples of their work being widespread throughout London and the south-east. By 1914 had moved to 10 Henrietta St, London, W.C., but appear to have left by 1918. In 1893 another firm, Cox & Edgley Ltd, 69 Berners St, London, appear in the *P.O. London Directory* as 'Memorial Brass Engravers', and may well be connected with the above. Typical examples of former's work in Christchurch Priory, Hants., one in memory of Sir Percy F. Shelley (1889), son of the poet; another to Lt. Col. C. L. (1908) and Charles G. Allan (1911), Chislehurst (St Mary's Church), Kent.

CREENY, Rev William Frederic (1825–97)
Ecclesiologist; President M.B.S. b Portaferry, Co. Down, N. Ireland 19 May. *Educ* St John's Coll Camb., BA 1853; MA 1860; C. St Mark's, Lakenham, Norf. 1853–55; Wellingborough, Northants. 1855–9; Chap to Bishop of St Helena, 1859–62, and St Leonard's, Is. of Ryde, Sydney, Aust., 1862–72; C. St John's, Upper Norwood, Surrey, 1873–4; Soham, Cambs. 1874–6; V. St Michael-at-Thorn, Norwich 1876–97. Keen musician. FSA elec. 14.1.1886, adm 4.5.1886 (see *SAP* 2 ser XI (1885–7), 139); exhib and spoke abt rs to Soc on many occasions. 'Fellows will remember the quaint way in which he described the monuments, and his humorous accounts of his difficulties in the pursuit of his work'. (obit *S.A.P.*); Member Norf. and Norwich Archaeol Soc, M.B.S.; Pres CUABC; Pres M.B.S. 1894–7. One of leading authorities of all time on continental brasses and incised slabs. On his death his colln of rs willed to BM, but some of those not reqd by BM went to Strangers Hall, Norwich in 1901 (with those of Rev C. R. Manning). A brass to his memory, engr by W. R. Weyer of

Norwich, and erected from 'Creeny Memorial Fund' set up by M.B.S. (See *MBS Trans* 3 (1897–9), 66), is on chancel wall of St Michael-at-Thorn, unveiled 21 June 1898; this suffered some damage when the church was bombed in World War II. *Pubns incl* (1) *Book of Facsimiles of Monumental Brasses on the Continent of Europe* (1884); (2) *Illustrations of Incised Slabs on the Continent of Europe* (1891). *Reviews of* (1) *Athen* 2997 (Apr. 4, 1885), 445–6; *Archael J* XLII (1885), 123–32; of (2) *Archael J* XLVIII (1891), 476–82 (by 'A.H' [artshorne]). (3) 'Brass of Leonardus Betten, 1607 . . . Musée Commonal Archael, Ghent' *CUABC* No. 7 (Feb. 1890), 2–6.
Died: 8 Orford Hill, Norwich, 18 Apr. 1897; *Obits:* (1) *SAP*, 2 ser XVI (1895–7) 364–5; (2) *MBS* 3, i (Apr. 1897), 1–2; (3) *Ann Reg* (N.S.), 1897, 153 (note).

CULLUM, Sir John (1733–85)
Antiquary: b Hawsted, Suff. 21 June. *e.s.* Sir John Cullum, 5th Bart (ob. 1774) and *w* Susanna (née Gery). *Educ* K. Edward VI Sch, Bury St Edmunds; Catherine Hall, Camb. 1756–8; R. Hawsted 1762–74; V Gt Thurlow, Suff. 1774–85. Bart 1774. FSA 1774; FRS 1775. Collected much antiq^{n}. material for history of Suffolk. Wrote *History of Hawsted and Hardwick* (pub 1784). Inspired Rich. Gough (q.v.) to write his *Sepulchral Monuments*, and with Gough and Craven Ord (q.v.) perfected a system of taking impressions of brs 'rolled-off' the top of the original plate; their coll^{n} is now in BM. For full details of the Cullum/Ord/Douce coll^{n} (Add MS 32478/9) see article by late V. J. B. Torr 'A Guide to Craven Ord' *MBS* IX, ii (Oct. 1952), 80–91; IX, iii (1954), 133–45. Cullum also acquired some of Thomas Martin's (1697–71) notes on Suffolk according to the former's obituary in the *Gent Mag*, which are recorded in *Brit Topog* Vol II, pp 242, 247. Martin is accredited with making the earliest surviving 'rubbing' (c 1764) – see p 79 above. Cullum married (1765) Peggy (née Bisson) who died 1810; his diaries and letters have survived.
Died: Hardwick Hse, near Bury 9 Oct 1785 (bur. at Hawsted). *Obits:* (1) *Gent Mag* 55 Pt 2 1785, p 836. *s.a.* DNB for full account and list of principle works.

DART, Rev John (ob. 1730)
Antiquary: Little known of early life; perpetual Curate, Yateley, Hants. 1728–30. Wrote some poor poetry, but best known for his *History and Antiquities of the Cathedral Church of Canterbury* (1726); and, *Westmonasterum, or, the History and Antiquities of the Abbey Church of St Peter, Westminster* (2 vols 1742), in which the notes and

engr of monuments and brasses (many since lost or mutilated) are the most valuable part, though of little artistic merit.
Died: Sandhurst, Berks., Dec. 1730.

DAVIDSON-HOUSTON, Constance Isabella Barton (1875–1970)
Dau Prof. Robert Caesar Childers (1838–76), oriental scholar; her brother was Robt. Erskine Childers (1870–1922), author of *The Riddle of the Sands; m* 11.2.1907 Lt Col. Charles Elrington Duncan Davidson-Houston, DSO (1873–1922), LtCol. Indian Army (see *Burke's L.G.* 18th edn Vol 2, p 319). Member Sussex Archaeol Soc 1924–50; Member M.B.S. from 1934 (Hon Member at time of death). She made a fine colln of rubbings of Sussex m.b. on which she was an authority; she usually wrote using her husband's initials, viz. C. E. D. Davidson-Houston, illus her work with her own rubbings.
Pubns incl: (1) 'Military costume on m.b.' *Sussex Co. Mag* 3 (1929) 560–64; (2) 'Female dress on Sussex brasses' *ibid* 6 (1932) 261–23 [21 illus] (3) 'Sussex monumental brasses'. *Sussex Archaeol Collns* (Pt I), LXXVI (1935), 46–8, [incl gen. bibliog of brs]; (Pt II) LXXVII (1936), 130–94; (Pt III) LXXVIII (1937), 63–125; (Pt IV) LXXIX (1938), 74–130; (Pt V) LXXX (1939), 93–147. (see also an 'Addenda' by R. Griffin, *Sussex A.C.* LXXXVI (1947), 118–25).
Died: 21 Feb. 1970.

DAVIS, Cecil Tudor (1854–1922)
Librarian, genealogist and author. b Upton St Leornards, Nr Gloucester. *Educ* Payswick G.S.; La Villette, Yverdon, Switz.; Cheltenham G.S.; Univ Coll; Dublin; G.S. teacher for 30 yrs; 1883–6 Snr Officer B'mgham Ref. Lib, Boro' Librn Wandsworth 1.12.1886–31.12.1920; *m* (1) Fanny Rachel (née Carr) – *5 s,* 1 *dau*; (2) Cecile Mary (née Bailey) of St Martin's, Jersey (1915); Member Archaeol Sectn. B'mgham and Midland Inst, also serving on Comm; Bristol and Gloucs. Archaeol Soc, Surrey Archaeol Soc (local sec for Wandsworth); Hon Corresp Memb B.A.A.; member Ex-Libris Soc (fd 1891); CUABC (from 1887); Hon Sec and Treasurer, Hon Librn and for time Hon Auditor MBS. Locally he was also Hon Sec and Governor Rumford Tech. Inst; on Comm Putney Sch of Art; Special Constable 1914–18; C/Warden St Margaret's Ladywood and Wandsworth Parish Ch (2 yrs); sidesman at latter 20 yrs; lay reader St Stephen's Mission Ch, Wandsworth; diocesan reader for Southwark; Editor *Wandsworth N. & Q.* Pubd many papers and articles on antiquarian and geneal. matters; transcribed Wandsworth C/Warden's Accounts pubd in *SAC* Vols 18–21, 24. *Pubns incl* (1) 'M.B. of Herefordshire

and Worcs.' *Birm & Midland Inst Trans* XII (1881), 52–75 (later re-issued as pamphlet, 1885); (2) 'MB in the Old or West Church, Aberdeen'. *MBS* 3 (1897–9), 183–6; *Archaeol. J.* 51 (1893–4), 76–80 (3) *M.B. of Gloucestershire* (1899 repr. 1969; orig pubd *Gloucs. N. & Q.* Vols 6 and 7 (1894–99)); (4) 'Zoology on brs, chiefly from Gloucs. examples' *BAA* (N.S.) 7 (1901), 189–204; repr *MBS* 4 (1901–3) 79–92; most of the above articles appeared previously in various Midland newspapers and journals incl *Gloucs. J.* June 1882–Sept. 1885; *Worcs. Herald* Mar.–Dec. 1883; *Evesham J. and Four Shires Advert* July 1886 *et seq;* (5) 'Merchants' Marks' *BAA* XLIX (1893) 45–54 *illus.*
Died: West Hill, Wandsworth 29 May 1922; *obit: Wandsworth Boro' News.* 2.6.1922.

DAVY, David Elisha (1769–1851)
Antiquary and collector: b ? Rumburgh, Suffolk. *Educ* Yoxford; Pembroke Hall, Camb. BA. 1790. FLS; succeeded to his uncle's estates at Yoxford (1803); Magistrate and Receiver-General for Suffolk (1795 +). Left Yoxford for Ufford and devoted himself to genealogical and antiquarian studies of Suffolk history. The DNB says that Davy's MSS are 'remarkable for their neatness and admirable arrangement'. Frequent contrib to *Gent Mag, Topog & Geneal,* etc. In 1852 his MSS and two cases of rubbings of Suffolk brasses given to BM (Add MS 32483–4).
Died: a bachelor and intestate at Ufford (near Woodbridge), Suffolk, 15.8.1851, aged 82. *Obit:* (Note) *Ann Reg* XCII (1851), 321.

D'ELBOUX, Raymond Herbert (1894–1961)
Antiquary; teacher; Vice-Pres M.B.S.: b 37 Halden Rd, Wandsworth 6 Jan.; *y.s.* Herbert Clare and Lydia Alice (née Kent). *Educ* County Sch, Beckenham 1905–12; Strand Sch 1912–14; Kings Coll, Lond., St John's Coll, Camb. 1919; BA 1921, MA 1945. Served E. Kent Regt 1914–18, awarded MC in France; Asst Keeper of Archaeol Nat. Museum of Wales 1921–4; teacher Bexhill G.S. 1931–57. Joined M.B.S. 1942; Council Member 1943–52; Hon Editor 1946–54; V.P. 1952–61; FSA 1942; Member Kent Archaeol Soc 1917–35 re-joined 1943; Council Member 1946–56; Hon Gen Sec 1950–51; Member Sussex Archaeol Soc from 1931; Hon Sec 1951–7; Hon Sec Harleian Soc 1947–61. Regular contrib to journals of above, with special knowledge of heraldry and genealogy on brasses; also contrib to *Archaeol Camb.* (esp 7th ser 1921–8) and *Archaeol J,* mainly on Welsh archaeology. Fine heraldic artist.
His private library incl a copy of Weever's *Funeral Monuments.* (1631), annotated by Sir Edward Dering (q.v.) *m* (1922) Eleanor

Mary Eliz. (née de Trafford) who died 1955. 2 dau. *Pubns incl* (1) 'Wardiewe brass at Bodiam, Sx.' *MBS* 8, i (1943) 10–16; (2) 'Stanstead Abbots [Herts.]' *ibid* 30–32; (3) 'An alphabetical list of post-Reformation brs of known authorship' (see under Esdaile, K. A. item 5); (4) 'Dual de Luda Casement' *MBS* 8, iii (Dec. 1945), 79–81; (5) 'Brass of Wenllian Walsche at Llandough'. *ibid* 94–5; (6) 'Commemorative Brass to Bishop R. W. Walpole from the Cloister at Strawberry Hill'. [with A. R. Wagner] *ibid* 99–102; (7) 'Rochester Cathedral indents' *MBS* 8, iv (Dec. 1946), 133–7; (8) 'External brasses' [Pt I] *ibid*, 150–7 [Pt II] 8, V (Dec. 1947), 208–19 (9) 'Dering brasses . . .' *Antiq J* 27 (Jan.–Apr. 1947) 11–23; (10) 'Sussex Mon Brs' *Sussex A.C.* 86 (1947), 118–25 [addenda]; (11) 'Reproduction of E. Anglian brasses'. *E. Anglian Mag* 6 (12), Aug. 1947, 653–7; (12) 'Lost brass of Sir Roger Somerville of Burton Agnes, York' [with H. S. London] *MBS* 8, vi (Dec. 1948), 260–63; (13) 'Unrecorded brasses in Kent' *MBS* 8, viii (Dec. 1950), 370–75; (14) 'Testamentary brasses' *Antiq J* 29, 3 and 4 (July–Dec. 1949), 183–91; (15) 'Brief account of brass rubbing' *Sussex Co. Mag* 24, iii (March 1950), 93–4; (16) 'Indents at Meldreth, Cambs.' *MBS* 9, i (Feb. 1952), 9–11 [additl note by A. C. Cole *MBS* 9, iii (July 54), 146–7]; (17) 'Kent brasses; some identifications' *MBS* 9, iv (Nov. 54), 160–63, (18) 'Lost brs of Willesborough, Kent). *ibid v*, (Dec. 1955). 221–6.
Died: Machynlleth, Montgom. 5 Jan. 1961; *obits* (1) *MBS* 9, ix (Nov. 1962), 539–4 [by 'H.N.M.'] with photo.; (2) *Archaeol Cant.* LXXVI (1961), 218–9 [by 'H.N.M.']

DERING, Sir Edward (1598–1644)
Antiquary: b 28 Jan. in Tower of London. *e.s.* Sir Anthony D. and Frances (née Bell). *Educ* Magdalen Coll, Camb. Knighted 1619. Bart - 1627. M.P. Hythe, Kent 1625. Kent. Co. 1641. Reformer of Church law; Royalist supporter; fined by Parliament 1644 for supporting Irish Catholics. Married three times and died in relative poverty. His most valuable antiq works are his collns of MS. notes and drwgs of Kentish brasses, monuments, etc. See: *Book of Church Notes; Book of Monuments* (1628) – a folio vol now in Soc of Antiq Lib (see ref to same by R. H. D'Elboux. *Antiq J* XXIX, July–Dec. 1949, 188). For example of one of his drwgs see *MBS* IX, v (1955) f.p. 222. Mr D'Elboux had Sir Edward's own annotated copy of Weever's *Funeral Monuments* (1631).

DILLON, Harold Arthur Lee, 17th Viscount (1844–1932)
Antiquary and author: b London 24 Jan. *e.s.* Arthur Edmund Denis Dillon-Lee, 16th Visc. and *w* Ellen (née Adderley); *Educ* privately at

Eltham 1855–60; Bonn Univ; joined Army 1862; Ensign Rifle Brigade 1862–74; Oxford L.I. 1874–91; First Curator of Armouries, Tower of London 1892–1913, during which time he became a great authority on European arms and armour, costume, etc, on which subj he wrote prefaces to sev of standard works; Chairman Trustees Nat Port. Gallery 1894–1928; Trustee BM 1905–12; Wallace Colln 1918–31 (where he became aquainted with Sir J. G. Mann (*q.v.*); Pres Roy Archaeol Inst 1892–8; Soc of Antiq 1897–1904; Fellow Brit Acad 1902; Antiquary to RA; Hon Member Armourer's Co. of Lond. (1903); CH, MA, DCL. First Pres *OUBRS*; member CUABC/MBS. *m* (1) Julia (née Stanton; ob. 1925); 1 *s*, 1 dau; (2) Margt. Louise Everard (née Ffoulkes). Some of his many contrib to his subjects are given in 'Bibliog of the works of the late Visc. Dillon' by J. G. Mann (*J Soc Army Hist Res*, 12 (1933), 135–7). Geo. Clinch (q.v.) dedicated his book 'English Costume' to Viscount Dillon. *Pubns incl* (1) FAIRHOLT, F. W. *Costume in England.* 3rd edn ed by Hon H. A. Dillon, 2 vols (Bell. 1885); (2) 'Some peculiarities and omissions on brasses' *OUBRS* I (1897–9), 2–3; (3) 'Brass plate at Ditcherly House, Oxford' *ibid*, 234–7; (4) 'Some military garments other than plate armour' *OUBRS* 2 iii (March 1912), 111–5; (5) HOPE, W. St John and DILLON, H. A. *Pageant of the birth, life and death of Rich. Beauchamp, Earl of Warwick, K.G.* (Longmans. 1914). *Died:* 18 Dec. 1932; *Obits:* (1) *Times* 20.12.32; (2) *Procs Brit Acad* XVIIII (1932), 335–44 (by C. Ffoulkes, with bibliog by J. G. Mann) (3) *J Soc Army Hist Res* 12 (1933), 131–7 – repr from item (2) above; (4) *Ann Reg* (n.s.) 1933, p 151.

DODSWORTH, Roger (1585–1654)
Antiquary: b Newton Grange Oswaldkirk, Yorks. 24.7.1585 (or earlier). *Educ* Abp. Hutton Sch, Warton, Lancs. Became antiquary at early age. *m* (1611) Holcroft (née Hesketh). 1 *s*, 3 *d;* visited nearly every ch in Yorks. collecting notes for a Monasticon Anglicanum, which was eventually pubd in 3 vols (2 bearing his name, the other that of Dugdale (q.v.) the editor, whose name is more commonly associated with the work). Dodsworth's numerous mss and sketches (incl many brasses) are in Bodleian Lib (*see* HUNTER, J. – *Three catalogues* [including] *Catalogue of manuscripts written and collected by . . . Roger Dodsworth and now deposited in the Bodleian Library* [*with memoir*]. *1838*).

DRUITT, Herbert (1876–1943).
Solicitor, author and ecclesiologist: b 15 High St, Christchurch, Hants., one of 15 child. (by two marriages) of James D. (1816–1904), solicitor and Town Clerk. Herbert also practiced as solicitor in town.

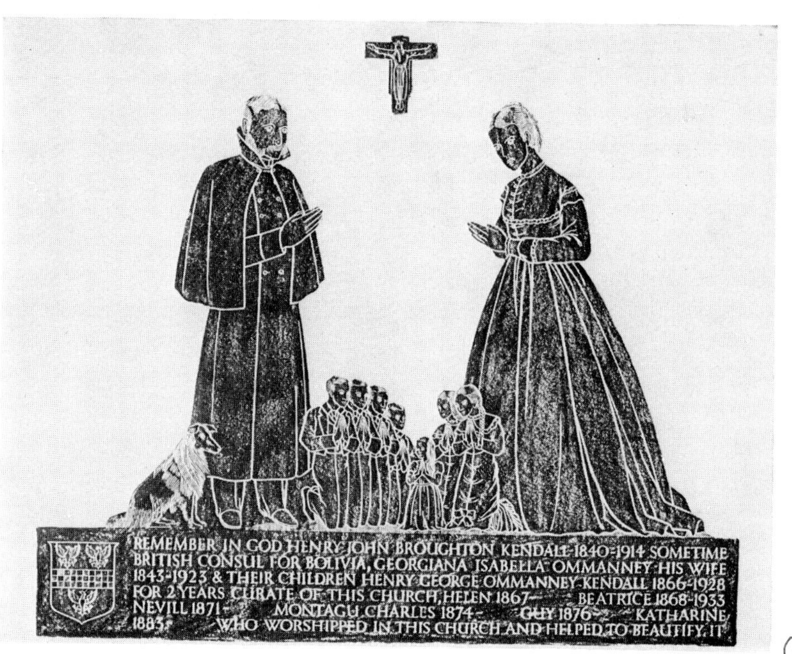

(*a*)

TE 13

Kendall family brass, St Mary's Church, Hatfield Hyde, Welwyn Garden City, Herts. gr. c. 1933); a very pleasing modern brass engr. by *Robt. Austin*, R.A. with figures in dern' dress. Overall size 61 cm high by 71 cm wide (24 by 28 ins approx.); (*b*) Ryce & e Hughes (1594), St Ippolytts, nr. Hitchin, Herts. A traditional late 'Elizabethan' s with kneeling figures at a prie-dieu; Ryce Hughes was apprenticed to Richard Davey 1582, who freed him 11 July 1589. Overall size 43.5 by 47 cm ($17\frac{1}{4}$ by $18\frac{1}{2}$ ins approx). bings by the author. Photos Peter Marshall

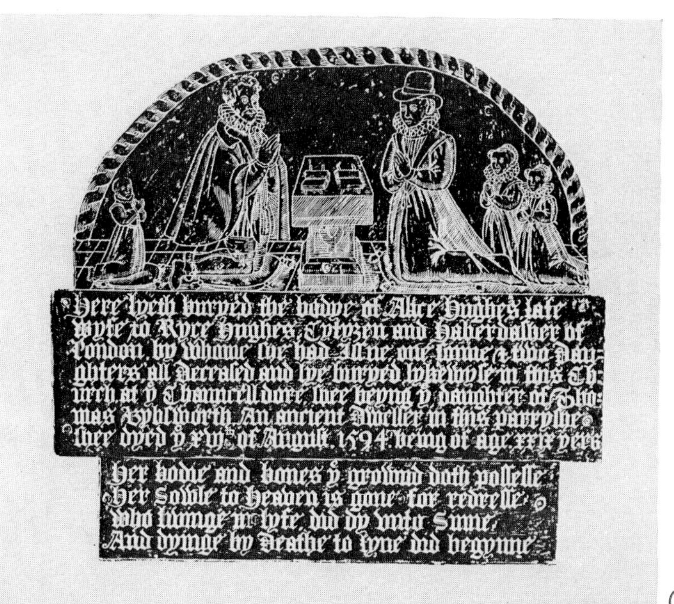

(*b*)

PLATE 14

(*a*) Richard Howard & wife Cecilie (1499), Aylsham, Norfolk. Quaint, grinning cadavers in shrouds; such brasses were popular in England between c. 1480 and 1510 particularly and were often laid down before decease; this example is from the local school of engraving. Figures 57.5 cm ($22\frac{1}{2}$ ins); (*b*) Brass Rubbings and Local History – an 'end of term' exhibition of a W.E.A. class at Sutton-in-Ashfield, Notts. Shows well how interest in local history can be stimulated or supplemented by brass rubbings (see also Chapter 4). Photos: (*a*) Peter Marshall. (*b*) Maltby & Griffiths Ltd. Kindly loaned by Mr W. Clay Dove, Tutor of the class in question who also made the rubbings illustrated.

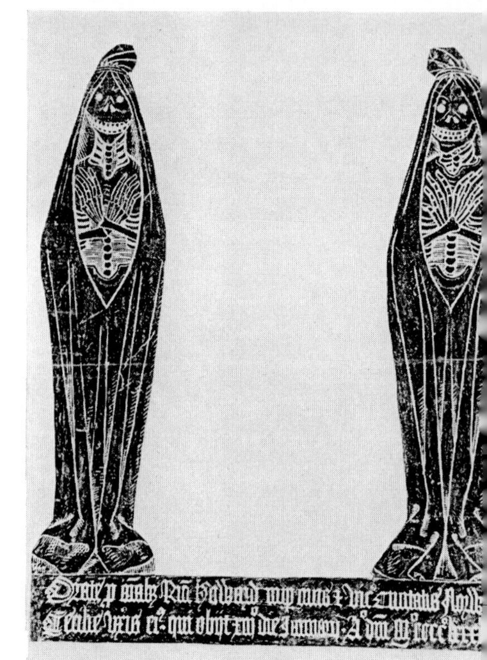

(*a*)

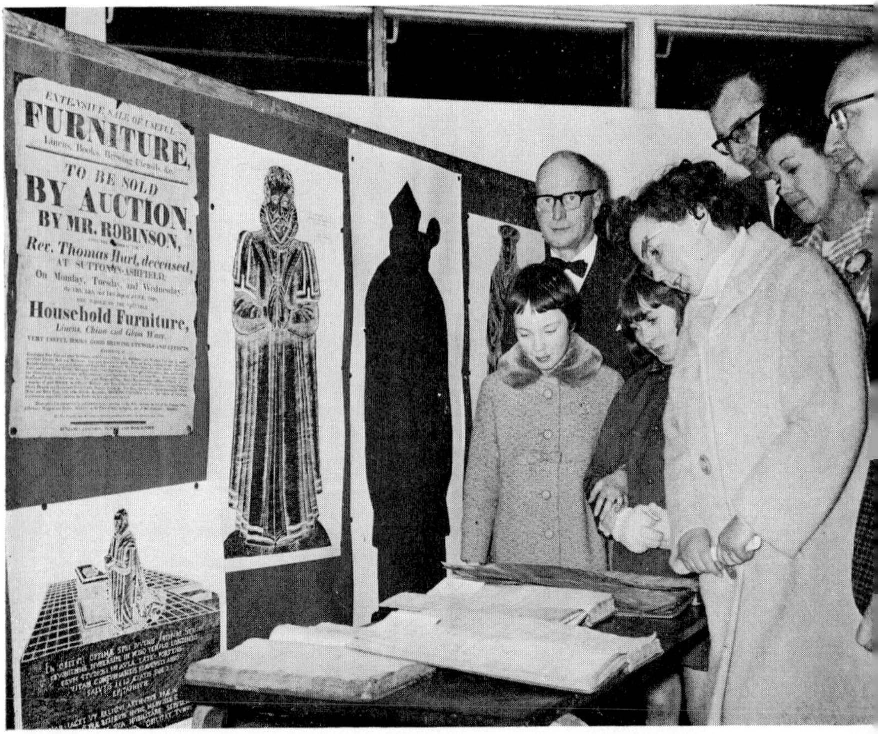

Took early int in local hist and brs. Joined M.B.S. 1902. Pub first book on subj 1906. Served on Town Council for time and in 1918 fd Christchurch Hist and Scientific Soc, of which he was Hon Editor and Curator. Owned famous 12th cent Constable's Hse, the Red Hse (now a Museum), and 'Woodstock', Barrack Rd, where he later lived and housed his colln of antiquities, rubbings, etc. The latter bldg is now called 'Druitt Buildings' and houses the Public Lib. Keen student medieval Latin; wrote series of articles on local hist for Parish Mag and other pubns. Married, his wife Charlotte survived him. His only book (No. 1 below) is a valuable and scholarly work which is now available again in a reprint. Reviews of it can be seen in (a) *Athen* 4102, 9.6.06, 707; (b) *MBS* 5 (1904–9), 125–6; (c) N. *& Q.* (Ser 10) VI, 14.7.06, 39–40 (d) *TLS* (1906), 279. *Pubns incl* (1) *Manual of costume as illustrated by monumental brasses* (1906 repr Kingsmead Repr 1970); (2) 'Notes on brasses remaining at Harpenden and Kimpton, Herts., August 1909' *MBS* 5, 409–19; (3) 'List of casements remaining in Christchurch, Hants., April 1907) *ibid* 191–204 (4) 'Gloucestershire Notes' *ibid* 159–60 (5) 'Cirencester . . . brass inscriptions subsequent to 1600' *ibid* 139–53. In No. 1 above a 'Bibliography of M.B's' was announced, but regrettably never appeared; in *MBS* 5 (1904–9), 235–41 is a 'List of illustrations in Druitt's *Costume on Brasses* . . . arranged topographically'.
Died: 16 Nov. 1943; *Obit: Christchurch Times* 20 Nov. 1943.

DUNKIN, Edwin Hadlow Wise (1849–1915)
Palaeographer, genealogist and ecclesiologist: b Greenwich early 1849; *e.s.* Edwin Dunkin FRS, FRAS (1821–98) and *w* Maria (née Hadlow) ob. 1899. Edwin (senior) was born in Cornwall where his father lived and worked, which prob accounts for E.H.W.D's early interest in that County; in later life his love was for Sussex. He not only published the fine work on Cornish brasses below (which Mill Stephenson in his review (*MBS* 2, iv (Sept. 1894), 137) says 'stands first as an example of how a book on a given county should be produced . . .') but also one on *Church Bells of Cornwall* (1882); his careful scholarship was directed for many years into transcribing calendars and records, mostly of Sussex registers, wills, etc. He also had a vast colln of Sussexiana which one writer in *Sussex Arch Collns* 85 (1946), 64 called 'the greatest of all collections of Sussex material, far outstripping even Sir William Burrell's . . .'. Some years after his death his wife, Mary Mercedes Dunkin, gave her husband's mss to the BM (221 vols, Add MSS 39326–39546) [see *Sussex N. & Q.* 21 (1928–9), 158.] Mr Dunkin was a leading figure in founding the Sussex Record Soc (fd 1900), was a member of the Sussex Archaeol Soc from

1873 and was elec FSA 1902. Some of his rubbings are now in the Sussex Archaeol Soc colln at Lewes. *Pubns incl Monumental Brasses of Cornwall* (1882 repr 1970).
Died: 10 Feb. 1915; his will was noted in *The Times* 24.4.1915, p 11 (d).

EDLESTON, Robert Holmes (1868–1952)
Antiquary and ecclesiologist: b Gainford, Co. Durham. *s* Rev Dr Joseph E., Vicar and Harriet Sophia (née Cumming). Encouraged from an early age by his sister Sarah Alice Cumming E. (ob. 1956), he took a keen interest in brs and incised slabs, later becoming an authority on the latter, noteably those of his own county; late in life he again studied brs, noteably continental examples, producing two suppts to Creeny's work which he greatly admired, and whom he had met at Cambridge. Elected FSA 6.3.1902. Consul, Republic of San Marina (later becoming the Baron de Montalbo); Gold Medal Italian Red Cross (1922); Knt Command Order of Francis I of Sicily and KGC 1926. Very keen horse breeder and had stud at Newmarket. Lay reader Diocese of Ely. Served sev societies incl Durham and Northumb. Archaeol Soc (from 20.6.1890); Surtees Soc (jd 1895; V.P. from 1908); Soc of Antiq Newcastle-upon-Tyne; Camb. Antiq Soc, Teesdale Record Soc; Norfolk Rec Soc and Peterboro. Archaeol Soc; he was also Chairman Gainford Psh Council and Lord of sev manors in Cambs., Norf., Yorks. and Durham. He had a fine colln of rs of brs and incised slabs many of which are reprod in the pubns below. A box containing copies of these and many others not pubd is at the Soc of Antiq, London. He was married (1899) to Maud (née Acland) who died 1915. *Pubns incl:* (1) 'Mon. brs' (additions and corrns to Haines' Manual). *Antiq* 21, (May 1890), 191–5; *ibid* (June '90), 251–6; *ibid* 22 (July '90), 12–15; (Aug. '90), 53–5. (2) 'Mon. brs of Spain' *Camb. Antiq Soc, Procs* XIX (1915), 50–2; (3) 'Note on the m.b. of 1510 of Cardinal Prince Frederick of Poland, in Cracow Cath' *SAP Newcastle* (1916), 164–6; (4) 'Notes on three fine brs (i) of Bruno de Warendorp . . . Lübeck, of 1369; (ii) of Bp Robt. Hallam . . . Constance Cath 1416, and (iii) of Bp John Avantage, in Amiens Cath, of 1456' *ibid*, 173–5; (5) 'Monumental Brasses' Pt I *Peterboro. NHSAS, 59th Ann Rpt for 1928–9*, 83–7 + 9 pl (pp xii-xx); Pt II *ibid 60th Ann Rpt for 1930–31*, 44–48 + pl 1–5 (pp vii–xi); (6) 'Incised Monumental Slabs' Pts 1 and II, *ibid 61 and 62 Ann Rpts* (*1933–4*), 9 p + 8 pl and 4 p + 8 pl respec'ly; *ibid* Pt III, *63rd Ann Rpt* (*1935*), 7 p + Pls I–XII; *ibid* Pt IV, *64th and 65th Ann Rpts* (*1936–7*), 8 p + pls I–XV; Pt V (1942) and Pt VI (1943) privately printed by author, 10 p + pls I–XII and 31p (incl XVI pls) – *Note:* Pts IV and VI cont mainly continental slabs, noteably France; (7)

'Continental brasses' *N. & Q.* clix (15.11.1930), 435–6; (29.11.30), 290–91; *ibid* clx, (3.1.31) 10–12; (9.5.31), 338; (23.5.31), 373; clxiv (26.8.33), 128–9. (Some of the above are replies to notes by W. E. Gawthorp and R. H. Pearson); (8) 'Illus. of incised monumental slabs on the Continent of Europe from rubbings and tracings: a suppt to Creeny'. Pts I and II (Privately printed. [1944]). Pt I: numbered pp. [1]–71; Pt II; numbered pp [73]–145; (9) 'Some tomb slabs in Teesdale churches'. *Trans DNAAS* 7, ii (1936), 223–34; (10) 'Incised monumental slabs in Northumb. and Durham' *Archaeol Ael* 4 Ser, XVI (1939), 71–86; (11) HARRISON, S. E. 'Mon brs and incised slabs' *Teesdale Rec Soc for 1939–40*, No. 5 (1940), 17–18 + 12 pls. [List of plates from rubbings by R.H.E., with refs to sources of articles cited].
Died: 30 Nov. 1952 aet 83; *obits:* (1) *Trans D.N.A.A.S.*, 10 (1946–54), 354–5; (2) *Antiq J* 33 (1953), 271, 272–3.

EDWARDS, Lewis (ob. 1969)
Ecclesiologist; President M.B.S.: Mr Lewis Edwards, MA joined the M.B.S. at its refounding in 1934, serving on Executive Council for many years and later succeeding R. H. Pearson (q.v.) to the Presidency on the latter's death in 1961. He was also a FSA (elec 1935), serving as Auditor, Council Member and Scrutator of the Ballot during his period of membership. His wide knowledge did not often appear in print, but the papers below are both classics of their kind. *Pubns incl:* (1) 'Professional costume of lawyers illus chiefly by mon brs' *BAA* XL (1934), 135–54; repr *MBS* 7, iii (Nov. 1936), 97–108, iv (Nov. 1937), 145–64' Illus; (2) 'The Historical and Legendary background of the Wodehouse and Peacock Feast Motif in the Walsokne and Braunche brasses'. *MBS* 8, vii (Dec. 1949), 300–11.
Died: 20 Apr. 1969.

ELLACOMBE, Rev Henry Thomas (1789–1885)
Ecclesiologist and Campinologist: b 15 May *s* Rev Wm. Ellicombe (ob. 1831). *Educ* Privately, Oriel Coll, Camb., BA 1812; MA 1816; during his years at Univ he studied engineering under Brunel. D 1816. Ord 1817. C Cricklade 1816–17; Bitton (Gloucs.) 1817–35; V Bitton 1835–50. R Clyst St George, Topsham, Devon, 1850–85. Married dau Rev Henry Nicholson (V of Bitton); 1 dau, Eliz. Rous. Changed his name to Ellacombe 1842. Author of sev psh hist, but best known for his books, articles on ch bells, bell-ringing, etc; devised good method of taking rs of bell inscr and marks (see p 88 above) but also int in brs. Ackn by Boutell (1847); Subscr to Haines. Freq contrib to *Notes & Queries.* Produced leaflet c 1875 *Instructions for taking*

Rubbings of Inscriptions on Bells, or other raised Letters. (Copy in BM Lib). A colln of rs by Canon Ellacombe of Bitton are in Bristol City Museum (see pp 165 above).
Died: 30 July 1885, aet 96, at Clyst St George; *obit:* (1) *N. & Q.* (6 Ser) XII, 8.8.1885, 120. (2) *Ch Bells*, 7 Aug. 1885, 847–8 (with port). (3) *Ann Reg* 1885 (N.S.) 174 (short note).

ESDAILE, Katharine Ada (1881–1950)
Ecclesiologist and author: b 23 Apr *d* Andrew McDowall and *w* Ada *Educ* Notting Hill High Sch, Lady Margt. Hall, Oxon. MA. Keen student of archaeology and English sculpture, making special study of 17th and 18th cent tombs and their makers. Won Leaverhulme Fellowship 1937. *m* Arundell James Kennedy E. (1880–1956), librn, bibliographer and Sec to BM 1926–40. Mrs E. was a frequent contrib to art and archaeol jnls, incl *Eng. Porcelain Circle Trans; Archaeol J, RIBA Jnl, RSA Jnl, Walpole Soc, Sussex N. & Q., Appollo, County Life, MBS Trans. et al.* She was also the author of several books. Member M.B.S. 1934–50, serving on Executive Council for a number of years.
Pubns incl (1) *English Monumental Sculpture since the Renaissance* (S.P.C.K. 1927); (2) 'Sculptor and the Brass' *MBS* 7, ii (1935), 49–56; (3) 'Three Monumental drwgs from Sir Edward Dering's Colln.' *Archaeol Cant.* XLVII (1935), 219; (4) 'Sculpture and Sculptors in Yorks.' *Yorks. A.J.* XXXV (1940–3), 363; XXXVI (1944–7), 78, 137; (5) 'An alphabetical list of post-Reformation brasses of known authorship . . .' [with R. H. D'Elboux] *MBS* 8, ii (Dec. 1944); *ibid* 8, iv (1946), 140–44; (6) *English Church Monuments* (Batsford. 1946) – complementing her earlier *Monuments in English Churches* (S.P.C.K. 1937); (7) 'Engraving of m.b.' [letter] *County Life* CIII (Feb. 20, 1948), 388.
Died: 31 Aug. 1950. *Obit:* (1) (note) *MBS* 8, viii (Feb. 1951) 388, (2) *Sussex Co Mag* 24 (1950), 427.

EVANS, Henry Francis Owen (1898–1966)
Ecclesiologist; Hon Sec MBS: b Denton, Kent 3 July *s* Rev Henry Charles Evans. *Educ* St John's Sch, Leatherhead; served in Army 1914–18 – Garrison Bombing Officer, E. Coast Defences; Defence Officer to Brit. Motor Corpn 1939–45; MBE 1942; FSA 1948. *m* (1924) Winifred (née Hughes). Joined M.B.S. shortly after its revival 1934; Council Member many years; Hon Corr Sec; Hon Sec 1961–6 on death of colleague R. H. Pearson (q.v.) Early interest in brs, becoming acquainted with Ralph Griffin (q.v.) and later Mr Pearson above, from whom he acquired considerable technical knowledge on cleaning and restoring brasses; had large lib of books on

brs (many now in Soc of Antiq), Heraldic MSS. and over 700 rubbings (now in Bodleian Library, Oxf.) *Pubns incl* (too many to attempt full listing): (1) 'Brasses of Canons of Windsor' *Oxf. Archaeol Soc Rpt* LXXXII (1937), 21–2; repr *MBS* 7, vi (May 1939), 259–60; (2) 'St Cross Church, Holywell, Oxford' *MBS* 7, v (June 1938), 222–4; (3) 'Incised slabs' *ibid* 219–21; (4) 'Tomb Grille with Latten inscr' *MBS* 8, vii (Dec. 1949), 314–5, (5) 'Cople, Beds.' *ibid* viii, 366–7, (6) 'Unrecorded brasses at Haddenham, Bucks.' *ibid*, 376–7, (7) 'Pygott brass at Whaddon, Bucks.' *MBS* 9, i Feb. (1952), 1–8; (8) 'Easton Neston, Northants.' *ibid* ii (Oct. 1952), 50–59, (9) 'Palimp br to Wm. Fermoure and W. at Somerton, Oxon.' *ibid* iii (July 1954), 98–104, (10) 'A brass in private possession' [Baddesley Clinton Hall, Warwicks.] *ibid*, 191–3; (11) 'Faces on brasses' *ibid* 205–6; (12) 'Eaton Bray, Beds.' *MBS* 9, v (Dec. 1955), 246–50; (13) 'Edlesborough, Bucks.' *MBS* 9, vi (Apr. 1958), 304–10; (14) 'Brasses at Penn and Edlesborough'. *Records of Bucks.* XVI, 2 (1957), 106–9; (15) 'The lady who died on the 30th February' *MBS* 9, viii (Dec. 1961), 362–3; (16) 'Brass damaged by a musket ball' *ibid* 364–5; (17) 'Latten lecterns' *ibid* 375–87; (18) 'Charterhouse, London' *MBS* 9, ix (Nov. 1962), 464–74; (19) 'Blisworth, Northants.' *ibid* 489–92; (20) 'Tomb of James Zouch in Oxford Cathedral' *ibid* 509–11; pp 527–33 of this issue also contain 19 short notes by Major Evans; (21) 'Peyton slabs at Stoke-by-Nayland, Suff.' *MBS* 10, i (Dec. 1963), 13–15; (22) 'Cardinal Nicholas de Casan' [1488]. *ibid*, 25–8; (23) 'Drake's plate of brass' *ibid* 30; (24) 'Fixing of brasses' *MBS* 10, ii (Dec. 1964), 58–62; (25) 'Two little known Holy Trinities' *ibid* 90–92; (26) 'Mon brs of St Albans Abbey' *Abbey Mag* Feb. 1965 [later repr as pamphlet for sale in Abbey]; (27) 'Elephant on brasses' *MBS* 10, iii (Dec. 1965), 128–35; (28) 'Malicious damage to brasses' *ibid* 186–91; (29) 'Find of palimps at Lit Walsingham, Norf.' *ibid*, 204–9; (30) 'Palimp brs at Ossington, Notts.' *MBS* 10 iv (Dec. 1966), 303–10; (31) ' "Brass" to Rowland Eyre, Esq, and W. Gertrude, 1924, at Gt Longstone, Derbys.' *MBS* 10, v (Dec. 1967), 393–6; (32) 'Elsfield, Oxon.' *ibid*, 384–6; (33) 'Palimp at Thame, Oxon.' *MBS* 10, vi (Dec. 1968), 492–3; (34) 'Knossington, Leics.' *MBS* 11, i (Dec. 1969), 32–6; (35) 'Tonsure on Brasses' *ibid*, 38–40. *Died:* Oxford, 14 Dec. 1966; *obits:* (1) *MBS* 10, v, 431–3 [by A. C. Cole and Augustus White], with photo. (2) *Antiq J* 47 (1967), 340 [note only].

FAIRBANK, Frederick Royston (1841–1913)
Antiquary: b Ecclesall Bierlow, Yorks. early 1841; *Educ* Rugby Sch, Manchester Medical Sch, King's Coll, Lond; MRCS Eng.; LRCP

Lond. 1862 practising first at Lynton then for many years at Doncaster; also consulting surgeon Doncaster Royal Infirmary; MD Heidelberg 1865; Fellow Roy Med and Chir Soc 1869; MRCP Edinburgh 1874; Fellow 1892; author of sev medical papers and a clinical note-book; FSA Elec 1.3.1888, adm 1894 (see *SAP* 2 ser XV (1894–5), 403); Doncaster Local Sec, Yorks. Archit Soc 1883–8; Member M.B.S. 1894–1913; OUBRS 1899; Hon Corr member BAA; Hon Local Sec (Dorking) Surrey Archaeol Soc from 1900. Moved to St Leonards, Sx., 1892 and later to Dorking from where he sold his practice c 1910 to return to Caversham nr Oxford. Twice married, his second wife, Dora, and three children survived him. Apart from his archaeol pursuits (incl some excavation at Roche Abbey) he gave a number of excellent papers on brs, nearly all well illus from his own rubbings. *Pbns incl:* (1) 'Brasses, with a series of illus of Military Brasses . . .' *AASRP* xviii Pt II (1883), 181–91 (2) 'Brasses in Howden Church, Yorks.' *Yorks Archaeol & Topog. Soc J* XI (1891), 169–73; (3) 'Ancient Memorial brs remaining in the old Deanery of Doncaster'. *ibid*, pp 71–92; (4) 'Pardon brasses' *MBS* 2 (1893–6), 9–11; (5) 'Thomas Garland, 1609, Todwick, Yorks.' *ibid* 145–8; (6) 'Ticehurst, Sussex' *ibid* 224–5; (7) 'Brass of Lambert von Bruun, Bishop of Bamberg (illustrated)' *ibid* 145–7; (8) *Catalogue of the Loan Exhibition at the Brassay Inst March 16th 1896 . . . [edited] by F.R.F. . . .'* (who wrote 72 p intro on hist of brs); (9) 'Brasses in Battle Church, Sussex' *OUBRS* I, iii (Dec. 1897), 99–103; (10) 'Rubbings of medieval engraved brasses' *Connoisseur* I, (Nov. 1901) 162–8; (11) 'Memorial Brasses in the County of Surrey'. *cont in* COX, Rev J. C. (ed). *Memorials of Old Surrey* (G. Allen & Sons, 1911), pp 52–81, illus; classified arrangement – good general survey. *Died:* Caversham, Oxford 3 Oct. 1913: obits: (1) *Lancet* 2 (18 Oct. 1913), 1154; (2) *SAP* 2 Ser, XXVI (23.4.1914), 165 (note only).

FARRAR, Rev Edmund (1847–1935)
Ecclesiologist: b Norfolk. *s* Edmund F. *Educ* Dedham and Rugby Schs, Caius Coll, Camb. Matric 1886. Ord Deacon (St Albans) 1878; C. Kelvedon 1878–81, Bressingham, 1881–5; Chap Luton Hoo, Beds. 1885–90; C. Rickingill Inferior, 1890–96; R. Hinderclay (Nr Diss) Norfolk, 1896–1915. Visited every church in Norf. and Suff. and comp lists of brs in each (see below); FSA Elec 27.5.1886; Adm 15.3.1898. Early member CUABC/MBS; Hon Member MBS; Farrar's colln of rs of Norfolk brs were acquired by Sir A. W. Franks (q.v.) who later gave them to Soc of Antiq (*see: SAP* (2 Ser) XVI, 1895–7, 149–51). *m* Florence Emily, who survived him. *Pubns incl* (1) *Church Heraldry of Norfolk* (1885, 1893) (2) *List of the Monumental brasses remaining*

in the County of Norfolk (1890) (3) *List of the monumental brasses remaining in the County of Suffolk* (1903)
Died: 8.4.1935 at Stoneham Parva. *Obit:* (1) *MBS Trans* VII (2) 1935, 89; (2) *Antiq J* 15 (1935) 397 (note only); (3) *Procs Suff Inst*, XXII, 2 (1935) 228–9.

FIELD, Rev Harry Eardley (1858–1955)
Ecclesiologist: b Whitechapel, London 25 Nov. *Educ* privately; King's Coll, London; Durham University; MA; Ord 1890, C St Marys Howden-le-Wear, Durham 1890–93, Carlton-in-the-Willows, Notts. 1893; V Ambergate, Derbys. 1893–1921. Member M.B.S. 1893 till death; made special study of Notts. and Derbys. brs but contrib to MBS Trans on other subjects as well; a Rev J. E. Field contrib a number of useful articles to *OUBRS Jnl* and other journals. *Pubns incl:* (1) 'Brs of Canons of Windsor' *Antiq* 15 (May 1887), 212–4. (2) 'Some suggestions for preserving records of the m.b. of England' *MBS* 2 (1893–6), 103–6 [incl suggestion of using pantograph for copying brs]; (3) 'Brass of an ecclesiasiastic, c 1400, Stamford-on-Soar Notts.' *ibid*, 215; (4) Matrix of Bishop Beaumont's brass, Durham Cathedral' *ibid* 291–4; (5) 'Note on the brass of Thomas Magnus, 1550, Sessay Ch, Yorks.' *MBS* 3 (1897–9), 44–7; (6) 'Notes on the brs in the churches of Wollaton and Strelley, Notts.' *ibid* 219–26; (7) 'Brasses in Clifton Ch, Notts.' *ibid* 249–53; (8) 'Monumental Brasses of Derbyshire' *ibid* 194–6, 209–15; 5 (1904–9), 1–7, 29–39, 101–111, 129–38, 171–80, 380–89; (9) *Monumental Brasses of Nottinghamshire* Pt I [with J. P. BRISCOE (q.v.)] 1904 (No further parts issued; see short reviews *MBS* 5; 99).
Died: Bridgwater, Somerset 16 Oct. 1955 *Obit: MBS* IX (7) Oct. 1960, 408 [by A. B. C(onnor)].

FISKE, George (1851–1902)
Traveller; ecclesiologist: b Boston, Mass., U.S.A. 28 Dec.. *s* Augustus Henry F. (eminent Boston lawyer) and Hanna Rogers Bradford F. *Educ* Privately in Boston; Harvard, BA; Guy's Hospital Medical Sch, London, 1 term only. *m* (1) Joanna Euling (London 14.1.1873); (2) Mary E. Rood (at Lynn, Mass., 13.12.1888). 1 *s* George F. (jnr.) b 27.11.1891 but died soon afterwards. Spent much of life travelling in Europe. Keen student m.b. and only American member at time of M.B.S.; gave large exhib of rs Trinity Church, Boston 1898, having one of largest collns of rs in U.S.A. The Fogg Art Museum, Harvard Univ, now has 279 rs by Fiske, given in 1912 by his widow. He also coll much material for a bibliog of m.b. shortly before his death (see *N & Q* 10 Ser, VI, 15 Sept. 1906, 210); it was never pubd. He was

also an active member and benefactor St George's Ch, Maynard, Mass. *Died:* 5 March 1902 at home in Concord, Mass. *Source of info:* (1) *Harvard Coll, Class of 1872, Seventh Rpt, 1898,* pp 32–3; (2) *ibid, Eighth Rpt of the Secretary, 1902,* pp 15–16; (3) Mrs K. D. Reiser, Asst Registrar, Fogg Art Museum.

FISKE, Stewart
In the colln of ms notes and letters in Univ Museum of Archaeol and Ethnol Camb., is a draft of an article written c 1907 for *N & Q* (but never published) entitled 'A Bibliographical Note' by Stewart Fiske of Mobile, Alabama, U.S.A. giving brief history of CUABC and listing their publications (see under CUABC for details).

FRANKS, Sir Augustus Wollaston, KCB (1826–97)
Antiquary and ecclesiologist: b Geneva, Switz. 20 Mar. *e.s.* Capt. Fredk. Franks, RN and *w* Frederica (née Sebright). *Educ* privately abroad; Eton (1839–43), Trinity Coll, Camb. 1845–9. BA 1849, MA 1852. From graduate days devoted himself to study of archaeology, when he began coll br rs and made aquaintance of Revs H. Haines and C. Boutell; Albert Way, J. G. Nichols *et al.* One of fdrs Camb. Archit Soc; early member Camb. Antiq Soc and Royal Archaeol Inst; Sec Mediaeval Exhib, RSA (1850); Asst Dept of Antiq BM 1851–66; Keeper Brit and Medieval Antiq BM 1866–96; took spec interest in ceramics and book plates. Most of his valuable private collns were given to BM in later years or under his will. FSA, 1853. Director S. of A. 1858–67, 1873–80. President 1891–6. Editor *Archaeologia* and freq contrib to *Procs* of Soc; Member Standing Comm BM Trustees; Hon Litt. D (Camb.) 1889; D.C.L. (Oxon.) 1895; CB 1888, KCB 1894, FRS 1874. Member Roxburghe Club. During his lifetime he gave his huge and valuable colln of some 3,000 rs to Soc of Antiq, many his own, others from collns of friends incl Rev Herbert Haines, J. G. Nichols, Albert Way, Rev E. Farrar; still others from early collns like that of Thomas Fisher (q.v.) In 1870's he gave a number of talks on brs of sev counties based on rs he was donating to Soc of Antiq; he also gave colln of engravings of monuments, incl many of brs. Herbert Haines' own, annotated, copy of his *Manual* was given by Franks to Mill Stephenson, who later gave it to Soc of Antiq. Franks was unmarried. Amongst his many pubns may be mentioned the following: (1) 'M.B. of Beds.' *SAP* (2 Ser), VI (1875), 310–3. (2) 'M.B. of Berks.' *ibid* 321–3; (3) 'M.B. of Bucks.' *ibid* 332–4. (4) 'M.B. of Cambs.' *ibid* 452–7. (5) 'M.B. of Cheshire, Cornwall and Cumberland' *SAP* (2 Ser) VII (1876), 21–4. (6) 'M.B. of Essex' *ibid* (1877), 147–54. (7) 'M.B. of Gloucs.' *ibid* (1878), 409–13, (7) 'On palimp-

sest sepulchral brs and more esp on an instance in Burwell Ch, Cambs.' *Camb Antiq Soc Misc Comm* Vol 2 Pt I. No. 1 (1848), 1–6 [with illus of obv and rev by the Wallers]; (8) 'Genealogical Hist of the Freville Family, with some account of their monuments in Little Shelford, Cambs.' *ibid* 2, Pt I No. 4 (1848–51), 21–31. [3 illus (Pls VI–VIII), 2 of exg brs, 1 of three lost brs from Cole's MS in BM]. *Died:* Westminster, 21 May 1897 *Obits:* (1) *SAP* 2 Ser, XVII (1898), 148–54; (2) *Art J* (1897), 167–9 [with photo]; (3) *Procs Roy Soc* LXI (1897), x–xii; (4) *Ann Reg* 1897 (N.S.), 158.

GAWTHORP, Thomas John (1832/3–1912)
Art metal worker: Founder of firm of T. J. Gawthorp & Sons 16 Long Acre, London, art metal workers to H.M. Queen Victoria and makers and engravers of memorial brasses (Est. 1859). An early catalogue of their work (of c 1865) is in the V & A Library; another of 1881; 'Designs and examples of monumental heraldic and memorial brasses' is listed in the BM Catalogue but could not be found when I applied for it (1970). T.J.G. (together with his son W. E. Gawthorp (*q.v.*) specialised also in the repair and restoration of ancient brasses, of which they made a special study, usually from old rubbings (or prints/drwgs if no other evidence survived). Many of their memorial plates are signed 'GAWTHORP & SONS, LONDON', but those dating from after c 1918 bear an additional name, viz. 'GAWTHORP & SONS, CULN LTD. LONDON' (e.g. Inscr in raised letters of 1929, in S.A. of Nave, St Michael and All Angels, Bournemouth); At Digswell Ch, Herts. is a stained glass window with brass plates below, one of which bears their trade mark with the word 'LATTEN' stamped across it. (date 1893); at Radlett, Herts. is an inscr to Albert Giles (ob. 1922) stamped 'CULN, GAWTHORP & SONS., LONDON'., other examples I have seen usually bear the word 'CULN' following 'sons'.
Died: 10 Oct. 1912 aet 80 (at 38 Clyde Rd, Addiscombe, Surrey).

GAWTHORP, Walter Edmund (1859–1936)
Ecclesiologist and metalworker: b 14 Nov. 2 *s* Thomas John G. (q.v.) of Long Acre and Addiscombe, Sy. *Educ* Whitgift G.S. Croydon 1871–5 when he entered his father's business. He remained with the firm (which held sev Royal Warrants) until his retirement in 1935; until abt 1926 the firm remained at Long Acre, then moving to 4 Trafalgar Sq, W.C.2. and (by 1932) to 11 Tufton St, S.W.1. When W.E.G. retired his premises were taken over by J. Wippell & Co. Ltd, makers of memorial brasses and church furnishings. The *P.O. London Dir* from 1914 onwards desc Gawthorp & Sons as 'brass,

wrought iron and repousée workers, monumental masons and memorial engravers, art metal workers to H.M. the King . . .'. W.E.G. jd M.B.S. 1897; member Exec Council; regular contrib to *Trans* and made spec study of old methods of engraving brs. Council memb St Paul's Eccles Soc; FSA Scot. elec 1911. *m* Clara (ob. 9.10.29) who bore him sev child; a Thomas Alfred, Gertrude Louisa and Ethel May Gawthorp are mentioned in wills of above. A Thos. Gawthorp of Coulsdon, Sy. (ob. 1929 aet 70) and a Thos. John Joseph Gawthorp (engineer) also lived in area at time, but I have not est their relationships. *Pubns incl:* (1) 'Some remarks on stones used for Ancient Brs and Incised Slabs' Builder CII (16.12.1912), 185–6; (2) 'Brass at Stoke D'Abernon, 1277, enamelled shield' *N & Q* (12 Ser) IX, 28.5.1921, 428; (3) 'Additional notes on repairs to brasses' *MBS* 6 (1910–14), 48–55; 202–13 [work by Messrs Gawthorp of Long Acre, mainly by T. J. Gawthorp]; subsequent notes appeared mainly in *N & Q*, noteably a series issued jointly with late R. H. Pearson 'Restoration of ancient brasses' in *N & Q* 1928–31. One letter in Vol CLX (Nov. 29th 1930), 390–91, mentions a fragt of br from Notre Dame, Nieuport 'found in a German metal dump' after 1914–18 war; (4) 'Ancient brass engraving' *N & Q* (12 Ser) X, 11.3.1922, 186–7; (5) 'Ancient and modern methods of engraving brs'. *Trans St Pauls Eccles Soc* 9 (ii–iv), 1922–8, 15–24, illus; (6) *The Brasses of Our Homeland Churches* (1923); (7) 'Chinnor, Oxon.' *MBS* 7, ii (Dec. 1935), 65–6; (8) 'Brs at Stoke D'Abernon' *ibid*, 84–5; (9) 'Denchworth, Berks.' *MBS* 7, iv (Nov. 1937), 165; (10) 'Mon. brs at South Weald and Layston' [palimp] *EAST* (N.S.) 20, ii (1933), 277–9.
Died: 5 Aug. 1936; *obit: MBS* 7, iii (Nov. 1936), 139.

GOUGH, Richard (1735–1809)
Antiquary: b Winchester St, London 21 Oct. *o.s.* Harry Gough and Eliz. (née Hynde). *Educ* privately under two tutors; adm Corpus Christi Coll, Camb. July 1752 but never attained degree, left July 1756. Did much travelling in his antiq researches, esp with his friend John Nichols the publisher. FSA 1767; Director Soc Antiq 1771–97; FRS 1775–95; *m* 18.8.1774 Anne; 4 dau of Thos. Hall of Goldings, Hertford; inherited estate at Enfield on death of mother in same year. Prob the most famous of the early antiquaries and the 'father' of serious study on mon brs. His *Sepulchral Monuments* in five huge vols incl many engravings of brasses by friends of the author, incl the Basires, John Carter and amateurs like Michael Tyson (q.v.), Craven Ord (q.v.), Rev Thos. Kerrick and J. Schnebellie. In vol 2, Pt II, are three folding sheets bearing impressions of (now lost) brs 'rolled-off'

the original plates. Most of Gough's huge colln of notes and mss are in the Bodleian Lib, Oxford. *Pubns incl:* (1) *British Topography* (1768 and 1780); (2) *Sepulchral Monuments of G.B.* (1786–99); (3) A revised edn of Camden's *Britannia* 3 Vol 1789 and 1806; 3rd edn 1806 (not completed). For full list of works see DNB or BM Catalogue. *Died:* 20 Feb. 1809 aet 74; bur. at Wormley, Herts. with his wife (ob. 1833) *s.a.* (1) DNB (2) FORDHAM, Sir G. 'Richard Gough'. *EHAS Trans* 7 (1923–7), 254–7.

GRIFFIN, Ralph Hare (1854–1941).
Antiquary and genealogist: b Ospringe, Kent 30 Apr. 2 *s* Rev W. N. Griffin, MA (Vicar of Ospringe and one of fdrs Camb. Camden Soc) and Eliz. (née Hurst); *Educ* Tonbridge Sch, St John's Coll, Camb. Called to Bar of Inner Temple (1881) where he practiced intermity until 1890; Registrar of Designs and Trade Marks, Patent Office 1890–1920. From 1920 until he died he gave unsparingly of his time to the study of the Middle Ages, especially brasses and genealogy on which he became a great expert; he did much towards the preservation and restoration of m.b. and was Member Cantab. and London Diocesan Advsry. Comm on Preservn of Churches; FSA – auditor; Sec 1920–29; joined M.B.S. 1902. V.P. many years and freq contrib to *MBS Trans*, with spec ref to Kent. His main work was cataloguing the colln of rs of the Camb. Antiq Soc, largely completing the coverage of U.K. brs. By 1939 he had 6,000 rs of the high standard he always reqd. (*see* RUCK, G. A. E. – 'Mon Brs, with spec ref to the Camb. Antiq Soc Colln . . .' *Camb. Antiq Soc Procs* 38 (1936–7) 50–59.) Also worked with Mill Stephenson at Camb. on M.S's *List* and *Appendix*. Many of his personal books and notes on brs are in Soc of Antiq Lib; others are at Univ Museum, of Arch and Ethnol, Cambridge. *Pubns incl:* (1) 'Sidney Tombs at Penshurst and Ludlow' *MBS* 5 (1904–9), 391–408; (2) 'Note on the br of Wm. Holyngbroke, 1375, in New Romney Ch, Kent'. *MBS* 6 (1910–14); 85–90; (3) 'Kentish items' *ibid*, 158–97, 181–202; 295–318; 354–71. [all well illus, repr in one vol 1915 repr MBS 1955]; (4) *Some illus of m.b. and indents in Kent* (1914, repr from articles in (3) above by MBS 1946; (5) *Drawings of Brasses in some Kentish Churches . . . by Thomas Fisher*, edited by R.G. (1913), (6) 'Mon Brs in Kent'. *Archaeol Cant.* 31 (1915) 131–54 [cont useful bibliog notes on sources + list of illus not in Haines (pp 137–54)]; 32 (1917), 27–75 [incl reprod of many Fisher drwgs]; (7) *List of M.B. remaining in the County of Kent 1922* [comp jointly with M. Stephenson who, according to Mr Griffin, wrote most of the text]. 1923; (8) 'Minister in Sheppey; note on two brs in the church' *Archaeol Cant* 36 (1923), 43–7; (9) 'Care of

rubbings of m.b. in Museums'. *Museums J* 32 (June 1932), 94–5; (10) 'Brass of Bp Yong at New Coll, Oxon.' *Antiq J* XIV (Oct. 1934), 379–82 [a valuable paper discussing the origin of the incised stone head of the fig based on old and recent rubbings]; (11) 'Mon brs, their care and preservation' *Ch Assembly Notes* 13 (Nov. 1936), 253–8; *ibid* (Dec. 1936), 278–81; illus bibliog. Later issued as pamphlet by S.P.C.K. (1937); *2nd edn* entitled *Care of m.b. and Ledger Slabs* rev by R. H. D'Elboux. S.P.C.K. 1946 (Pamphlets on the Care of Churches); (12) *Cotman's Suffolk Brasses 1819* (Privately printed. 1937); (13) 'Mon brs in Kent' *MBS* 7, v (June 1938), 200–3 [add Notes to items (7) above]; (14) *List of M.B. in Great Britain* (1926); *Appendix* (1938) by R. Griffin and M. S. Guiseppi; (15) 'Brass once in Biggleswade Church' *MBS* 7, vi (May 1939), 251–8 [Rudying brass]; (16) 'Brass once in Staplehurst, Kent' *ibid* 271–9; Mr Griffin also contrib a valuable series of 'Bibliographical Notes' on early books on brasses to *MBS* 5 and 6.
Died: Warren Hse, Micheldever 20 Aug. 1941; *obits:* (1) *MBS* 7, vii (Sept. 1942), 374–6; [by Dr G. H. S. Bushnell]; (2) *Archaeol Cant.* LIV (1941) 77–8 [by F. W. Cook]; (3) *Antiq J* 22 (1942) 73–5 [by 'L.C.G.C.']

GRIGGS, William (1832–1911)
Photo. Lithographic printer: b Woburn, Beds. Self-educated, he came to London in 1848, and with Charles Griggs helped to photograph and produce exhibits for Indian Court at Gt Exhibition of 1851. In 1855 appt as technical-asst at Indian Museum, Leadenhall St. In 1858 Dr John Forbes Watson, his chief, helped him set up photo-lithographic studios and workshops at India Office. Following research he undertook there, he invented photochrome-lithography and an improved method of photo-lithographic transfer. Est. his own photo-litho works at Peckham 1868; later became chrome-lithographer to Queen Victoria and King Edw. VII. Also reproduced many old mss and texts with equal skill, incl the illus for the famous Furnivall edn of Shakespeare's works (43 vols 1881–91). In our context his best work is seen in the illus to Creeny's and Beloe's works (*op cit*). Up to 20 Dec. 1906 his firm was privately owned, but on that date W. Griggs & Sons became a public company, in conjunction with his two sons. He resigned his directorship in January 1910, and died the next year. His wife, Eliz. Jane (née Gill) whom he married in 1851, died in 1903. Some scrap-books and papers belonging to Griggs are now in the St Bride Printing Library.
Died: 7 Dec. 1911 at Worthing, Sussex. *Obits:* (1) *Times* 8.12.1911; (2) *J Indian Art* Jan. 1912 [for full account see *DNB* Suppt. I; 1901–1911].

GRIMM, Samuel Heironymous (1734–94)
Antiquary and topographical artist: b Burgdorf (Nr Berne) Switz. Came to London, 1769 where one of his early drwgs engr by James Basire (q.v.) Employed by Sir Rich. Kaye to make topog drwgs in Derbys. and Notts., but best known for his work for Sir Wm. Burrell's (q.v.) 'Sussex Collections', now in the BM. He worked chiefly in water colours or pen and ink.
Died: Covent Garden 14.4.1794.

HAINES, Rev Harry Fowler (1869–99)
b Gloucester. *y.s.* Rev Herbert Haines (q.v.) and *w* Rosina. *Educ* College Sch, Gloucs.; St Catherine's Coll Oxon.; MA. Followed his Father's interests and made marginal notes in the latter's own copy of his *Manual;* founder, May 1893, Oxford Univ Brass Rubbing Soc (q.v.) and its first Vice-President. He was soon to be taken ill and died suddenly at Hoxne, Suffolk in the Spring of 1899. (see note *OUBRS Procs,* 2 (i) 1900, 49). He was a member also of the Norfolk and Norwich Archaeol Soc at the time of his death.

HAINES, Rev Herbert (1826–72)
Ecclesiologist: b Hampstead 1 Sept., 7 *s* Dr John Haines, surgeon, and *w* Jane. *Educ* Coll Sch, Gloucs., Matric 1843; Exeter Coll, Oxon. Oct. 1844–49. BA 1849, MA 1851; C Delamere, Cheshire Sept. 1849–1850; second Master College Sch, Gloucs. 22.6.1850–1872. *m* (16.1.1851) Rosina (née Dugard) 4 *s*; Chaplain Gloucs. County Asylum 1854–9; Barnwood House Asylum 1859–72. When Haines died his friends and colleagues opened a fund for a memorial to him and to assist his widow to complete the educ of the eldest-surviving son. The memorial brass to his memory, paid for by the Old Boys of College Sch, was designed by Capel N. Tripp and made by Messrs Heaton, Butler & Bayne (q.v.); it is now in S. Ambultory of Choir of Gloucs. Cath. Haines is justifiably best remembered for his fine *Manual of Monumental Brasses* which has remained the standard work almost since pubn in 1861; it was based on his earlier *Oxford Manual* (1848), compiled for the Oxford Archit Soc while still at the University. Haines had a large colln of rs of his own, later bought by Sir A. W. Franks, a close friend, now mostly in Soc of Antiq Lib; others are in the Mus. of Archaeol and Ethnol. Camb. and Gloucs. City Lib. Haines met or corresponded with many interested colleagues incl Boutell, Way, Weale, J. B. Nichols, J. G. Nichols, the Wallers and the Revs Addington, Birch and C. R. Manning. Haines' own annotated copy of his 1861 *Manual* is in Soc of Antiq Lib. *Pubns incl* (1) *Manual for the study of M.B. . . .* ['Oxford Manual'], 1848; (2) *Manual of*

M.B. . . ., Pts I and II (1861, repr with new biog intro by R. J. Busby, 1970 [Adams & Dart. £5.25]); (3) 'M.B. in the Cathedral and County of Hereford' *BAA* 27 (1871), 85–99; 198–203, 541; (4) 'Brasses and monumental slabs in Sundridge Church' [Kent]. Letter dd 20.12.1871. *Archaeol Cant.*, XVI (1886), 275–6.
Died: Hampden Hse, Barton St, Gloucs. 18 Sept. 1872 aet 46. *Obits:* (1) *Archaeol J* 30 (1873), 434; (2) *Gloucs. N & Q* 2 (1884), 186–7; (3) *Gloucs. Chronicle* 28.9.1872 (4) *Guardian* 27, 25.9.1872, 1203 [repr from No. 3 above]; (5) *Athen* 2345, 5.10.1872, 438 [brief]; For full details see my new intro to reprint of *Manual* (*op cit*) pp 5–22.
Add note: see under Sparvel-Bayly, J. A. below.

HARDMAN, John, jnr (1811–1867)
Ecclesiastical metalworker and stained glass mafr; b Birmingham 7 Aug. *s* John Hardman, metal-button-maker; jnd father's firm early in life but in 1838 est his own firm of ecclesiastical metalworkers and stained glass mfrs 'in which' says Boase, 'he enjoyed a practical monopoly'. Specialised in church plate, using old medieval designs and methods, closely associated with the Gothic movement, especially with A. W. N. Pugin (q.v.); he collected together and trained many young and old workmen in precious metals in an attempt to revive old crafts; the firm exhibited at the Great Exhibition in 1851. The *J. of Design and Manufactures,* II (Sept. 1849–Feb. 1850), p 54, describes H's "labours in latten, brass and iron", remarking that it was difficult to accept that his products were only made "in the baser metals". H. designed a number of figure brasses (some listed on pp 237–42 of Haines' *Manual*), and many memorial plates, usually bearing the firm's name or mark. John H. came from a strong R.C. family and lies buried in St Chad's Cathedral, Birmg'hm' which he helped to build and where he was a chorister for 18 years. His son, John Bernard H. succeeded to the business after his father's death.
Died: 3 Clifton Pk. Bristol, 29 May 1867 aet 55; *Obits:* (1) *Art J.* (N.S.) VI, 1867, 172; (2) *Builder,* XXV (1867), 408 (brief); *s.a.* (1) *Connoisseur,* 165 (663), May 1967, 29–35; (2) TIMMINS, S. *Industrial History of Birmingham* (1866), 521–5.

HARDMAN, John & Co. (London and Birmingham)
Ecclesiastical metalworkers and stained glass manufacturers: Fd 1740 by John Hardman, snr as firm of metal button-makers in Pardise St, Birmingham. John H. jnr (1811–67) joined the firm in early life, but after meeting A. W. N. Pugin decided to branch out into ecclesiastical metalwork. He combined the production techniques of two local firms, Hammond, Turner & Sons (button-makers) and G. R. Elkington

(metal-workers) in 1837 to become the first 'medieval metalworker' of the Victoria era. In 1838 the new firm of John Hardman & Co. was established. When Hardman snr died in 1844, his son went into partnership with Jeremiah & Charles Iliffe, and a year later est. a separate factory in Gt Charles St with the help of his nephew Wm. Powell (jnr) specialising in eccles metalwork made by electro-plating and electro-typing methods, normally on a common base-metal. Their trade mark was registered 22.9.1845. The firm made a number of figure brasses but mainly memorial tablets and plaques and continued to do so until after the First World War. Most of their work bears their name in the lower right hand corner, (e.g. Georgina Bathurst (1874) Cirencester, Gloucs., signed 'John Hardman & Co., Birm[m]'). The original day-books of the firm still survive at the John Hardman Studios, 44 Newhall Hill Rd, Birmg'm*, where stained glass is now their principal work. For further details see valuable article by Shirley Bury 'In search of Pugin's Church Plate. Pt I Pugin, Hardman and the Industrial Revolution'. *Connoisseur* 165 (663), May 1967, 29–35. illus.

HART, SON, PEARD & CO. LTD, London and Birmingham
Ecclesiastical metalworkers: Est. by 1866 in London as Hart & Son, and in 1867 in Birmingham and principally engaged in making brassware; most of their memorial brasses are inscription plates or plaques, with varying degrees of border decoration and colouring. A 20-page catalogue of examples of their work (with illus) '*Memorial Brasses and Mural Tablets*, published c 1900 is in the V.&.A Library. The present survivor of the above firm is the Hart Foundry, Grosvenor Works, Grosvenor St West, Birmingham. Many signed examples of their wall plaques, frequently cast with raised letters within a decorative plain or coloured border can be found. At St Mary's Parish Church, Chislehurst, Kent is an inscription of 1866 signed 'HART & SON. LONDON' and another of January 1901 signed 'HART, SON, PEARD & CO.' In 1904 their London address was 138 and 140 Charing Cross Road.

HARTSHORNE, Rev Charles Henry (1802–65)
Ecclesiologist and antiquary: b Broseley, Salop., 17 Mar. *o.s.* John H. of Liverpool. *Educ* Shrewsbury; St John's Coll, Camb., BA 1825; MA 1828; C Benthall (Salop.) 1825–8; Little Wenlock (Salop.) 1828–30; Cogenhoe (Northants.) 1838–50. R Holdenby (Northants.) 2.11.1850 to death. Founder-member B.A.A. and Inst 1844; FSA; Close friend of the Waller brothers, whose *Series* . . . is jointly dedicated to him; subscr Haines' Manual (1861). Had large colln of rs later bought by Sir A. W. Franks and given to Soc of Antiq. Author of the first book

*Since deposited in Birm'[m] Reference Library.

attempting to describe the brasses of a single county. His wife Frances Margaretta, and two sons Albert and Bertram Fulke survived him. Albert contrib an interesting article 'On the Brass of Sir Hugh Hastings in Elsing Church, Norfolk' to *Archaeoligia* LX (1905), 24–52, following the discovery of one of the figures from the side shafts of the canopy of the Hastings brass. *Pubns incl: An Endeavour to Classify the Sepulchral remains of Northamptonshire or, a Discourse on Funeral Monuments in the County; delivered before the members of the Religious and Useful Knowledge Society of Northampton* (1840). A reprint of the above was announced by Gerald Coe Ltd, Wilbarston, Market Harborough, Leics., in 1969, but has not appeared to date (Dec. 1971).

HEATON, Clement (1824–82)
Glass painter and ecclesiastical metalworker: b Bradford, Wilts. *s* Rev James H., Wesleyan Minister (ob. 1862); known to be practising glass painter/designer in Warwick 1850; fd firm of Heaton & Butler [later Heaton, Butler & Bayne (q.v.)] 1857; ardent Gothicist; firm specialised in stained glass, mosaics and other church decoration, incl memorial brasses (see below); Heaton was also very keen on natural history on which he had extensive knowledge; he and his wife were early members Watford Nat. Hist Soc from its foundn in 1875 (until H's death). His wife, Mary Louisa, and brother, Ignatius, survived him.
Died: Bournemouth 24 Feb. 1882; funeral 1.3.82. *Obit: Builder* XLII, 2040, (11.3.82) 298.

HEATON, BUTLER & BAYNE LTD (London and New York)
Ecclesiastical metalworkers and stained glass mfrs: Fd 1857 as Heaton & Butler, glass painters and church decorators of London; by Clement Heaton (1824–82) [q.v.] an ardent Gothicist; and Timothy Butler, artist. Most famous for their decoration of Trinity Coll Chapel, Camb., Eaton Hall, Manchester and Rochdale Town Halls, Banbury, Ascot, West Newton and Sandringham Churches. The business continued under Heaton's son, A. Clement Heaton, and held a Royal warrant under Edward VII; the firm exhib their work many times between 1884 and 1893 at the RA (see Graves). A catalogue of the firm of c 1910 in the V&A names them as makers of 'Stained glass, mosaics, church decoration, memorial brasses, etc' advertising their metal as 'genuine "latten". Brass – the fine old metal engraved in Flemish, and afterwards in English, workshops of nearly seven centuries ago – which remains today the only suitable material for memorial brasses'. Six pages of illus follow. Their most famous figure brass is that made

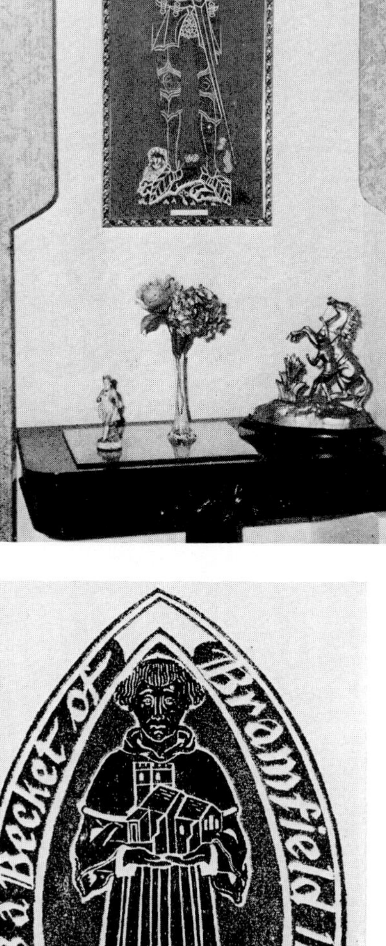

(*a*)

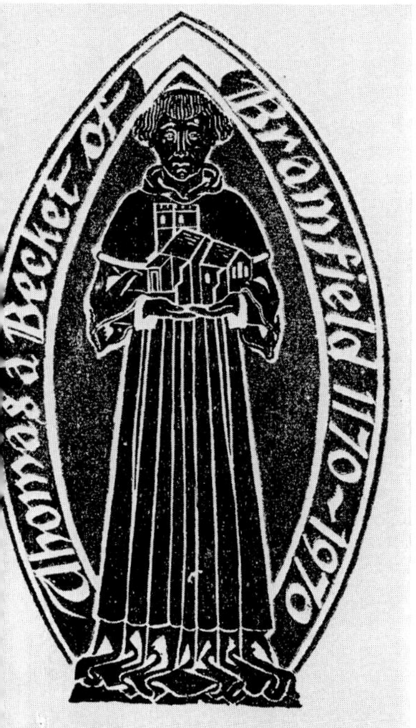

(*b*)

Plate 15

Brass Rubbings for decoration and display: (*a*) In the Home: Showing how, with good lighting, simple framing and competent mounting, a rubbing can be used to good effect in an alcove like the above; chimney breasts and stair wells offer similar scope. The rubbing shows the brass of Sir Robert Eyre (1459), Hathersage, Derbys. Photo kindly supplied by W. Clay Dove; (*b*) In Graphic Art work: A very simple, pleasing design used as the emblem of the Bramfield Becket Festival held at Bramfield (nr. Hertford), Herts in 1970. Designed by Dr Rene Pudifoot and reproduced with acknowledgements. Photo Peter Marshall (from original coloured Festival programme).

(*a*)

The
Kings
Head
Pebmarsh

MENU

Sir William Fitzralph 1323

PLATE 16

(*a*) The Menu and Wine List covers of the King's Head, Pebmarsh, Essex, making cle use of the famous Fitzralph brass in the parish church; the original shows the brass in g on black and is from a rubbing and reproduction by the skilled hand of Mr S. A. Illes of Essex (who also makes fine miniature reproductions of brasses); (*b*) The 'Fitzral Room in the King's Head at Pebmarsh, Essex; the room takes its name from the br illustrated above of Sir William Fitzralph (1323); note the other brass rubbings decorat the walls of the room. Copies of (*a*) above and the photograph adjoining kindly suppl by Mr & Mrs Peter Scott, Licensees of the King's Head (see Chapter 5)

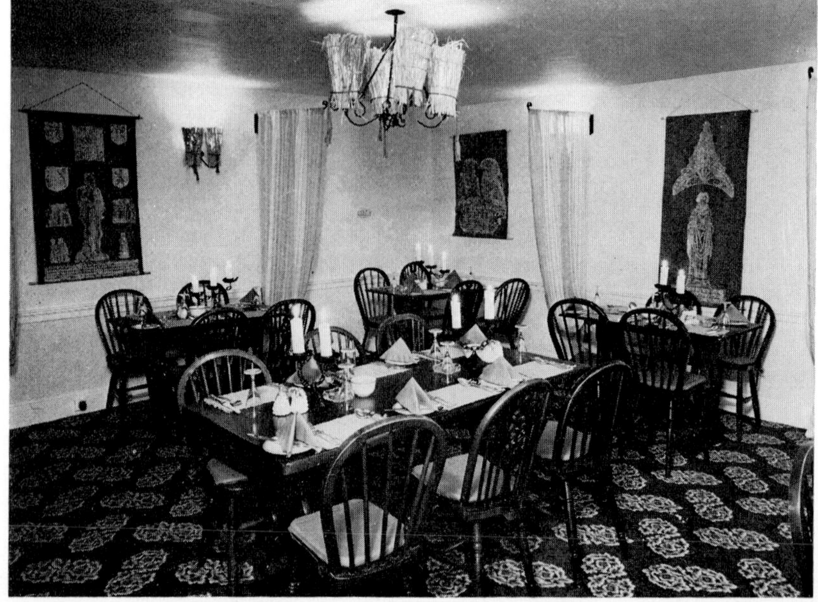

(

for Rev Herbert Haines (q.v.) now in Gloucester Cathedral. Examples of their wall plaques abound, usually signed in the lower right hand corner of the plate. A typical example can be seen at Whitchurch Canonicorum, Dorset (John Rich. Wykeham Stafford, vicar (1880–1921)) a raised letter inscr signed 'HEATON, BUTLER & BAYNE. LONDON.'

HEAVYSIDE, John Smith (1812–64)
Wood engraver: b Stockton-on-Tees; worked chiefly in London and then mainly for firm of J. H. Parker at Oxford on their antiquarian publications. Examples of his work are in Haines & Boutell, usually signed "I.H.S." Many of the drawings for the *Oxford Manual* (1848) were specially made by P. H. Delamotte and engraved by Heavyside.
Died: Kentish Town, London. 13 Oct. 1864.

HOLLAR, Wenceslus (1607–77)
Engraver: b Prague 13 July *s* Jan Hollar, lawyer; served Royalist Army during Civil War in England; c 1754 joined House of Fairthorne, engravers, and on accession of Charles II became 'His Majestie's designer'. Provided many of engr for antiquaries of day incl Thoroton's *Antiquities of Nottinghamshire* (1677); Dugdale's *History of St Paul's Cathedral in London* (1658) and the latter's *Antiquities of Warwickshire* (1656. 2nd edn in 2 vols 1730). All cont. engr of brs, mostly of inferior design, those of the latter being of such poor quality as to make one writer supposed Hollar had probably never seen the originals (see KIRBY, H. T. 'Some notes on Hollar's drawings for Dugdale's Warwickshire' *Apollo*, 38 (July 1943), 15–7.
Died: 28 Mar. 1677. *s.a.* (1) DNB (2) VERTUE, G. – *A description of the works of W. Hollar . . . with some account of his life* (1745).

HOLLES, Gervase (1606–75)
Antiquary: b Grimsby, Lincs. 9 Mar.; only surv. son Frescheville H. and Eliz. (née Kingston); *Educ* privately; adm Middle Temple 3.5.1628; *m* (1) (?) 17.6.1630 Dorothy (née Kirketon; ob. 1634–5); 1 *s* 1 *dau* (ob. 1634). (2) Eliz. (née Molesworth; ob. 1661); 1 *s* Freschville. G. H. was M.P. for Grimsby 1640, 1661–75; Oxford 1642; Royalist supporter, took part in Battle of Edgehill; Governor of Lynn, Norf. 1644; Colonel Royalist Army, serving in Holland. Retd to Grimsby 1661. Collected great many mss now in BM of antiquarian value, esp relating to Oxon., Lincs. and Notts.; incl sketches of and notes on brs and many more concerned with heraldry (esp Harl MS 6829).
Died: 10 Feb. 1675.

HUDSON, Franklin (1818–53)
Author: Of his early life I have been unable to trace details; a Franklin Hudson of Ewell, Surrey, obt the Licence of the Soc of Apothecaries 21.5.1840, and his name appears in the London Sectn of the *Medical Directory* from 1845–49 at 24 Alexander Sq, Brompton. He presumably married soon after 1849 as the intro to the small paper edn of the work below mentions a 'wife and infant daughter'. His dau, Sarah, was baptised at Braunston 9.7.1853, and the parish register names Franklin and Sarah Hudson as parents. There is no entry for the father's death, in the same year, in the burials register of Braunston. Hudson's book (and the births Register above) describe him as a 'surgeon', giving his address as 'The Willows, Braunston, Daventry'. He was a member of the Northants. Archit Soc in 1852. His sole work was published posthumously by Thomas M'Clean (q.v.), publisher, 26 Haymarket, London, who wrote a prefatory note about Hudson, dated Nov. 1st 1853. Hudson's own intro is dated July 1853, a few months before his death following a serious illness. Published in two edns, a large and small paper edn, the plates were made from rubbings by the author, and were engraved in tinted lithograph and bronze; it was first issued in four parts between about April and Nov. 1853, being divided into deaneries. Many illus are poor and, says Ralph Griffin 'the letterpress is of the most indifferent kind and is really quite worthless' (*MBS Trans* VII (3) Nov. 1936, 108–112). The large paper edn appears to me to be worse than the small in respect to the quality of the plates. M. H. Bloxam (q.v.) is said to have assisted in the work. *Pubn. Brasses of Northamptonshire* (T. M'Clean: Pub under the Patronage of the Soc of the Archdeaconry of Northants.; 1853).
Died: Oct. 1853 aet 35.

HULLMANDEL, Charles Joseph (1789–1850)
Lithographer: b Queen St, Mayfair 15 June; *s* of German musician. After period abroad retd to Somers Town, Lond. and in 1818 pubd first bk of litho drwgs. Made special study of preparing litho stone and in 1824 pubd his now famous *Art of Drawing on Stone*, explaining what was then a little understood process in England. His researches lead to many other improvements in the art, including his perfection of the graduated and litho-tint. Established his own business of litho printers, Hullmandel, Day & Haghe, and Rawlins, who produced several of the best plates in the Cambridge Camden Society's *Illus of M.B. of G.B.* (1840–46), noteably Pts 2–4 (1840–41) e.g. Sir Thomas de Cruwe and lady, Wixford, Warwicks. (1411) – repr in *Apollo* XXXVIII (July 1943), 17, and the brasses of Prior Nelond

(1433), Cowfold, Sx., and Archbp Harsnett, Chigwell, Essex (1631). *Died:* Gt Marlboro. St, London 15 Nov. 1850. *Obit: Art J* (N.S.) 3, 1 Jan. 1851, 30.

HUTCHISON, Rev Aeneas Barkly (1819–66)
Ecclesiologist and collector: b London *e.s.* Robert Hutchison; *Educ* Q. Coll, Camb., sizar 1845. Matric 1853. BD 1855. BD Oxon. 1856. Deacon Salisbury 1848. Curate St James the Gt, Devonport 1848–50; Ord Pr (Exeter) 1850; Chap Keyham Dockyard and Factory 1858. Perp. Curate St James [new church] Devonport 21.8.1850–1866. Hon Local Soc Exeter Dioc. Archit Soc; member Incorp. Soc for Promoting Enlargement of Churches and Chapels; Subscr Haines' *Manual* (1848 and 1861). Gave large colln of rubbings (rolled) to BM (Add MS. 32489). Published two works of local interest only (*see* BM Cat. or Boase for details).
Died: 25 Dec. 1866 at Harrogate.

JEANS, Rev Canon George Edward (1848–1921)
Latin scholar and ecclesiologist: b 1848 *e.s.* Rev Geo. J. of Tetney, Lincs. *Educ* Privately; Pembroke Coll, Oxon. 1867–72. BA 1872; Hertford Coll, Oxon, MA 1875. Asst Master Haileybury Sch, Amwell, Herts 1874–87; (Housemaster Bartle Frere 1879–87; Chaplain to servants). C Shorwell, I. of Wight. 1887. R Shorwell-with-Mottiston. 1887–90; Hon Canon of Winchester. R Diss, Norf. FSA adm 28.1.1892. *w* Mary Violet J., who survived him. Early member M.B.S. Author of sev guide books, incl those on Hants., I. of Wight and Lincs. *Pubns incl: List of the Existing Sepulchral Brasses in Lincolnshire* (1895) [Repr from *Lincs N&Q*].
Died: 7 Aug. 1921 at Shorwell Vicarage; *Obit:* (1) *Times* 8.8.21, 10 (d); 11.8.21, 13 (c). (2) *Antiq J* 2 (1922), 313, 314. *s.a. Haileybury Register* 1862–1961, p 2.

JEWERS, Arthur John (1848–1921)
Palaeographer and antiquary: Lived many years in Plymouth and later in London, taking special interest in the preservation and transcription of parish registers. He was elected FSA 6.3.1879, but resigned in 1892–3. He contrib sev articles to Devonshire Assn Trans Vol 33 (1901) *et seq*; Ex. Libris Soc J and edited Vol 28 of Harl Soc Registers (1901) of special interest in the present context are the 4 Vols of mss, drwgs and notes of *Monumental Inscriptions of the City of London* (1919) now in the Guildhall Lib, cont many refs to brs, and commissioned by the Corporation of London. Married, his wife Emily died 18 Apr. 1920, Mr Jewers dying a year later in Hampstead

Pubns incl: Parish registers and their preservation . . . (1884). *Obit: A. J. Jewers: an appreciation* [by R(ichard) H(olworthy)]. 1921; with portrait.

JEWITT, [Thomas] Orlando [Sheldon] (1799–1869)
Wood engraver: b Duffield, Derbys. 3 *s* Arthur J. and Martha (nèe Sheldon); Thomas' elder brothers were Rev A. G. Jewitt (author) Llewellyn Jewitt, FSA (antiquary); he had three other younger bros as well. Entirely self-taught, at 16, he illus his eldest brother's *Wanderings of Memory* (1815) and his father's newspaper *Northern Star*, with aquatints and engrs. From abt 1818–1857 he worked almost exclusively for Parkers of Oxford (q.v.) (see advert. at end of some edns of Boutell's *Brasses* (1847)), doing many of the engrs. for their famous *Glossary of Architecture* and some for Boutell's *Brasses* and *Heraldry* and Haines' *Manual* (1848 and 1861), a number of them previously appearing in the Archaeol Inst's pubns. He later moved to London where he worked for *Building News;* Murray's 'Guide Books to the English Cathedrals', etc; Member Oxford Archit Soc, Archaeol Inst (to whose jnls he contrib). Also a keen botanist. One obituary (No. 2 below) calls him 'the last of the old school of wood-engravers'. He usually signed his work 'Orlando Jewitt'.
Died: Clifton Villas, Camden Sq, London, 30th May 1869; *Obits:* (1) *Art J* (N.S.) 1869. 251–2; (2) *Builder* 27 (1375) 12.6.1869, 461.

KIRKE, George Wistor (fl 1890–1910)
American ecclesiologist: Elected member Church Club of New York 1893, serving as Vice-President 1906–9. Contrib several articles on brs to Club journal *Living Church*, two of which are noted in early issues of MBS Trans viz: (1) *Living Church* Nov. 18, 1899, incl account of brass of Abbot Thomas de la Mare, St Albans. (see note *MBS* 4) 1900–03), 40); (2) *ibid* 12 July 1902 'Rubbings of some Ancient Brasses in the collection of the New York Church Club.' (see *MBS* 4 (1900–3) 292 which says illus very small and 'letterpress inaccurate').

KITE, Edward (1832–1930)
Ecclesiologist and genealogist: b Devizes, Wilts. 14 May *s* of local grocer; *Educ* Long St Sch, Devizes, then entered his father's business (which he cont after latter's death) from 1875–7 when he began his writing and antiqn researches once again. Earlier he had been Asst Sec to Wilts. Archaeol Soc, having charge of the library for a time, but left following a disagreement with the Society's Council. Later in life he was re-instated and became the only Hon Member at the time of his death. His interest in brasses was in early life, and his only book on

the subject is a model of its kind; one obituary says that it was the 'only work he ever wrote or cared about', and is still the only complete volume covering Wiltshire; K.'s orig ms notes were purchased for Wilts. Archaeol Soc Museum, Devizes for only £12.10.0 in 1931 (see *Wilts. Mag* XLV (Dec. 1931), 471). He made the drwgs for this work on zinc plates, and also for the rev edn of Aubrey's *Wiltshire* (1862). Later his interests turned to heraldry and genealogy; in 1929 he suffered an illness imparing his hearing, though not his eye-sight, from which he never fully recovered. *Pubn Monumental Brasses of Wiltshire* . . . (Parker. 1860; repr Kingsmead Reprints 1969).
Died: 9 Jan. 1930. *Obits:* (1) *Wilts Gaz* 16.1.30 (with photo.); (2) *Wilts Archaeol & NH Soc Mag*, XLV (162), June 1930, 94–9 (incl long bibliog of his works).

LEVERET, Albon (fl 1618–50)
Athlone Pursuivant 1618–50: Made a number of drawings of sepulchral monuments in Ireland of better quality than those of contemporaries like Dineley (or Dingley). A good illus of his work, a drwg of Archbishop Talbot's brass formerly in St Patrick's Cathedral, Dublin, is in an article in *J Roy Soc Antiq of Ireland* (6 Ser) 7, (1917) f.p. 120.

LEWIS, Rev Robert Walter Michael (1866–1954)
Ecclesiologist, genealogist; President MBS. b Tonbridge, Kent. *Educ* Dulwich Coll, Corpus Christi Coll, Camb. 1889–1892; BA 1892, MA 1896. Ord D 1893, Pr 1894. C Christchurch, Erith '93–7; Sth Norwood, Middx. '97–1900. V Dersingham, Norf. 1910–23. R Morley, Derbys. 1925–9; Proctor in Convacn, Lower Hse of Cantab 1925–9; C Beckenham, Kent 1929–45. FSA 1945; Pres M.B.S. 1934–54. Began brs rubbing 1888; attended early CUABC meetings 1889, joined 18.12.89; Hon Corr Sec 1889–92; V.P. 1892. Helped re-found M.B.S. 1934. Married, his wife Mary Priscilla survived him. *Pubns incl* (1) 'Complete list of the brasses of the Isle of Wight' *CUABC* II, i (1893) 2–6; (2) 'Palimp. inscr Erith, Kent' *MBS 3* (1897–9), 203–5; (3) 'Lord Edward Bruce's heart brass' *MBS* 7, ii (Dec. 1935) 78–81; 7, iii (Nov. 1935). 114–5; (4) 'An Indent in old St Pancras Church, London' *MBS* 7, iv (Nov. 1937), 184–5; (5) 'Early days of our Society' *MBS* 8, v (Dec. 1947), 161–4.
Died: Warblerswick, Suff. 9 Oct 1954; *Obit & Port MBS* 9, iv (Dec. 1955), 212 [by R. H. Pearson].

LINNELL, Rev Charles Lawrence Scruton (1913–64)
Ecclesiologist and author: b 10 Jan. *Educ* Gresham's Sch, Norf.; Keble Coll, Oxon. MA; Ely Theol Coll where he became Chaplain; R

Letheringsett, Norf. 1951–1961; Librn and Asst Chap, Keble Coll 1961–64. FSA; Council Member and V.P. Norfolk Archaeol Soc and regular contrib to *Norfolk Archaeol, E. Anglian Mag* and other jnls. Member M.B.S. 1934–61; Pres Oxford Univ Archaeol Soc Hilary Term 1939; funds for relaying brs at Little Walsingham, Norf., after fire of 1961 met by Rev Linnell and his friends. *Pubns incl:* (1) 'On Brasses' *E Anglian Mag* July 1935, 52–4; (2) 'East Anglian Chalice brasses' *MBS* 8, i (1943) 51; (3) 'Scargill Memorial, Mulbarton, Norfolk' *ibid* 8, iii, (Dec. 1945), 91–3; (4) 'Brasses at Cley-next-the-Sea, Norfolk' *ibid* 8, v (Dec. 1947), 196–202; (5) 'East Anglian Chalice brasses' [Cont.] *ibid* 8, viii (Dec. 1950), 356–65; cont. under title 'Chalice Brasses' *MBS* 9, ii (Oct. 1952), 76–9; 9, iv (Nov. 1954), 168–9; (6) 'Mannington, Norfolk' *ibid* 9, iv, 170–71; (7) 'Wiveton, Norfolk' *ibid* 9, i (Feb. 1952), 12–16; (8) 'Chrysoms' *E Anglian Mag* Apr. 1953, 335–6; (9) *Norfolk Church Monuments* [with S. J. Waring]. 1952; (10) 'Oxnead, Norf.' *MBS* 9, v (Dec. 1955), 236–44; (11) 'Some notes on Cotman's *Brasses*' *ibid* 9, vi (Apr. 1958), 329–30; (12) *Shell Guide to Norfolk* [with W. Harrod]. 1964.
Died: 13 March 1964; *obits:* (1) *Times* 17.3.64, 12e; (2) *Nor Archaeol* 33 (1962–5), 242 [by R.W.K.C.]

MACALISTER, Robert Alexander Stewart (1870–1950)
Archaeologist: b Dublin 8 July. *s* Alexander M.; *Educ* Rathmines Sch, Dublin; privately in Germany; St John's Coll, Camb., MA, where he took early interest in brs until c 1900 when he devoted his energies to archaeological research and excavation; Dir of Excavation, Palestine Exploration Fund 1900–09, 1923–4; Prof Celtic Archaeol U.C. Dublin 1909–43; Pres Roy Irish Acad 1926–31; member Roy Soc of Antiq of Ireland, Pres 1925–8; Pres Cambrian Archaeol Assn 1932–3, 1934–5; Chairm. Ancient Monuments Advisory Council; Hist MSS Comm; early member CUABC; Hon Manager, Sec and Treas 1890; worked with C. J. P. Cave and O. J. Charlton on list of Cambs. brasses 1893–c 1900; editor MBS Trans 1897–9. *Pubns incl* (1) *Ecclesiastical vestments; their Development and History* (1896) – incl a few illus from brs as well as textual refs comp with help of F. R. Fairbank (2) 'Brasses of Cambridgeshire' (see under Cave, C. J. P.); (3) 'Brasses of Old St Paul's *MBS* I (1894), 54–60; (4) 'Durham Cathedral: an account of the lost brasses' *MBS* 2, viii (Jan. 1897) 338–42.
Died: 26 Apr. 1950 at Cambridge.

MACKLIN, Rev Herbert Walter (1866–1917)
Antiquary and ecclesiologist; President MBS: b 4 Aug. Brixton (Sy.) *s* Horace Samuel M. *Educ* Q. Eliz. G.S., Cranbrook; Manor Hse,

Hastings; St John's Coll, Camb., adm 8.9.1884. Matric 1885; BA 1888; MA 1892. Ord (Truro) 1889; Priest 1890; C St Ives, Cornw. 1889–91; Princetown, Devon 1891–3; Somersham with Pidley-cum-Fenton and Calne, Hunts. 1894–7; R Houghton Conquest, Beds. 1897–Oct. 1914. Asst Chaplain Nice 1900–01. President M.B.S. 1903–14, and author of one of most competent handbooks on brasses ever written (No. 1 below); he was gifted with a concise and clear style of writing, and his books were used as models by later writers like Beaumont and J. S. M. Ward. His *Brasses of England* (1907) received many favourable reviews (see: *MBS Trans* 5 (1904–9), 205–11; *J Brit Archaeol Assn* (N.S.) XX (i) March 1914, 49–50; *Athenaeum*, 4161, July 27, 1907, p 104). As recently as 1962 Canon Rutter referred to it as 'the best general introduction' (*MBS Trans* IX (ix), 1962, 463); it went through four edns before going O/P (4th edn 1928); several of his original notebooks (and some rubbings) are now in Univ Mus of Archaeol and Ethnology, Camb. *Pubns incl:* (1) *Monumental Brasses* . . . 1890 et seq, 7th rev edn 1953; 8th completely rev and re-written edn by J. C. Page Phillips (1970). Older edns (esp 5th edn 1905, pp 113–22) contain useful annotated bibliog; (2) 'Brasses of Huntingdonshire) *MBS* 3 (1897–9), 144–60; 167–82; (3) 'Value of despoiled slabs' *OUBRS*, 2, i (Feb. 1900), 28–34; (4) *Brasses of England* (1907) – see note above, and *s.a.* 'List of illus in . . . Macklin's *Brasses of England*, arranged topographically' *MBS* 5 (1904–9) 235–41; (5) 'Brasses at Chipping Norton, Oxon'. CUABC No. 7 (Feb. 1890), 14–15.
Died: 16 Jan. 1917; *obit: Times* 18.1.1917.

M'CLEAN, Thomas (1788–1875)
Publisher and Bookseller: of 26 Haymarket, London W.; estab 1825 at 69 Haymarket, but had moved to former address by 1831 (see *Post Office London Dir* 1831); specialist in coloured lithographic printing and most famous for his prints of Sir Edward Landseer's paintings, Gillroy's works and humorous sporting prints. Also published Frankn. Hudson's *Brasses of Northamptonshire* (q.v.) for which he [M'Clean] wrote preface following Hudson's early decease in 1853. When M'Clean retired the business was handed over to his son.

MALCOLM, James Peller (1767–1815)
Engraver and antiquary: b Philadelphia, U.S.A. and chiefly known for his drawings in Lysons' *Environs of London*. Vol I (1800); for *Gent Mag* betw 1792 and 1814; Nichol's *Leicestershire*, etc. He also published several topographical works himself, including *Lives of the Topographers and Antiquaries* . . . (1815) and the fine *Londinium*

Redivivem. 4 vols 1802–7; he made a number of tinted drwgs of brasses in the 1790's when working/living at 34 Charlton St, Somers Town, several of which, of good standard, can be seen in an annotated copy of Lysons' *Environs* given by A. J. Jewers to the Guildhall Lib London.
Died: 5 Apr. 1815.

MANN, Sir James Gow (1897–1962)
Antiquary and author: b 23 Sept. *s* Alexander M. *Educ* Winchester; New Coll, Oxon., MA BLitt; Asst Keeper Dept of Fine Arts, Ashmolean Mus., Oxon. 1921–4; Asst Keeper Wallace Colln 1924–32; Depy Dir Courtauld Inst of Art 1932–6; Dir Wallace Colln 1936–62; Master of Armouries, Tower of London 1939–62; FSA (1924); Dir Soc of Antiq of London 1944–49; Pres 1949–54. Surveyor of the Queen's Works of Art 1952–62; Chairman Nat Bldgs Record; Governor Nat Army Museum, etc. KCVO, FBA, leading authority on European armour. Made careful study of military brs for their value in illus the devpt of armour, and coll series of rubbings of 'Milanese' brs for comparative purposes for Wallace Colln. Wrote many books and articles on this subj and re-wrote the fine catalogue of arms and armour in the Wallace Colln (pub 1962 in 2 vols); went to great pains to correct faulty nomenclature of terms describing pieces of armour used by older writers, incl those on brasses; the catalogue also has a valuable glossary of its own (Vol. I pp, xxxii–li) and Vol II a long bibliography, pp 629–666. *m* [1] Mary (née Cooke (ob. 1936)); [2] Evelyn Aimée (née Hughes); 1 *dau. Pubns incl* (1) *English Church Monuments 1536–1625* (Walpole Soc 21 (1933)). (2) 'A 15th cent description of the brass of Sir Hugh Hastings at Elsing, Norfolk' [with Sir A. R. Wagner] *Antiq J* XIX (4) Oct. 1939, 421–8; (3) *Monumental Brasses* (King Penguin. 1957); (4) 'Nomenclature of Armour' *MBS* 9 (viii) Dec. 1961, 414–28; (5) 'Armour in Essex' *EAST* (N.S.) XXII, ii (1939), 276–98 [sev illus from brs.]
Died: 6 Dec. 1962; *obit:* (1) *Proc Brit Academy* 47 (1963), 407–11, with port [by F. J. B. Watson] (2) *Antiq J* XLIII (1963). Pt II, 187–8, 365.

MANNING, Rev Charles Robertson (1825–99)
Ecclesiologist: b Diss, Norf. 2 July; 2 *s* Rev Wm. M. (ob. 1857) Rector of Diss; *Educ* privately; Corpus Christi Coll, Camb. BA 1847, MA 1850; Ord Deacon (Norwich) 1848; Pr 1850; R (and Patron) Diss 1857–99; Hon Canon of Norwich; Rural Dean Redenhall; Member (a) Norfolk and Norwich Archaeol Soc and Jt Hon Sec 1852–95; V.P. 1895–1899; (b) Suffolk Inst of Archaeol; (c) Royal

Archaeol Inst; (d) FSA 1886; (e) Hon Sec Archit Sect, Beds. Archit and Archaeol Soc in 1880's (Pres then M. H. Bloxam; V.P. Rev H. Addington); (f) M.B.S. *m* (1) Emilia (née Upwood), ob. 1855; (2) Florence Charlotte (née Waller; ob. 1899). 1 *s* Charles Upwood *b* 1857; Compiler while at Camb. of first list of brs in U.K. (pub 1846), to which that of Rev Herbert Haines, pubd two years later (ie. *Oxford Manual* 1848) was indebted and to which Rev M. was a subscriber; also knew Boutell and many other famous antiquaries of 19th cent. *Pubns incl* (1) *List of the M.B. remaining in England, arranged according to counties* (1846). Some corrections by F. S. Growse appeared in *N&Q* X, 4 Nov. 1854, 361–2, 520–21; (2) '*Norfolk Archaeology: general index to the first ten vols* comp by Rev C.R.M. (1847). His own contrib began in Vol 3; (3) 'Matrix of a br in St Paul's, Bedford' *N&Q* 6 (4) 1881, 145–6 (refuting existance of Beauchamp slab, 1208); (4) 'Monumental brass inscriptions in Norfolk omitted in Blomefield's History of the County' *Norf Archaeol* X (1886–91), 192–224; XI (1892), 72–104, 182–207. illus.

Died: 2 Feb. 1899; *obits:* (1) *Eastern Daily News* 3.2.1899, repr *MBS* 3 (1897–9) 227–9; (2) *Norf Archaeol* XIV, i (1899), iv–v.

MANNING, Percy (1870–1917)

Antiquary: b Leeds, Yorks. *Educ* Clifton Coll, New Coll, Oxon., MA; Interest in antiq matters began in student days, esp in local hist of Oxfordshire; collected large series of books, drwgs, engr etc, on same. Sec and V.P. Oxford Archit and Hist Soc, having spec interest in late Celtic pottery and folklore, on which he contrib papers to *Folk-Lore J* and *SAP* Founder-member OUBRS (May 1893); joined National Reserve of Oxford and Bucks. L.I., att rank of Q.M.; died during military service. FSA elec 4.8.1896; removed from Register 23.4.1907; re-elected 18.6.1908. *Pubns incl* (1) 'Notes on the m.b. in Chipping Norton Ch, Oxfordshire. *OUBRS* I, i, (Feb. 1897), 3–10; (2) 'M.B. in Queen's College, Oxon' *ibid* ii (June 1897) 67–79; (3) 'M.B. in the churches of St Aldgate and St Peter-le-Bailey, Oxford' *ibid* iii, (Dec. 1897) 103–9; (4) 'M.B. in the Deanery of Henley- on-Thames, Oxfordshire' *ibid* v, (Oct. 1898) 237–54, *ibid* vi (May 1899) 286–306; (5) 'On several M.B. now in private possession' *SAP* (2 Ser) XVIII, May 17, 1900, 186–89; (6) 'List of brs in Lancaster Parish Church' *MBS* 5 (1904–9) 90–3; (7) 'Palimpsest brs from Quarrenden, Bucks. and Stanton St John, Oxfordshire' *OUBRS*, 2, iii (March 1912), 153–7.

Died: Southampton, 27 Feb. 1917 aet 47. *Obit: SAP* (2 Ser). XXIX, 23.4.1917, 156, 162.

MORLEY, Henry Thomas (1861–1951)
Antiquary, artist and collector: devoted most of his life to the study of Berkshire history on which he became an authority; he maintained a long association with the Berks. Archaeol Soc being Treas 1918–24; Excursion Secretary 1924–49; Secretary 1930–9; V.P. (with Mrs E. Morley) 1946–19 Mar. 1949 when he resigned the office; he was then made an Hon Life Member. He was a JP for the County; Hon Curator Reading Museum; FRHistS; MSP; FSA(Scot) – elec 1931; FSP and FRSA; he also had a BSc (Archaeol). He wrote a great many articles in his lifetime as well as publishing a valuable book on the brs of his own county; his rubbings are now in the colln of the Berks. Archaeol Soc (see p 153 above). His effects were willed to Henry Thomas Morley, printer. *Pubns incl* (1) *Monumental Brasses of Berkshire* (1924;* repr announced for pubn early 1972, by Thames Valley Press, Maidenhead, Berks. price abt £5.00). A review by W. J. Greenstreet appeared in *Berks. Archaeol J* 28; i (Spring 1924) 58–60; (2) 'Shroud brs of Berks.' *Berks. Archaeol J* 33, i (Spring 1929), 34–9; (3) *Old and curious playing cards* . . . (Batsford. 1931); (4) 'Lettering on some m.b. of Berks.' *Berks. Archaeol J* 48 (1944–5), 43–46; (5) 'Notes on Arabic Numerals in Mediaeval England' *ibid* 50 (1947), 81–6 [incl many examples from m.b.'s].
Died: Reading, 10 Jan. 1951, aet 89; *obit: Berks. Archaeol J* 53 (1952–3), 27–8 by F. M. Underhill (with port as frontis).

[NATIONAL] SOCIETY FOR PRESERVING THE MEMORIALS OF THE DEAD.
Fd 1881; inaugural meeting May 10, 1882 (see *Antiq* 5 (June 1882), 275) aim 'to preserve memorials in parish churches and churchyards . . . ' *Patron* Archbishop of Cantab.; many distinguished vice-patrons. First Secretary Wm. Vincent; Hon Monumental Conservator, R. Davison. Long list of members; early lists incl names of sev persons cited in this *Who was Who* incl J. L. André (who contrib a paper 'English Monuments; Mediaeval, Jacobean and Georgian' to Vol I of Society's *Journal* (pp 175–92)); R. T. Andrews (brother of W. F. Andrews above); Rev C. G. R. Birch; C. A. Buckler, R. H. Edleston and Andrew Oliver (who was Council Member 1892–3); First *Journal* Vol I, No. 1, issued 1882; includes many notes and papers on brasses, esp where loss or damage has occurred. On p 38 of the same volume is a letter dd 16 Sept. 1882, from Rev G. E. Haviland of Warbleton Rectory, asking how his brasses should be protected. Mill Stephenson

* A copy of the original prospectus (4 pages) in Herts. C.R.O. gives sample illus. and full list of subscr., which incl Dr G. H. S. Bushnell, Mill Stephenson and W. H. S. Short.

commented on the Society's advice on protecting brasses with 'lead sheeting' with some amusement!

NICHOLS, John (1745–1826)
Antiquary and publisher: b London, *Educ* Islington and later apprenticed to Wm. Bowyer (jnr) with whom he went into partnership in 1866. Editor of sev imp literary antiqn works; prop *Gents Mag* 1792–1826; publisher *Bibliotheca Topographica* (10 vols 1780–1800) and author and publisher, under imprint of J. Nichols & Sons, of the famous *History and Antiquities of the County of Leicester* (4 vols in 8 pts 1795–1809). The first two vols of a reprint of the above appeared 20 May 1971; being re-printed by E.P. Publishers Ltd in 8 vols with new intro (£100 the set or £13.75 per vol; it is hoped to publish 2 vols per year); this massive work contains many references and some illus of varying quality of brs, mainly engraved by Barak Longmate, Jnr (1768–1836). Married, J.N.'s eldest son, John Bowyer N. (q.v.) succeeded his father to the business.

NICHOLS, John Bowyer (1779–1863)
Antiquary and publisher: b London 15 July *e.s.* John N. and *w* Martha. *Educ* St Paul's Sch till 1796, when he entered his father's publishing business. *m* 1805, Eliza (née Baker) who bore him 14 child of which 3 *s* and 4 *dau* survived. Jt Editor *Gents Mag;* proprietor 1833 with Wm. Pickering; sold interests to J. H. Parker (q.v.) 1856. In 1818 fd firm of J. Nichols, Son & Bentley of Red Lion Passage, Fleet St, and 25 Parliament Sq' Printer to Corpn of London; Master of Stationers' Co. 1850. Publisher of many of 19th cent county histories and of Wallers' *Series . . .* (1843–64); FLS 1812; FSA 1818. Orig Member of Athenaeum Club. (fd 1824). Archaeol Inst, Numismatic Soc and Roy Soc of Lit, His eldest son, John Gough N. (1806–73) followed his father into the printing business and was responsible for pub Hoare's *Wiltshire* and sev imp jnls incl *Herald & Genealogist* (1863–74); *Register & Mag of Biography* (1869); *Topographer & Genealogist* (1846–58); *Collectanea Topog et Geneal* (1835–43). Some of J.G.N.'s brass rubbings given by Sir A. W. Franks (q.v.) to Soc of Antiq.
J.B.N. *died* at Ealing, London 19 Oct. 1863; *obits:* (1) *Gent Mag* 1863 Pt 2, 794–8; (2) *Athen* 24.10.1863; (3) *SAP* 23.4.1863, 393–4.

OLDFIELD, Henry George (fl 1789–1805)
Topographical artist: Free-lance draughtsman who worked for John Meyrick, FSA (father of the famous Sir John Rush Meyrick, authority on arms and armour); made valuable series of 194 drwgs of Hertford-

shire brasses betw c 1789–1800, now part of Dimsdale Colln in Herts. C.R.O., as well as working in other counties. His drawings were generally accurate, tinted with yellow wash, but not to scale. Another (amateur) artist, John Pridmore (1762–1837) made copies of many of the above and has been acredited erroneously with the originals on occasion.
S.a. HALL, H. R. Wilton – Notes and memo . . . *StAAS* (1895 and 1896), 29–152.

OLIVER, Andrew (1858–1927)
Architect and ecclesiologist: b Alnick, Northumb. early 1858. From early life a keen student of brs and archit; ARIBA; practised mainly in London. Contr. articles on brs and other matters (incl London history) to many archit, archaeol and antiq jnls incl *Ars. Quatuor Coronatorum* [Lodge Quatuor Coronati No. 2076, London], tho. he does not appear in the Lodge's records as a member. Member: StAHAAS (and contrib talks during excursions, plus notes to their Trans); Salisbury Field Club; Brit Archaeol Assn from 1889, and Council member on sev occasions; corr Member CUABC/MBS – accepted editorship of revn of Camb. sectn of Haines' List (5.5.1890); gave many rs to Soc. Had sev reprod of brs printed at own expense, plus many others reprod in *The Builder* during 1880's and 1890's of high standard, with accomp notes. After 1914–18 war little heard of him, and his death is scantily recorded; he left two sisters, Mary Elizabeth and Katherine Janet to whom probate was granted. *Pubns incl* (1) 'Brasses of the 14th and 15th centuries' [Read 6.1.1888 to Archit Assn]. *AAN* II, 18 (1888–9); *Build News* 54 (1888), 9 and 68; *Brit Archit* 29 (1888), 34 with notes on making rs; *Builder* 54 (1888), 30–32 [Hist and notes on br rg.]; 50, 74, 144 (letters); *Archit* 39 (1888), 25. (2) 'A Brass Society' (letter dd 12.3.1888] *ANN* II (13) Apr. 1888, 248 (note on form^{n} CUABC); (3) 'Notes on Flemish Brasses in England' [a lecture read at Pub Lib, St Albans 12.11.1889] St Albans: W. Cartmel. 1889 (off-print); *ibid* read before CUABC 10.3.1890 (see *CUABC Trans* IX (1891), 16; *AAN* XII (1897), 37–9, 53–5; *BAA* (N.S.) 8 (1902), 195–208. (4) 'Notes on English m.b.' *Salisbury Field Club, Trans* I (1890–93), 57–76. (5) 'Eng. m.b. of the 13th, 14th and 15th centuries'. Read at St Albans 4.12.1890; pubd *AAN* 18 (1903), 17–21. (6) 'Brs in London Museums' *Archaeol J*, XLVII (1891), 286–9; also *Antiq* 25 (May 1892), 197–200. (7) 'Brass of Andrew Evyngar in All Hallows, Barking' *St PES*, III (1891), iv, v; *BAA* XLVIII, 263–4. (8) 'Brasses and the Archit Assn Excursion' [Etchingham, Ticehurst, Penshurst and Canterbury] *AAN* XI (114). Sept. 1896, 84–5. (9) 'List of m.b. in the City of London' *AAN* XI (115) Oct.

1896, 104–6; (10) 'Notes on the matrix of a br in Woodbridge Ch, Suff.' *MBS* 2 (1899), 11–12. (11) 'Note on the brasses of Berks.' [Read at Reading Congress BAA 18.7.1905] *BAA* (N.S.) 12 (1906), 12–17. *illus.* (12) 'Notes on the br of Robt Honeywood, St George's Chapel Windsor' *MBS* 5 (1904–9), 111–2; *Berks, Bucks & Oxon Archaeol J* (N.S.) 12, i (1906) 6. (13) 'Flemish brs in Eng.' *ibid*, 5–6. (14) 'M.B. in the City of London'. *Antiq* (N.S.) 5 (1909), 54–9. (15) *Incised Effigies of Staffordshire* (Sprague. 1913.) 23 p + 40 pl. Pub by subscr with 40 line drwgs to scale, each with short descr notes. Subscr incl Beloe, Christy, Gawthorp, Rev H. F. Oliver, Prideaux, Sanderson and Mill Stephenson (q.v.) (16) Oliver also prop pub by subscr *Mon Br of the County of Derby;* price 13/6d per copy; 35 plates, but this never appeared (see *MBS* 3 (1897–9), 268). Mr F. A. Greenhill (*Incised Slabs of Leics. & Rutland* p 22) says the former work (15 above) is 'poor and incomplete'.
Died: 5 Queens Gdns, Hyde Pk, 20 Sept. 1927 aet 69. *Obit* (1) Note of death at RIBA meeting 21.11.1927; no details (2) *Times* 16.1.1928, 15d – will noted.

ORD, Craven (1756–1832)
Antiquary: b London *y.s.* Harry O. and Ann (née Hutchinson); most closely assoc with Sir John Cullum (q.v.) in prompting Rich. Gough (q.v.) to write his *Sepulchral Monuments*, with which Ord asst. In Sept. 1780 he made an extensive tour of E. Anglia (with Gough and Cullum) in search of brs, and helped form fine colln of impressions of brs in S.E. England. Their *modus operandi* is described briefly in my *Beginner's Guide* (p 26) and in other works on brasses. Engravings from Ord's work, mainly by the Basires (q.v.) appeared in *Archaeologia*, to which O. also contrib on antiqn and other matters. One of the most frequently seen reproductions is from his impression of the Hasting's brass (1347) at Elsing, Norf. showing it almost complete (for e.g. see article by R. H. D'Elboux (q.v.) *E. Anglian Mag* 6 (12) Aug. 1947, p 653). A little known drwg by Ord, dd. 10 Oct., 1777, of a now lost br at Cherry Hinton, Cambs. is repr in *MBS* 8, v (Dec. 1947), f.p. 77. Ord's colln of rs were purchased by Thorpe, the bookseller, in 1830 for £43/1/– in two huge folios over 6 ft high; these now in BM with those of Cullum (Add MSS 32478–9); sale catalogues of his fine library of books and MSS, esp of Suffolk material, are also in BM (pubd 1829 and 1830); much of the contents of the sale also in BM (Add MSS 7101–2; 8986–7). *m* (1784) Mary (née Smith); *5 s*, 1 *dau.*
Died: Woolwich Common, Jan. 1832 *Obit: Gent Mag* 1832, Pt I, 469–70. *S.a.* TORR, V. J. B. 'Guide to Craven Ord' *MBS IX*, ii (Oct. 1952), 80–91; IX, iii (1954), 133–45.

OXFORD LADIES ARCHAEOLOGICAL & BRASS RUBBING SOCIETY (o/w. Ladies Brass Rubbing Society of Oxford).
Fd Nov. 14th, 1894 at the house of James Parker (jnr), the Oxford publisher. First *President* Miss Swann. *Hon Secs* Misses Parker and Stone. Early notes record 25 members and 1 corresp member. They also had a room in Polstead Rd, where they had a library of books and rubbings. Visiting speakers inc. E. T. Beaumont (q.v.); talks covered antiquarian as well as brass rubbing matters. Their reports and notes were issued jointly in the *Berks, Bucks and Oxfordshire Archaeol J* until 1927 (see: Vol 31 (2) Autumn 1927, 199 when Miss Swann, Secretary, reported the disbanding of the Society).

OXFORD UNIVERSITY BRASS RUBBING SOCIETY (OUBRS)
Fd: 1893 by Rev Harry Fowler Haines (q.v.), son of Rev Herbert Haines, Percy Manning (q.v.) *et al.* 'for the study of monumental brasses and kindred subjects'. Its parent might be said to be the Oxford Archit Soc, of which Revs Herbert Haines and Charles Boutell were early members. The OUBRS held its first meeting in May 1893 under its President elect, Hon H. A. Dillon (q.v.); it pubd its own *Journal* (price 5/– p.a. or 1/9d each) of which only nine issues appeared, viz. Pt I, No. 1 (Feb. 1897) – 6 (May 1897), Pt. II No. 1 (Feb. 1900); No. 2 (1901) and No. 3 (March, 1912). A *Portfolio* was first issued in a limited edn of 200 copies from 1898–1901, then becoming defunct; *Series 2* was issued betw 1950–55 (Pts 1–5) and this year [1971] an attempt is being made to revive it once again. The *Journal* contains some articles of high standard, and has some valuable book reviews and literature surveys; the Society also issued numerous pamphlets and broadsheets of their meetings and activities, incl one entitled *A plea for the better preservation of mon brs*, In 1901 the OUBRS was absorbed into the Oxford Univ Antiquarian Soc, but had to be 'resuscitated' again in 1911, it was disbanded during the 1914–18 war, but was reconstituted and renamed the Oxford Archaeol Soc in 1919 under the guidance of Mr E. T. Leeds and now continues to grow. The President in Hilary Term 1939 was the Rev C. L. S. Linnell (q.v.) One of the most successful pubns on brs is the valuable handbook *Notes on Brass Rubbing*, first issued by the O.A.S. in 1941 and now in its 6th rev edn (1969). For a brief history of the Society see P. W. Dixon. *The Oxford University Archaeological Society 1919–1969: an outline history*. Pub by the Society, 1970 (price £0.10); 21 pages; typescript.

PARKER, John Henry (1806–84)
Antiquary and publisher: b London 1 Mar, *s* John P.; *Educ* Manor Hse Sch, Chiswick, entered bookselling 1821 and in 1832 succeeded to firm

of Joseph Parker of Oxf., publrs and bksellers. A keen archit student he pubd (1849) his famous *Intro to the Study of Gothic Archit*, a sequel to his earlier *Glossary of Terms* . . . (1836 *et seq.*) containing notes on brasses, incised slabs, etc by Albert Way (q.v.) Parker also pubd and/or sold, Boutell's and Haines' works, and materials for rubbing; he was a good friend to both men, espec Haines, and met or knew most of famous antiquaries of day; FSA 7.6.1849 and freq contrib to *Archaeologia;* Hon MA Oxon. 27.6.1867; keeper Ashmolean Museum 1869/70–1884. V.P. Oxford Archit Soc; Brit. and American Archaeol Soc of Rome; Archaeol Inst (whose *Journal* he pubd). *m* Frances (née Hoskyns). 1 *s* James, who succeeded to business; 1 *dau* who was founder member Oxford Ladies Brass Rubbing Soc (q.v.)
Died: 31 Jan 1884. *Obit: SAP*, 2 Ser X (1883–5), 79–81.

PEARSON, Reginald Hammond (1878–1961)
Ecclesiologist and engineer; President M.B.S.: Joined M.B.S. 1906, making special study of continental brs and in later years in the repair and refixing of brasses; as Managing Director of his own firm of aerial ropeway engineers, his engineering experience and a long association with W. E. Gawthorp (q.v.) helped a great deal to enlarge his technical skill in his former interests. In the early 1930's the two men wrote a series of articles for *Notes & Queries* giving details of some of their work and findings. The present writer had the privilage of watching Mr Pearson's skilled work in progress in 1956 when some of the famous brs at Digswell, Herts. were re-laid with his help and advice. Mr Pearson was largely responsible for the re-birth in 1934 of the M.B.S.; he was Hon Sec and Treasurer from 1934–60 and President 1960–61. He was elected an FSA in 1944, at the same time becoming Hon Keeper of the huge colln of br rubbings at the Society. His skill as a draughtsman is seen in his reconstruction of the Flemish brass from which the palimpsest fragments at Walken (Herts.), Marsworth (Bucks.) and Lee (Kent) were cut (see illus *MBS* 9, iii (July 1954), 109); the orig. copy of the drawing is in the Univ Museum of Archaeol and Ethnol, Cambridge and is dd. 3.12.1933). He left a widow at his death. *Pubns incl:* (1) 'Recently discovered palimpsest brasses'. *MBS* 7, i (Dec. 1934), 18–23; (2) 'A hidden br in the Church of St Jacques at Bruges' *ibid*, ii (Dec. '35), 71–5; (3) 'Palimp br in St Giles Cath, Edinburgh' *ibid*, iii (Nov. '36), 130–5; (4) 'Brasses in private possession' *ibid*, iv (Nov. 1937), 178–80; (5) 'Medieval M.B. at Antwerp'. *ibid*, v (June 1938), 216–28; (6) 'Brasses to the Arundell family at Mawgan-in-Pyder, Cornwall'. [with M. Stephenson]. *Antiq J* Apr. 1939, 125–46, repr *MBS* 7, vii (Oct. 1940), 303–20; (7) 'Kelmarsh, Northants' *MBS* 8, ii (Dec.

'44), 66; (8) 'Two fragments at Bruges'. *ibid*, iv (Dec. '46), 148–9. *Died:* 27 Feb. 1961 at Croydon; *obits:* (1) *MBS* 9, viii (Dec. '61) 411–12 by H. F. O. E[vans] and Augustus White (with photo); (2) Antiq. *J* 41 (1961), 278 (note only).

PHILIPOT (or PHILPOT), John (1588/9–1645)
Somerset Herald: b Folkestone, Kent. 2 *s* Henry P. and Judith (née Leigh); Henry (ob. 1603) has a br inscr in Folkestone Ch. *Educ:* privately; apprenticed 20.6.1604 to Edm. Houghton, a London draper being adm to Draper's Co. 1611. His strong interest in heraldry and antiq soon caused him to leave business and in 1613 he was nominated Blanch Lyon Pursuivant Extraordinary; promoted 19.11.1618 to Rouge Dragon Pursuivant in Ordinary; 14.6.1624 bought office of Somerset Herald. Adm as member Lincolns Inn 8.8.1635, but does not appear to have been called to Bar; appt Registrar College of Arms 1637. Employed many times on Visitations by Wm. Camden during which time he made many of his heraldic and topog notes. Betw 1621 and 1640 P. was fined or cautioned for various offences connected with his duties. Appt land and water Bailiff, Sandwich, Kent. 1623. M.P. for Sandwich 1623. M.P. for Sandwich 1627/8; Steward of Royal Manors of Gillingham and Grain. Royalist during Civil Wars and accomp'd King to Oxford (where P. rec'd degree of DCL) and later Gloucester; captured 1645 and returned to London a prisoner where he died 'in great obscurity'. He was buried at St Benet's, Pauls Wharf, the Heralds' Church. *m* 1612 Susan (née Glover) who died 1664/5. 2 *s* 2 *dau* (named in will PCC54 Fines). P. also colld much material for hist of Kent but it was never pubd under his name, altho. his son Thomas did produce one in 1659 cont material by his father; other antiquaries like Weever (q.v.) and Camden also made good use of P's notes. Many of P's books and some MSS are now in Coll of Arms; others in BM (esp Harl M.S. 3917 and Egerton MS 3310 on Kentish hist). For very full account of P. see valuable article by H. S. London 'John Philipot MP. Somerset Herald, 1624–45'. *Archaeol Cant.* LXI (1947), 24–53, 134 (repr as pamphlet 1948). The DNB only contains a very brief account. *See also* 'A book of Church notes by John Philipot, Somerset Herald (BM Egerton MS 3310)' *ed* by C. R. Councer and contained in: *Kent Records: a seventeenth century miscellany* (Kent Archaeol Soc Pubns) XVII (1960), 68–114. This contains many repr of sketches of glass, tombs and brasses, with notes.
Died: London, 22 Nov. 1645.

PORTEOUS, William Wade (1872–1963)
Ecclesiologist: b 22 March, Saffron Walden, Essex. *s* George P. *Educ:* Saffron Walden G.S. *Employed* Quaker Bank; Gibson, Take & Gibson

(where he met Miller Christy (q.v.) who was then a junior clerk, and with whom his name is most closely associated). Began rubbing 1884; betw 1893 and 1913 collab. with Christy in recording over 300 Essex brasses. Joined M.B.S. 1894, Hon Auditor 1898–1905; *m* Gwendoline Elsie who survived him. For pubns see under *Christy, Miller*. Also, *MBS* II, 6 (Dec. 1895), 213–5 'On two brasses from Braughing now in Saffron Walden Museum'.
Died: Tunbridge Wells, Kent 4 Oct. 1963; *obit: MBS Trans* X (1) 1963, 35 [short note by 'N.R.B.'].

POWELL, Rev David Thomas (–1848)
Antiquary and genealogist: b London; *s* Thomas P. *Educ* Privately, Magdalen Coll, Oxon. Matric 21.3.1798, BCL 12.6.1805; jnd 14th Light Dragoons, attaining rank of Lt; served at Cork, Flanders and Brabent, 1794; coll notes for *Topographical Account of Tattershall* [Lincs.] (1813); v keen student of heraldry and geneal, accumulated large colln of books, MSS and drwgs etc of inscr, monuments and brasses, now in 8 vols in BM. (Add MSS 17456–63) viz: vol I Beds. and Bucks.; II Berks.; III Cambs., Hereford and Herts.; IV Devon and Dorset; V and VI Essex; VII Leics., Lincs. and Norfolk; VIII Somerset. Colln sold by auction 31 July–4 Aug. 1848. For e.g. of one of his drwgs of brs see *MBS* 8, iii (Dec. 1945), f.p. 74 (Fitzralph br, Pebmarsh, Essex, c 1323).
Died: Tottenham, London 9 June 1848. *obits:* (1) *Gent Mag* 1848 Pt II, 438–9; (2) *Ann Reg* 89 (1848), 232 note only.

PRIDEAUX, William de Courcey (1862–1923)
Ecclesiologist and Inventor: b Wellington, Somerset. *Educ* privately, qualified as dentist (LDS Eng. 1899), practiced in London for few years, then joined his brother's (C. S. Prideaux) practice in Dorchester; later est own practice at Weymouth. Pres Wessex Branch, Brit. Dental Assn; best known nationally for his invention of the Prideaux or Mk IIIx steel feed belt links used in Vicker's Machine guns during Great War; despite official inertia and unreward in London, he was awarded the Chevalier de l'Étoile Noire for his services to France; flew with Hawker against Von Richthofen, the German air-ace; LSD, RCS Eng.; FRSM, FSA. Joined Dorset NH and AFC 1900 – V.P.; Member Somerset and Devon Archaeol Socs; contrib to antiquarian and dental journals. His wife Mary and 3 child survived him. Died through anxiety over his wartime inventions and overwork. *Pubns incl* (1) 'Ancient Memorial brasses of Dorset' *Procs Dorset Nat Hist and Antiq Field Club.* XXIII (1902), 195–208; XXV (1904), 144–55,

XXVII (1906), 234–8; XXVIII (1907), 226–44; XXIX (1908), 273–80; XXXII (1911), 213–25; XXXIV (1913), 158–66; XXXV (1914), 75–80; XXXVI (1915) 225–9; XXXVIII (1916) 124–32; XL (1919), 48–51. Illus; (2) 'M.B. of Dorsetshire' *Jnl BAA*, (N.S.) XIII (1907), 209–26. illus.
Died: 8 June 1923 at Herrison, Nr Dorchester, Dorset; *obits:*(1) *Southern Times* 16.6.1923; (2) *Procs Dorset NHAFC* XLV (1924), lxxxvii–viii; (3) *Brit Dental J* (1923), 723; (4) *Dental Record* (1923), 724; (5) *Antiq J*, 4 (1924), 322, 325.

PUGIN, Augustus Welby Northmore (1812–52)
Architect and ecclesiologist: b London 1 Mar. *s* Augustus Charles P. (1762–1832) Catherine (née Welby). *Educ* Christs Hospital; Trained as archit by his father. *m* (1) 1831 Ann (née Garnett) ob. 1832 (2) 1833 Louisa (née Burton) ob. 1844, (3) 1848 Jane (née Knill). 8 children. Opened archit supply shop 1831 which failed; settled first in Ramsgate where he designed own house; wrote first book on archit 1835. Ardent Gothicist whose work found great favour in new revival. Appt Commissioner of Fine Arts, Gt Exhib 1851, but work too much for him and he was committed to an asylum; died shortly afterwards at home. During early years worked closely with John Hardman (q.v.) of Birmingham, another Gothicist and R. C.; Pugin became R.C. in 1834; taught eccles antiq at Oscott 1838–44, designed several brasses for firm (see p 40 above) Coll fine library of books, prints and MSS on medieval art. His eldest son Edward Welby (1834–75) carried on his fathers practice. P. pubd many books on Gothic art, as well as having a large private library of his own, and his influence was long felt on Victorian architecture and design. In his famous work *An Apology for the Revival of Christian Architecture in England* (John Weale. 1848), Pugin includes notes on 'Sepulchral Memorials' (pp 33–7), showing how contemporary fashions can be adapted to brasses and other monuments. In Pls V and VI he shows actual examples of such brasses of his own design, the two in the latter Plate being particularly fine; one is in memory of Lady Gertrude Fitzpatrick (ob. 30 Sept 1841), showing her kneeling under a fine Gothic tabernacle surmounted by a cross; the other in memory of Dame Margaretta Sarah Morris (ob. 13 Jan. 1841), showing an ornate octofoil cross (similar to that on the Paris br (1408) at Hildersham, Cambs.) within a heavy marginal inscr with Evan. symbols at corners. The influence of Pugin's work can be clearly seen in many Victorian brasses, especially ecclesiastics. For account of his life and work (though almost none mention his designs for brs), see: (1) CLARK, Sir K. – *Gothic revival* (1928. 2nd edn 1962); (2) EASTLAKE, C. L. *Hist of*

the Gothic revival (1872 repr Leics. U.P. 1969); (3) GWYNN, D. – *Lord Shrewsbury, Pugin and the Gothic Revival* (1946) (4) STANTON. P. A. – *Welby Pugin and the Gothic Revival* (Thesis: Univ of Lond., Courtauld Inst. of Art, June. 1950.) At the time of writing (Aug. 1971) a book by the above was also announced '*Pugin*' (Thames & H. £2.95 (£1.50 pbk)); (5) TRAPPES-LOMAX, M. – *Pugin, a Medieval Victorian* (1932) (6) DELANEY, J. J. *and* TOBIN J. E· – *Dict of Catholic Biog* (1962), p 963.
Died: 14 Sept. 1852 at Ramsgate.

RICHARDSON, Henry Samuel (1812–1905)
Printer and bookseller: b Stockwell St, Greenwich where he inherited his father's printing business in 1834 from his mother Harriett; in the same year he pubd a history of Greenwich. Early member Brit Archaeol Assn from 1844, before whom he exhib some rubbings at Winchester Congress (1845) and again in 1847. R. ran his house and shop in Stockwell St until late in the 19th cent, the firm finally being dissolved after World War II. Best remembered in our context for his invention and marketing of 'Richardson's Metallic Rubber and Prepared Paper for Monumental Brass Rubbing', first produced in 1844 (see notices (a) *Athen* 888 (2.11.1844), 1004 (b) *Gent Mag* Sept. 1844, Pt II; (c) *Archaeol J* I (Sept. 1844), 206; (d) *Art Union* No. 84 (1.8.1845), 271) It never obtained the universal popularity of black heel-ball because of its dark finish. R's help is acknowledged in preface to Haines' (1861) and both Boutell's works on brs (1847 and 1849); the latter also has advertisements for R's products for which J. H. Parker (q.v.) G. Bell and Stephen Austin (of Hertford), publishers, were agents. Some rubbings (largely black on white, but some 'metallic') in 3 albums by Henry S. Richardson are in the Greater London Record Office and Library, some with letters from incumbants giving permission attached; most appear to be of late19th cent date. R. was a member of Surrey Archaeol Soc and served once as Auditor and three times as Council Member (resigned 1876); several notebooks belonging to him, one with examples of his work as printer, another of early reminiscences of Greenwich (handwritten in 1901) are now (1971) in the Local Hist Centre, Greenwich Pub Libs. An edited selection from latter is in *Procs Greenwich and Lewisham Antiq Soc* for 1970. A small, privately printed and undated pamphlet signed by Richardson entitled *Monumental Brasses: a descriptive list of 'Rubbings' in the possession of H. S. Richardson* is in the colln of the Camb. Antiqn Soc at the Univ Museum of Archaeology and Ethnology, Cambridge (q.v.) The 'metallic rubbings' cited were chosen for a lecture, and each is described briefly; four are illus (3 in colour). This

is the only copy of this 16 p pamphlet I have seen to date. *m* Mary Ann, who survived him; 1 *dau.*
Died: 163 Algernon Rd, Lewisham 29 Jan. 1905 at 93.

ROWE, Rev George (1824–82)
Theologian; amateur archaeologist: b London 28.2.1824. *Educ* Camb. Univ MA (1854); Deacon (Ely) 1851. Priest. 1852. *C* Swyshead, Beds. 1851–3; Vice-Principal and Chaplain Female Training Sch, York. 1853–64. Principal York Diocesan Trg Sch for Masters 1864–74. Member Yorks. Archt and Topog Soc; prepared Index to first 8 vols of Assoc Archit Socs Reports and Papers. [1867]. *m* Harriett Eliz. (née Barker). Made large colln of rubbings now in BM Add MSS 32481 – A – X (arr. topographically). His wife survived him.
Died: 16.10.1882 at York.

SANDERSON, Harold Kennedy St John (1865–1936)
Schoolmaster, musician, ecclesiologist: b Warwick 20 Feb. *Educ* Shrewsbury; Trinity Coll, Camb. 1883–6. MA 1886. Taught in Army 1886–90. Sept. '90 to July '28, 6th Form Classics Master Bedford Sch; Editor School Mag *Ousel* '98–1910. Keen amateur musician and composer; wrote sev of sch songs; member Bedford Musical Soc; lover of books, esp Greek and Roman classics. *m* (1890) Charlotte Joanna (née Hull) who also taught at Sch '10–'15 (ob. 16.6.1930). 2 *s* (1 killed in action 1918). Int. in m.b. began at Camb. where he helped form CUABC; V.P. M.B.S. nearly 40 yrs; prepd. valuable paper on Cambs. brs with Rev A. Brown (see; *CUABC* VIII (Sept. '90), 25). Although his interest never flagged, his other duties left him little time in later life to study brs or make rubbings. Rev H. W. Macklin acknowledges his help in his *Brasses of England* (1907). *Pubns incl* (1) 'Merchant's Marks' *CUABC* No. 6 (1888); (2) 'On the S.S. Collar, and others' *CUABC* No. 7 (Feb. 1890), 6–11; (3) 'Bucks. notes' *MBS* 2 (1893–6); 3 (1897–9) 115–8; 4 (1900–3), 31–6, 165–76, 246–9; (4) 'Brasses of Bedfordshire' *MBS* 2, 33–45, 74–90, 117–33, 153–74, 193–213, 275–91; *ibid* 3, 31–41; (5) 'Brasses of Wells Cathedral *MBS* 2, 140–2; (6) 'Norton Disney, Lincs.' *ibid* 216–23; (7) 'Newark, Notts.' *ibid* 226–33; (8) 'Somerset Notes' *ibid*, 343–4; (9) 'Contribn to a complete exploration of Northants. . . .' *ibid*, 345–6; *ibid* 3, 47–53; (10) 'Lincoln Cathedral' *ibid* 2, 314–25; 3, 67–87, 119–42; (11) 'Merchant's Marks' *OUBRS* I, ii (June 1897), 30–41 enlarged version of No. 1 above.
Died: 16 Rothsay Pl, Bedford, 18 Jan. 1936. *Obits:* (1) *Ousel* [Bedford Sch Mag] N.S. 40 (1936), 18–19; (2) *Old Bedfordians' Y.B. 1936*, 154–8; (3) *Beds. Times and Indep* 24.1.36.

SCOTT-GATTY, Sir Alfred Scott (1847–1918)
Herald, genealogist and composer: b Ecclesfield, Yorks. 26.4.1847. 2 *s* Rev Dr Alfred Gatty and *w* Margaret. Assumed addit. surname and Arms of Scott 1892. *Educ* Marlboro'; Christ Coll, Camb. *m* Elizabeth (née Foster) 1874; 2 sons. Rouge Dragon Pursuivant 1880–86; York Herald 1886–1904; Acting Registrar Coll of Arms 1899–1904; Garter Principal King of Arms 1904–18; CVO 1906; KCVO 1911. Knt. 1904; Kt Com. Royal Norwegian Order of St Olaf (2nd Class); Kt Justice of Order of St John of Jerusalem and Genealogist of same. FZS; FSA. Founder member of Oxford Univ Archaeol Soc; Consulting Herald, CUABC 1887–93; Hon Heraldic Adviser M.B.S. Member (and contrib.) E. Riding Archaeol Soc; Hunter Archaeol Soc. A composer of music for children.
Died: Wendover Lodge, Welwyn, Herts. 18 Dec. 1918. *Obits:* (1) *Ann Reg.* (N.S.) 1918, p 211; (2) *Genealogist* Apr. 1919, 241–2 (by K. W. Murray); (3) *Music* Jan. 1919, 19; (4) *Welwyn Parish Mag* No. 556 (Jan. 1919). 1.

SHEPHERD, George (fl 1800–1830)
Water colour and topographical artist: Worked on several famous early 19th cent topog works incl C. Clarke's *Archit Antiq of England & Wales* (1819); *Beauties of England & Wales;* W. H. Ireland's *English Topographer* . . . (1828), etc Exhib. RA 1820–29; Soc of Brit Artists. 1827–30. Some of London drwgs reprod in *London Topog Soc Pubns* Nos. 27, 29 and 33. His son, George Sidney S. (ob. 1858) was equally talented. Some tinted drwgs of brs and monuments made c 1820 are in Crace Colln in BM (Add MSS 16966–67).

SHORT, Rev Canon Frederick Winning [Hassard-Short]. (1873–1953)
Ecclesiologist: Hon Sec MBS: b London 5 Aug. *s* Frederick Hugh Short and Maud (née Davies). *Educ* Blackheath Prop. Sch; Christs Coll, Cambs. BA 1895, MA 1899. Ord (Cantab.) 1897. C St James, Tunbridge Wells, 1897–1901; St John Baptist, Cardiff 1901–6; St Mary's, Chatham 1906–9. Asst Master Kings Sch, Rochester 1906–7. Chap Territorial Army 1911–33. V St Albans, Dartford 1907–23; V St Luke's Bickley, 1923–53. Hon Canon Rochester 1934–53. Rural Dean Bromley 1941–53. Hon Chap to Forces 1933–53. Member Dartford and Bromley Bd. of Guardians 1911–33. Chairman Automobile Assn. 1942–53. FR Hort Soc 1931 on. Changed name to Hassard-Short 1919. Hon Sec M.B.S. 1899. Comp index to C. T. Davis' *Gloucestershire Brasses* (1899).
Died: Bromley, 12 Feb. 1953.

SIMPSON, Justin (1832–96)
Antiquary: b Stamford *s* James Simpson, seedsman. *Educ* Stamford G.S. left 1845; joined Stamford Rifle Corps. 1860; keen student of genealogy, heraldry and numismatics, with spec ref to Lincs. Member Harl Soc freq contrib to *Gents Mag, N&Q; Old Lincolnshire; Fenland N&Q; Lincs. N&Q; Herald and Geneal; Reliq and Illus Archaeol, Athen and Stamford Mercury*. FSA; Pub one of earliest lists of English brasses; subscr to Kite (1860) and Haines (1861). *Publns incl. List of the Sepulchral Brasses of England; alphabetically arranged by counties* (1857).
Died: Stamford, Lincs. 26.2.1896; *obit:* (1) *Times* 3.3.1896, p 10f. (2) *Stamford Mercury* 28.2.1896 (repr *N&Q* (8th ser) IX, 7.3.1896, 200).

SPARVEL-BAYLY, John Anthony (1845–96)
b Swanscombe, Kent 21 March. *Educ* Privately; Camb. Univ; BA; JP for Essex from 22.2.1881, FSA resigned 4.5.1886. Churchwarden at Swanscombe until he left village in 1874 for Burghstead Lodge, Billericay, Essex where he later died. A keen yachtsman, he was for time Rear Commodore of Royal Corinthian Yacht Club, receiving a special presentation from the Club in 1882. He was elected to Council of Essex Archaeol Soc in 1877, serving until 1882 and contrib sev articles to the *Transactions;* his keen interest in antiquities are indicated in the obituary below and at the time of his death he was assisting with an *Encyclopaedic Index to Essex;* he was also a member of the Vigilance Committee of the Council on Progress of Church Restoration from 1882, set up by the Essex Archaeol Soc. From c 1880 his interest in the bibliography and history of brasses appeared in print as the pubns mentioned below indicate: those on individual counties are too discursive to be of great value. The most interesting fact I have discovered is a reference in George Gatfield's little known bibliography *Guide to Books & MSS relating to Genealogy & Heraldry* (1892; issued in a limited edn of 300 copies) on p 234 of which is a reference to 3 vols of Ms. notes by Sparvel-Bayly, then (1880) 'in the possession of Arthur Vicars, Esq, Vicarage Library, Clyde Rd, Dublin'. This I take to be Sir Arthur Vicars, later of Kilmorma Castle, Co. Kerry, whose home was destroyed when he was shot in April 1921. Despite extensive enquiries of institutions and individuals I have been unable to locate the work above, which was said to be notes the compiler collected for a revised edition of Haines' *Manual* of 1861. Probably they perished in the fire above. Mr Sparvel-Bayley was twice married: (1) on 9.6.1870 to Edith Anna (née Williams), by whom he had 4 child; (2) on 23.7.1884 to Mary Jane (née Pye) who

gave him 6 child. When he died suddenly following a short illness, and after some severe financial losses, his family was left destitute and his researches cut short long before completion. *Publns incl:* (1) 'Essex brasses' [addns and corr to Haines' *List*] *Antiq* IV (Oct. 1880), 151–3, (2) 'On mon brs' [corr and addns to Haines]. *Antiq* V (1882), 8–10; *ibid* VII, 4 (Apr. 1883), 165–7; *ibid* (May 1883), 213-5, (3) 'Some addns to Haines' *Manual of M.B.'s ibid*, XVIII (Oct. 1888), 183; (4) 'Mon brs of Northants.' *Northampton Herald* 24.5.1890; (5) 'Mon brs of Bedfordshire' *Beds N&Q* 3 (1893), 65–73; (6) 'Mon brs of Hertfordshire' (1890's – source unknown, but copy in my possession). His rubbings of Essex brs were presented to Soc of Antiq in 1884 (*SAP*. 2 Ser, 8 (1884), 542).
Died: 13 Dec. 1896; *obit: Essex Rev* 5 (1896), 14–16 [anon., but with add note by Alfred Cotgreave, Chief Libn of West Ham].

SPRAGUE & Co. Ltd, London
Photo-lithographic printers fd c 1880 as Sprague & Co. (with Robert W. Sprague) at 22 Martin's Lane, Cannon St, London E.C.; by 1892/3 had moved to East Harding St, and again in 1915/6 to 69–70, Dean St, London. By 1921 had amalgamated to form Sprague & Havecock Ltd, but by late 1920's appear to have left London or dissolved company. In the present context Sprague's are best known for their photo-lithographic reproductions of brasses in the pre-1914 volumes of the *M.B.S. Portfolios;* they also printed the series of illus in *The Builder* in the 1880's and 1890's from rubbings by Andrew Oliver (q.v.) and those for Belcher's *Kentish Brasses.*

STEELE, Edward (fl 1710–58)
Professional church painter and decorator; amateur antiquary and artist: Little known of his early life; prob living in Herts. c 1710 where he was compiling notes for a revised edn of Sir Henry Chauncey's *History of Hertfordshire* (1700) and doing some painting in local churches, incl Great Gaddesden. He made many MSS notes and drwgs of monuments and brs, most of which are now in the Gough Colln. (Herts. MSS 4) in the Bodleian Lib; his drwgs are made in pen and ink, uncoloured, and not to scale; they are mainly of historical rather than artistic importance. A single vol of notes on Gt Gaddesden, Herts., made c 1713, is in the Lewis Evans' Colln, St Albans City Libraries. In 1744 Steele was in Bromley, Kent, but moved to Jerusalem Ct., St John's near Clerkenwell soon afterwards. In the BM are two printed catalogues of a sale of his colln on 12 and 27 Apr. 1758. For further details see article by J. H. Busby 'Topographical notebooks of Edward Steele'. *Herts. Archaeol* II (1970), 105–8; for example of

his work see Pl II in same work, accompanying an article on the brs at Gt Gaddesden by the present author (pp 82–7), or Pl 8*b* above.

STEPHENSON, Mill (1857–1937)

Antiquary and ecclesiologist: b Hull, Yorks. *Educ* Gonville and Cauis Coll, Camb., BA 1880 Adm to Bar of Inner Temple 1885, shortly after which his interest in brs and antiq began, under able guidance of Sir A. W. Franks (q.v.); joined CUABC 1887, Council member and auditor. When Rev H. W. Macklin resigned as Editor of a new list of brs (1894) M.S. took over General Editorship and set standard for what was to become a life's work. When M.B.S. fd M.S. became first jt editor of *Portfolio*, 1897–9 (with C. J. P. Cave); later he became Hon Sec and Treas and Hon Ed of *MBS Trans* with C. T. Davis (q.v.) until 1914. Blessed with private means he was able to devote himself ungrudgingly to his interests, and made a special study of palimpsest brs and those of three English counties (see below); he also did much voluntary and invaluable work at the Soc of Antiq Lib, noteably on sorting and cataloguing the rubbings and books, as well as the Roman and Medieval antiquities in which he was keenly interested; he gave a number of valuable items from his own colln to the BM; FSA elec 7.6.1888; early member Surrey A.S. from 1889 when he was Jt Hon Sec, resigned in 1897, council member 1897–1937; V.P. 1930. Apart from his prolific special studies and articles on brs, he is best known for his classic *List of M.B.* (1926, with Appdx 1938) on which revision is once again beginning only this year (1971). Most of his notes, mss and rs now at Soc of Antiq; it seems doubtful that the work of men like Stephenson and Ralph Griffin can ever be repeated by a single individual. *Pubns:* These are far too numerous to list here and only some of the most important or comprehensive are noted; the definitive bibliography is yet to be compiled: (1) 'On a brass in Stoke D'Abernon Church' *SAC* X (1891), 283–7 [Ann Norbury, 1464]; (2) 'M.B. in the E. Riding' *Yorks Archaeol & Top J* XII (1893), 195–299 (with add notes *Yorks Archaeol J* Pt 95 (1917), 269–74); (3) 'M.B. in Surrey' *SPEST* III (1891–4), 186–94; (4) 'M.B. in Shropshire' *Archaeol J*, LII (March 1895), 47–103; *Trans Shrop. A.S.*, 2 Ser VII (1895). 381–442; (5) 'Notes on the m.b. of Middx.' *SPEST* IV (1895–8), 221–33; (6) 'M.B. in the West Riding' *Yorks Archaeol J* XV (1897–8), 1–60, 119; (7) 'M.B. in the North Riding' *ibid* XVII (1899), 1–81; (8) 'M.B. of William, Lord Zouch and his wives' *SAP*, 2 Ser, XVII (1897–9), 51; (9) 'Notes on the Zouch-Over brass at Okeover, Staffs.' *MBS* 3 (1897–9), 187–93; (10) 'Palimpsest brs in Surrey' *SAC* XV (1900), 27–39; (11) 'List of Palimpsest Brasses in Gt Britain' *MBS* 4 (1900–3), 1–31, 97–135, 141–64 (re-issued as book. 1903); (12) 'List of

palimpsest brs in Herts.' *HCM* VIII (1906), 270–74, IX (1907), 19–24, 99–102; (13) 'List of Palimp brs in G.B.' *Additions: MBS* 5 (1904–9), 19, 77–90; 215–315; 6 (1910–13) 75–90; 224–51; (14) 'Notes on the m.b. of Kent' *SPEST*, V (1903–4), 129–48; (15) 'M.B. formerly in Gt Marlow Ch [Bucks.] *MBS* 5, 112–25; (16) 'List of papers on m.b. in the Surrey Archaeol Collns Vols I–XII [1887–99] *MBS* 37 (1897–9), 57–60; 206–8; (17) 'List of m.b. in Surrey' *SAC* XXV (1912) – XXXIII (1920) [9 parts]. Issued in book form 1921; again repr Kingsmead Reprints (with new preface and appendix by J. M. Blatchly) 1970; (18) *List of M.B. in Great Britain* (1926; *Appendix* (1938); repr in one vol by M.B.S., 1964; (19) 'Brasses to the Arundel family at Mawgan-in-Pyder, Cornwall [with R. H. Pearson]. *Antiq J* (Apr. 1939) 125–46; *MBS* VII, vii (Oct. 1940), 303–30. (20) 'Brs in Tattershall Ch, Lincs.' *MBS* 5, 326–37, 371–80.
Died: London, 29 July 1937; *obits:* (1) *MBS* VII, iv (Nov. 1937), 194–5 (Ralph Griffin); (2) *SAC* XLV (1937), 167–71 by M. S. G[uiseppi].

STOTHARD, Charles Alfred (1796–1821)
Artist and engraver: b London 5 July. 2 *s* Thomas S. and Rebecca (née Watkins). *Educ.* Privately; adm Royal Acad 1811 and in same year issued first number of his fine series of tinted engrs of monuments and brs. *Monumental Effigies of Great Britain* (12 pts in all, 10 by Strothard, 2 completed after his early death by other artists). Finally pubd 1832. 2nd rev edn 1876. Also made drwgs for Lysons' *Magna Britannia* and of Bayeaux Tapestry; FSA 2.7.1819 and historical draughtsman to Society. *m* Feb. 1818 Anna Eliza (née Kempe). Died following fall from ladder while making drwg of stained glass window at Beerferris, Devon, where he was buried.
Died: 28 May 1821.

STUKELEY, William (1687–1765)
Antiquary: b Holbeach, Lincs. 7 Nov. *s* John Stukeley and *w* Frances (née Bullen) *Educ* Free Sch Holbeach. 1692. Corpus Christi Coll, Camb. M.B. 1707–8; MD 1719. Entered medical practice 1710; FRS 1717–18. Helped estab Soc of Antiq of London 1718. Sec 1718–27; FCRP 1720. Spalding Soc 1722; Ord 1729. Freemason; *m* (1) Frances (Williamson) 1728 (2) Eliz. (Gale) 1739. 3 *daus* by 1st *w*. Most famous for his researches and pubns on Stonehenge (1740); *Itinerarium Curiosum* (1724. 2nd edn 1776). He also made a number of useful notes and sketches of brasses, most of which are now in Gough

Colln in Bodleian Lib (see repr f.p. 113), noteably of St Albans Abbey, Herts.
Died: 3 March 1765.

SYMONDS, Richard (1617–(?)95)
Collector and antiquary: An officer of the Court of Chancery ('cursitor'), Royalist and member of King Charles' bodyguard during Civil Wars, for which he was fined 1/6th of his estate in 1646 (£295); keenly interested in archaeological matters and made extensive colln of prints and engravings while in Italy and France between 1649 and c 1652. Best known in our context for his extensive colln of notes and sketches of brasses, monuments, stained glass, etc, made in diaries between 1643–5. Most of original MS now in BM (Harl MS. 965) covering Oxford, Worcs. and Berks. especially, and some West Country churches. Extracts appeared in facsimile, with notes, in the Camden Soc Pubn named below. *See* (1) *Diary of the Marches of the Royal Army during the Great Civil War kept by Richard Symonds now first published from the Original MS in the British Museum: Ed by Charles Edward Long*. (Camden Soc Pubn. LXXIV, 1859 [a reprint of this is listed in the Johnson Reprint Corpn catalogue, price $20.00]). (2) OGDEN, Henry and Margaret. 'A seventeenth century collection of prints and drawings'. *Art Q*. XI (Winter 1948), 42–73. (3) GRAHAM, R. – Oxford Church Notes, 11043–4 . . . *Oxf Hist Soc Pubn*, 47. (4th Ser) 1905.

TALBOT, Rev Thomas Sugden (1778–1832)
Artist: b Wymondham, Norf. *Educ* Caius Coll, Camb., MA. Spent most of his life at Sprowston Hall and is buried at his birthplace. Best known for his fine series of some 100 drwgs of brasses made 1793–4 when only 16 years of age; in two vols, the pen and ink sketches are on 70 leaves, and have a light yellow wash; many are of brasses now lost or damaged. In Vol I are add notes by the artist Clere Talbot (his daughter) dd. Aug. 1883; in Vol II is inserted a letter from Rev W. F. Creeny stating value of work and adding a few pencil notes. The two vols were given to the Norfolk and Norwich Archaeol Soc by A. M. Talbot, grandson of the above. For full description, list, and specimen illus see valuable article by H. O. Clark 'An Eighteenth Century Record of Norfolk Sepulchral Brasses'. *Norfolk Archaeol* XXVI (1936), 85–102.

THACKER, Francis James (1870–1932)
Librarian and ecclesiologist: Member of staff Birmingham P.L. 1886–1901 when he left to follow a career in business. Retd to former at end

of 1915 where he became Chief Cataloguer in the Ref Dept and later second Officer, Routine Sectn; Hon Treas Birmingham and District Lib Assn 1920–23; Hon Sec 1923–33. Estab Frances J. Thacker Scholarship for asstg trainee librns. Married, he had one son. Authority on Worcestershire brasses, of which he had a fine colln of rubbings given to Birm. and Midland Inst in 1938 and now in Birmingham Reference Library. *Pubns incl:* 'Mon. Br of Worcs.' *Worcs Archaeol Soc Trans* (N.S.) 3, 1925–6, 107–27, *ibid* 4 (1926–7), 129–55. Well illus, some with Arms in colour; series completed after his death by A. E. B. Barnard (q.v.) and J. F. Parker.
Died: suddenly at Birmingham 14.12.1932; *obit: Lib Assn Rec* (3rd Ser) III, i, Jan. 1932, p 28 [by H. M. Cashmore].

THORNELY, James Lamport (1865–1900)
Solicitor and author: b Liverpool *s* James Thornely, solicitor (ob. 1898) of Thornely & Cameron of Liverpool; adm as solicitor Feb. 1889, first certificate issued 16th of that month by Law Soc. Member firm of Thornely & Cameron 1889–1900 (London agents Field, Roscoe & Co.); Comm Member Liverpool Athenaeum; active supporter university extension movement in Liverpool, noteably of Univ Coll, where he was a pt time student for some years and an active member of the Soc of Lit, Hist and the Fine Arts from its early days; freq contrib to various College Mags. His first love was poetry and he wrote and pubd in later life *Stanley* (a verse drama; 1890) and *Moments Apart* (short poems. 1894). His only pubd bk on brs (see below) was illus with engr from author's own rbs; varying in merit it was not well received on pubn. Mill Stephenson's review (*MBS Trans* 2, iv, Sept. 1894, 137) notes it as 'unfortunately an example of a book in which the author has rushed into print before he has exhausted or digested his material', regretting the method of illus and absence of an index. *The Antiquary*, XXVIII (Apr. 1893), 177–8, offers similar criticism and 'cannot recommend' the work. Short reviews also in *N&Q* (8th Ser), III, 17 June 1893, 479–80. Thornely was an early member CUABC; member Incorp Law Soc. *Pubn:* (1) *Mon. Br. of Lancashire and Cheshire* (Hull: Wm. Andrews; London: Simpkin Marshall), 1893.
Died: 5.12.1900 (buried Anfield Cemetery) *obit:* (1) *Law J* 22.12.-1900, 706 (short) (2) *Sphinx* [Liverpool] *Univ Coll, Student's Mag*, 8 (1900), 143–4.

TORR, Valentine John de Jersey Berry (1895–1965)
Ecclesiologist b 3 Sept. *s* James Fenning T. and Beartrice de Jersey (née Moore). *Educ* St Paul's Sch, London. From early age keen

student of Kentish history and brs on which he was to become an authority; prominent member Friends of Kent Churches, on which subject he produced a book in 1954 with H. R. P. Boorman. Gave many talks where his forthright views sometimes brought him into conflict with his audiences; frequent contrib to *Archaeol Cant.* and *MBS Trans;* Council Member both societies. Staged fine exhib of rs at All Hallows, London Wall, 24 Sept.–13 Oct. 1962 (see p 130 above.) *Pubns incl:* (1) 'On the br of an unknown coped pr in St Peter's Clapham'. *MBS* 7 (Dec. 1934), 28–32; (2) 'The Iden brass' *MBS* 7, ii (Dec. '35) 69–70; (3) 'Adisham indent' *ibid* v (June '38) 204–7; (4) 'Oddington shroud br and its lost fellows' *ibid,* 225–35; (5) 'Chronological list of early male civilians' *ibid* 240–2; (6) 'Chron. list of priests in Cassock'. *ibid* vi (May '39), 265; (7) 'Pr in cassock and other brs at High Halstow, Kent' *ibid* 261–4. (8) 'Brasses and the M.B.S.' *Amateur Hist.* I, 5 (Apr.–May 1953), 159–62; (9) 'Guide to Craven Ord' *MBS* 9, ii (Oct. 1952), 80–91, *ibid* iii (July '54), 133–45. (10) 'Note on Charlton-on-Otmoor' *ibid* 114–7; (11) 'Re-discovery at Eastling, Kent' *MBS* 9, vii (Oct. '60) 388; (12) 'The Countess Pillar' *MBS* 9, ix (Nov. '62), 485–8; (13) 'Re-dating and other notes' *MBS* 10, iv (Dec. 1966), 299–302; (14) 'Thomas Magnus' *MBS* 10, ii (Dec. 1964), 75–6; (15) 'Chigwell and its brasses' *MBS* 10, iv (Dec. 1966), 238–9; (16) 'Et reliqua' *ibid,* 240–43; (17) 'Unrecorded items, ancient and modern', *ibid* 299–302. *Died:* London 11 March 1965; *obits:* (1) *MBS* 10, iii Dec. (1965), 220–21 [by A.W.] (2) *Archaeol Cant.* LXXX (1965), 298; (3) *Times* 22.3.1965, 12(e).

TYSON, Michael (1740–80)
Engraver: b 19 Nov. *Educ* Corpus Christi, Camb., BA 1764, MA 1767; began painting for own amusement c 1770 and caught attn of sev prominent people. Worked for Soc of Antiq from 1768 and Royal Soc from 1779. Made some drwgs of brasses and monuments for Richard Gough's *Sepulchral Monuments of G.B.*, in the preface of which he is mentioned as a 'friend' of the author.

ULLATHORNE, Francis, SONS & CO. (fl c 1820–1930)
Shoe thread manufacturers and wholesalers; tow spinners: warehousemen and makers of heel-ball for brass rubbing: Appear to be first manufacturers whose heel-ball was used for brass rubbing in the late 1830's or early 1840's. The firm of Francis Ullathorne & Co. first appear in *Pigot's London and Provincial Directory* (1823–4) at 12 Gate St, Little Turnstile, Lincolns Inn, London, E.C. as 'shoe thread manufacturers'. The *Post Office London Directory* for 1831 (p 408) cites them similarly

but adds 'and wholesalers' to the description and names their premises as a 'Grindery Warehouse'. Although not separately listed, by 1844 they also had premises (or a shop) in Long Acre, since Albert Way (q.v.) and others refer to 'Messrs Ullathorne' as being at this address (e.g. *Archaeol J* I (Sept. 1844), 205); Way calls them the 'sole manufacturers of heel-ball', supplying both small pieces and pieces 'about three inches in diameter', noting also that they proposed to supply 'a waxy compound of a yellow colour in order that the rubbings may assume some resemblance to the original brass'. By 1846 the Gate St premises had changed ownership, being listed as 'William Ullathorne & Co.', but with the addition of 'Flax Mills' at Barnard Castle, Durham and Startforth, Yorks. (many of the family remained in Yorkshire as Somerset House death's Registers show). William Ullathorne died on 22 Oct. 1859, and his will names him as of 'Mound House, Notting Hill and Gate St, Lincoln's Inn; Barnard Castle, Durham and Startforth, York., Flax and Tow Spinner and Warehouseman'. Legatees under the will were his widow Anne Hoare U.; Alexander and William U. (sons) and Geo. Hutton U. (nephew) of the same addresses and occupation. The firm continued to use the Gate St warehouse and grindery for the next sixty years or so, but at some time separate companies were formed; by 1912 the *P.O. London Directory* lists them as Ullathorne & Co. 'shoe-thread manufacturers'; Ullathorne, Hartridge & Co. 'Leather merchants' and '*Ullathorne, Francis. Heel-ball maker*', with their premises now renumbered as 7 and 9 Gate St. In about 1926 the firms had all moved to 46 Castle St, Long Acre, but by now the owners of the warehouse business were C.B. and W. J. Ullathorne, with other premises in Australia and New Zealand. Francis Ullathorne remained at that address until 1929, after which his name does not appear again. By 1931 only Ullathorne, Hartridge & Co. remained at the premises, but by 1932 they had also gone and the premises were vacant; it was then taken over by the 'Film Transport Co. Ltd'. Ullathorne's heel-ball is last mentioned in print in 1913 when E. T. Beaumont (q.v.) mentions 'Ullathorne's two penny sticks, obtainable from a leather merchant . . .' (*Ancient Memorial Brasses* 1913), p xv). Their small cakes (about 3 cm in diameter) were embossed with a crown, and an old piece I saw recently was stamped 'FRANCIS ULLATHORNE, LONDON'. The firm appears to have been dissolved by the end of the Second World War.

UTTING, Robert Brooke (1817–86)
Wood Engraver: Made many of woodcuts for Boutell's works, notably the *Mon Br of England* (1849), where he receives special

mention in Preface (p XII), and 450 cuts for *English Heraldry* (1867); a few also appear in Boutell's earlier work. Utting appears to have been one of a team of engravers employed by J. H. Parker (q.v.), publisher, contempoarry with T. O. S. Jewitt, J. R. Jobbins and others. Utting's engravings also appear in Haines' *Manual* (1861), though mostly borrowed from other pubns or journals from the House of Parker. I have been unable to discover any notice of his death or many other details about him; he appears in the *Post Office London Directories* between 1856 and 1877, first at 34 College St North, Camden Town, and latterly at 33 Camden Rd, London, N.W. *Died:* 14 July, 1886.

WALLER, John Green (1813–1905)
Artist, ecclesiologist and antiquary: b Halesworth, Suff. 30 Sept. *e.s.* John Waller and *w* Susanna (née Green); *educ* privately with his brother L. A. B. Waller (q.v.) in Suffolk and Maryland Point, Epping; pupil with G. F. Watts, J. C. Horsley and W. P. Firth at Sass Art Sch; entered R.A. Schools and won life scholarship 1838; specialist in designing painted glass and memorial brasses; won many prizes for his work; designed Chaucer window in Westm. Abbey. Began rubbing brs in 1830's, when use of heel-ball first began (possibly helping to begin the practice) with his brother; some of their rs now in Soc of Antiq colln; close friend of Charles Roach Smith (ob. 1890) and Albert Way (q.v.) with whom he founded Brit. Archaeol Assn (1844); also helped estab London and Middx. Archaeol Soc 1855, Hon Member of same, V.P. 1876 and Council Member many years; very learned in London topography. Also Hon Member Essex and Surrey Archaeol Soc; FSA elec 27.5.1886, but first exhib to Soc 1838–9; close friend of Sir A. W. Franks for over 50 yrs. V.P. Quekett Microscopical Soc (fd 1865). Apart from the fine series of engr of brs pub betw 1842 and 1864 with his brother, he gave many papers on this and other subjects, esp London history. He also designed and helped restore many brasses for the firm of Messrs Waller of Long Acre, who also made stained glass windows; in 1851 the firm exhib a large brass at the Gt Exhibition (see p 40 above); they also designed and made br of John Gough Nicholas (q.v.) in Holmwood Ch, Sy. On 9.1.1896 he stated his intention of giving 50 of his and his brother's drwgs of brs to Soc of Antiq (see: *SAP* 2 Ser, XVI (1895–7), 51); his rubbings at Soc of Antiq incl set from Camberwell made before fire of 1841 (see *MBS* 6 (1910–24), 377–8). He never married. *Pubns incl:* (1) *Series of m.b. from the 13th to the 16th century, drawn and engraved by J.G. and L. A. B. Waller* . . . Pts I–X (1842–64). The work was dedicated to Charles Roach Smith, Albert Way (q.v.) and Rev C. H. Hartshorne (q.v.) 'Early friends of the authors . . .'. *See also* (a)

ROSE, N. – 'Monumental brasses' [topog index to plates and illus in above.] *N&Q* (10 Ser) VI, Sept. 15, 1906, pp 210–11; (b) GRIFFIN, R. 'Bibliographical Notes.' *MBS* 5 (1904–9) 185–91; (2) 'Monuments of the Cobham family at Lingfield'. *SAC* IV, 186–99; (3) 'Brass of Sir John Northwood and wife, c 1330, Minster, Isle of Sheppey' *SAP*, 2 Ser, VIII (1879–81), 442; (4) 'Brasses in Northumberland and Durham' *Archaeol Ael* (N.S.) XV, 76–89; 207–311; (5) 'Brass in the possession of the Surrey Archaeol Soc' *SAC* X, i (1890), 126–9.
Died: Blackheath, 19 Oct. 1905 aet 92; *Obits:* (1) *Athen* 4070, 28.10.1905, 585 (by Sir E[dward]B[rabrook]); (2) *Lond & Middx AST* (N.S.) 2, (1911–13) 1–8 by Sir E. Brabrook; with portrait; (3) *SAP*, 2 Ser, XXI (1905–7) 159–61; (4) *MBS* 5 (1904–7), 93–5 (extracts from No. 3); (5) *Builder* 89 (28.10.1905), 453.

WALLER, Lionel Askew Bedingfield (1816/7–1899)
b Halesworth, Suff. 2 *s* John and *w* Susanna (née Green). *Educ;* with his brother, J. G. Waller (q.v.), in Suffolk; Maryland Point, Epping; Sass Art Sch; and showed equal promise in art. Betw 1842–64 the two brothers produced the now famous *Series of M.B.'s* (see under J. G. Waller). He never obtained the fame in antiquarian circles that his brother enjoyed, and died with even less publicity.
Died: Blackheath, 27 Oct. 1899 aet 82. *Obit note: Times* 30.10.1899, p 6e.

WARD, John Sebastian Marlow [Mar John, titular Archbp of Olivet] (1885–1949)
Ecclesiologist, freemason and sectarian: b Belize, Brit. Honduras. *s* Rev H. M. Ward. *Educ* Mcht Taylors Sch; Trinity Hall Camb. 1906–11, BA, 2nd Cl. Hons Tripos. (1908); FRHistS; H/Master Diocesan Boys Sch, Rangoon; Director Intelligence Dept, Fedn Brit Ind. 1918–Jan. 1930. In Nov. 1928 Ward and his wife Jesse began a series of 'spiritual exercises' leading to their founding the Confraternity of the Kingdom of Christ at Hadley Hall, Barnet on 24.6.1930; the 'Abbey of Christ the King' was dedicated by Bp of St Albans 14.2.1931, but was disbanded in 1934. On 12.9.1935, after returning to the Autonomous African Universal Church, Ward was ord Deacon and priest of the sect, severing relations with the C. of E. After re-consecration the New Barnet Chapel became the Orthodox Catholic Church in England, with Ward as its primate from Dec. 1938. After an unfortunate court case and other mishaps, on July 13th, 1946 Ward (now titular Bp of Olivet), his wife and others, mysteriously left Barnet and went to Cyprus where Ward died in July, 1949. Apart from the above, W. was

a great authority on freemasonry and occultism, writing several books on the former. He initiated Isaac Newton Univ Lodge (No. 859) 28.5.1906; Rangoon Lodge (No. 1268) 1912–30; Fdr Member Industries Lodge No. 4100 (1920 res'd 1930). His interest in brasses was an early one and his little book was a useful, if unoriginal, work at a remarkably low price (see review in (a) *Archaeol J*, 2 Ser, 69 (1912–13), 379 [by M. Stephenson]; (b) *Builder* CIII, 13.12.1912, 711–12; (c) *MBS* 6 (1910–14), 253–5). *Pubns incl:* (1) *Brasses* (Camb. U.P. 1912); (2) 'Archit details in m.b.' *Builder* CII (19.1.1912), 69–71; *ibid* (16.2.1912), 183–5. For further details of Ward's life see also (a) ANSON, P. F. *Bishops at Large* . . . (Faber. 1964), esp pp 282–90; (b) *The Pilot* (Q Organ for Soc for Promoting Catholic Unity) 5, IV (Winter 1951), 94. Ward's colln of rubbings is now in the V&A Museum, London.

WAY, Albert (1805–74)
Antiquary and ecclesiologist: b Bath, Som. 23 June, one of 9 child Rev Lewis Way (1772–1840); *Educ* Privately, often abroad. Showed early promise as a child, reading a great deal and collecting items of ecological interest; also made number of competent sketches on his travels, noteably in 1822–3, encouraged by his sister Drusilla; Trinity Coll, Camb. BA 1829. MA 1834; FSA 7.3.1839; Director Soc of Antiq 15.12.1841–19.11.1846; one of founders and Hon Sec Archaeol Inst of G.B. (1844); one of V.P. St Albans Archit Soc 1845–6 where he met Rev Charles Boutell (q.v.) Keen student medieval hist and antiq, taking early interest in brs on which he wrote some excellent articles (notabley Nos. 1 and 2 below). He assisted or advised Boutell, the Wallers, Haines and others to whose work he was a subscriber; built up fine private lib and valuable colln of rubbings of brs some of which now in Soc of Antiq Lib; Boutell (*Mon Brs* (1847), p 147) says Way coined the term 'palimpsest' in respect to brs. His influence on the early writers on brasses, and his erudite and competent 'state of the art' articles are now often overlooked. When he died, his widow (Emmeline, *y.d.* John Thomas, 1st Lord Stanley of Alderley, *m* 30.4.1844) gave 150 vols of dictionaries and glossaries, 2 vols of his drwgs of prehistoric and other remains and his fine colln of impressions of medieval seals to Soc of Antiq; lived most of his life at Wonham Manor, near Reigate, Surrey. *Pubns incl:* (1) 'Sepulchral Brasses and Incised Slabs' *Archaeol J* I (Sept. 1844), 197–212; (2) Articles on *Sepulchral Brasses, Incised Slabs, Metalwork & Encaustic Tiles,* plus 'much varied and recondite information on many other subjects' for J. H. Parker's *Glossary of Terms used in Grecian, Roman, Italian and Gothic Architecture* 3 vols 3rd edn 1840 *et seq*, but notably 5th edn

1850 where his article on *Brasses* (pp 82–90) offers one of the concisest general summaries I have seen.
Died: Le Trouvelle, Cannes 22 Mar. 1874; *Obits:* (1) *SAP* 2 Ser, VI (1874), 198–200; (2) *Illus Lond News* No. LXIV (1874), 331, 397, 398, 475 (with portrait); (3) *Ann Reg* 115 (1874), 147–8. *See also:* STIRLING, A. M. W. *The Ways of Yesterday* (Butterworth. 1930).

WEALE, William Henry James (1832–1917)
Antiquary and publisher: b Marylebone, Lond. 8 Mar. *Educ* Kings Coll, Lond. Spent most of middle years in Belguim where he made valuable studies of funeral monuments and brasses and wrote a history of Bruges, where he lived and worked from c 1860 on; his first pubn appeared 1859; with Rev W. F. Creeny he might be described as the father of the study of continental brasses. Member Roy Soc of Fine Arts, Ghent; Archaeol Soc of Mons; Royal Flemish Academy; Order of Leopold. His work remained virtually ignored in England until 1890 when he was appt Keeper of the Art Lib, Sth. Kensington [V&A] Museum – retired Aug. 1897. His obit in *The Times* describes the poor treatment he received from his native country. Weale was a Roman Catholic, often writing under the pseud. of 'Recusant'; he ed several catalogues of items in National collections, e.g. BM, V&A, Burlington Fine Arts Club. *m* Helena A. Watson. 4 *s* 5 ***dau.*** Subscriber to Haines' *Manual* (1861); acknowledged by Creeny. Most of Weale's rubbings are now in the V&A Museum's colln. *Pubns incl:* (1) 'Tombe plate en cuivre de Sire Louis van Leefdael . . . à Thielen (Anvers)'. *Messages des Sciences Historique* . . . XXVIII (1860), 169–83. Illus in colour; (2) 'Notes on foreign brasses and incised slabs' [c 1890] (typescript copy at V&A Mus Lib and Soc of Antiq). 76 p; (3) 'Note sur les lames funéraires en cuivre conservées à Bruges'. *Bull de la Gilde de St Thomas et de St Luke, Bull de Scéances.* Tom. XIII (1900), 153–190; (4) '*Catalogue de froitures de tombes plates en cuivre et pierre.* [nd.]; (5) *Monumental Brasses and Incised Slabs of Northern Europe.* Announced but regrettably never published, 1859.
Died: 26 Apr. 1917 at Clapham Common, Surrey; *Obits:* (1) *Times* 28.4.1917, 3 (b); (2) *Ann Reg* 1917 (New Series), 169 (note).

WEEVER, John (1576–1632)
Antiquary and poet: b Lancs. *Educ* Queen's Coll, Camb. 1594–8. First works pub 1599, spent early years of 17th cent travelling abroad studying antiquities, finally settling in London; most famous for his. *Ancient Funerall Monuments* . . . (1631) in which many lost brasses

are recorded, though his accuracy is not good; an orig copy of the pubd work given by Weever is in Q. Coll Lib; the original MSS and notes are in the Soc of Antiq. Largely of value as written before great fire and Civil Wars. 2nd edn 1661. 3rd edn with add notes by Wm. Tooke, 1767.

Died: London and was buried St James Clerkenwell (since rebuilt).

Indexes

INDEX OF NAMES

Note: This index includes personal and corporate names, book titles, plus a number of titles of periodical articles where of special interest; book titles are printed in italic for ease of reference. Persons or bodies given full biographical entries in the Appendices are not normally included below, unless they also appear in the main text, footnotes or references.

In all indexes the letter (B) after a title or page reference indicates a book or pamphlet, and the letter (A) a periodical article. Numbers in parentheses following a main page reference refer to the relevant item in the Chapter Notes on pages 134–51 (e.g. 134(14) refers to page 134, note 14).

INDEX OF PLACES*

* Boundaries of English counties follow those used in Mill Stephenson's list, and take no account of recent changes in local government areas.

INDEX OF SUBJECTS